Endorsements for
Full Gospel, Fractured Minds?
by Rick M. Nañez

The greatest explosive movement of any kind in history has been the expansion of the kingdom of God in the last sixty years. By some estimates, seventy percent of this expansion has come at the hands of Pentecostal, Charismatic, or Third-Wave believers. Clearly, God has honored these believers, and they have much to teach other parts of the body of Christ. That's the good news. The bad news is that this part of Christ's body has, sadly and unnecessarily, been anti-intellectual for far too long. This has not only hurt the health of a more Spirit-oriented fellowship, but it has prevented them from having a greater impact on their more traditional evangelical brothers and sisters.

With gratitude to God, I am delighted to celebrate the publication of *Full Gospel, Fractured Minds?* by Rick Nañez. Standing squarely within the Pentecostal-Charismatic tradition, Nañez cannot be dismissed as an outside critic or faulted for not knowing the community he challenges. I know of no book like this. Its uniqueness lies in being a distinctively Pentecostal-Charismatic call to the life of the mind. This is must reading for all Pentecostal-Charismatic believers, and those outside this camp will gain much insight into and encouragement about their Pentecostal-Charismatic sojourners. Nañez's book is sure to help bring about a deeper love and unity throughout the body of Christ.

J. P. Moreland, Distinguished Professor of Philosophy
Talbot School of Theology, director of Eidos Christian Center,
and author of *Love Your God With all Your Mind* (NavPress)

Finally, a book long overdue but timely, given the emergence of Pentecostals and Charismatics in the theological academy! For laypersons in the pew who are a part of these movements, Nañez opens up the possibility of cultivating the life of the mind in a way that does not quench the Spirit. A must read for all first-year undergraduates at institutions that cater to Pentecostal-Charismatic constituencies.

Amos Yong, Ph.D, Book review editor, *Pneuma: The Journal of the Society for Pentecostal Studies*, and Associate Research Professor of Theology, Regent University School of Divinity

It was most encouraging to read this full-blown, discerning, culturally sensitive, and bracingly Christian defense of intellectual life. The book offers exceptionally helpful commentary on the general plight of learning in modern society as well as unusually shrewd observations on the tragic consequences when churches abandon responsible intellectual effort. The book's wisdom is heightened by the fact that its author says what needs to be said about Christian intellectual endeavor while maintaining his own Pentecostal convictions with integrity.

Mark A. Noll, McManis Professor of Christian Thought, Wheaton College, and author of *The Scandal of the Evangelical Mind*

This book is a clarion call for clarity of thought as well as fullness of the Spirit among Pentecostals and Charismatics. Nañez makes a good case for the famous phrase of Bishop J. O. Patterson to Pentecostal students, "Get your learning but keep your burning."

Vinson Synan, Dean, Regent University School of Divinity, and author of *The Holiness-Pentecostal Tradition: Charismatic Movements in the Twentieth Century*

FULL GOSPEL, FRACTURED MINDS?

A CALL TO USE GOD'S
GIFT OF THE INTELLECT

FULL GOSPEL, FRACTURED MINDS?

RICK M. NAÑEZ

ZONDERVAN™

GRAND RAPIDS, MICHIGAN 49530 USA

ZONDERVAN.COM/
AUTHORTRACKER

Full Gospel, Fractured Minds?
Copyright © 2005 by Rick M. Nañez

Requests for information should be addressed to:

Zondervan, Grand Rapids, Michigan 49530

Library of Congress Cataloging-in-Publication Data

Nañez, Rick M.
    Full gospel, fractured minds? : a call to use God's gift of the intellect / Rick M. Nañez.
      p. cm.
    Includes bibliographical references and indexes.
    ISBN-13: 978-0-310-26308-1 (hardcover)
    ISBN-10: 0-310-26308-5
    1. Pentecostal churches—Doctrines. 2. Pentecostals—Intellectual life. 3. Faith and
reason—Christianity. I. Title.
BX8762.Z5N36 2005
230'.994—dc22

                                          2005010116

Interior design by Beth Shagene

Printed in the United States of America

06 07 08 09 10 11 • 10 9 8 7 6 5 4 3

Contents

Foreword

I congratulate Rick Nañez as a Pentecostal author for his insight into our need for sharpening Pentecostal minds. Though there has been a significant increase in the number of Pentecostals who are seeking higher education, too many still do not see the need. True, I have learned much from sincere Christians with little education — and that keeps me humble. Yet God definitely led me to the University of California, where I studied science, then to Gordon Divinity School, Harvard University, New York Theological Seminary, and Central Baptist Theological Seminary. I learned that in depth study of the Bible, biblical languages, archaeology, psychology, philosophy, other religions, and church history sharpened my appreciation for the truth of God's Holy Word and helped me to realize my dependence on the Holy Spirit for guidance. All of my writing has come from study of God's Word and prayer. God has continued to guide me throughout the eighty-eight years of my life.

Rick Nañez has come from a different background but has been led by the Spirit of God in his education as well. His in-depth understanding of many important subjects is reflected in his research and in the writing of this book. He dares to point out weaknesses and call Pentecostals and Charismatics to seek a balance between mind and Spirit. This book will stir you to seek all that God has for you. After you read it, read 1 Corinthians 15 and pay attention to how Paul logically defends the truth of the resurrection. As Rick Nañez emphasizes, we all need to be able to take part in the defense of the gospel. Enemy forces are all around us. This book will help you find and use God-given resources.

STANLEY M. HORTON, TH.D.

Acknowledgments

From around 1989, I began to chat with influential minds in the Pentecostal – Charismatic movement about the value of the life of the mind as well as of our lack of discussion on this matter. One by one, these people shared their concern over our indifference and, at times, antipathy toward intellectual involvement in the Full Gospel faith. Year after year, I monitored lists of new releases to see if someone from within our ranks had penned a volume on this vitally important topic. After ten years, I sensed that the Lord was dealing with my heart, nudging me toward being that person. I was, and still am, humbled at the thought that he would use me to speak to this critical issue.

The book that you hold in your hand has been written with professors, students, pastors, *and laypeople* in mind. I know that this is a broad spectrum, but I have strived to make this a readable volume for as many as possible. Pentecostal – Charismatic scholars are making marked headway in their various disciplines, but it seems that there is a gap in the literary market between academic endeavors and the call to intellectual spirituality on the lay level. With this book, I hope to contribute to the closing of that gap. In order to do this successfully, we must not only continue to work on a scholarly level, allowing our findings to trickle down to the people, but we must place tools into their hands that can help them to meet the scholar halfway. In this way, the healing of our fractured mind will take place more speedily, which will, in turn, help us to become what we already confess to be — Full Gospel.

I want to give a word of thanks to those who have helped bring about this work. I am so very grateful for the Pentecostal – Charismatic movement. Without the love, passion, and guidance of some of her choice servants, I would be wandering in the labyrinth of life, stricken with angst, and chasing after the winds of an elusive life-calling. There was Bill, a Full Gospel friend who introduced me to Christ, and James, a Charismatic leader who taught me early on of the indispensable value of prayer. Charlie and Phil, two Spirit-filled missionary statesmen, were the first to stir my soul for world missions; and two Pentecostal professors, Hank and John, first provoked me to place my rational faculties at the disposal of my heavenly Father.

Furthermore, I was privileged to bump into a few authors early in my spiritual expedition who pricked my mind to offer it to the Architect of my mind. Isaac Watts' *The Improvement of the Mind*, A. G. Sertillanges' *The Intellectual Life*, and John Stott's *The*

Mind Matters have each helped me to think about thinking as a Christian calling. I also want to thank my perennial professors, my thought-breeders: Francois Fenelon, Søren Kierkegaard, C. S. Lewis, David Martyn Lloyd-Jones, Francis Schaeffer, Carl F. Henry, Peter Kreeft, and Philip Yancey. These are the mentors I've turned to when in need of compassionate, balanced, inflamed, Christian minds that tower and shine like beacons over the sluggish, hazy contour of our modern intellectual landscape. These are the friends I've consulted again and again in order to know that I am not alone.

I am equally grateful for the friends within arm's reach who encouraged me all along the way as I fought to remain focused. I offer my thanks to Jim and Lori, Andy and Wendy, Wendell and Laura, who believed in the project and demonstrated it in so many ways. I also want to make known my appreciation to the quality people — the sheep of my former pasture — at Victory Bible Church. For over eleven years they helped me to develop as a pastor. They smiled and loved me as I tried my hand at blending the intellectual with the devotional. They provided me with freedom and gave me courage to seek and teach a balanced faith.

I wish to record my indebtedness to Zondervan for their willingness to partner with me in somewhat untested waters. In a sense, this book is the first of its kind; thus, with courage and faith they have crossed the threshold with me. Without their vote of confidence, the message contained within this volume may never have made its way into the minds of the reading public. Again, I am humbled and grateful.

I owe a hefty word of thanks to Jack Kragt, academic marketing manager at Zondervan, along with the whole marketing team. Their intense, thorough, and distinct approach to the success of a new title is impressive. They do so with enthusiasm and class — much like a proud father does when heralding the arrival of his firstborn.

Through my editor, Verlyn Verbrugge, I have learned that one need not be smug and indifferent in order to work in the world of revision. Verlyn has gently guided me around the potholes and barriers that could have otherwise unnecessarily hindered the flow of my message. With wit, skill, and kindness he has taken a block of manuscript and chiseled out a recognizable sculpture for the viewing public. He is truly an example of one who possess the gift and art of editorial ministry.

I must make mention of my sons, Joseph and Christopher, at this juncture. I am fully aware of the sacrifice they made, leaving friends and familiar surroundings for the sake of moving to a quieter setting where I could research and write. No doubt many times during the year that I wrote, their drums and trumpets were silenced because of my need for solace and thought. I am likewise pleased that they are young men who are cultivating a thinking faith.

Finally, I am greatly indebted to my wife, who has bore with patience the life with a bibliomaniac. I could not have written this book without her tolerance while I held her dining room hostage for months on end, littered with crumpled copies of half-baked chapters and fortressed by barricades of reference books. I am honored to have a wife who was willing to leave a comfortable eleven-year pastorate for the sake of wading into the uncertain waters of a writing sabbatical. When questioned by less enthusiastic onlookers, Renee believed in the cause. Without such a soul mate, the message in this book would have never materialized. For all this, I thank her — and I thank God for her.

Introduction

The year was 1985; the occasion was the annual summer camp meeting of a well-known Charismatic leader. I had only known the Lord in a personal way since August of the previous year and had experienced an infilling with the Holy Spirit the following November. During a ten-month period, I had sat under the teaching of several prominent Pentecostal – Charismatic personalities within a several-hundred mile radius of my hometown, Wichita Falls, Texas — well-known speakers such as Kenneth Copeland, Oral Roberts, Jimmy Swaggart, Kenneth Hagin, Bob Tilton, Norvel Hayes, and Billy Jo Daugherty. Each one placed a brick in my soft but growing foundation. Though my traveling companions and I belonged to a local Pentecostal church, we were once again on our weekend trek to gain more spiritual treasures from the anointed teaching of yet another Spirit-filled preacher.

On that trip I devoured a book written by the man whom we were traveling to see. Up to this point, my literary diet had consisted of those books gifted to me by my Pentecostal and Charismatic friends in the faith — books like *They Speak With Other Tongues*, *The Late Great Planet Earth*, *Angels on Assignment*, *Armageddon 198?*, *The Miracle of Seed Faith*, *I Believe in Visions*, *Pigs in the Parlor*, *God's Formula for Success and Prosperity*, and *Understanding the Anointing*. One by one, these works challenged me and spurred me on in the life of faith. This trip was no different from the rest; I was primed for a miracle!

During that camp meeting so many years ago, one of the greatest miracles of my life did take place, but not in the way I had anticipated. It all began when the host speaker challenged the participants to empty our minds and to battle the temptation to think about anything at all. We were instructed to refuse to allow reason to get in our way and to restrain our heads from blocking the route to our hearts. When most had complied with the speaker's authoritative directives, he then told each one of us to turn to the person behind us and prophesy into his or her life. I stood bewildered by the unthinking obedience of the thousands who were participating in what seemed like a dangerous and mindless exercise.

I was a baby Christian who had been nurtured for only a short time in biblical teaching. But it seemed to me that what was taking place was a mishandling of people's minds and that there were philosophical implications in the mental gymnastics I was witnessing. I became aware that this group of professed believers both undervalued and misunderstood

13

the place of the intellect in the enterprise of worship. Haunting and hounding questions plagued me following the incident. How could adults so easily forfeit their reasoning faculties? Did they think of their minds as mere mechanized calculators twice removed from the spiritual life? Or was I the only one perhaps out to lunch; maybe I didn't recognize the full meal deal when I saw it.

Ever since that episode, I have watched and listened, and I have pondered why so many Pentecostals and Charismatic believers minimize the "life of the mind." The situation would be confusing enough if we were simply neutral about our views concerning the connection between the intellectual and spiritual life. But we seem to go a step further; we are often suspicious of reason and give the impression that we actually distrust the mind.

Don't get me wrong. I deeply love the Pentecostal – Charismatic movement. It is within her realm that I choose to make my theological home. I have elected to worship and minister in the "Full Gospel" environment for many reasons. Without a doubt, she has been a phenomenal blessing to the worldwide body of Christ. Her spiritual enthusiasm, passionate pursuit of the transcendent, and openness to the restoration of many gifts of the Holy Spirit have captured the attention of and enriched God's people around the globe. Millions outside of Spirit-filled circles have been drawn away from the numbness of a formal, stale faith into meaningful, vital spirituality through her influence. Countless others have discovered through their contact with Full Gospel folk that they need not possess holy orders to study the Holy Scriptures or to participate in the priesthood of the kingdom.

Our movement is most often a place where brotherly love is exhibited and where robust leadership is encouraged and cultivated. An open willingness to confess the wonders of Christ, liberating emotional expression in worship, and encouragement to participate in the ministry of the Spirit are all trademarks of this great ecclesiastical force. In many ways, this body of believers has aided the extended church in its quest for a profound and satisfying experience with Christ. Added to this are the emphases that this movement has placed on power encounters over mere human endeavor and on God's willingness to bless his children with all of our temporal needs as well as some of our wants. And who can argue with the powerful effect that Pentecostals have had on the world of missions? To these positive characteristics many could be added, and for all of these we praise God!

For myself personally, as I have worshiped and ministered over the past twenty years within this community, I have continued to experience the presence of the supernatural. I desire greatly that the Holy Spirit be my guide; his infilling is my strength, the gifts of the Spirit are active in my life, and the out-of-the-ordinary still intersects my spiritual sojourn. Visions, dreams, an occasional rendezvous with the demonic realm, and the voice of God have accompanied me on my kingdom pilgrimage.

I consider myself, in other words, a "Full Gospel" believer by the common Pentecostal – Charismatic definition, but my understanding of the term "Full Gospel" has changed radically — in my estimation, for the better. Combined with the above spiritual activities, I have come to realize that *our intellect is an essential part of the image of God in human beings, especially in the life of born-again human beings.* Our abilities to reflect, reason, contemplate, and think creatively are indeed gifts from our Maker. Thus, to count these aspects of our nature as second rate, to court a prejudice against matters of the mind, or to hold our intellectual commodities in suspicion is not only classical anti-intellectualism, but is sin.

Furthermore, to champion a so-called *Full* Gospel belief system, yet to pit experience against logic, faith against reason, and spirituality against rigorous mental exercise, is to fall far short of operating within God's *full* counsel as communicated in his written revelation. In the following pages, my aim is to admonish my Pentecostal and Charismatic brothers and sisters to reconsider some of the popularly-held misconceptions concerning the intellect in order that we as a movement may modify some of our thinking about thinking and change our minds about the importance of "the life of the mind."

Though we have made headway in the arenas of education, politics, and scholarship, we are still a movement that has sheltered deep within its soul a definite predisposition against the more cerebral aspects of the faith. We are a substantial subculture that, for the most part, has mass-produced an army with supernatural aspirations, while at the same time allowing many to maintain superficial intellectual lives.

I am fully aware, of course, that there are those within our movement who have labored to develop their minds to the fullest as well as those who have dedicated their lives to cultivating the intellectual soil of others' souls. I tip my hat to them, and my heart goes out to them, because many of these have had to cut against the grain and paid a hefty price to do so. Though this is true, we remain a people who are deeply concerned about physical healing, but exceedingly leery about intellectual healing. Let me state it bluntly: Possessing full hearts with vacant heads or burning spirits with sluggish minds makes for mediocrity at best and disaster at worst.

There are a host of benefits that may be harvested as a result of maintaining well-trained minds — minds on fire — and my desire is to demonstrate many of these in the pages that lie before you. The ultimate goal in *sharpening our Pentecostal iron*, however, must be to reflect the image of our Maker, who invites us to come and reason with him (Isa. 1:18) and commands us to get our minds ready for action (1 Peter 1:13). In turn, we will become better prepared to adequately defend and correctly contend for Full Gospel Christianity. In doing so, we will surely learn to glorify and love our Lord with all of our minds as well as with all of our hearts and souls (Matt. 22:37).

PART 1

ANATOMY
OF THE
FRACTURED
MIND

1

The Heart and the Head: What the Bible Teaches about the Mind

The Protestant clergy were filled with "head knowledge"; they were not taught
of the Spirit and were therefore ignorant, even "anti-intellectual" because
God's wisdom can never be acquired by the mere "human" mind.
EARLY PENTECOSTAL LEADER, 1915

"Teacher, which is the greatest commandment in the Law?" Jesus replied: "Love the
Lord your God with all your heart and with all your soul and with all your mind."
JESUS CHRIST

Carnal and proud minds are contented with self; they like to remain at home; when they
hear of mysteries, they have no curiosity to go and see the great sight, though it be ever
so little out of their way; and when it actually falls in their path, they stumble at it.
JOHN HENRY NEWMAN

Christina was a twenty-seven-year-old mother of two who was diligently pressing her
way through life. She was active in sports, loved poetry, and worked as an enterprising
computer programmer. Life was good to her, but a nightmare-come-true would soon dash
her hopes and ambitions.

A day before a scheduled gallstone surgery, Christina had an unnerving dream that the
members of her body refused to follow the commands of her mind. Oddly and tragically,
within twenty-four hours her nocturnal vision came true. She could not stand, her hands
wandered, she couldn't feed herself, her posture slumped, and even her voice was erratic.
"Something awful has happened," she cried out. "I feel disembodied." Christina's body
members were refusing to include her mind while performing their duties. In essence, her
mouth, hands, and feet were in rebellion against her mind!

The above account isn't fiction; it is documented in Oliver Sacks' national bestseller
The Man Who Mistook His Wife for a Hat. In the prime of life, Christina was permanently
handicapped by a rare disorder in which the parietal lobes of the brain failed to receive
communication from other parts of the body. Christina's lobes were in excellent working
order, but, as Dr. Sacks puts it, "they had nothing to work with." As a result, the patient had
no tendon or joint sense at all, and her movements were clumsy. Though her emotions and
feelings were very sensitive, she realized that her body was "blind and deaf to its mind."[1]

By accident, Christina had brought on her own "body blindness." In an attempt to strengthen her health, she had consumed sizeable amounts of vitamin B – 6. In moderation B – 6 is a good thing; however, she had overdosed on it.

Approximately two hundred years before Christina encountered her frightening disorder, another body began to experience similar symptoms. The condition of this other body was also self-induced. She too overdosed on good things; she gorged herself on emotion, intuition, and experience. Her name wasn't Christina, but Christian. And the wreckage was not to be found in a physical body but in a spiritual body — the body and bride of Christ.

WHEN THE MIND BECAME SUSPECT

Beginning about 1800, much of the church in America began to undergo a radical mutation. For various reasons (dealt with throughout this book), it started to separate the heart from the head, faith from reason, experience from logic, believing from thinking, and intellect from emotion. In a nutshell, the *mind* and the *spirit* were set up against each other as archenemies. Thus, just as Christina's physical body had refused to hear the commands of her head, so also the body of Christ failed to listen to its Head. Though Jesus has clearly commanded his followers to love God with all their minds (Matt. 22:37), and though the great apostle Paul challenged the body of Christ with the words "in your thinking be adults" (1 Cor. 14:20), teaching on the importance of using one's brains for God's glory began to fade. What had been a relatively rare teaching throughout church history began to spread like a plague during the nineteenth century.

During the formative stages of "revival religion" in the new republic of America (1800 – 1850), many among the Christian masses slated science as an adversary of faith and of the Bible. The healthy art of critical thinking was relabeled as "negative thought" and was placed in the same category with atheistic criticism of the Scriptures. God-given reason was inaccurately lumped together with the "goddess of reason" and was thus redefined as an enemy of belief. Furthermore, many believers began to confuse an education in the liberal arts with the secularization of education through liberal*ism*. The spiritually revitalized but intellectually passive multitude of the nineteenth-century evangelical revival reclassified faith as an urge or a feeling and mistakenly separated reason and emotion — the Siamese-twins of the soul.

Instead of pointing out that non-Christians were twisting the definitions of science and maligning the origins and proper use of reason, the intellect, and logic, many nineteenth-century believers simply exited from these arenas of contention. Rather than responding with an offensive strategy and defending the faith once for all delivered to the saints, they simply retreated from study in such areas. Thus, human reason (or, as we say, "the head") came to represent the fallen faculty of worldly creatures — the part of a human being that cannot help but get one into trouble, especially in matters of faith. By contrast, emotion (or, as we say, "the heart") was appointed as the ruling monarch of the spiritual life.

When the church separates the head from the heart and reason from revelation, she becomes guilty of driving an artificial wedge into God's unified reality. It is true, of course, that this is the same mistake that was made by those outside of God's kingdom. Religion was for the private world of feeling; the mind was for dealing with the problems of life. Thus, it shouldn't surprise us to witness within the church a general confusion about life when she attempted to carve up God's reality as the world did. In some respects, therefore, in forfeiting the honorable origins, definitions, and place of human intellectual faculties, nineteenth-century evangelicalism (along with fundamentalism and Pentecostalism later) seems to have actually helped foster the fragmented worldview that is so prominent today.

Like the victim of the neurological defect described at the beginning of this chapter, the voice of the church has been weakened in the world. Its abilities to stand intellectually, to hold a strong moral posture, and to offer its helping hands have been affected greatly. Moreover, like Christina, so many within the twenty-first-century American body of Christ struggle to feed themselves, are without tone, and lack flexibility in their "intellectual sinews." While in mental convalescence, Christina's emotions, though vibrant, were out of touch with her body. In much the same way, hosts of Full Gospel believers excel in the devotional, emotional, and experiential aspects of their faith, but they leave much to be desired in the sphere of the life of the mind.

Only through ongoing, rigorous, mental exercises did our young, ailing pilgrim make progress, training the *physical* members of her body to once again follow the commands of her *mind*. And it will only be through the same type of painstaking effort that the Pentecostal – Charismatic movement can recover from her comfortable but flawed approach to issues concerning the intellect.

HEAD AND HEART

It is surprising (at least, to this writer) that in light of the generous amount of teaching in the Scriptures on "the mind," so little has been written about this subject, especially by authors who identify themselves as "Full Gospel." Moreover, in Pentecostal and Charismatic churches, I have detected a notable scarcity of preaching on this and other related topics. Though subjects like "baptism with the Holy Spirit," "spiritual gifts," "spiritual warfare," "the Lord's Supper," and "tongues" are mentioned only a few times in sixty-six books of God's inspired revelation, they are referred to relatively often in our churches. The Bible refers many times, however, to issues concerning the intellect, yet seldom do we hear teaching on such themes. To brush aside either at the expense of the other is negligent. Yet it appears as if we have given little thought to our neglect of such an important and central biblical topic.

It is important for us to keep in mind that the "Full Gospel" believer is one who passionately pursues *all* of God's counsel. But we are just as guilty of being piecemeal Christians as any other group. We call ourselves "Full Gospel" as compared to Christians who purposefully leave out the *charismatic* aspects of New Testament faith, yet we downplay the *intellectual* aspects of New Testament faith. In the final analysis, which of the following is worse? To neglect the relatively elusive charismatic gifts that visit us only at God's discretion (1 Cor. 12:11), or to fail to actively civilize and fervently exercise our God-given intellectual endowments that follow us every moment of our existence? I suggest neither is worse. When cold reason rejects the fire of God's manifest presence, disillusionment and injury rise to the surface. Likewise, when the *charismata* are not tethered to good thinking, the same confusion and injury surely follow.

Our fear of getting what we call "the head" (intellect) involved in "heart" (spiritual) issues has blinded us to the Bible's directives on loving God with our minds. The first step, then, in clearing up these myths is to go to God's Word and examine what the mind of our Maker says on the matter. In light of this, we will begin by seeking to determine how the terms "head" and "heart" are used by the One who created them both.

THE VENERABLE HEAD

The idea that our heads are, *by nature*, a hindrance to the spiritual life (heart activity) is *totally* foreign to the text of God's Word. Biblically, the head is *not* viewed as the home of godless reason, *set in opposition* to the heart or spirit, where devotional communion takes place. Rather, the head is described as a symbol of *prestige* and *respect*. The Old Testament word *ro,sh* denotes the place of *gesture*. The head was shaven in times of grief (Ezek. 7:18) and during the time of a vow (Num. 6:5), and it was covered with ashes as a sign of penitence (2 Sam. 13:19). In addition, the Old Testament believer saw the head as the *source of one's life* or likened it to the headwaters of a stream or river (Gen. 2:10; Isa. 1:6). Lastly, *ro,sh* signified one who occupies a position of *superiority* (Judg. 10:18).[2] It doesn't appear that Moses, David, Solomon, Isaiah, or any other Old Testament saints ever thought of the head as a mere necessary body part that is full of mischief.

In New Testament Greek, the head (*kephale*) is recognized as a place of *honor* and *dignity* (Rev. 4:4; 19:12). As with *ro,sh* in the Old Testament, the New Testament refers to the *kephale* as the part of the human being that represents an *individual as a whole* (Acts 18:1, 4, 6). In references such as 1 Corinthians 11:2–15, where Paul discusses headship, the term "head" denotes the *source, origin*, or, even *ruler* of another. In close relationship with this last nuance, Paul uses the word in Ephesians 4:15–16 to emphasize the *nurturing* and *guiding* aspects of the Christian's dependence on Jesus as the Head. Finally, Christ as the *Head* over every power demonstrates his supreme *authority* as well as his *life-giving* capacity (Col. 2:10).

The word "head" occurs approximately 360 times in the Bible, but nowhere does it appear to have the negative overtones that many modern-day believers pin on it. The head is not a logical reasoning device that merely transmits and stores information. As a matter of fact, as far as God's Word is concerned, the head isn't even referred to as the place where reasoning occurs.

In modern American culture, we understand "the head" as the place where thinking, reasoning, and understanding occur, whereas the heart is "the seat of emotions." When Christians assign stale, rationalistic traits to the head, then mistakenly equate the head with the mind, and, finally, detach the mind from the heart, they have succeeded in constructing a dangerous, unbiblical, and self-defeating doctrine that can become fatal to one's faith. But this is what has happened — seemingly without alarm. It shouldn't surprise us, then, that this widespread miscalculation has had cataclysmic repercussions in the realm of the life of the mind among professed believers.

As a result of confusion over these terms, we hear a well-known Pentecostal – Charismatic minister saying things like, "Had I kept *my mind* out of the situation," in contrast to letting it "come up in *my heart*." This Full Gospel spokesperson refers to the dangers of being "led by our *heads*" and points out that "there is a big difference in *head knowledge* and *revelation knowledge*." But this whole idea of "reasoning in the mind versus obedience in the spirit" (a direct quote from this popular preacher) is foreign to the biblical text. We can certainly reason without obeying, but can we ever actually obey without the involvement of our mind? Even the believer who speaks in a tongue must think in his or her mind: *Am I willing to launch out in faith? Will I choose to let the Lord use my lips? Have two or three attendees already given a message in tongues? Is somebody else speaking right now?* — and so on.[3]

There is no doubt that we can *think* without *doing* and *do* without *thinking*. Our mind may fight against what God has declared, or we may act in apparent obedience but do so out of wrong motives. We are also prone to say with our lips what we don't feel in our emotions or even believe (Isa. 29:13). And the human race has been known to spin alternative plans to God's plain will — like Saul (1 Sam. 13), for example. To suggest that any of these scenarios (in which we malign truth) indicates a *fundamental* hostility between the mind and the spirit is itself a maligning of truth — a fabrication of the human brain. We will see now why this latter dichotomy between head and heart or reasoning and believing is a myth spun by the modern mind rather than reality as revealed by God.

THE THINKING HEART

It's easier to accept that the "heart" in the Old Testament is the location of reason and thought when one realizes that there's no separate term for "mind" in the Hebrew language. In light of this, functions of what we call "the mind" are said to be performed by the heart. The Old Testament word for "heart" is *leb*; it is translated in three primary ways. To the Hebrew understanding, the *leb* was "mind," "soul," and "heart;" the seat of a human being's *spiritual*, *emotional*, and *intellectual* life. The popular idea that emotions, intellect (or reason), and "the will" operate from different places contradicts biblical teaching. The heart is the place of thought (Gen. 6:5), recollection (Deut. 4:9), intellectual objection (Gen. 17:17), meditation (Ps. 19:14), decision-making (2 Sam. 7:3), judgment (1 Kings 3:9), understanding (Prov. 8:5), planning (Isa. 10:7), and comprehension (44:18 – 19).[4]

It is interesting that while the above are all *heart* functions, they are also rational in nature. Though the Scriptures make it clear that "the heart" is our "reasoner," we seem to have a struggle with reconciling this fact with the spiritual life. Are we not a bit like the atheist who inadvertently uses arguments that actually best fit the worldview that says: "There must be a God"? This professed skeptic criticizes the worldview that, in reality, provides some of his most fundamental arguments. In a similar way, many Christians who are skeptical of "the intellect" seem to have no problem with using and even leaning heavily on it — that is, until it is pointed out to them that they have actually defended its importance by depending on its aid. The best solution (though not always simple) is to accept what the Bible reveals about this matter.

Most of us are familiar enough with Proverbs 23:7 (as rendered in the King James Version) to fill in the blank: "As a man thinketh in his _____, so is he." Of course, the missing word is *leb* — "heart" — the origin of *belief* or *denial* (Ps. 14:1). The heart manifests its operations in that it wills (1 Chron. 6:7 – 8), envisions, weighs ideas (Ex. 36:2), reasons (Deut. 29:2 – 4), and knows (Ps. 90:12). It's also where a person's "inner" conversation takes place (Joel 2:12) and where the functions of conscience carry on (1 Sam. 24:5). According to the Old Testament Scriptures, the heart is man's "organ" of thought; it is where those made in God's image think.

The New Testament uses the word "heart" in the same vast array of mental, intellectual, and rational attributes. This is somewhat peculiar, seeing that the Greek language, unlike Hebrew, does have a separate word for "mind" (*nous*). In spite of this, the heart (*kardia* in Greek) is designated as the part of a human being that decides (Matt. 5:28), draws conclusions (9:4), produces ideas (12:34), doubts (John 14:1), defends and judges (Rom. 2:14 – 16), receives knowledge (2 Cor. 4:6), thinks (Mark 7:21; Heb. 4:12), and reasons (Rom. 1:21). The notion that the head or mind is the seat of menacing, rational thought, and that the heart is the sole sanctuary of emotion and love, is novel but is not biblically sound.

WILL THE REAL "THINKER" PLEASE STAND UP

Of course, it would be wrong to suggest that the heart is merely a thinking entity. We see in both the Old and New Testaments that the *heart* also expresses emotion and possesses the ability to commune with its Maker. And though this is true of the heart, the *mind* too is said to have the capacity to enjoy sweet communion with God. Both of these human facets are described as having the capability to be friendly toward *or* at enmity with God. Even the casual reader of the Bible discovers that the *soul*, too, wills itself *for* or *against* its Creator and that the human *spirit* can both praise and curse God.

While each of these terms may carry a special nuance and seems to lean slightly toward a particular function, the difficulty lies in the fact that each of them — the soul, spirit, mind, and heart — can be found operating in all of the mentioned functions. That is, all four are said to carry the aptitude for thought, emotion, and will. Once again, the idea that the mind or head is rational and inferior and that the heart is emotional and superior is folklore. To put it simply, defining the functions of one's inner components isn't as cut and dried as some make it out to be.

I am not suggesting that there's no difference between the heart, the head, and the mind. Our heart beats in our chest but is the term used for the center of being in a person. Our head sits on our shoulders and contains the brain, without which we can't talk to God. And our mind, wherever it is, somehow uses the tangled gray matter sandwiched into our skull in order to experience God and his creation. Though we don't have it all figured out, one thing we can be sure of is this — the mind matters!

The Scriptures bear out the fact that our nonphysical components are intertwined and share responsibilities. First, the *heart* thinks, but it is also the seat of human volition or will (Deut. 8:2; Acts 8:22) and is the "location" from which human feelings and moods radiate (1 Sam. 1:8; Acts 2:26). Second, the *soul* ponders (1 Sam. 20:4), desires and longs for (Ps. 63:1; Matt. 6:25), knows (Ps. 119:14), and remembers (Lam. 3:20) — the same activities represented by the *heart*. Third, the human *spirit* is also presented as the thinking or reasoning element of a human being (Isa. 29:24; Mark 2:8; 1 Cor. 2:11). In addition, the spirit constitutes the seat of emotions (Ps. 143:4) and of the will (1 Chron. 5:26; Matt. 26:41), serving the same functions as heart and soul. Fourth, the *mind* engages in thought (Luke 24:45; 1 Cor. 14:14–15, 19), emotions, and affections (Eph. 4:17; 1 Tim. 6:5; Titus 1:15), and it wills or purposes as the organ of moral consciousness (Rom. 7:23, 25; 8:7, 27).[5]

All this is to say that not only do these varying terms represent elements of our non-bodily being that function in like capacities, but the terms themselves (*heart, soul, mind, spirit*) seem to be used interchangeably. Spirit-filled theologians Guy Duffield and N. M. Van Cleave point out that at least nine different terms are used in the Bible to refer to the inner part of the human being: the four above, plus *life* (Mark 8:35); *strength* (Luke 10:27); *self* (1 Cor 4:3–4); *will* (1 Cor. 7:37), and *affections* (Col. 3:2). On this matter, they are in agreement with the greater majority of prominent theologians and scholars.

There are scores of other verses supporting the view set out in this chapter; but I trust the above list of Scripture references is sufficient to settle the issue of the danger of pitting our heads and minds against our hearts and souls. If God does not pit these against each other, it is safe to say that we *must* not! If the term head doesn't carry negative overtones, if the mind is not simply a cold rationalistic gatherer of information, and if the heart operates in an intellectual capacity (among others), then to be anti-intellectual is to be, in essence, "anti-heart" and dangerously unbiblical.[6]

CONCLUSION

The fact that God's Word so often ascribes the same cognitive activities to the heart as it does to the mind and the fact that so few Pentecostal or Charismatic believers seem to acknowledge this indicate the breadth of our problem. Furthermore, the truth that the Bible frequently challenges the Christian to intellectual excellence and that many Full

Gospel folk carry anti-intellectual tendencies, combined with the reality that so small a number have spoken out on anti-intellectualism in Spirit-filled circles, speak to the depth of our dilemma.

Christianity with zeal and emotion, yet without knowledge and intellectual prowess, fits ideally into a society such as ours, where a nonrational, feelings-oriented, subjective way of life is customary. Yet as children of the kingdom, God urges us to be radically distinct from the unregenerate populace around us. We ought to acknowledge that reason and logic are gifts from God; that the mind and intellect are, in large measure, his image in us; and that science, education, and the arts are at their best when under the dominion of those called out from the blinding clutches of a fallen worldview. Besides, will not the pseudo-wise of this present age easily shrug off the voice of the church if she is unable to contend for and defend her faith and if she is unable to render superior reasons as to why she has placed her hope in God's Word and God's Son (1 Peter 3:15)?

But how can we love God with our minds in these crucial ways unless we prepare? How can we prepare if we don't even understand the value of our intellectual gifts? The answers lie in accepting that the heart is the place of thought and in seeing that there is no fundamental war between our minds and souls — between our heads and hearts. To approach this vital biblical subject in any other way is to do so haphazardly and with prejudice, which in turn is irresponsible and self-defeating.

For far too long, Pentecostals and Charismatics have maintained that true Bible-believing Christians should be suspect of the intellect. It is time to turn back the tide, prevail over this self-induced injury, and discontinue our practice of exporting it to other cultures. Emotions, personal experiences, and "Spirit-leadings" have their place in the life of faith; however, to leave our minds out of the mix is to encounter our own variety of "body blindness," like the young woman in the beginning of this chapter — it's a nightmare we cannot afford to leave uninterrupted. Our goal, then, is to continue to fan the fires of Pentecost with passion while at the same time endeavoring to cultivate the gardens of our minds with care and persistence.

NOTES

1. Oliver Sacks, *The Man Who Mistook His Wife for a Hat* (New York: Harper Perennial, 1985), 44 – 51.

2. G. Bromiley, "Head," *International Standard Bible Encyclopedia*, rev. ed. (Grand Rapids: Eerdmans, 1982), 2:639 – 40.

3. Joyce Meyer, *Battlefield of the Mind: Winning the Battle in Your Mind* (Tulsa, OK: Harrison House, 1995), 86 – 89.

4. T. Sorg, "Heart," *The New International Dictionary of New Testament Theology*, ed. Colin Brown (Grand Rapids: Zondervan, 1976), 2:180; J. P. Moreland and David M. Ciocchi, *Christian Perspectives on Being Human* (Grand Rapids: Baker, 1993), 34 – 35.

5. Even the *bowels* and *kidneys* (*reins*) are mentioned in several places in Scripture as closely connected with, or functioning like, the *heart* or *mind* (Ps. 7:9 – 10; 26:2; 73:21; Jer. 4:19; 17:10; 20:12; Phil. 1:8; 2:1; Rev. 2:23; see KJV on these).

6. Marvin Vincent, *Word Studies in the New Testament* (Peabody, Mass.: Hendrickson, 1991), 4:52; Kenneth Wuest, *Wuest's Word Studies From the Greek New Testament* (Grand Rapids: Eerdmans, 1973), 1:238; F. F. Bruce *1 & 2 Thessalonians* (WBC 45; Waco, TX: Word, 1982), 130; William Hendrickson, *Exposition of I and II Thessalonians* (Grand Rapids: Baker, 1979), 141 – 42; Sorg, "Heart," 2:180; in addition, Brown includes at least ten articles in this work on the subjects of "Mind," "Heart," "Head," and "Understanding." Donald Guthrie, *New Testament Theology* (Downers Grove, Ill.: InterVarsity Press, 1981), 167 – 71; Walter Elwell, *Evangelical Dictionary of Theology* (Grand Rapids: Baker, 2001), 331 – 32, 527 – 30; Moreland, *Christian Perspectives*, 31 – 44; A. T. Robertson, *Word Pictures of the New Testament*, 4:38.

2

The Life of God in the
Minds of Human Beings

God, who is abstract wisdom, and delights that his rational creatures should
search after it, and that his ministers should study to propagate it,
He expects that you will be foster-fathers of knowledge.
EARLY PURITAN LEADER, 1600S

He who understands truth without loving it, or loves without
understanding, possesses neither one or the other.
BERNARD OF CLAIRVAUX

Thus, we might conclude, it is subhuman merely to drift along,
unreflectively surrendering to external forces and conditions,
implicitly agreeing to be the plaything of outside forces.
DAVID GILL, EDUCATOR

You've probably heard about the man who was convinced that he was dead. Of course, that is ridiculous because a person's ability to reason about his or her own condition proves, ipso facto, that he or she is alive. But as you can imagine, this poor fellow created quite a dilemma, not only for himself but also for his concerned physician. After trying every measure in the book to convince his client of his true condition, the doctor hatched a brilliant scheme.

The first step was to get the patient to admit that living persons bleed and dead men don't. Only after this could he help prove to the delusional man that he was yet a living creature. Through various experiments, including pricking the skin of a number of deceased persons in the mortuary, the doctor succeeded in convincing the man that dead people in fact do *not* bleed. This otherwise frustrated physician knew he had found the solution for his deluded counselee — or so he thought!

When the doctor quizzed the previously confused man, the man replied, "It is true, dead men don't bleed." The doctor then informed the man that, since he thought of himself as being dead, then if he in fact bled, there was something seriously wrong in his thinking. The patient agreed without argument. After the doctor pricked the man with a pin, as expected he began to bleed. The prudent guide knew he had him — glorious day!

28

When the patient was asked if this whole matter was now settled in his mind, the man exclaimed, "Why, yes, it is settled; it is all clear to me now: *Dead men do bleed!*"

Like the problem presented in this silly anecdote, anti-intellectual*ism* is quite elusive in character. Its causes and symptoms are numerous and its influence is widespread. In brief, anti-intellectualism can be defined as *a prejudice against the careful and deliberate use of one's intellect*. Given this definition, almost anyone (especially Christians) can claim that they are free from its tyranny. This, in itself, is part of the nature of the problem — that is, an unwillingness to recognize and admit to its presence. Few admit to its hold on them, many have failed to escape the clutches of this prejudice.

In the previous chapter I attempted to dispel the notion that the head and heart are mortal enemies. I demonstrated this simply by drawing attention to the functions — according to Scripture — of the head, heart, and mind. The general purpose of this chapter is the same: to explore how the activity of the mind is woven into the very fabric of the spiritual life as well as how some of the biblical heroes of the faith put to use their God-given intellects for his glory. Granted, after reading this chapter, some may still retort, "*Christians don't think!*" It's my hope, however, that some of those who struggle with the mind's relationship to the spiritual life will see, perhaps for the first time, that a fair share of experiencing the *abundant life* is found in the cultivation of the *life of the mind*.

THE DOUBLE STANDARD: BODY, MIND, AND "THE SPIRITUAL"

We generally have no problem believing that Adam possessed a perfect physique and that he had unspoiled spiritual communion with the Father. Moreover, it seems widely accepted that this "son of God," made in his Father's image, was extremely intelligent; in other words, he had a profound intellect. Anyone naming every creature in existence had to have been pretty sharp (Gen. 2:19 – 20).

So, how do we relate to this? Through medical science, nutrition, and supplication, we do almost everything within our ability to extend our physical lives, scrambling to recapture even a portion of those ninety-three decades that Adam enjoyed. By way of Scripture reading, prayer, fasting, and praise, we attempt to garner a measure of that garden-variety communion with our Maker that our federal head (Adam) forfeited in the Fall. But when it comes to the *intellect*, many Pentecostal – Charismatic believers are apt to rejoin, "Be careful, lest it [the intellect] lead you astray." I admit that *over*emphasizing the intellect at the expense of other spiritual exercises is detrimental; but so is taking pride in one's devotional life or spiritual gift, or approaching the buffet at the local KFC with gluttonous intentions.

Thus, those who claim that we must be careful with our intellects because of their fallen nature receive a hearty "amen" from this author. There is no doubt about it: Our entire being fell when, in Adam, we acted unreasonably in the garden — and, of course, this includes our minds. But to be consistent, we can't argue against cultivation of the intellect *because* it's fallen and yet feed, pamper, exercise, groom, medicate, protect, and pray for healing of the physical body, *in spite of* its fallenness. That's dishonest and unbalanced. Undoubtedly, we should treat our fallen physical shells with respect in light of the fact that they are the temples of the Holy Spirit (1 Cor. 3:16 – 17; 6:19). But we must also treat the mind with at least equal respect, seeing that our minds are, in large part, the very image of God in man! It's important to remember that our bodies will either decay or be transformed at the Lord's coming, but also that the transformation and renewal of the mind is a lifelong project in the here and now (Rom. 12:2; Col. 3:1 – 10).

In addition to the common contradiction mentioned above, Pentecostal and Charismatic believers tend to confuse the matter even more when bringing into the mix the issue of "spiritual gifts." We appear to have no problem accepting the notion that God may grant a "word of wisdom" or a "word of knowledge," revealing information about ordinary life in an extraordinary way — and this is good. Yet many of us seem reluctant to embrace the idea that the Christian can glorify God by diligently studying ordinary or religious topics for the sake of mastering them and sharing them with others. Hundreds of times I've seen believers awed and impressed by the one who claims a "word of knowledge." Yet hundreds of times I've seen the same believers bored at the words of knowledge that were mined through arduous prayer and study. Why is this?

Mishandling and/or misunderstanding certain Scripture passages about the nature of knowledge and the mind can easily lead to this tainted approach. Often combined with this is an unhealthy lust for the sensational (i.e., craving melodramatic manifestations of the *charismata*). Other than these two pitfalls, there seems ultimately little excuse for this contradictory way of thinking. But it's this very line of reasoning (or lack of reasoning) that has hampered us in the realm of recapturing the intellectual dimension of paradise lost.

THE WORD OF GOD AND MIND OF MAN

The Bible assumes that the human being is a rational being, that God communicates his will through knowledge, and that human beings are capable of understanding that knowledge — even with a fallen mind. God expects us to comprehend, take to heart, and apply his words. Some argue that the non-Christian is unable to understand God's truth. But this poses at least three serious problems. First, how can an unbeliever ever become a believer if he can't make sense of the command to repent? Second, how can God hold us accountable for the truth if we cannot even understand it? Third, if unbelievers did not understand Isaiah, John the Baptist, Jesus, Peter, and Paul, then why were these people sawn in two or crucified, and why did some have their heads presented as trophies? Was it because the audiences couldn't quite make out what these prophets were trying to get across, or because they understood them all only too well?

When Adam fell, he hid because he understood that he was no longer a guest in God's house but a fugitive in the doghouse (remember, in Hebrew thought the "heart" *is* the mind). Adam knew and understood God's ways but decided against walking in them. He chose not to *think* God's *thoughts*. Instead, by suppressing the truth (Rom. 1:18, 28), he voluntarily allowed his *mind* to be blinded (2 Cor. 4:4) and so became an enemy of the Father in his *mind* (Rom. 8:7).

When God summons us to come back to him, he declares, "Let the evil man [forsake] his thoughts" (Isa. 55:7). In doing so, he is calling to repentance those whose thinking has become futile (Rom. 1:21). The word "repent," in its strictest sense, means to change one's mind or thinking. Thus, the act of repentance is said to bring us to the knowledge of the truth — back to reality (2 Tim. 2:25). This explains why those who once walked "in the futility of their thinking" (Eph. 4:17) are commanded to be made new "in the attitude of [their] minds" (v. 23) and to continually be transformed by "the renewing of [their] mind" (Rom. 12:2; in Greek, "thinking" and "mind" come from the same root, *nous*). And those who desire to engage right thinking must allow "things above" to occupy their minds (Col. 3:1 – 10) and to respond to the mandate to prepare their minds for action (1 Peter 1:13).[1]

As a repentant sinner receives the Spirit of truth, God opens that person's mind (Luke 24:45). He is granted a sound mind (2 Tim. 1:7), thus enabling him to love God with all of his mind (Matt. 22:37). Like the demoniac in whom dwelt Legion, those who are set free from mental/spiritual bondage (Rom 8:7) are found to be in their right mind (Mark 5:15), for those who were enemies of God in their mind now possess the "mind of Christ" (1 Cor. 2:16). Paul puts the whole matter succinctly in Romans 8:5 – 6: "Those who live according to the sinful nature have their minds set on what that nature desires; but those who live in accordance with the Spirit have their minds set on what the Spirit desires. The mind of the sinful man is death, but the mind controlled by the Spirit is life and peace." Without question, the mind is a huge factor in our relationship to our Maker.

MEN OF FAITH, MEN OF LEARNING

Not only is the mind an important element of entering into the life of faith, but how we use that mind throughout our faith *walk* is also vital. First, we will think better about think-ing and learn more about the nature of learning when we recognize that God does not carve chasms between knowledge and spiritual excellence. Neither does he drive wedges between knowledge in the brain and knowledge in the heart or between information gath-ered by perspiration and that garnered by intuition. Second, God's Word demonstrates that knowledge, for all intents and purposes, is neutral. Because of this, God is more con-cerned with how knowledge is used than with whether or not it is simply possessed. Third, it is impossible, of course, to apply knowledge unless that knowledge is first possessed.

Regardless of how much knowledge our brains contain, there are three basic attitudes toward knowledge itself. Because of mere suspicion or sheer laziness, we can spurn the idea that gathering knowledge is important. Or, we can seek, find, and hoard knowledge, use it for our own gain, and get all puffed up over what we know. Finally, we can passion-ately pursue knowledge in humility and then use what we know for the sake of serving others, for furthering Christ's kingdom, and for glorifying our God.

So, again, the contrast isn't between so-called "head knowledge" and "revelation knowledge," or between the intellectual life and the spiritual life. The contrast, rather, is between the *obedient* heart or mind, and the *disobedient* heart or mind. In God's economy, knowledge *with* action is the converse of knowledge *without* action (Mark 4.24), and knowledge accompanied by pride is the evil counterpart to knowledge with humility. Ultimately, however, the supreme disparity (as far as our intellects are concerned) is this: passionate, intentional use of the mind for God's kingdom and glory — or not!

It is interesting that many influential Bible characters came from cities that were known for their educational excellence and intellectual intensity. Abraham was raised in Ur of the Chaldees, where one of the most voluminous libraries of antiquity has been unearthed in recent years. Among the hundreds of thousands of "books" (stone tablets) found there, many deal with business, government, medicine, law, mathematics, and literature. Daniel too, who lived in Babylon, receiving an education par excellence (Dan. 1).[2]

Moses was the beneficiary of extraordinary learning in Egypt. Paul hailed from the home of the famed "Tarsus University," and Apollos was reared in the shadows of one of the great wonders of the ancient world, the legendary library of Alexandria (Acts 18:24). It may be more than coincidental that one-fourth of the Old Testament was written by Moses, of whom it is said that he was "instructed in all the wisdom of the Egyptians" (Acts 7:22, ESV); while in the New Testament, "Doctor Luke" and "Paul the learned" are responsible for 50 percent of its total content. With this in mind, we will turn to three primary biblical examples of men who received God's help with and stamp of approval on their intellectual excellence.

PAUL, GOD'S SCHOLAR

That Paul was an ardent student and that he used what he learned isn't a secret. He admits to having sat under the tutelage of the great Gamaliel, the administrator of the most distinguished academy of first-century Judaism (Acts 22:3). Whether or not he also attended "Tarus University" we don't know. But we're certain of at least these three facts: Paul knew Greek philosophy and literature (Acts 17:27 – 28; Titus 1:13 – 14); others recognized his sophisticated level of intellectual training (Acts 26:24); and he didn't spurn his secular education but put it to use at every turn. Even the Spirit-inspired Peter points out that the Spirit-inspired Paul was complex in his thought and that "ignorant" people struggled with his writings (2 Peter 3:16). This in itself carries immense implications as to God's use of human brain power.

Think about it! How could it be said that one portion of biblical revelation exceeds another section of Scripture in intellectual finesse and complexity unless the writer's intellectual expertise was taken into consideration? It is no accident that God handpicked Paul to receive (via the Spirit) and dispatch (via his mind) the New Testament masterpiece on justification by faith (the book of Romans) — the Magna Carta of the Christian faith!

In addition to penning beautiful, powerful, and complicated letters, Paul also regularly used his intellectual, rhetorical, and apologetic abilities on his missionary journeys. In Thessalonica the Holy Spirit inspired him and empowered him to build a mountain of proofs, showing that the Old Testament prophecies of the Christ were fulfilled in Jesus (Acts 17:1 – 4). In Athens, he put to work for the kingdom his aptitude for reasoning; he engaged in cultural dialog and even quoted from two Greek poets before commanding the Athenians to repent (17:17, 22 – 31). From his oration on the "altar to an unknown god" to the altar call to meet the one true God, Paul demonstrated his intellectual distinction.

The story in Corinth and Ephesus is the same. There he repeatedly reasoned, persuaded, refuted, debated, and argued for the saving of souls (Acts 18:4 – 5, 13, 19; 19:8 – 10). Like the giants of the faith (Justin Martyr, Augustine, Aquinas, Luther, Edwards, Wesley, etc.) who would follow in his footsteps, Paul found no contradiction between calling on God's supernatural intervention and calling on his reasoning abilities if it meant drawing a lost person one step closer to heaven's gate.

Of course, just because God elects to use some scholarly servants doesn't mean that he requires or prefers academicians for his kingdom labors. It does indicate, though, that God did *not* go out of his way to recruit men who were *without* higher learning. Not only has God used men of learning, but he has also prepared them for ministry *by way of* sharpening their intellects. Paul is a prime example. If he was set aside for God's use at birth (Gal. 1:15), then it seems that his "great learning" (Acts 26:24) was, most likely, preparation for his ministry some thirty years later! The same goes for Joseph, prime minister of Egypt; for Moses, heir to the throne of Egypt and president of the nation of Israel; and for Solomon, builder of God's earthly temple, to whom we now turn.

SOLOMON, GOD'S MAN OF KNOWLEDGE

In the case of Solomon, God is the motivating factor behind the genius of this brilliant individual. Like Paul and Apollos, Solomon was wise in the Scriptures. And like the others, he excelled in what we often refer to as "secular knowledge." Of course, it's evident that neither Solomon's great learning nor his knowledge of God's Word averted him from a life of adultery and idolatry. And although this is true, that in itself does not mean that we can take the quantum leap (as so many do) and purport that knowledge automatically leads us away from intimacy with and humility before our God.

The argument that Solomon wandered from the Lord because of his pursuit of so-called secular knowledge (as some have suggested) bears no more weight than does the argument that he roamed from his spiritual roots because of his wealth of knowledge *about* God. Whether plumber, philosopher, or prophet, each of us must always be prepared and willing to participate in — to act on — the truth that has been revealed to us. Otherwise, in the spiritual quest, we accomplish little more than chasing after the wind. Solomon's problem wasn't one of knowing too much but of living too little according to what he knew.

First Kings 4:29 tells us that "God gave Solomon wisdom and understanding exceeding much, and largeness of heart" (the RSV translates it "largeness of mind"). Again, Solomon's wisdom wasn't limited to so-called "sacred" knowledge (as if it can be separated from the secular), but encompassed many disciplines of thought. He seems to have been an expert biologist, natural scientist, zoologist, botanist, philosopher, poet, musician, politician, and lawyer. His dealings with foreign delegates, ingenuity in court cases, comprehension of wildlife and flora, literary abilities, architectural engineering, and artistic talent made him a Renaissance man born out of time (1 Kings 3 – 6; Eccl. 1 – 2). There's little doubt that Solomon would have been right at home in the company of colossal minds such as Aristotle, Augustine, Aquinas, Copernicus, Blaise Pascal, Jonathan Edwards, C. S. Lewis, and others like them.

God blessed Solomon with intellectual excellence as he wearied himself studying and devoting himself to investigating and exploring God's wisdom (Eccl. 1:13; 12:9 – 12). The knowledge that Solomon accrued was not shot into his mind like a sovereign injection, but it came little by little as he grew through applying his God-given intellect (Eccl. 1:16). All of this was a gift from the Lord. "The Lord is a God who knows" (1 Sam. 2:3), and he made the world according to wisdom (Ps. 104:24; Prov. 3:19). Fools think wisdom is acquired easily (Prov. 17:16), but the wise seek God's knowledge with passion (4:7). Note too that the Creator reveals his thoughts and wisdom to human beings (Amos 4:13).

DANIEL AND THE BOYS

One final biblical example where God was directly involved in placing his approval on secular learning is Daniel, the remarkable seer of the sixth century B.C., who was a devout man of prayer, fasting, and spiritual warfare (Dan. 6:3; 9:1–27). Like Solomon, he was a learned man; but unlike the poet of Proverbs, this prophet of God's panoramic history lived a circumspect life.

In Daniel 1 we read that Nebuchadnezzar, king of Babylon, captured Jerusalem (1:1 – 2). Afterward, he called for his chief court official to choose some of the captive Israelites to be trained for service in his palace (1:3 – 4). The king was specific about his standard for the new recruits. Among the requirements, intellectual distinction seemed to be the most important. He called for young men who showed aptitude for every kind of learning, guys who were quick to understand and were well informed (1:4). The training for these children of God (Daniel, Shadrach, Meshach, and Abednego) consisted of cultural, linguistic, and literary classes. The duration of their schooling was to be three years (1:5), and its objective was to prepare Daniel and his friends to serve in the palace of the king.

It is clear from Scripture that God brought Israel into Babylonian captivity (because of their disobedience) under the reign of Nebuchadnezzar (Jer. 27:6; 29:4). We know that Daniel and his friends were gifted by God in their intellectual abilities (Dan. 1:4, 6). We also read that God aided them in their learning (1:17 – 20) and that in supernatural fashion, he came to their rescue on more than one occasion (Dan. 3; 6). What all this tells us is that God superintended the lives of these sophisticated students in a detailed and personal way. As with Paul, the Lord had prepared these young men for their future ministry and stations in life. Perhaps the most stunning aspect of their story is that their training took place in a severely secular atmosphere that promoted pagan studies!

Based on this information, it is fair to say that, in itself, there was nothing inappropriate about Daniel, Shadrach, Meshach, and Abednego applying themselves to the higher learning of the Babylonians. In addition to advanced mathematics (in relation to the times, of course), astronomy, engineering, and administration, these young believers would have studied Chaldean deities and mythology before securing their Babylonian A.B. degrees. As Daniel 1:4 indicates, literature was likewise to be one of their mainstays, and the Mosaic manuscripts would most definitely *not* be the basis of that study.

It is interesting that nothing negative is said about the academic, religious, and cultural training that these Jews received. In fact, as mentioned, God actually caused the four young men to eclipse everyone else in the entire kingdom in their intellectual excellence:

> To these four young men God gave knowledge and understanding of *all kinds of literature and learning.* . . . In every matter of wisdom and understanding about which the king questioned them, he found them ten times better than all the magicians and enchanters in his whole kingdom. (Dan. 1:17a, 20, italics added)

Not only did God enable these men to learn Babylonian academics "ten times better" (Dan. 1:20) than the others, but he empowered them to stand spiritually firm in the midst of a radically pagan society. They wouldn't give an iota when it came to compromising God's Word. When commanded to eat foods that were not in harmony with Mosaic dietary laws, they were stalwart in their determination to refuse (1:8 – 16). Likewise, when it was decreed that the three friends worship an image of gold and when Daniel was notified that prayer to *his* God was forbidden, each defied the edicts that cut against the grain of God's revealed will.

These servants of God who found themselves in the Chaldean camp avoided the futile practice of swallowing camels and straining at gnats (cf. Matt. 23:24). If this sounds too broad-minded, read the book of Daniel and take it to God; he is the One who sent them to Babylon to study, caused them to excel, and directed Daniel to refer to the other three by their pagan names. If they would just as soon die in a roaring furnace than to disobey God, yet partook freely in the academia of the day, then the only sound conclusion we can draw is that they viewed their studies as pleasing to God. Though assailed by the attacks of the enemy, these godly examples managed to assimilate their newfound knowledge into lives lived for their Creator. They treasured their secular learning, used it for God's glory, and exhibited distinctive lives regardless of whether they resided in a pious or pagan culture. Along with Paul, Solomon, and Daniel, this, too, is our calling.

CONCLUSION

The task of thoroughly investigating the topic of "the life of the mind and the Bible" is nothing short of gargantuan. But this is to be expected in light of the fact that God has created the human being as a *rational* being, revealed his truth in an *intelligent* way, and has even made available illustrations of saints who valued and employed their intellectual gifts for his glory. Our Lord challenges us all to gird up the loins of our *minds* (1 Peter 1:13, KJV), commands us all to love him with *all* of our *minds* (Matt. 22:37), and promotes the development of our minds as we take captive every *thought* for the sake of Christ and his kingdom (2 Cor. 10:5).

Lordship is not limited to the so-called "religious" dimension of our lives but includes our logic, mental efforts, intellectual endowments, and all other cerebral endeavors. As Paul clearly explains in Romans 12:1, the only "reasonable" (see NIV note) response to God's mercy is to offer oneself as a living sacrifice — this embraces not only charismatic abilities but cognitive aptitude as well, not only our bodies but also our brains.

Clearly, God desires that his followers not only be people of prayer, guardians of the spiritual gifts, and demonstrative worshipers, but also an assembly of excellent thinkers. Nothing less than a unified, holistic discipleship will do for those in the service of the King. Yet, too often many of us within the Pentecostal – Charismatic community fail in our conviction of and passion for this approach to the life of faith. We tend to worship the act of worship itself, retaliate against detailed, doctrine-packed sermons, court a fondness for entertainment in the sanctuary, and exhibit marks of addiction to the "feel-goods." Our fascination with fame, fads, and fashion are indications that thinking Christianly is not necessarily at the top of our spiritual wish-list.

I would hope that the kind of positive biblical information concerning the intellect shared in this and the previous chapter will satisfy those who are suspicious of the mind. But I have learned by experience that that is often not the case. As a case in point, a dear friend of mine has the relentless habit of listening to my "positive" arguments and then merely retorting, "Yeah, but what about where the Bible says...?" Instead of dealing with the proofs that I present, he tries to lure me into his territory without even acknowledging my evidence. He knows that this gets my goat, and so he answers this way mainly out of sport. Nevertheless, I have met scores of Christians who honestly think that this is a viable way to answer those with whom they disagree. Because this is such a common maneuver, we must turn our attention to some of the "yes buts."

NOTES

1. J. Goetzmann, "Conversion," in *New International Dictionary of New Testament Theology*, 1:355.
2. David Beck, *Opening of the American Mind* (Grand Rapids: Baker, 1991), 175, 179; A. R Millard, "Ur," *ISBE*, 4:951 – 52.

3

The Apostle Paul and His Anti-Intellectual Verses

We live in a time of one of the most anti-intellectual periods in Western Christianity. That is, we are anti-mind; and it has become a (so-called) virtue among Christians.
R. C. SPROUL, TEACHER AND PHILOSOPHER, 1999

I must be frank with you: the greatest danger besetting American Evangelical Christianity is the danger of anti-intellectualism.
CHARLES MALIK, FORMER LEBANESE AMBASSADOR TO THE U.S.

When it was to his [Paul's] purpose, he cited Greek authors, just as he at other times employed the subtle rabbinic lines of reasoning. . . . Ambrose, Jerome, and Augustine, following Paul, learned to appreciate and utilize classical learning.
FRANCIS SCHAEFFER, CHRISTIAN PHILOSOPHER

In a fuming rage, my great-grandfather took his Belgian, T-Barker double-barrel shotgun to a neighboring city. Hunting down a sworn enemy, with one sizzling blast he delivered the soul into the arms of his Maker. The weapon used in the crime had been hidden for decades, only to surface in the 1980s as an item gifted by my grandfather to my dad. Thus, the folkloric saga went unchallenged — until. . . .

One day my dad received a call from a far-flung relative endeavoring to make contact with those who had fallen far from her family tree. In the course of their conversation, the woman relayed to my dad that her aunt knew the above story in full and that her aunt was, in fact, not only the daughter of our legendary ancestral shooter but was also the daughter of the *victim*. How could this be?

Contrary to the commonly-accepted chronicle of the antiquated crime, the woman told the rest of — and the truth of — the story. The perpetrator hadn't been my great-grandfather after all, as I had believed for so long; rather, it was my great-grandfather's brother who had wielded the weapon in that sweltering West Texas twilight so many years ago. And he did, in fact, fire the now-vintage shotgun. In a day and age when drive-by shootings were less of a news item, my great, great-uncle drove by his girlfriend's place, shot her through a veiled window (only injuring her), and raced off to confirm his pre-manufactured alibi. In five minutes, by shedding light on the story of her aunt's parents (the female victim and the male perpetrator), an otherwise total stranger had managed to melt away the myth that had been spun one hundred times over — at least the rendering that we'd been accustomed to hearing, sharing, and believing.

THE POWER OF MYTH

The power of myth is immeasurable. Adventurous souls throughout the ages have gambled their lives on the allure of an Atlantis, on the endowments ascribed to a Fountain of Youth, or on the recompense of an enigmatic El Dorado. The power of myth has exhausted adolescent empires and assigned multitudes to the death camps of many a madman. Believing half-truths or half-believing out-and-out falsehoods has mesmerized nations, fettered suffering humanity in the shackles of slavery, and imprisoned the minds of susceptible subcultures. The Pentecostal – Charismatic movement is one of those subcultures; and one myth that we tend to cling to is that of believing that the Bible minimizes the reasoning faculties of a human being.

It's not as rare as you might think that Christians fail to distinguish between fables and the facts of Scripture. For example, even though many believers assume differently, the Scriptures do not tell us that Samson's hair was cut by Delilah, that Noah's ark rested on Mount Ararat, or even that three wise men visited Jesus at his birth. There is *not* a book of Revelation*s* in the Bible, Absalom was not caught up in a tree by his hair, and we are not told that the "mark" placed on Cain was a sign of judgment or curse. Furthermore, God did not limit Noah to housing two of every kind of animal on the ark, nor does the Bible indicate that money is the root of all evil. To these could be added dozens of other commonly-accepted untruths.

Of course, we are all prone to believe these kinds of floating fictitious data-bits, and one may argue that there is little harm in referring to the book of Revelation as if its title were plural. But far too many go a step further and believe totally erroneous concepts that are, otherwise, peddled as biblical truth. For example, instead of embracing the biblical idea of "faith," which most often indicates radical trust leading to action, many Christians speak of faith as an emotional inkling, to be used when there's little evidence to support one's case. Some liken faith to a magical creative force by which they can manufacture their every wish, and there are those who have been led to think that faith is equal to simply confessing that something is true.

Or take the case of the modern-day concept of "church." For the most part, when we think of "church," we almost automatically envision a bricks-and-mortar facility constructed to keep us out of the rain. By contrast, the Bible refers to *people* at every mention of the word. In the tangled terminology of pop Christianity, "worship" too has morphed, becoming that part of the gathering of the saints when voices are raised to crescendo while accompanied by an orchestra of mechanized instruments. As a result of segregating the biblical concept of "reverent submission" (the true meaning of "worship") from our everyday lives, we fail to integrate the Lordship of Christ into the so-called mundane duties of life, while glorifying that narrow slice of the "church service" when we sing songs to God. Some refer to the results of this fallacious and fuzzy thinking as "worship of worship."[1]

I could go on about how we think that true "fellowship" hasn't come to pass until pie is served, and of how we question whether or not "good preaching" has taken place if there hasn't been a display of high emotion and earsplitting volume. In addition, when we as Full Gospel believers speak of "the gifts," we almost always mean just the showy and mysterious gifts of ecstatic speech. And what about the biblical concept of tithing, which to many has come to mean "giving anything I want to give"; and evangelism, which has been reduced to telling a lost coworker that you go to a good church where there's good preaching and good fellowship?

The basic notion of "missions" has also been caught up in the same web of misinterpretation. In the thought of many, you aren't doing mission work unless you have first crossed a large body of water. "Prayer" is often equated with only asking and receiving. "Revival" has degenerated into a cluster of planned meetings with a special speaker. And, being "born again" is all too frequently equated with quoting a short prayer at an emotion-packed altar.

I could go on to cite our skewed conceptions of discipleship, holiness, the end times, and the like. My point is that we are apt to receive certain definitions as truth (however distorted they may be) and then go on about our spiritual business with little desire to revisit them for the sake of clarification or modification.

As I carve out this chapter, I have sitting before me twenty-one volumes with approximately 6,500 pages — utterly packed with false information that is commonly held as reliable. These works disclose 1,500 superstitions, conspiracies, myths, and half truths that people of every walk of life have held to enthusiastically. These fallacious fragments have only two things in common: They are all false, and at various times in history, the majority of the populace has believed these renditions to be true![2]

Again, it will probably never matter whether we mistakenly call London's famed clock tower "Big Ben" (only the bells themselves carry this title). Nor will we thwart world evangelization by continuing to surround baby Jesus' manger with three wise men (we are not told there were three, and they did not show up at the time of his birth). But if we exchange a fundamental aspect of the Scriptures (e.g., the life of the mind) for myths, we will surely pay a price — and that we have! When we believe these half truths, we begin to do strange and illogical things, such as using our intellects to promote anti-intellectualism or using our reasoning capabilities to defend the doctrine of "faith, not reason."

As long as we misunderstand the relationship between the gift of faith and the gift of reason, we will fail to live and minister as we should. We also deal an inestimable measure of damage to the kingdom of God by way of describing the Christian experience with the all-too-common mythical decree, "It ain't a head thing, but a heart thing." We can change this! In order to do so, however, we must plumb our minds with the mind of God; we must think critically, ponder philosophically, exercise our intellects, and engage in mental discipline.

God wants us to enhance the inner world of our mind and imagination, and he invites us to see the interconnectedness of all of life. We must no longer restrict "the life of the mind" merely to what we *think about*. Rather, we must become mature in these matters, paying closer attention to the way we think — that is, *why* we think *what* we think, and *why* we think the *way* we think. Only through these types of intellectual enterprises will we succeed in girding up the loins of our minds (1 Peter 1:13) and so become adept at bringing every thought captive and obedient to Christ (2 Cor. 10:5). The first step in accomplishing this was taken in chapters 1 and 2. The second step requires us to deal with the fraudulent interpretations that many modern-day believers attach to the so-called anti-intellectual verses.

THE "ANTI-INTELLECTUAL VERSES"

A Pentecostal pastor, a Full Gospel evangelist, and a missionary with the Charismatic movement — all three had visited our home at different times and all three pointed to the same handful of verses when challenging the ideas presented in this book. The biblical passages subpoenaed by my houseguests are the standard comebacks that I have heard countless times since becoming a Christian. Two verses come from 1 Corinthians; the first deals with the futility of the "wisdom of the world" (ch. 1) and the second warns that "knowledge puffs up" (ch. 8). A third verse quoted in opposition to my subject is from 2 Corinthians 3: "The letter kills, but the Spirit gives life." We must now examine how these "anti-intellectual verses" have been misunderstood and how we can wrestle them back into their rightful context.

1 Corinthians 1:17 – 2:5: "Wisdom of the World"

> For it is written:
>
> *"I will destroy the wisdom of the wise;*
> *the intelligence of the intelligent I will frustrate."*
>
> Where is the wise man? Where is the scholar? Where is the philosopher of this age? Has not God made foolish the wisdom of the world? (1 Cor. 1:19 – 20)

The idea that Paul by and large downplays the intellect, debate, philosophy, secular learning, or the life of the mind is without substance. Granted, a superficial perusal of these two verses may cause the reader to think that Paul pits the intellect against spirituality and human scholarship against the cross, but a closer look affords quite another meaning.

Paul begins 1 Corinthians by thanking God (1 Cor. 1:4) and complimenting the Corinthians (1:5) for their richness of *knowledge*. Then, in 1:10 – 11, he reveals the purpose for which he is writing to them: "that you may be perfectly united in *mind* and *thought*" (italics added). Third, the focus of the early chapters of this letter deals with the Corinthians' tendency toward pitting various personalities (Apollos, Paul, and Peter) against each other (1:12; 3:3 – 9, 22 – 23; 4:6). They craved "being someone" (at least, vicariously) by attaching themselves to the most recent rising star. Paul states that this conduct is worldly, that they are acting like "mere men" (3:3), thinking that they have somehow "arrived" by casting their vote for the most eloquent speaker or the one they imagine as exhibiting the deepest insight (4:6 – 21)!

Some of these believers are now despising Paul (1 Cor. 4:1, 6, 18; 9:1 – 27) and are tempted to view his message of the cross as merely one of many options or as being too elementary for them, now that they think of themselves as kings (4:8 – 21). By placing their faith in human beings (2:5), they are in danger of discarding the only "Amen" to God's promises (cf. 2 Cor. 1:20) and so forfeiting the power and value of Christ's death and resurrection.

In light of the situation in Corinth, Paul defends his apostolic commission as well as the exclusive truth of the gospel. He informs them that God does not choose people because of their nobility or special insights (1 Cor. 1:26 – 31). Rather, in spite of their lowliness, God chooses them to be heirs of his salvation. He reminds them that they did not come to God *because of* their own "wisdom"; therefore, they must not think themselves as wise in a worldly (arrogant) way. If they did in fact receive the message of Christ *by grace*, then they have no reason to boast (4:7). If they do boast, they indict themselves, because the very act of boasting empties the cross of its meaning for them (1:17). That is, a person cannot simultaneously be both "cross-dependent" *and* self-sufficient!

Paul is basically saying something like this: "If you were so wise, why didn't you figure it all out before I came with God's revelation of the cross?" (1 Cor. 1:21). Those whom Paul refers to as "wise" are wise in their own humanistic eyes and so refuse the wisdom of Christ's work on Calvary. His point is that divine revelation is the only well of information from which one may draw in order to accurately understand humanity's true condition and the remedy for that condition. In addition, the power of Christ's resurrection confirmed the divine origin of that revelation. If anyone claims "human wisdom" *over* divine revelation, then, in essence, they are purporting that the death and resurrection of Christ are just another exciting philosophy, neither distinguished among the many nor holding absolute reign.

But God doesn't condemn wisdom *carte blanche*. We know this because in 1 Corinthians 2:6, Paul refers (in a positive way) to "a message of wisdom among the mature." There's no doubt that God does frustrate the intelligence of the intelligent — but only when the "intelligent" are attempting to define reality and salvation *apart* from his Son. Also, the scholar or scribe who seeks salvation through good works or morality is just as lost as the babbling pagan who bows before a silent stone image. Nevertheless, without the faithful copying and linguistic labors of the scribes, the Scriptures would have never survived the dark ages of Israel's history.

God doesn't stigmatize secular learning, philosophical acumen, scholarly endeavor, or marked intelligence. But he does condemn *trusting for salvation* in any belief system other than "faith in his grace through the cross of Christ." This is why Paul purposed to preach only this message when he stayed among them (1 Cor. 2:2), and this is why he didn't use the emotional form of rhetorical persuasion often used by hired speakers (2:1, 4). Paul is well aware that feelings-based, psychological manipulation is a powerful tool; remember that he grew up in Tarsus where the schools were recognized for their expert training in the art of persuasive speaking. Paul knew that by beguiling his hearers emotionally, the power of his message would be emptied.

It is not that Paul is against persuasion or argumentation. As a matter of fact, when Paul first preached in Corinth, he is said to have "reasoned in the synagogue, trying to persuade Jews and Greeks" (Acts 18:4, 19). To Paul, there is a considerable difference between manipulating minds with technique and persuading minds with a reasoned defense. For one and one-half years Paul utilized the latter (18:11), and as a result, he witnessed much spiritual fruit among them.

Finally, according to 1 Corinthians 1, we should note that miracles are also among the culprits that can hinder belief in Christ. Since this is the case, we (especially Pentecostals and Charismatics) should broach the emphases of this chapter with exceptional care. If the intellect (1:19), scholarship (1:20), philosophy (1:20), and wisdom (1:21) are in themselves detrimental to or hindrances to Christianity, then miracles (1:22) must likewise be unsuitable. But, of course, Paul is not proposing that these elements of the human experience are, *by nature*, harmful to spirituality. Rather, Paul is trying to convey that each of these *can* become an impediment to faith *when* emphasized above the work of the cross. That is the very core of his argument.

Paul writes clearly that it is just as wrong for the Jews to place their faith in miraculous signs as it is for Greeks to place their faith in their own intellectual troubleshooting. Neither may take the place of God's revelation of his Son, nor can they provide salvation for the soul. Moreover, a careful reading of the Gospels bears out that an adulterous generation is more typified by miracle-mongering than by wisdom-seeking (Matt. 12:39; 16:4; Luke 11:29)! Ultimately, it is never the intellect, miracles, material things, or works that are the targets of God's hit list. Rather, it is the *trust* we place in these things over and against God's grace through Christ that ushers us into the crosshairs of his jealous wrath (1 Cor. 1:18).

In summary, those within the Full Gospel movement who struggle with anti-intellectualism would do well to learn at least five things from this portion of God's Word. (1) The focus of 1 Corinthians 1 is not centered on the negative character of the intellect, learning, miracles, and philosophy; rather, it focuses on the problem of wrong attitudes about them.

(2) Whether one admits that he or she is demanding miraculous signs or not, there's a danger of emptying the power of the cross in one's life by constantly asking for supernatural confirmation before obeying God's Word. Requiring that certain gifts be manifested

in a church service before deeming it as "spiritual" is also closely related to "demanding miraculous signs" (1 Cor. 1:22).

(3) We who belong to the Pentecostal – Charismatic movement tend to possess a weakness for following personalities. Too many of us chase after the man or woman of the hour because of their charisma, technique, or outward apparent success. Our Maker declares that this, too, is worldly.

(4) Because many Pentecostals have witnessed God's manifest power in remarkable ways, there's the perpetual temptation to think that we have arrived, that we as a movement are more spiritual, or that we have a corner on the market of truth and experience. We must be careful not to possess an attitude of superiority — an attitude that says, "If you get what I have, you too can be one of God's special people." Paul has a few choice things to say to those who act like royalty (spiritual giants among religious dwarfs), to those who have already become kings (1 Cor. 4.8).

(5) When we substitute loud, shallow preaching with little substance for rich exposition, when we deem that answering an altar call equals salvation, and when we rely on emotional manipulation or heart-tugging music to fill the altar, we are in danger of doing what Paul refused to do. The "eloquence" to which he refers in 1 Corinthians 2:1, 4 is reliance on atmosphere and emotional finesse rather than on the content or truth of Christ's message.

1 Corinthians 8:1: "Knowledge Puffs Up"

> Now about food sacrificed to idols: We know that we all possess knowledge. Knowledge puffs up, but love builds up.

Like the passage just dealt with, this one makes little sense without taking into account its immediate context. It is apparent that what is being taught here has something to do with "puffyness" or pride in connection with knowledge, but the nature of this knowledge is hidden until we probe a bit deeper. The verse cannot possibly mean that *all* knowledge produces pride. If this were the case, then knowing that knowledge puffs up would, ipso facto, bring guilt to the person who acknowledges this truth. This reduces the verse to sheer nonsense.

Once again, Paul is dealing with an *attitude* toward knowledge, not knowledge itself. The Son of God knows more than does every earthling combined (Col. 2:3), but he is not puffed up! He knows subatomic physics, calculus, the laws of thermodynamics, and the detailed anatomy of every living creature. As 1 Corinthians 8:6 points out, all of these things have come from the Father and through the Son, all of this and more — but he is not puffed up with pride.

Even while Jesus walked among us, he had greater knowledge of the Father and of human beings than any others who lived before, during, or after his walk of humanity. He was a thinker's Thinker, a logician's Logician, and the intellectual's Intellectual — but he was not puffed up in light of the knowledge he possessed. Of course, Jesus had an unfallen mind, which made all the difference in how he handled his knowledge. This is exactly what Paul is dealing with in this verse — encouraging followers of Jesus to handle knowledge the same way Jesus did.

Instead of working out the Beatitudes, the Corinthians are guilty of exhibiting bad attitudes; attitudes that scream — "It's all about ME!" In the case of 1 Corinthians 8, some of the believers are eating food that has been sacrificed to false gods. They are able to do this with clear consciences because they possess the knowledge that "an idol is nothing" (8:4). Their crime isn't to be found in the actual eating of such foods but in the attitudes that they exhibit in lieu of their capacity to eat these sacrifices. That is, some of the weaker believers, who do not acknowledge this freedom, are upset and confused over the fact that others are taking the liberty to eat lunch at the idol buffet (8:7).

Paul is basically revisiting the problem he had dealt with in 1 Corinthians 1 and will deal with in chapters 11 – 14. In the earlier passage, he addressed those who said, "I have knowledge of Peter, you only have knowledge of Paul"; in the latter, he will speak to those who say, "I don't need you, I have plenty of gifts and knowledge on my own." Paul nails them/us all by declaring: "If I can fathom all mysteries and all knowledge . . . but have not love, I am nothing" (13:2).

Through Paul, God shows his concern that the exercise of freedom by some is destroying the faith of others (1 Cor. 8:9 – 11). He challenges the stronger believers to choose to withhold some of their privileges for the sake of helping these weaker brothers (8:13; 10:28 – 29). If the stronger Christians continue to take their liberty in accordance with the knowledge they possess (i.e., that idols are nothing), then the weaker will be tempted to do what they still consider to be sin (8:10). Paul reminds the *knowledgeable* Corinthians that Christ died for the weak brothers and that to meddle with their faith is serious business. As a result, he instructs them to do that which builds up the body: Love the weaker brother — don't let them be destroyed by what you *know* (8:11)!

In the case of 1 Corinthians 8, the reality that "an idol is nothing" is portrayed as a positive thing and a sign of the Corinthians' maturity (at least in this matter). By nature, knowledge does not automatically puff up the one who possesses it. But if people use that knowledge in a selfish way, they sin. On the contrary, if knowledgeable believers are like Christ — that is, willing to humble themselves for the sake of others (Phil. 2:5 – 8) — they prove that they love God *and* that they are counted as among the children of God (1 Cor. 8:3, 13).

2 Corinthians 3:6: "The Letter Kills, but the Spirit Gives Life"

> He has made us competent as ministers of a new covenant — not of the letter but of the Spirit; for the letter kills, but the Spirit gives life.

One day, while perching on the railing of a bridge that overlooked our Bible college campus, I was approached by a good brother who "had a word" for me; you know, the God-told-me-to-tell-you variety. It concerned my activity while on the bridge — I was reading a book. I had known the Lord for only about a year, so it baffled me when this self-appointed seer looked me in the eye and declared, "The letter killeth, but the Spirit giveth life." He went on to counsel me of the dangers to be found in "dead letters," that is, books written by mere men. In light of the fact that this was coming from a fellow who was attending a Bible college, paying for textbooks, and sitting at the feet of learned men, the whole episode seemed rather curious to me. Moreover, I was reading a book on the guidance of the Holy Spirit, which made his word even more ironic.

I cannot count the times that the above fragment of Scripture has been parroted to me throughout the years. Being the custodian of a substantial personal library has made me a prime target for the superspiritual who seem never to find the need to graze on wisdom from the seasoned spiritual writers of the ages. Of course, I have found that these tend to be the same ones who untiringly pedal their own variety of wisdom.

In any case, the idea that "the letter" to which Paul refers is the printed page of non-biblical (or biblical) writings is ludicrous. Can reading — with too little prayer and a lack of communion with Jesus — diminish the soul's love for the things of God? You better believe it! But so can the inordinate love of golf, money, sports, fame, success, position, and even family (Matt. 10:37). But this isn't at all the issue that Paul is dealing with in 2 Corinthians 3:6.

The "letter" that Paul refers to is simply the old covenant law (2 Cor. 3:3, 7, 14). The law is God's way of showing the whole world that people have fallen short of his standard (Rom. 3:19). If anyone keeps the whole law and yet fails at just one point, he is guilty of breaking all of it (James 2:10). This bondage, as Paul duly depicts in Romans 7:7 – 20, is like trekking on a torturous eternal treadmill. It produces only exhaustion, temptation, frustration, condemnation, and damnation. Thus, whereas "the letter" (the law) causes us to see our own failure before, and separation from, God (death, 2 Cor. 3:7), the Spirit, who brings righteousness as a gift (3:9), offers life (salvation).

Paul goes on to write that the message of Christ was the liberating factor in the Corinthians' lives and that, as they turned to Christ (2 Cor. 3:16), their dull "minds" were enlightened (3:14). Because they received the truth of the new covenant, they also encountered the ministry of the Spirit and, in turn, obtained freedom from the demanding bondage of "the letter" (the law) and of sin. Thus, Paul goes on to declare that where the Spirit of the Lord is, there is "freedom" and there is "life" (3:6, 17).

Yes, Paul does contrast "letters of ink" with "letters written on the heart" (2 Cor. 3:1 – 3). The salvation of the Corinthians was the result of Paul's ministry to them. So, by way of this communiqué, Paul reminds them that their newfound freedom — their liberty in the Spirit — came as he preached Christ among them. Speaking for himself and his associates, he declares: "You . . . are our letter, written on our hearts" (3:2). This is why he is *writing* this letter of ink to the Corinthians.

CONCLUSION

Years ago, while sitting in a class dedicated to the study of the Holy Spirit, a student made a statement that has been branded onto my memory. This young zealot, who was known for his agitated demeanor and elevated suspicion of things demonic, was in hot debate with our instructor over the use of tongues in a corporate setting. This youthful mystic argued that there should be no limit placed on the quantity of ecstatic messages given in a church service. The professor noted that Paul, writing to the Corinthians, directed them to allow only two — or at the most three — congregants to speak forth a message in tongues in any one meeting (1 Cor. 14:27). With vexation on his countenance and provocation in his voice, the student shouted to the teacher, "I don't care what Paul says; how can you tell *the Holy Spirit* to shut up?"

Many Pentecostals and non-Pentecostals alike have used the Scripture passages dealt with in this chapter as battering rams against the fortifications of the intellect, the mind, logic, philosophy, higher learning, hermeneutics, apologetics, the sciences, the pursuit of knowledge, and the reading of great literature. Because ideas have consequences, we must all strive to be more cautious when interpreting the so-called "anti-intellectual verses." Otherwise, we may find ourselves thinking what the young man actually said — that is, "I don't care what Paul says; I won't tell *my preconceived notions and interpretations* to keep quiet."

NOTES

1. O. Michel, "Faith," *New International Dictionary of New Testament Theology*, 1:599 – 605; Merrill C. Tenney, *Pictorial Encyclopedia of the Bible* (Grand Rapids: Zondervan, 1976), 5:969 – 75; Elwell, *Evangelical Dictionary of Biblical Theology*, 95 – 97; Wuest, *Word Studies*, 3:109 – 24; James Hastings, *A Dictionary of the Bible* (Peabody, MA: Hendrickson, 1988), 2:412 – 13.

2. Among the more fascinating volumes on these subjects are: "The Bible Tells Me So," "Offbeat History," "The 60 Greatest Conspiracies," "Extraordinary Popular Delusions and the Madness of Crowds," "Studies in Contemporary Superstitions," "The Dictionary of Misinformation," "Architects of Conspiracy," "Fads, Follies, and Delusions of the American People," "Legends, Lies, and Cherished Myths of American History," "The Dark Side of Church History," and "The Rewriting of America's History."

4

Matthew, Luke, and John on Matters of the Intellect

Step one generation away from the New Testament writers to meet the men who were discipled by the apostles and you find treatises, apologies, and circular letters of stunning intelligence from those intensely devoted Church Fathers.
DAVID HAZARD, CHRISTIAN EDUCATOR

Eddication don't give a man the power of the Spirit. It is grace and gifts that furnish the real live coals from off the altar. St. Peter was a fisherman — Do you think he ever went to Yale College?
POPULAR NINETEENTH-CENTURY PREACHER

We went to extremes in despising learning and earthly culture.... If increased culture will now add to our achievement, and thereby increase the glory of God, we shall welcome it. Culture to whom culture; learning to whom learning; refinement to whom refinement; but for us all, the touch of God upon our souls.
DONALD GEE, PENTECOSTAL LEADER; *COMMENTS ON ACTS 4:13*, 1946

By 1976, at age twelve, I had already been involved for four years in the sport of racing homing pigeons. In the spring of that year, I was blessed with a newfound friend. A beautiful, promising prodigy hatched from my best breeding pair of homers. One day the little guy fell from his nest box and was made sport of by the other birds in his section of the loft. They managed to peck him so hard and for so long that his soft skull had been chipped away at — exposing his brain. The natural thing to do, in the pigeon-eat-pigeon world of racing, was simply to dispose of the suffering squab, but I didn't have the heart to do so. Furthermore, as I watched this bird, I thought I recognized something of greatness in his character.

With the help of hand-feeding and some mysterious salve that was supposed to work miracles, the little fellow made it. He didn't look like much — but he made it. Because of his squab-hood wounds, his eyes protruded in a ghastly fashion, his nose was disfigured, and his head was totally void of feathers. Though his registered number was an imposing "AU – 76 – WF – 32," I referred to him affectionately as "Scrub." Scrub went on to win first prizes against hundreds of other birds from the hundred-mile, two hundred-mile, and three hundred-mile race stations. He would win the cherished "Young-Bird Hall of Fame

Award," and went on to become a sensation among my breeding stock, producing a dozen great prize winners. At the youthful age of six, this passionate, strange little speckled bird died of a brain tumor. At first glance, he was only a ragged racing pigeon; but with fairness and time, I recognized an "otherness" about him. With closer scrutiny I came to see that he was more, not less, than your average bird. He was a mind on fire and not a scrub after all.

Whereas Paul the apostle has been noted as the slick scholar of New Testament lore, few have accused Peter, John, and Matthew of possessing heady prowess. In light of their humble statures in their B.C. lives, some who criticize rational involvement in heart affairs have championed the above trio as heroes of the anti-intellectual hall of fame — common, uneducated, crude, mental *scrubs*. At first glance one might think that they were mere illiterate, intellectual slouches who taught that the less training and learning one possesses, the greater potential for spiritual power and purity. But with closer scrutiny we can detect that they were more than just your average anti-intellectual. Like my feathered friend, all that these guys need is a fair chance to prove that they are not only "minds on fire," but individuals who promote the same — and not scrubs after all!

Matthew, the uncouth tax collector who wrote that heaven was hidden from the "learned" (Matt. 11:25), was also the gospel writer who noted that the greatest commandment of God was to love him with all of one's heart, soul, and *mind* (22:37). John, "Son of Thunder," who said that we don't need mere human teachers to instruct us (1 John 2:27), utilized the ancient philosophical concept of *the Logos* — Logic Incarnate — to aid in elucidating Christ's deity (John 1:1 – 18). And, Peter, the lowly fisherman, who (along with John) was reckoned as an ignorant and unlearned man (Acts 4:13), pleaded with his hearers to prepare their *minds* for action (1 Peter 1:13).

Though it's virtually effortless and painless — at least momentarily — to place our faith in an interpretation of Scripture that best suits our situation, it's neither prudent nor painless in the long run. We may feel better about ourselves because of our lack of education, we may feel justified in our dislike of cocky but unspiritual intellectuals, or we may sleep better knowing that we spend twenty-five hours a week in front of the TV (or partaking in our favorite diversion) instead of investing in the betterment of our minds. But this doesn't make our false interpretations of the so-called anti-intellectual verses any more accurate.

In addition, aren't false interpretations of isolated passages of Scripture the material that cults and sects are made of? The idea of baptizing for the dead, Christian demon possession, white supremacy, legalisms of every stripe, and hundreds of other dangerous doctrines derive from hackneyed hermeneutics — which, in the end, are the result of slipshod thinking.

If this is the case, then we must be that much more careful when interpreting the verses that deal with matters of thinking, learning, and the mind. Though I believe it is false to claim that demons can inhabit a Christian, I am convinced that if the enemy of our souls can poison our thinking about thinking, he will have abundant opportunity to inhibit our spiritual journey in hundreds of ways. In the previous chapter, we examined some of Paul's supposed slams on the intellect; let's look now at Luke's apparent praise of Peter's and John's ignorance, Matthew's censure of the wise and learned, and John's conjectural caveat against human tutors.

UNLEARNED AND IGNORANT MEN

> Now when they saw the boldness of Peter and John, and perceived that they were unlearned and ignorant men, they marvelled; and they took knowledge of them, that they had been with Jesus. (Acts 4:13, KJV)

Like the Scripture portions that we dealt with in the previous chapter, this verse is frequently perceived as downplaying the intellect by those who court an anti-intellectual bias. Those who glare through the narrow lenses of prejudice when explaining verses such as this one often speak with dogmatism and facility, "It says what it says — they were ignorant and unlearned!" When the shoe is on the other foot, though, these same brothers and sisters cry "foul," demanding that context be given its due respect.

For example, when those who refuse women a place of leadership in the church quote Paul that "women should remain silent in the churches" and "I do not permit a woman to teach" (1 Cor. 14:33 – 34; 1 Tim. 2:12), most Full Gospel believers maintain that you have to take Greek meanings and the cultural milieu into account in order to properly ascertain the true meaning of these verses. We do the same when someone quotes from Paul's charismatic corpus: "Do all speak in tongues?" (1 Cor. 12:30); "where there are tongues, they will be stilled … when perfection comes, the imperfect disappears" (13:8 – 10); and, "in the church I would rather speak five intelligible words to instruct others than ten thousand words in a tongue" (14:19).

As I sit here, scores of these scenarios come to mind, where double-standard maneuvers are made for the sake of protecting our preconceived notions. It seems that almost everybody (whatever camp we may belong to) exhibits this slanted approach at one time or another; yet it also seems that practically nobody ever admits to it — strange.

When those who promote the life of the mind take a verse like Acts 4:13 and attempt to explain it in context, the anti-intellectual should (for the sake of integrity) allow for this supposedly clear verse to be clarified further. It is dishonest to claim that *we* explain verses to further *our* cause and yet claim that *others* merely misuse verses when their insights dash one of our pet doctrines. The Holy Spirit is the "Spirit of truth"; therefore, it will serve us well to honor his namesake as we approach controversial passages.

First of all, if John and Peter, deemed as "unlearned and ignorant men," were like their Master (cf. Acts 4:13b), then one must concede that Jesus, too, was an ignorant and unlearned man. This, of course, doesn't set too well — especially in light of the fact that Colossians 2:3 informs us that in Christ "are hidden all the treasures of wisdom and knowledge." If everything was created through Jesus (John 1:3), if he sustains all things

(Col. 1:17), and if he is the Author of all the principles regulating the universe, it is difficult to view him as an "ignorant and unlearned man."

Second, if the "ignorance" and lack of learning refers to secular knowledge, then, again, we have no hope of lining up with "apostolic ignorance." Most of us have gone to school to learn math, English, spelling, science, geography, history, writing, and the like. Whether we have cheated our way through school (we *learned* to cheat), learned architectural geometry as an engineer, been trained in burger temperature as a cook, or studied theology at the Ph.D. level, *all* of us have *learning*. Moreover, if we believe that this verse condemns learning in general, then why do we boast when our child gets an "A" in algebra, is the valedictorian of her class, or has been accepted into medical school? Clearly, Christian people are not in practice — in reality — against all learning. Neither was Jesus; he too studied the multiplication charts (at least up to 70 times 7; Matt. 18:22), knew how to interpret meteorological conditions (16:2 – 3), and grew in knowledge and wisdom with God *and man* (Luke 2:52).

Why, then, do so many believers speak as if they are suspicious of cultivating the mind for the glory of God and base their conviction on Scriptures such as the one at hand? Personally, I believe that the roots of the matter are varied. (1) Because our spiritual leaders have neglected the call to challenge us as believers to love God with all our minds, we are oblivious to this need and privilege.

(2) We are encumbered by false definitions of learning, false dichotomies between our sacred and secular life, false views of God's creation, and inadequate views of his Lordship. Also, many lack the willingness to invest the essential sweat, tears, time, energy, and money into something that will not materialize tangible (and relatively rapid) gain. Thinking this way, we search for Scriptures that will help us to justify our lack of interest in matters that combine the intellect and the kingdom of God.

(3) If this passage *teaches* ignorance as a virtue, then why is it that the apostles are found teaching everywhere they go? And how is it that believers are commanded to learn? Proverbs 1:5 charges the wise to "add to their *learning*"; Romans 15:4 declares that "everything written in the past was written to teach us." Dozens of verses from the Bible can be added. Furthermore, it seems odd that God throughout church history repeatedly chose men of great learning to bid his business, if in fact he viewed learning as a hindrance. Just think of some of them: Justin Martyr, Clement of Alexandria, Augustine, Aquinas, Wycliffe, Tyndale, Luther, John Calvin, John Owen, Jonathan Edwards, John Wesley, and many others — all people of great learning!

(4) The real key to Acts 4:13 lies in the meaning of the words "ignorant" and "unlearned." These words have to do with a *special kind* of rabbinical training and official position. The passage carries the idea of: "How did these guys come to know what they know? They did not go to *our* schools." The experts in the law were surprised that these men, who were laymen, had such authority when discussing the issues of the law. The Greek word for "unlearned" literally means "unlettered," indicating that they were con-

sidered illiterate when it came to the rabbinical training of the day. The term "ignorant" is the Greek word *idiotes*, denoting that these men did not hold official positions; to the "experts," they were but civilians.

What astounded the onlookers was *not* that these men were so *un*intelligent, but that they were so knowledgeable and so confident in that knowledge (4:13, 29, 31). It would be like the senators of Athens arguing with Plato, taking note that he didn't belong to their particular political guild but that he was more than able to hold his own in their presence, and then remembering — ah, yes, he spent years with Socrates! For at least three years the apostles had been with Jesus, the One in whom all knowledge resided. Jesus, the great Rabbi, poured his life and knowledge into the men who attended daily the School of Christ.

In some respects, the apostles were very educated — just not in the particular schools that the Jewish elders had attended. Just think of it this way: If Peter and John sat under Christ's teaching for even two hours per day, in forty-two months each would have put in more "class time" than a four-year university student of today would.

As far as the "experts" were concerned, Peter and John were men who possessed no special qualifications. They had no technical training in the intricate man-made regulations of the law and its interpretations (Matt. 15:2, 3, 6; Mark 7:3, 5, 8, 9, 13), but they did know the Old Testament inside and out. It is also helpful to keep in mind that they were Jews in a Jewish nation, reaching Jews, preaching "*the* Jew," and debating with Jewish authorities over the Jewish Scriptures and traditions. To the Jewish rulers, it was strange that these fishermen had not attended their Jewish rabbinical schools, yet knew what they were talking about! This shows that Jesus places a premium on learning, not on ignorance, and that this learning, *combined with the power of the Holy Spirit*, brings about a refreshing and revolutionary boldness in proclaiming the content of God's Word.

God's sanctioned standard for Christians is not ignorance and deficiency in learning. His criterion is neither brilliance nor ignorance, but cultivation and putting to good use the mind that he has afforded to each. Both Peter, the rough-cut fisherman, and Paul, the polished one-time Pharisee, point out that sharpened minds are better tools in the hands of God than are dull, underdeveloped minds (e.g., 1 Peter 1:13; 2:15; 3:15; 4:7; 2 Peter 1:5, 12 – 15; 3:1, 16; and Acts 9:22; 17:2, 24 – 31; 18:4; 19:8 – 9; 2 Tim. 1:7; 2:15; 4:5). I think we all know that this is true in the realm of our temporal, earthly, vocational calling. The present challenge, then, is to apply the same principle to our eternal, heavenly calling.

HIDDEN FROM THE WISE AND LEARNED

> At that time Jesus said, "I praise you, Father, Lord of heaven and earth, because you have hidden these things from the wise and learned, and revealed them to little children." (Matt. 11:25)

This verse, too, has frequently been taken to mean that if a person has a healthy appetite for intellectual nutrition or seeks wisdom, he or she is in danger of missing out on the things of God. But we can be certain that this understanding is untrue, for God himself repeatedly commends the wise and challenges the unwise to become wise.

In Matthew 10, Jesus commands his followers to be "wise as serpents" (Matt. 10:16), and in chapter 11, only four verses after declaring that the Father has "hidden these things from the wise and learned" (11:25), Jesus invites the humble in heart to come and learn from him (11:29). Also, Paul was a very learned man (Acts 26:24), yet he had the things of God revealed to him in powerful proportions (Acts 9; 2 Cor. 12:2). One need only to take a fleeting glance in any concordance at the words "wise," "knowledge," "learn," and their derivatives to see that the Scriptures are satiated with declarations of their worth.

Clearly, the "wise" that Jesus is referring to here are not the academically wise, the "learned" are not simply knowledgeable, and the "babes" are not literally infants. What Jesus is saying is that to those who view themselves as too wise to submit to God, who think of themselves as so learned that they don't need Christ, and who refuse to follow a humble Savior, the Father's salvation is truly hidden. The same basic principle is established for the so-called "righteous," "rich," and "healthy." In their cases, it is not that they are hindered from entering the kingdom of God because they possess actual spiritual wellness, material wealth, or physical health, but that they view themselves as not needing Christ (Matt. 9:12 – 13; Luke 12:16 – 21).

By contrast, to those who are humble in heart (Matt. 11:29) — those who are dependent on a Savior (like little children who are unrelentingly reliant on others) — these are the benefactors of God's revelation of redemption through his Son. These are the ones who take note of and confess their interior lack, whether they happen to be rich or poor, religious or worldly, Jew or Gentile, fit or fat, erudite or ignorant, sign-seeker or secular. Intellectual aptitude is not at all the issue in Matthew 11; rather, the primary concern is the *attitude* of the hearers — that is, whether they are arrogant (filled up with themselves) or hungry in their heart of hearts.

As Spirit-filled people, we are convinced that speaking in tongues is a good thing; yet we also acknowledge that if we speak in tongues but fail to exhibit love, we are only clanging cymbals; and as Paul adds, we are "nothing" (1 Cor. 13:1 – 2). And though we believe that cheerful giving is a blessing to both us and the kingdom (2 Cor. 9:7), we also recognize that those who think they appease God by pitching money at the plate are in grave spiritual danger. In like fashion we admit that baptism and participation in the Lord's Supper are extremely important. But we also believe that if we trust only in such physical actions for spiritual salvation, we are barking up the wrong tree.

Moreover, who among us would want to argue that prayer is a negative thing? Yet we know that prayer turns out to be worthless when it is expressed with wrong motives (James 4:3), when it is presented as mere protracted babble (Matt. 6:7), or when it is generated from a root of pride (Matt. 7:21 – 23; Luke 18:13 – 14). All of this is to say that we cannot make a case against learning, knowledge, or education because of verses like Matthew 11:25, any more than we can make cases against prayer, fasting, giving, or tongues just because we are warned not to place our faith in our participation of these practices.

Make no mistake about it, we are to use our minds when comparing religions, when weighing the evidences of Christianity (otherwise, we can't fault the Mormon convert), and when interpreting the Scriptures. Some may claim that this is mere rationalism. But I suggest that those who flirt with unprincipled rationalization, yanking isolated verses from Scripture out of their contexts, playing with their interpretations for the sake of protecting pet doctrines, refusing to acknowledge good arguments contrary to their dogma, as well as majoring on minors and minoring on majors — these, I suggest, come closer to courting rationalism than do those who dissect the grammar, syntax, and context of a text.

We are quick to take Jesus at face value when he says that the kingdom is hidden from the learned, and yet so slow to use the same "simple" principle when he declares, "Blessed are you who are poor, for yours is the kingdom of God" (Luke 6:20). Most of us refuse to believe that a person must be poverty-stricken to receive eternal life, especially since other passages speak of God's material blessings (6:38). Consistency mandates that we regard Christ's statements on "the wise and learned" in the same way, seeing that elsewhere he commands us to "learn" from him, to "be wise as serpents," and to love him with all of our *minds*.

YOU DO NOT NEED ANYONE TO TEACH YOU

> But the anointing which ye have received of him abideth in you, and ye need not that any man teach you: but as the same anointing teacheth you of all things, and is truth, and is no lie, and even as it hath taught you, ye shall abide in him. (1 John 2:27, KJV)

In 1990 I began teaching the letter of 1 John verse by verse. When it came time for me to teach the latter portion of chapter 2, I naturally read the last few verses, including verse 27. After quoting the above passage, a loud "amen" resonated from a couple attending the study that night. In 1999, while lecturing in a foreign country, I quoted this same verse, intending to elaborate on how we as Pentecostals often misunderstand its meaning. Again, three or four prominent "amens" came from the college classroom before I could express my intent. In the summer of 2001, I was teaching on the value of preparing our minds for the defense of the faith. After quoting 1 John 2:27, a conspicuous "amen brother" radiated from the front row. This type of reaction is yet another of the telling signs that many Full Gospel people not only embrace varying forms of anti-intellectualism but have built their case on false interpretations of verses like this one.

On one of the above occasions, I paused, and in a lighthearted fashion I asked the one who was "amening" what it was that he was lauding. I explained to him that it sounded as if he was "amening" the *teacher* (me), who was quoting John, who in turn was *teaching* that we did not need *teachers*. The good brother simply sat silent displaying a mischievous grin, recognizing his self-spun catch–22. The couple whom I mentioned above was less malleable, for they later presented to me a stack of spiral notebooks that contained "revelations" they had supposedly received directly from God. Of course, these documents had been divined without the help of a meddling mediator — at least not one of a terrestrial nature. These, I was told, were soon to be used as teaching material for a small-group study. Yikes! I no longer had to speculate why they shouted "amen" when I quoted 1 John 2:27.

During my twenty years of ministry among Pentecostals and Charismatics, I have known scores of Full Gospel believers who faithfully and passionately plumb the pages of the Bible. These search, contrast, match up, and apply what they believe the Scriptures reveal. In a real sense, we are a people who love and know the importance of God's Word. Nevertheless, for varying reasons, many also tend to treat, as special pets, those Scripture portions that seem to pit ethereal intuition against propositional instruction. It's the old Bible-versus-Spirit, doctrine-versus-experience, reason-versus-revelation debate, which often swings out into the hinterlands of mysticism and rationalism — a battle wherein the participants forget that both extremes are unbalanced and that elements of both the rational and the mystical constitute our makeup.

From my own spiritual journey, I have learned how easy it is to enroll oneself in the infantry of the intuitive camp, especially when we've been set free from a diet of correct, yet cold, lifeless instruction; and when organized but passionless minds have informed us but failed to inspire us. Furthermore, when we've experienced supernatural direction, peculiar but precise "words of wisdom," God-ordained confirmation, and spine-chilling illumination, the mystical inclinations of our psyche begin to construct a theology that suggests that we only get "the good stuff" *directly* from heaven. If we continue in this line of thought, we link the few genuine intuitive experiences with others that are little more than wishful thinking, forming an ideological rule out of the exceptions. We have then set ourselves up to become suspicious of earthly teachers. There's much more to it than that, but this provides a hint of the general and dangerous process.

In light of the foregoing, there seems to be a widespread notion that what John is teaching in this passage is that if we "have the Spirit," we are to seek to acquire spiritual information from God without human mediation. Of course, as Pentecostals and Charismatics, we are persuaded that God not only can, but also does (at his own will) reveal otherwise unknown knowledge to us (1 Cor. 12:8). Of course, that knowledge must line up, in principle, with his already-revealed Word. It is quite another matter, however, to go a step further and declare that we need no one to teach us. But this is what some claim (and many more believe but do not verbalize) when they misinterpret the text under consideration.

There are several main points that are vital to the proper understanding of this passage in 1 John. First, when the Scriptures indicate "anyone," "any man," "anything," or "whatsoever," they don't necessarily mean it in the absolute sense; the context must decide the scope. For example, when Mark writes, "Whatever you ask for in prayer, believe that you have received it, and it will be yours" (Mark 11:24), there are conditions. The one praying must not be unforgiving (11:26), and what is asked for must be requested in the name of Jesus (John 14:13a).

In other words, Mark 11:24 does not mean that simply mouthing the words "in the name of Jesus" is sufficient to receive what we ask for; otherwise, the power of prayer is reduced to a sanctified vending machine. Rather, the idea is to ask for that which brings glory to God through Christ (John 14:13b). If the "anything" in John 14:14 and the "whatever" in Mark 11:24 literally mean "whatever we want," then it stands to reason that two believers could pray for the opposite thing and both would come true — wrong! Moreover, under these circumstances, if someone prayed "in the name of Jesus" for the death of an enemy, the Lord would be bound to deliver a corpse. The simple answer to this dilemma is that there are conditions placed on these promises.

Many other verses fall into this same category. For example, when the thinking reader is told that "all things are possible with God" (Mark 10:27), he or she surely realizes a few things that are not possible for God. God himself tells us he cannot lie (Num. 23:19). Neither can he create another God, make 2 + 2= 5, or cease to exist. Again, when Paul writes, "I can do all things through him who gives me strength" (Phil. 4:13), he does not intend to convey that he can run a one-minute mile, fly to the moon unassisted, or create another universe *ex nihilo*, if he really, really believed; rather, he is trying to teach us that he has learned to be content under any circumstance, no matter how difficult or delightful (4:11 – 12).

Having said all this, in the case of 1 John 2:27, the "any man" cannot mean absolutely anyone, for John himself is a teacher and declares that his teaching is the truth. He goes so far as saying that "whoever knows God listens to us; but whoever is not from God does not listen to us" (4:6). The problem with the church in Ephesus (the probable recipient of the letter) was that false teachers were attempting to confuse the church body. John distinctly tells the reader, "I am writing these things to you about those who are trying to lead you astray" (2:26). The "any man" in this case (2:27) means "anyone *else*" — that is, anyone other than those who teach what the apostles taught.

In the first three verses of 1 John 1 alone, John uses the words "we" eight times and "us" two times: "We have heard," "we proclaim...." This language sets the tone of the letter, denoting the authority of that which the believers have received "from the beginning" (1:1 – 3). Whereas the apostles preached that Jesus is the Word of life (v. 1), was from the Father (v. 2), and is God's Son (v. 3), and that "the blood of Jesus ... purifies us from all sin" (1:7), the false teachers were saying that Jesus was not the Christ (2:22), that he had not come in the flesh (4:3, 15), and that they had no sin (1:8, 10).

These are not peripheral issues that are being disputed, but *the very heart of the gospel itself!* If the Christians of John's day yield to the message that says, "Jesus is not really the Son of God," their hope to overcome the world and have eternal life will be dashed (1 John 5:4 – 5, 11 – 12). In light of all this, the Spirit, through John, announces that the body of Christ has no need of these supposedly enlightened yet heretical teachings of the false prophets in their midst.

The Holy Spirit, who abides within (John 14:16), is unquestionably the Spirit of truth (16:13), and he has brought truth to those whom he baptized into his body. The emphasis in this passage is on a deposit of information that was sent by the Holy Spirit into the minds of the apostles and then distributed to the believers. He clearly teaches that the message that they have "heard from the beginning" is that to which they must hold fast (1 John 2:24). The deposit of truth poured out on them through the proclamation of the apostles (the fact that Jesus is the Son of God and the way to salvation) has remained in them, and they must guard it with all of their might! Their baptism into the body of Christ qualifies them to be recipients of that truth, yet other teachers (false teachers) are attempting to replace that truth with lies.

In view of this, John tells them that they don't need these teachers. It's somewhat like the Corinthian scenario (1 Cor. 1), where Paul had already preached the message of the cross and the Corinthians needed no "other" wisdom; so also the Ephesians have received the apostolic truth of the gospel, and thus they do not need another "salvation message," from "other" so-called apostles.

The fact that Christ has given the gift of teachers to his body (Eph. 4:11) tells us that John does not intend to include all teachers in his warning. Also, Timothy was commanded to teach others who could in turn "teach" yet others (2 Tim. 2:2), and Paul himself taught in Corinth for eighteen months (Acts 18:11) as well as in Ephesus for nearly three years (19:10). Learning at the feet of others has been *the* method of spreading God's truth since he has entrusted us with his revelation. To imagine that John in 1 John 2 is instructing believers to avoid human teachers not only neglects the context of John's teaching but reduces the verse to sheer nonsense, seeing that John himself was a teacher!

CONCLUSION

Though there are other passages of Scripture that believers who struggle with anti-intellectualism wield, those dealt with in this and the preceding chapter are the most commonly quoted. My sincere prayer is that the eyes of many hearts have been enlightened, or at least that help has been provided for some who deal regularly with individuals who maintain a prejudice against the mind. If those who harbor prejudice against the mind are not open to the few foregoing expositions, then it's questionable whether they will be moved if one were to write:

Dear elect strangers in the world:

    Let me explain this to you; listen carefully to what I say (Acts 2:14b). Prepare your minds for action (1 Peter 1:13a), for it is God's will that by doing good you should silence the ignorant talk of foolish men (1 Peter 2:15). Always be prepared to give an answer to everyone who asks you to give the reason for the hope that you have (1 Peter 3:15). The end is near. Therefore be clear minded (1 Peter 4:7a). For this very reason, make every effort to add to your faith goodness; and to goodness knowledge (2 Peter 1:5).

    Dear friends, this is now my second letter to you. I have written both of them as reminders to stimulate you to wholesome thinking (2 Peter 3:1). Paul also wrote you with the wisdom that God gave him. His letters contain some things that are hard to understand, which ignorant and unstable people distort as they do the other Scriptures (2 Peter 3:15 – 16). Therefore, dear friends, since you already know this, be on your guard so that you may not be carried away by error. Grow in the grace and knowledge of our Lord and Savior Jesus Christ. To Him be the glory both now and forever! Amen (2 Peter 3:17 – 18).

Affectionately, The Scrub Fisherman

5

Early Pentecostals and the Life of the Mind

Education is killing Christianity. I had an uncle who couldn't read or write, but he got saved, and after that God taught him to read the Scriptures. But now head knowledge gets into religion.... The less education, the more quickly you can accept salvation.

EARLY PENTECOSTAL, 1908

Many people have a mistaken idea that the baptism in the Holy Spirit does away with all need of hard work but it is not a labor-saving device. You might say, "I suppose I won't need to study; I won't need to think."

DONALD GEE, EARLY PENTECOSTAL LEADER

I don't think; I leave that to God.

JOAN OF ARC

Some men have intellectuality, but the Christian is supposed to be the possessor of the Spirit. There should never be any misunderstanding along these lines.

JOHN G. LAKE, EARLY PENTECOSTAL LEADER

In the second century before Christ, Lucius Apuleius, a native of Numidia, scrawled a prose narrative that has proved influential long after his death. The work he's best remembered for is entitled *The Golden Ass*. In this partially autobiographical allegory, Lucius charts the story of a man's metamorphosis from the image of an ignorant donkey into that of a man.

In books 4 – 6 of this work, the author chronicles the story of "Cupid and Psyche." Here, he sets out to create a religious metaphor — one that not only served to express his original intent but also serves, in a sense, to connote the intellectual dilemma in which we are entangled today. Cupid (the daughter of love, emotion, romance, and beauty) is depicted as radiating a divine dignity, sought after by all, and marrying early in life. Meanwhile, her sister Psyche (denoting the soul or rational aspect of man), though aware of her own worth and beauty, had little to show for her intellectual endowment. She wept over her barrenness, for though she had much to offer, she alone was unwedded among all of her sisters.

Eventually Psyche is assigned a husband — her mate is "that evil serpent-thing" from the shadows of Styx (the underworld). The ruler of the kingdom in which she lived escorts her to "her deadly bridal," where the god of Hades "impelled the hapless Psyche to her fate." When the inhabitants of the land realized they had lost their beloved Psyche, they went out looking for her on the grassy hills of the kingdom. After finding her, she revealed that she had *not* been consumed by the beast of hell but was living in "a dwelling-place, built not by human hands." It was a palace clad with gold, cedar, ivory, and silver, fashioned by a carpenter, who possessed a "divine or half-divine" nature and who had breathed his very soul into the edifice. The house in which she lived is further described as "fashioned for the conversation of gods with men!"[1]

In much the same way as Cupid was preferred over Psyche, so also the Pentecostal – Charismatic movement as a whole has frequently favored the romantic forces of emotion, feeling, and experience, all the while assigning the power of reason to the lower regions of the earth. As we have seen, though, the life of the Psyche (i.e., the place of the mind) is a gift of God, crafted by the divine Artisan (the Logos) and dwelling within the inner sanction of our being. Though Cupid plays a vital part in the overall spiritual scheme of life, without the Psyche, one cannot even spell the word "Cupid," define "life," or discern what is good or spiritual.

There are a number of voices from without and a growing number from within our movement that bear witness to our prejudice against the intellectual dimensions of the spiritual life. These challenge us to reconsider the beauty of our God-given minds and the part they play in the life of worship. I encourage the reader to approach the remainder of this book with the words of Pastor Jack Hayford in mind. In a 1990 *Charisma* article, where dealing with the importance of a balanced Charismatic life, he writes:

> A good beginning would be to trust more readily the intentions of sympathetic critics. Rather than judging appeals to greater carefulness in theology as a threat to our style or liberty, we might listen to them.... But too often the response of charismatic leaders and laity, who have been burned by past criticism, is outright rejection of such suggestions. So part of the challenge before us is to cultivate a new tolerance and wisdom toward those who question us.[2]

VIEWS FROM WITHOUT THE CAMP

Historian John Nichol, whose 1966 publication of *The Pentecostals* sparked new scholarly interest in American Pentecostalism, wrote of the apparent anti-intellectualism of many of the early Pentecostals and of how antagonism toward education was problematic to a host of Protestants. From that time forward, many others began to write about our lack of theological depth, our tendencies of building doctrine on experiences, and our vulnerability to anti-intellectualism.[3]

English writer Michael Green, who penned *I Believe in the Holy Spirit* (1975), underscores the tendency of our movement to "dub doctrine unimportant." He stresses how becoming nonrational in our approach is little, if any, better than being *too* rational. Noted leader and author John R. W. Stott also indicated in the mid-1970s that "one of the most serious features, at least of some" Pentecostal Christians, is their avowed anti-intellectualism. "Not doctrine, but experience," he maintains, is the battle cry of far too many Full Gospel believers. Yet in his customary balanced manner, his suggestion for those who have "zeal without knowledge" is that they take heed not to fall into the error of "possessing knowledge without zeal"; the aim, he asserts is "devotion set on fire by truth."[4]

Wheaton professor Mark Noll contends that Pentecostalism has contributed its part to the modern "disaster for the life of the mind" and has aided many other movements in bringing damage to evangelical thought in twentieth-century America.[5] Still others point out that Charismatic people often seem to be bored by intellectual formation, that we provide too little theological base for our experiences, and that our methods of interpreting Scripture can be extremely subjective. With varying measures and in an assortment of ways, non-Pentecostal censors are basically saying that we are rather ambivalent toward rational checks and theological balances against error.[6]

There are, of course, those who go out on a ridiculous limb attempting to indict our movement as unmitigated madness. Consider the following outlandish allegation: "Charismatics are incapable of logic and too incapacitated by their emotionalism and spiritual blindness to handle the Word of God honestly and effectively."[7]

It should be noted that the above-mentioned concerns were voiced in works spanning forty years. In other words, outsiders have alluded to this problem over a considerable length of time. And though dozens of equivalent statements can be mined from older works, it's more important to allow our outside critics to speak to more contemporary times. Besides, our own earlier representatives make a strong enough case by their own anti-intellectual statements.

It should also be noted that of the critics that I have listed in the endnotes for this section, all but one have *positive* things to say about the Pentecostal – Charismatic movement. This is important! Most admit that it's our openness and passion for the Spirit's personal involvement in everyday life that challenges their overly-reserved traditions. In other words, these men are not against everything we believe. They have the sense and balance to know that throwing out healthy babies with dirty bathwater is self-defeating. In light of this, we should be careful so as not to be found doing the same with their corrective exhortations.

VIEWS FROM WITHIN THE CAMP

One of the most prominent voices within our movement who has articulated concerns over the mind's involvement in the hermeneutical process is Gordon Fee. Fee, a New Testament scholar, contends that we demonstrate a lack of consistency and excellence when interpreting Scripture and that we are apt to ignore or even scorn our historic roots. Others of like mind point out that we have made only feeble attempts at producing theological literature and that we are less willing to support advanced theological training than we are to provide for schooling in areas of secular study. Doctrinal malformation, a rejection of intellectual analysis of our religious experiences, and a reluctance to engage in Pentecostal scholarship — these are further cognitive weaknesses that are pointed out by some within our Full Gospel fellowships.[8]

Russell Spittler, an exceptional Pentecostal scholar, has for many years fought patiently for excellence and distinction in the domain of Full Gospel thinking. He has lamented the fact that "Pentecostalism is a largely anti-intellectual tradition" and that few Pentecostals accept the findings of even Spirit-filled scholars. Spittler urges those within the Pentecostal sector to become "thinking Christians," in order to better affect a fallen human culture for the glory of God. He further enunciates the call for Pentecostals to seize the day, acknowledging our opportunities and responsibilities to reach an ever-rising educated population. After challenging the believer to proclaim an experiential faith, he declares, "But there is more to do on a theological level.... Let us not leave unreached the reflective thinkers who also search for reality."[9]

Another leader within Pentecostalism who has given consideration to the matters at hand is Gordon Anderson. Anderson, while commending the validity of a true and unique Pentecostal method of Bible interpretation, writes about our sometimes faulty approach to doctrinal matters: "Pentecostals are not well known for good exegesis, hermeneutics, and theology, that is just a fact." He notes that we often come to doctrinal decisions having approached the matter through "a simplistic sense of Bible reading and through problematic practices such as allegorizing"; moreover, "Pentecostals have developed doctrines and practices supposedly based on the Bible, yet their methods have been called into question." He has also spoken of the dangers connected with gleaning doctrine from prophetic utterances and depending too much on emotion, both of which can lead to uncritical "acceptance of leaders, doctrines, and practices that should be rejected."[10]

God is raising up those within our ranks who dare to speak to our suspicion of education, marked anti-intellectual bias, shameful hostility to history, and languor in the courtyards of American culture. This slight contingency of discriminating analysts is also beginning to make mention of the Full Gospel forfeiture in the fields of philosophy, of the general castigation of our cognitive faculties, and of our apathy toward apologetics.[11]

It is important for the reader to recognize that these who contend for intellectual vigor and who summon the Spirit-filled throngs to gird up the loins of their minds *also promote* the experiential, emotional, and ecstatic elements of the faith. Thus, while striving to advance the academic and cognitive standards of a movement, which has lagged behind in these affairs, they continue to preach the need for the Holy Spirit's constant influence. Full Gospel believers cannot afford to discount the voices of this growing "cloud of witnesses." It is by grace that God is attempting to get our attention. He is sounding the alarm so that after having become a people of zeal and blessing, we will not look back regretfully, realizing that by neglecting the mind, in the long run we may have actually forfeited the very soul of our movement.

The Pentecostal – Charismatic movement is a phenomenon. As an ecclesiastical current, this modern-day descent of the Spirit has woven its way into the fabric of many nations. Her influence has aided in filling up the haunting spiritual emptiness of hundreds of millions, bringing hope and providing an outlet through which a direct experience with God is facilitated. Her contagious jubilation and enthusiastic expectation have tapped deep into the substratum of a humanity that lay as an existential wasteland in the wake of two world wars.

Without question, the Pentecostal – Charismatic movement is fulfilling a decisive role in rescuing multitudes from the icy waters of conventional, yet often lifeless religion. Personally, I am inclined to believe that through his sovereignty, God allowed various men and women (such as the early Pentecostals) to "see," to intuit the currents of collective thought, and to prepare to tip the scales away from mechanistic humanism toward the weight of his glory. I don't know this for certain, but I do know that something much like the Pentecostal – Charismatic movement was needed at the very time she emerged onto the stage of history.

Whatever else may be said about this movement, one thing is sure — she is playing an integral part in a contemporary and global religious renaissance. Even though our movement has struggled with imbalances and excesses and even though we have unnecessarily minimized the art of and importance of excellent thought, her message has been a revivifying breath of fresh air to the hopeless dry bones of modernity. For these reasons, she is my choice, my movement, my home. Furthermore, because this is the particular sacred milieu into which God has planted, nurtured, and made use of me, it is with a sense of duty that I talk and write about the elements within her makeup that at times hinders God's work through her.

ANTI-INTELLECTUALISM IN EARLY PENTECOSTALISM (1901 – 1930)

In the remainder of this chapter, I will provide a brief survey of the anti-intellectual temper that colored the earliest years of our Spirit-filled tradition. We now enter into the coliseum where pairs of companions — the heart and the head, the intellect and experience, reason and revelation, as well as great minds and great mystics — have been *unnecessarily* and tragically forced into mortal combat!

Charles Parham (1873 – 1929)

It came as no surprise to me when I first discovered that the man whom many consider the "Father of Pentecostalism" and "Founder and Projector of the Apostolic Faith Movement" exhibited varying symptoms of anti-intellectualism. Charles Parham, who has been called "the single most important individual in the rise of the Pentecostal movement," tended to pit what he deemed "Spirit-education" against study, the intuitive against the rational, and private interpretation against biblical, orthodox hermeneutics.

Though it was at a school (Bethel Bible School) that a twentieth-century Pentecost made its first substantial splash into the pool of American Christianity, the radiating influence of the movement didn't necessarily carry with it a notable regard for those elements that are ordinarily associated with genuine education. Critical thought, scrupulous accuracy, gallant fairness, cultural concern, and careful reasoning were neither the strong suits of Parham nor of his direct spiritual progeny.[12]

Parham himself had enrolled to prepare for ministry in the fall of 1891. During his brief stay at Southwestern Kansas College, he struggled with whether or not to dedicate his life to the ministry. At one point he felt led to reroute his studies toward medicine. Later, however, he announced, "It was the devil who tried to make me believe I could be a physician and a Christian too."[13] Upon deliverance from medical ambitions, he claimed to have received a revelation that education hinders the heart's true service to God in ministry. After coming to these conclusions, he left this establishment, never to return to formal schooling. As a teenager who had studied less than one year, he denounced institutional learning (Parham was not quite twenty years old at the time).

Despite his professed anti-school, anti-establishment disposition, Parham established Bethel Bible School in October of 1900. Within a few weeks, twenty-five to thirty students were enrolled and commenced their studies. Parham's approach to Bible education reveals his prejudice against the value of men's ideas — that is, *other* men's ideas. The curriculum basically consisted of reading Scripture and giving his personal comments on various Bible texts.

It is important to note that Parham's methods were patterned after those of Frank Sanford's "Holy Ghost and Us Bible School" in Lewiston, Maine. That name says it all. Parham was merely one in a long line of loners who have viewed all those going before them as unreliable in terms of doctrinal teaching and biblical exposition. For a hundred years (1800 – 1900), a throng of independent spirits who had been injected with a double dose of self-contained individualism set out to set straight all who had become set in their ways! Whatever good Parham carried out, it was often overshadowed by a tone of self-contradiction and an aura of superiority.

The ultra-simplistic approach of what has been called "Bible-onlyism" may sound noble, but it also smacks of super-spirituality, exclusivity, and naïveté. It is unthinkable that a modern-day physician would forego all that has been written on the practice of medicine for 2,400 years, referencing only the "pure" teachings of Hippocrates (460 – 377 B.C.). But this is precisely the approach of many of the world's religious pioneers: "All we need is the Bible and the Holy Ghost." This has often been their sole statement of belief, that is, only until they could figure out how to get the "other" creeds into print.

Granted, without the Scriptures and the Spirit's aid we are doctrinally and spiritually lost. Nevertheless, whenever scholarship and history have been neglected, scores of contradictory doctrines inevitably crop up. The act of abstaining from so-called academic enterprise leads, at best, to reinventing the wheel and, at worst, to shaky foundations that shift with every current of opinion and "special leading." While starting out to fulfill the Spiritual Hippocratic Oath, most "Bible-only" activists devolve into hypocrisy by insisting that they expect others to take *their interpretations* of the truth as *the only* truth.

Though Parham had voiced that institutional education for ministry was a detriment, he nevertheless opened a Bible school. The "faith school" that he had started in October of 1900 endured only a few months, closing in the spring of 1901. Moreover, he discouraged others from hanging on the words of men, yet traveled far and wide in order to discover the latest doctrinal trends. And though he believed that the Bible was the only text one needed to study, he wrote voluminous articles, printed pamphlets, published a biweekly journal, and wrote at least two books. This passionate promotion of his theological findings was achieved with the help of a printing press he conveniently maintained in his Topeka home.[14]

Parham fought voraciously for his doctrinal findings, yet firmly stated that "truly spiritual people do not quibble over points of doctrine." Though he disdained the concept of hierarchical, spiritual establishments, he battled furiously to hang on to the leadership of the Pentecostal movement when his waning influence was evident to most. In addition, he insisted that when he preached, his "mind took no part," yet he meticulously manuscripted his messages in order to print them in newsletters and in his published sermons, *A Voice Crying in the Wilderness*.[15]

Parham did have strong doctrinal convictions. But by refusing to acknowledge the wealth of theological treasures provided by men of the past, he tended to tangle his twines of theology. He taught that water baptism was not necessary but later advocated that "triple baptism" was in keeping with the biblical injunction. In his estimation, Anglo-Saxons were the literal ten lost tribes of Israel; Hindus were the descendants of Abraham; and, the black, red, and yellow races belonged to "the heathen." He also taught that the gift of tongues was given to enable the recipient to preach in the language of any hearer to whom he was sent. This, he suggested, would keep missionaries from wasting their time with the mundane duty of studying languages.[16]

Historian Edith Blumhofer says of Parham's theological methodologies:

> Parham exercised considerable inventiveness with various doctrines. His preference for rooting doctrine in his private meditation on Scripture and his conviction that the Holy Spirit communed directly with him, undoubtedly influenced the character of his teaching.... His uncompromising rejection of recognized religious leaders contributed to his impatience with traditional views that diverged from his own.

She goes on to speak of his response when men of learning and equilibrium attempted to address his doctrinal looseness: "As the Movement attracted some who were concerned to balance spiritual experience with doctrinal orthodoxy, he responded by emphasizing anew his private interpretation of Scripture."[17] In many respects, Parham's life itself is a classical case study of anti-intellectualism, and to varying degrees, we are his children!

William Seymour (1870 – 1922)

Parham's credibility and influence began to wane as repeated reports of alleged unscrupulous activities surfaced. At this critical juncture, God saw fit to bring William Seymour, a Black Holiness preacher, to the forefront of the Pentecostal Movement. In 1906 Seymour had enrolled in Parham's newly-established school in the city of Houston, Texas. Parham's teachings consisted primarily of sharing his personal slant on various biblical passages. Innovative "Spirit-teaching" was also transacted, where prophesying new insights and instructing through the use of foreign tongues and interpretations was often the mode of education. It was there that Seymour heard and was convinced of the doctrine of Holy Spirit baptism.[18]

Though he didn't experience this phenomenon in the few weeks that he had sat under Parham's teaching, he did encounter the Spirit's infilling a couple of months later while pastoring a small congregation in Los Angeles. Two days after this encounter he moved his small flock to a newly acquired facility. The physical location of this meeting place has been forever linked with the national and international spread of modern Pentecost. The street on which the little lackluster, wood-framed, Methodist chapel was situated was named "Azusa." With the above in mind, it shouldn't surprise us that some of the same anti-intellectual drifts, intrinsic within Parham's philosophy of Christianity, were also evident in Azusa's outpouring.

Azusa: Revivalism, Pentecostalism, and Anti-Intellectualism

Beginning with the first volume of *The Apostolic Faith*, Azusa's monthly newspaper (edited by Seymour), her intellectual atmosphere was established. A tone of exclusivity promoting "knowledge without study" is apparent throughout its premier edition. Take for example, Seymour's comments made about Parham and his followers as to the way they came to discover truth concerning "Pentecost":

> After searching through the country *everywhere*, they were unable to find *any* Christians that had the *true* Pentecostal power. So they laid aside *all commentaries* and *notes* and waited.... They had an experience that measured up with the second chapter of Acts, and could understand the first chapter of Ephesians.[19] (emphasis added)

Seymour then reports of a young man who had been filled recently with the Holy Ghost and began writing in foreign languages which he had *"never gone to school to study;"* and that "the Lord has given languages to the *unlearned*, Greek, Latin, Hebrew." Also, "Do not puzzle yourselves by *theorizing*, but tarry in Jerusalem.... He will reveal the whole Word from Genesis to Revelation" (emphasis added). The age-old adage of "presenting oneself as a worthy workman of the biblical text" took a direct hit. It was replaced with "just wait, God will do the work for you." Of course, this works just fine until two godly saints get two vastly different interpretations of Genesis 1:1![20]

For the next three years, this tabloid was sent to upwards of 80,000 households on a monthly basis. Imagine the sway this had in the minds of the subscribers. During this foundation-laying period of Pentecostalism, hundreds of thousands read of the wonderful works wrought in the lives of those attending the meetings. Their faith was bolstered by the chronicled wonders and their hopes were lifted because heaven-sent help was on the way. For all of this we are grateful; however, the multitudes were also exposed to a mindset that bred a prejudice against the importance of the intellect and beauty of the mind. The effects would be, and are, seen even a century later.

Again and again, sprinkled throughout the pages of this "Full Gospel" paper are blatant fruits as well as latent seeds of mindless spirituality. Many who were "unschooled" and who "did not learn in books" were pointed out as prophets of the Lord. It is certainly reasonable that God can use uneducated people to speak his Word, but this isn't the point. The problem lies in the continual accentuation of the fact that spiritual accomplishments were regularly done by uneducated people. It was stated over and over that the truly hungry were being touched by the Spirit, while thinkers and theologians refused him. Simply put, they glorified noncognitive activity and criticized the intellectual virtues through the incessant marrying of two concepts: "lack of learning" and "spirituality."[21]

Seldom, if ever, was any activity of the mind, study, or intellect commended. Medical ministry was counted as carnal, and books and sermons written by mere men were condemned to the fires of Judgment Day. In many meetings, it was said that there was no preaching at all. But when there was, only messages that "the Lord preached" were allowed. Theology and creeds were considered enemies of revival; thus, when interpretation of Scripture was needed, only the Holy Spirit himself could get the job done.[22]

Regarding the approach of various congregations in praise services, it was stated: "We *do not need these song books of earth* ... we have no need of organs or pianos ... the Holy Ghost plays the piano in all our hearts and then gives the interpretation of the song and sings it in the English language" (emphasis added).[23] I'm not questioning whether or not this happened; I'm simply pointing out an attitude that suggests that truly spiritual things sidestep the mind! I suppose that the highly intellectual hymns of Luther, Watts, Wesley, and Crosby paled in the assessment of those who were directly inspired — or so one might conclude. Finally, when instruments *were* eventually utilized, leaders claimed that the music was not of man but was the supernatural result of God's granting gifts of playing instruments. Whether dealing with personal study or preached sermons, missions or music, it is not hard to ascertain that in the earliest days of our movement, the cerebral elements and intellectual disciplines of the spiritual life were at best dwarfed and often denigrated.

The 1910s and 1920s

In the 1910s and 1920s a number of "Spirit-filled" believers continued to castigate matters of the mind. Though some of the early Pentecostals were well educated, many believed that neither religious nor secular instruction should be a concern of "Spirit-filled" people and that it was even harmful to spirituality. Various leaders of the embryonic Pentecostal church denounced involvement in politics and social issues and railed against the arts and sciences.

Some even saw organization in itself as anathema. Take, for example, the sentiments of Frank Bartleman, a key leader in the first twenty-five years of the Pentecostal movement: "The truth must be told. Azusa began to fail the Lord also, early in her history. God showed me one day they were going to organize.... Sure enough, the next day I found a sign outside Azusa."[24]

Believing that the mainline churches had fallen prey to the enemy, scores of Pentecostals were convinced that any type of alliance with them would bring a spiritual collapse to their standing. When asked about staying in the denominational churches, E. N. Bell, first chairman of the Assemblies of God, replied, "I see no way how one can be true to God ... and yet stay in these churches."[25] A few among the Full Gospel top brass deemed that almost all churches that were not Pentecostal were "against God" and "anti-Christian." With this cast of mind, it is easy to see how, in the first twenty-five years of the Pentecostal movement, little is said of utilizing the deep wells of Protestantism's doctrinal treasures. So, even though we witness a bubbling caldron of spiritual fervency during these formative years, we can also detect a coalescent philosophy that, when dissected, smacks of cultural conceit and theological narrowness.

As briefly noted, engaging one's mind and efforts for political causes fared just as poorly as did educational and organizational involvement. After becoming Pentecostals, many shunned all political involvement. A. J. Tomlinson, first general overseer of the Church of God (Cleveland, Tenn.), while referencing his conversion stated, "I have never taken any part in politics since, nor gone to the polls and cast a ballot"; he followed this up by, "I will vote only for Jesus." In a 1922 *Pentecostal Evangel* article, chairman of the Assemblies of God W. T. Gaston said, "I don't believe any Christian is ever authorized in the Word of God to put his nose into political business."[26] I wonder how the Puritans (1620s), founding fathers (1770s), abolitionists (1850s), and civil-rights activists (1930s – 1960s) would respond to this political posture.

Politics aside, it appears that there was little if any interest in the major socio-scientific issues of the day. Remember, the Pentecostal movement was being formulated in the very heyday of the Darwinian debate (Scopes Monkey Trial, 1925); but one searches far and wide to find Full Gospel leaders who dealt persistently and comprehensively with the issue. One Pentecostal historian cites the consensus of the early Pentecostals on the matter, writing: "There was agreement that 'God did not want scholars and clever persons. He had no need of science. All he wanted was pure hearts.'"[27] This mirrors the demeanor of the Holiness movement thirty years earlier; for as another author puts it: "Satisfied in their own minds that the Bible was the Word of God, the Holiness people largely abandoned the futile fight with science."[28]

There was also the suspicion toward what many referred to pejoratively as "book learning." They complained that those who gleaned information with their *mere human mind* were filled with only "head knowledge" and so had automatically forfeited the influence of the Spirit's teaching. Howard Goss, Charles Parham's successor, made this statement on the topic:

> While *we* poured in the Holy Scriptures, and heated our part by prayer ... *others* succumbed to being bookworms. *Those*, He [God] gently steered toward quiet, shallow waters where we lost sight of them. They could be satisfied with less, so less they got! Why? Because books are in themselves only dead things. (emphasis added)[29]

The ironic thing is that you read this very statement in a *book* that Goss published.

The foregoing are all manifestations of the reluctance of Pentecostalism's founding generation to engage the intellect in the issues that have now come to saturate our society. A prejudice against the mainline churches caused us to forego vast measures of theological wealth that could have reinforced the mortar of our foundations. The hands-off policy in relation to politics surrendered the voice of a growing mass who could have aided in bringing about much positive change in the destiny of our national life. And a monastic-like retreat from the arena of science crippled our ability to speak to, and help form, the gigantic effects of science on our culture. I hope that we see today the twisted ideological wreckage that in large part is the result of leaving our collective national mind in the control of those who do not know their Maker. The fault, of course, cannot be attributed only to Pentecostals; there was an anti-intellectual attitude as well throughout much of fundamentalist Christianity.

EDUCATE, INDOCTRINATE, AND DEBATE

Though many within the avant-garde of Pentecost's initial leadership exhibited evidence of classical anti-intellectualism, there were those who not only possessed excellent and educated minds but who called for a deeper and wider educational base for those pursuing ministry. True, agreeing that there's value in preparing for ministry is not necessarily equal to "loving God with one's mind"; however, it *can* be a step in the right direction to recover lost intellectual ground. Schooling can be anything from nursing at the bosom of Aristotelian academia to feeding off of the "prophesied doctrine" of a self-appointed teacher. Most of us are aware of educational malnutrition, which is rampant in our progressively dumbed-down society — a society brimming with every kind of school imaginable. This, in itself, proves that there *can be* vast chasms separating true intellectual cultivation and mere attendance in academic sessions.

Though a minority band of Spirit-filled believers fought for some theological training, we shouldn't automatically assume that the minds of the students of these early schools were learning to engage their intellects for the glory of God. Mere indoctrination (being taught *what* to think, not *how* to think) doesn't count when measuring true education, for programming a mind with mere data not only fails to sharpen one's "intellectual iron," but in reality *blunts* the edge of the intellect by brainwashing its subjects into believing that their minds have in fact been sharpened!

Thus, even though many schools were established in the initial decades of Pentecostalism, most did not train their students to read widely, think critically, and defend the faith. All in all, the circle of ministers and prominent laymen that eventually became the Assemblies of God seemed to attract more than their fair share of those who saw warrant for institutional preparation for ministry. At the first Council held by the Assemblies (April, 1914), five primary objectives for their gathering were given. Among these five, the group recommended "a proposition to lay before the body a general Bible Training School with a literary department for our people."[30]

These educational endeavors met with all manner of resistance. Some went so far as to claim that those who chose the path of education could no longer rightfully call themselves Pentecostals. They maintained that education automatically took the place of the power of God. Others deduced that it was this very shift from experience to intellect that had hoodwinked and then hurled the denominations down the abysmal slopes of a backslidden state.[31]

When we consider the overall attitude of early Pentecostals, it is not surprising that it took thirty-five years before an Assemblies of God school would offer its first full-fledged four-year degree. It would be sixty-two years from Parham's day before the first Pentecostal university was launched, and sixty-nine years until the founding of the first fully-accredited Pentecostal theological seminary. Compare these figures to the founding of Harvard in 1636, especially in light of the fact that the Puritans had only *begun* to settle Boston in 1630! The Puritan Fathers, whose intellectual credo was "All truth is God's truth, wherever it may be found," were convinced that a godly nation without deep cultivation of the mind fell far short of God's plan for America.[32]

CONCLUSION

This, then, is a short survey of the intellectual life of Pentecostalism's earliest years. We must not condemn those early Pentecostal pioneers who may have misunderstood the relationship between the head and the heart and between experience and knowledge. Rather, we should learn from their miscalculations and prejudices. And like the holy remnant of Nehemiah's time, we must build up the wall of God's city, all the while carrying "sharpened iron" at our sides lest we advance in one area at the expense of another (Neh. 4:17 – 18).

The millions among us who pant for the manifest presence of the Holy Spirit must realize that by bearing dull intellectual implements, we will be found wanting when called upon to defend the reality of that very presence. Rather than ignore, downplay, justify, or lambaste the Pentecostal pioneers who shunned matters of the intellect, we must learn humbly and pray ardently that the passion of these pioneering fathers be conferred on our comfortable souls, all the while avoiding antipathy toward the life of the mind that some of them exhibited.

With souls afire and with sacrificial commitment, these Pentecostal trailblazers dauntlessly carved a century-long course along which the charismata of Christ would navigate. With God's help, let us — today's Pentecostals and Charismatics — as pioneer missionaries to a *new* century, dare to pay the price that our whole being might be set ablaze, furnishing a promising path for the generations to come. In other words, let us resolve to love God with *all* of our hearts *and* minds. With the guiding hand of the Master, we surely *can* — O that we *will*!

NOTES

1. Lucius Apuleius, "Cupid and Psyche," in *The Golden Ass*, ed. F. R. B. Godolphin, *Great Classical Myths* (New York: Random House, 1964), 412–28.
2. Jack Hayford, "A Remedy for Imbalance," *Charisma and Christian Life* (September, 1990), 74.
3. John Nichol, *The Pentecostals* (Plainfield, NJ: Logos International, 1966), 77–78; Millard Erickson, *Christian Theology: One-Volume Edition* (Grand Rapids: Baker, 1983), 836; idem, *The Evangelical Mind and Heart* (Grand Rapids: Baker, 1993), 200.
4. John R. W. Stott, *Your Mind Matters* (Downers Grove, IL: InterVarsity Press, 1972), 6, 7, 9, 10; Michael Green, *I Believe in the Holy Spirit* (Grand Rapids: Eerdmans, 1975), 204, 208.
5. Mark Noll, *The Scandal of the Evangelical Mind* (Grand Rapids: Eerdmans, 1994), 24.
6. Martin Marty, "Pentecostalism in the Context of American Piety and Practice," in *Aspects of Pentecostal–Charismatic Origins*, ed. Vinson Synan (Newberry, FL: Bridge-Logos, 1975), 205–6, 209; Carl F. Henry, *Toward a Recovery of Christian Belief* (Wheaton, IL: Crossway, 1990), 27; Donald W. Dayton, *Theological Roots of Pentecostalism* (Peabody, MA; Hendrickson, 1991), 23. Watson Mills, *Speaking in Tongues* (Waco, TX: Word, 1967); Victor Budgen, *Charismatics and the Word of God: A Biblical and Historical Perspective on the Charismatic Movement* (Harrisburg, PA: Presbyterian & Reformed, 1985), 181; H. J. Stolee, *Speaking in Tongues* (Minneapolis: Augsburg, 1963), 134–35; Quentin Schultze, *Televangelism and American Culture* (Grand Rapids: Baker, 1991), 84; George Marsden, *Religion and American Culture* (San Diego: Harcourt Brace Jovanovich, 1990), 151–59; Tom Smail, *The Love of Power* (Minneapolis: Bethany, 1994), 13–19; Arthur Clement, *Pentecost or Pretense?* (Milwaukee: Northwestern, 1981), 56, 133, 140–41; George Dollar, *The New Testament and New Pentecostalism* (Sarasota, FL: Nystrom, 1978); O. Talmage Spence, *Charismatism: Awakening or Apostasy?* (Greenville, SC: Bob Jones, 1978), 98ff.; Arthur Johnson, *Faith Misguided: Exposing the Dangers of Mysticism* (Chicago: Moody Press, 1988); Harold Bloom, *The American Religion* (New York: Simon & Schuster, 1992), 179; Richard Culpepper, *Evaluating the Charismatic Movement* (Valley Forge, PA: Judson, 1977), 10; Richard Quebedeaux, *The New Charismatics* (San Francisco: Harper & Row, 1976), 40; Richard Lovelace, "Evangelical Spirituality: A Church Historian's Perspective," in *Journal of the Evangelical Theological Society* 31 (March 1988): 33.
7. Bob Jones, "Foreword" to Spence, *Charismatism*, viii. Of all the above authors, Jones appears to be the only one who cannot find it within himself to unearth a single positive trait of Pentecostalism. This statement, in itself, seems to have been made by one whose logic has been incapacitated by his emotional bias on the subject!
8. Gordon Fee, *Gospel and Spirit: Issues in New Testament Hermeneutics* (Peabody, MA: Hendrickson, 1991), x–xi; idem, "Hermeneutics and Historical Precedent — a Major Problem in Pentecostal Hermeneutics," in *Perspectives on the New Pentecostalism*, ed. Russell P. Spittler (Grand Rapids: Baker, 1976),

122; William G. MacDonald, "Pentecostal Theology: A Classical Viewpoint," in *Perspectives on the New Pentecostalism*, 69; R. Hollis Gause, "Issues in Pentecostalism," in *Perspectives on the New Pentecostalism*, 114; Clark Pinnock, "The New Pentecostalism: Reflections of an Evangelical Observer," in *Perspectives on the New Pentecostalism*, 185.

9. Russell Spittler, "Maintaining Distinctives: The Future of Pentecostalism," in *Elements of a Christian Worldview*, ed. Michael Palmer, (Springfield, MO: Logion , 1998), 10; idem, "The Theological Opportunity Lying Before the Pentecostal Movement," in *Aspects of Pentecostal – Charismatic Origins*, 243.

10. Gordon Anderson, "Questions, Problems, Challenges;" side one of Tape #1 in the cassette series "Pentecostals at the End of the 20th Century"; idem, "Doctrines" and "Problems, Evaluation, Conclusion;" on Tape #4 in the cassette series "The Prophecy Movement"; idem, "Pentecostals Believe in More Than Tongues," in *Pentecostals From the Inside Out*, 56 – 56; cf. also Stanley Burgess and Gary McGee, *Dictionary of Pentecostal and Charismatic Movements* (Grand Rapids: Zondervan, 1988), 57, 773.

11. L. Grant McClung Jr., "Salvation Shock Troops," in *Pentecostals From the Inside Out*, 86; William Menzies, "The Movers and Shakers," in *Pentecostals From the Inside Out*, 40; William G. MacDonald, "Pentecostal Theology: A Classical Viewpoint," in *Perspectives on the New Pentecostalism*, 69; R. Hollis Gause, "Issues in Pentecostalism," in *Perspectives on the New Pentecostalism*, 114; Clark Pinnock, "The New Pentecostalism," 185; Gary McGee, Conversation with Del Tarr, partially recited in Tarr's article entitled "Transcendence, Immanence, and the Emerging Pentecostal Academy," in *Pentecostalism in Context*: *Essays on Honor of William W. Menzies*, ed. Wonsuk Ma and Robert P. Menzies (Sheffield: Sheffield Academic Press, 1997), 204.

12. Claude Kendrick, *The Promise Fulfilled* (Springfield, MO: Gospel Publishing House, 1961), 37; Menzies, *Anointed to Serve* (Springfield, MO: Gospel, 1971), 85; James Goff Jr., "Questions of Health and Wealth," in *Pentecostals From the Inside Out*, 67.

13. Charles Parham, *A Voice Crying in the Wilderness* (Baxter Springs, KS: Joplin Printing, 1944), 15 – 19; Robert Anderson, *Vision of the Disinherited* (New York: Oxford Univ, Press, 1979), 58; Sarah Parham, *The Life of Charles F. Parham: Founder of the Apostolic Faith Movement* (Joplin, MO: Tri-State Printing, 1930), 6 – 10

14. Charles Parham, "The Old Time Pentecost," in *Apostolic Faith* (September, 1906), 1 – 2; Edith Blumhofer, *The Assemblies of God: A Chapter in the Story of American Pentecostalism*, 2 vols. (Springfield, MO: Gospel, 1989), 1:76 – 77; Sarah Parham, *Life*, 48; Menzies, *Anointed to Serve*, 35 – 36.

15. Charles Parham, *Voice*, 31; idem, "Hell," *Apostolic Faith* (September 1912), 11; Anderson, *Vision*, 58; William Connally, *History of Kansas State and People* (Chicago: American Historical Society, 1928), 3:19; Sarah Parham, *Life*, 53 – 54; Blumhofer, *The Assemblies*, 1:91.

16. Charles Parham, "Baptism," *Apostolic Faith* (October 1912), 5; Parham, *Voice*, 101 – 18 (esp. 106 – 7); Blumhofer, *The Assemblies*, 1:74, 75, 89, 90; Sarah Parham, *Life*, 6 – 10.

17. Blumhofer, *The Assemblies*, 1:74, 91.

18. See note 104 on page 396 of Blumhofer, *The Assemblies*, 1:396, n. 104; see also Parham, "Free Love," *Apostolic Faith* (December 1912), 4; see also *Apostolic Faith* (October 1912), 6; (March 1927), 5; Vinson Synan, *The Holiness-Pentecostal Movement in the United States* (Grand Rapids: Eerdmans, 1971), 112 – 13; J. Stolee, *Speaking in Tongues* (Minneapolis: Augsburg, 1963), 63; Nils Bloch-Hoell, *The Pentecostal Movement* (Oslo, Norway: Universitetsforlaget, 1964), 19.

19. Seymour, *Apostolic Faith* (September 1906), 1 – 4.

20. Ibid., 3 – 4

21. *Apostolic Faith* (October 1906), 1 – 2; (September 1907), 1.

22. *Apostolic Faith* (September 106), 4; (October 1906), 3 – 4; February – March 1907, 4 – 5; (May 1908), 1.

23. *Apostolic Faith* (January 1907), 2.

24. Frank Bartleman, *How Pentecost Came to Los Angeles: As It Was at the Beginning* (Los Angeles: Bartleman, 1925), 67 – 68.

25. E. N. Bell in *Weekly Evangel* (January 20, 1917), 9; Bartleman, *How Pentecost Came*, 158; *Pentecostal Holiness Advocate* (June 28, 1917), 2.

26. A. J. Tomlinson, *Answering the Call of God* (Cleveland, TN: White Wing, n.d.), 9.

27. Walter Hollenweger, *The Pentecostals* (Peabody, MA: Hendrickson, 1988), 472.

28. David Womack, *Wellsprings of the Pentecostal Movement* (Springfield, MO: Gospel, 1968), 83.

29. Howard and Ethel Goss, *Winds of God: The Life of Howard Goss* (Hazelwood, MO: Pentecostal Publishing, 1958), 65.

30. General Council Minutes, 1914, 7.

31. See "Our Bible School Men Speak Concerning Education," General Presbytery Minutes, August 14 – 20, 1951.

32. Milliard Collins, "Establishing and Financing of Higher Educational Institutions in the Church Body of the Assemblies of God" (Austin, TX: Collins, 1959), 31 – 36. Menzies, *Anointed to Serve*, 355; C. M. Robeck Jr., "Seminaries and Graduate Schools," in *Dictionary of Pentecostal and Charismatic Movements*, 774 – 75 (Oral Roberts University was the first Pentecostal University and Charles Mason Theological Seminary was the first fully accredited Pentecostal Seminary). See also Samuel Eliot Morison, *The Founding of Harvard College* (Cambridge MA: Harvard Univ. Press, 1935), 432.

6

The Spirit-Filled Mind in Modern Times

There is a need for the Pentecostal churches to . . . add to our fervent
testimony of experience . . . a more determined intellectual effort to define our
faith. We ought not enjoy deep emotion at the expense of shallow *thinking*.
DONALD GEE, PENTECOSTAL LEADER, 1935

Believers are not supposed to be led by logic. We are not ever to be led by
good sense. The ministry of Jesus was never governed by logic or reason.
KENNETH COPELAND, POPULAR CHARISMATIC LEADER, 1975

Reasoning opens the door for deception and brings much confusion. . . . It is difficult
for human beings to give up reasoning . . . but once the process is accomplished, the
mind enters a place of rest. . . . I don't want to reason, to figure and to be logical.
JOYCE MEYER, POPULAR CHARISMATIC PREACHER, 1995

In the early 1970s, a major earthquake hit Southern California, the epicenter being near
the heart of the Los Angeles downtown area. Within a short distance of the epicenter sat
a newly-constructed, pristine, Presbyterian church building. After the quake, the people
congregated to observe their cherished property in order to determine what measure of
damage, if any, the building had sustained.

The congregation was both astonished and delighted when they arrived. Not a single
window had been cracked, and as far as the eye could ascertain, the structure was safe and
intact. Just to be on the safe side, they called in engineers to examine the structure more
scrupulously. What the engineers found after their close investigation was that during the
tumultuous tremors, the entire building had shifted from its otherwise firm foundation.
The verdict was in: The facility was utterly unsafe, placing in jeopardy anyone daring to
ignore its haphazard condition. The entire edifice was demolished. The foundations were
then reworked and the footings modified, thus bearing up better under the fury of future
quakes. The undertaking was costly, but the building would now be competent to house its
most precious commodity — the people of God.

In the previous chapter, we witnessed how many of the prime movers of early Pentecostalism failed to deposit sufficient shares of cognitive reinforcement within the soft
mortar of its foundation. Even though they laid long and wide experiential footings, their
intellectual base was alarmingly narrow. Pentecostalism was birthed in tumultuous times,
issuing from an extended period of extreme individualistic spirituality and continental

religious and philosophical convulsions. She witnessed the damaging effects of mixing man-centered modernity with religion and of championing reason over revelation. Thus, Pentecostalism became the next reactionary pass on the ever-oscillating pendulum where the masses swing from experientialism to scholasticism and back. Our movement settled on the shifting soil of anti-intellectualism, but like the rattled church building (which, by the way, was just down the street from Azusa), she too would face multiplied tremors shortly after her establishment.

Within twenty-five years of Azusa's revival, the "War of the Worlds Part I" had taken place, the legs of Wall Street had been knocked out from underneath her, and the American economy began her descent into a neck-deep Depression. Furthermore, the ghosts of Darwin, Nietzsche, and Wagner were already stirring up a potion of furor to pour into the mind of a little Austrian madman. Freud was marketing his psychoanalytic wares and loads of liberal European theology were being imported to American Christian consumers. As for Pentecostalism itself, there were controversies over the significance of tongues, the nature of sanctification, and the person of Christ (the "Oneness" debate), which splintered our fledgling Full Gospel fraternity. During the decades of our formation, there was indeed a whole lot of shaking going on!

So, what did we do in light of all the quaking? Did we follow in the vein of American pragmatism and claim, "If it's working, don't try to fix it?" Did we revisit the vistas of history and recognize the value that the church had traditionally placed on the "life of the mind" when forging and formulating their future courses? Did we acknowledge that the Scriptures promote the cultivation and use of the intellect? In general, I think we felt that our foundations were fairly secure and so engaged in little *self*-criticism. With eschatological eagerness, we continued to develop on the unsettled foundations of an experiential faith rather than on a more balanced base of emotion *and* reason, experience *and* intellect, piety *and* knowledge.

The principle of self-criticism is an indispensable and basic condition for any kind of growth: social, philosophical, moral, intellectual, or spiritual. When we refuse to engage in self-criticism or ignore scrutiny from without, we construct a refuge of willful ignorance that most often brings with it intellectual stubbornness and spiritual arrogance. The feeble reasoning, which goes something like, "How can you argue with our success," or "God wouldn't bless us if we were wrong," is the result of a kind of pious idolatry that is often the result of oversimplistic and naïve views of God's Word. These shallow arguments sound right until we realize that the Mormons and Muslims, the Baha,i faith and Buddhism, and the likes can all claim the same.

If we desire to possess truth, enjoy genuine certainty, maintain skill in processing ideas, and participate in lifelong learning, it is necessary for us to be adept at recanting our errors. But before we can do so, we must be able to *recognize* our errors. This calls for self-correction, which, in turn, is dependent on our ability to take criticism. At the thirty- or forty-year mark, our movement was still making impressive headway. She was a devout organism marked by miracles and zeal. She was comprised of witnessing, praying,

God-seeking, God-loving people. She was not, however, a people who had a passion for loving God with all their minds. Augustine of old, when reflecting on his preconversion drama, stated: "My sin was all the more incurable because I imagined that I was not a sinner." Most Pentecostals imagined that they were not at all anti-intellectual, and thus their prejudice was all the more incurable.

In this chapter, we will meet one of the dominant engineers who arrived shortly after the quaking crossroads of the nineteenth and twentieth centuries to inspect our foundations more scrupulously. He tried desperately to stimulate our thinking about thinking and proposed insightful counsel for remedying our imbalances. In addition to his attempts, I will provide some of the varying shapes of and means by which anti-intellectualism has trickled down to us Full Gospel moderns.

IS THERE AN ENGINEER IN THE HOUSE?

Donald Gee (1891 – 1966) was a Spirit-filled "seer" — a scrutinizing engineer — in the early days of Pentecostalism's history. For half a century, Gee traveled around the world both confirming the power of God in the movement as well as communicating the need for a well-balanced Pentecostal message. He took up the difficult and unpopular responsibilities that most often go with prophetic territory. Because of his love for the Pentecostal movement, he confronted her potential pitfalls, plunging his finger into the raw nerves of the excesses and inconsistencies that, more often than not, accompany the ecstasies of a highly emotional faith.

Gee was by no means a dreary stuffed shirt who winced at the thought of demonstrative praise and was disquieted by heaven-sent phenomena. He was fervid for the perceptible presence of a holy God, yet maintained an intellect on fire — a rare combination in Pentecostal – Charismatic ranks at that time. On the subject of God's miraculous intervention, Gee contended that the manifestation of supernatural healings not only birthed and ignited new church works but that they were, in a real sense, the very life of Christ that emanated from the hands and hearts of the members of his body. Bringing equilibrium to the doctrine, however, he rebuked those who exaggerated claims of healing or who denied one's evident physical malady for the supposed glory of God.[1]

The same cogent balance can be detected within all of the various themes on which he taught. During the war years he avidly supported the Allied cause, yet warned the Pentecostal masses against the all-too-common pitfall of mechanical allegiance to our government's policies. "Unthinking patriotism" he called it — an impulsive devotion based on mere emotion. On the phenomena of "the anointing" and of spiritual gifts, he believed that these supernatural interventions enabled God's servants to exceed by far what they otherwise might accomplish with even the finest of natural abilities. At the same time, he argued that "God-given ministry should not be confused with the lazy slipshod habit of some preachers who waste precious hours that should be spent in preparation.... *A true prophet* needs preparation!"[2]

In the midst of abundant cultural and philosophical convulsions, Donald Gee continued to hold up a standard against the tantalizing trends of the age. But after fifty years of observing his cherished movement, Gee was not impressed with her intellectual improvement. In the closing years of his ministry, he lamented over the scores of professedly Spirit-filled believers who paraded themselves as spiritual superstars. He was disappointed that after sixty-five years of history (1966), the Pentecostal people, in large part, still exhibited an obsession toward the emotional, the spectacular, and sign-seeking. The manufacturing of doctrine plucked from isolated texts, interpretation of Scripture based on mere opinion, mistaking feelings for faith, and sidestepping responsibility in lieu of so-called Spirit leadings — all were indictments that he leveled against the Full Gospel fellowships of his era.[3]

Furthermore, Gee was convinced that as long as Pentecostals exploited Scripture in superstitious ways and believed that "the anointing" came as a result of shouting Bible verses, there would be little progress made in the intelligent employment of God's Word. He also spoke of the temptation among Pentecostal people especially to confuse the stirring of emotion with the moving of the Holy Spirit. For Donald Gee, the gifts of the Spirit operated "through the understanding, or the mind, or the intellect of the believer filled with the Spirit." On one hand, he knew that believers must be encouraged with sound instruction. On the other hand, he realized that those who needed coaching the most often possessed "an unwillingness to be taught" and were apt to deem themselves always right because they *felt* that they had been divinely led. These caveats are in keeping with the tenor of prophetic pronouncement: simultaneously ancient and yet contemporary, as refreshing as they are rare, and as exceptional as they are essential![4]

Brother Gee has been remembered as "The Apostle of Balance," "The Apologist of Pentecostalism," and as one who "ranks on the highest level of contribution to the American Pentecostal Movement." Another writer says of Gee, he was "extremely important to the success of the Pentecostal movement when a growing fanaticism and tendency to emotional excess threatened our survival." Furthermore, the well-known historian of Pentecostalism, Edith Blumhofer, gives this impressive judgment of the man: "A remarkable man, noted for wrestling thoughtfully with troublesome and controversial issues, Gee was widely revered as a Pentecostal statesman and was arguably the most astute spokesman the movement had yet produced."[5]

So, again, the question could be asked: How did the Spirit-filled movements of the 1940s, 1950s, and 1960s respond to Gee's directives? Did the Pentecostal churches take to heart the prognosis provided by this engineer, a diviner who deemed portions of our foundation as "needful of repair"? Did we seek to dig deeper the wells of our otherwise shallow thinking? Or did we possess an unwillingness to be taught, having been summoned once more by divine leadings and unquestionable unctions, prompting us, yet again, to follow our own infallible feelings? Only their future would bring to light the answers to these questions — and we are their future!

ANTI-INTELLECTUAL SUBTLETIES

There is no doubt that by the end of Gee's ministry, the sharp and blatant anti-intellectualism that was so evident in our earliest years had been blunted. Nevertheless, in a host of ways, the prejudice continued to manifest itself. One way this took place was through the subtle influence of popular literature. In the limited space below, I will provide just a few examples of how this predisposition has bled through the printed page and oral speech.

It is important to keep in mind that those personalities highlighted in the foregoing chapters, in this chapter, and in the two following ones each addressed millions, in person or in print. This is significant, and it brings about colossal consequences. Often it is those who are exceptionally popular among the common Christian public who promote a prejudice against the mind. This, in itself, has major repercussions for those of us who are local pastors, missionaries, or disciple-makers. When a popular book has dropped from the bestseller's list, or when the evangelist and his or her crew has gone off the air or exited the city, we are left to the difficult task of shepherding those who have been swayed by the powerful voice of a household name — the voice of one who has sown seeds of skepticism about the value of the intellect into the hearts of the hearers or readers.

In the 1940s, Carl Brumback penned an admirable apologetic for the Pentecostal experience entitled *What Meaneth This?* His case for the Pentecostal cause contains many excellent and persuasive points. And although there was, and still is, a need for more works of this nature, it appears that, in places, he promotes a slight bias against the commodity of God-given reason. Of course, any time one attempts to address a long-neglected topic, he or she runs the risk of appearing unbalanced (present company not excepted). Again, it's not that the book is patently anti-mind; yet we all know the power of subtleness — elusive, yet potentially injurious.[6]

It's true that throughout Brumback's volume (which was highly promoted for three decades), the author demonstrated that believers of the Pentecostal persuasion *could* defend Trinitarianism and the biblical doctrine of Holy Spirit infillings. Nonetheless, he failed to help Pentecostals see that it is the intellect and the use of reason that we are primarily dependent on in order to execute that very defense! This is a fundamental mistake made by many who attempt to campaign for the supernatural and experiential work of the Spirit. Donald Gee, by contrast, covers this base in stating, "If the fullness of the Spirit is emotional, it is also intellectual," and, "Let us be quite clear that the Baptism means intellectual apprehension of truth."[7] The latter, more judicious approach both defends the experience as well as provides for *the means* to defend it.

While dealing with Paul's teaching on tongues, Brumback hammers on the notion that the human mind cannot possibly fashion the kinds of words associated with tongue-speaking. They are "not understood by the mind," for they have "nothing whatever to do with the mind or intellect of man." And with a twist of sarcasm, he inquires, "What did you say, Paul? Your understanding was unfruitful when you spoke with a tongue? Do you mean that in your Spirit-filled life you actually experienced times when your marvelously illumined mind was passive?" Though there is truth to be found in his propositions, this droning on and this type of caustic castigation unnecessarily furnish fodder for anti-intellectual appetites.[8]

True, there is certainly such a thing as deifying reason; thus, the believer must be on guard against falling into this error. But this definitely is *not* the problem in the Pentecostal–Charismatic realm. Our obstacle is anti-intellectualism. And since this is the case, one must be careful not to reinforce this problem; however, that's exactly what statements like the above tend to do. For by them, one might get the impression that some equate abstinence from thought with depth of spirituality (the same impression given by the early Azusa papers). Paul does instruct us to stop thinking — but, to stop thinking *like children* — and to think like *adults* (1 Cor. 14:20)!

We know that mere rational investigation can neither *discover* the otherwise veiled truth of God nor play even the slightest part in *meriting* salvation; but neither can bodily nutrition, and yet without nutrition, we die. We openly discuss the value of nutrition without demeaning God's supernatural intervention, for we know that both play their part in the life of well-being. Thus, just because the intellect or reasoning power is unable to do some things doesn't mean that it can do nothing. If I can write a book on the value of the "intellectual life" without having to slander the supernatural, so also one should be able to write on the validity of Spirit baptism without downplaying the life of the mind.

Brumback's book is a thought-provoking work of notable worth, especially for those who are struggling with the pertinence of tongues for today. However, I find that it unnecessarily reinforces the very specter that haunts us — prejudice against the mind. It's interesting that in his closing remarks, Brumback ends up doing what so many others have done when arguing against the commodity of reason. Note what he says: "We trust that this Pentecostal answer to the Pentecostal question, 'What meaneth this?' is *reasonable enough to satisfy your mind*" (emphasis mine).[9] There are two lessons that we can learn from this statement. First, it takes the use of reason, applied through the mind, to prove that the supernatural intervention of God in our lives is reasonable. Second, it requires reason to prove that reason is not our all-in-all! Surely, it's not impossible to synthesize the two.

THE 1960S AND BEYOND

Though training institutes abounded in Pentecostal–Charismatic camps, resurgent waves of anti-intellectual affections swept over her adherents. There is little doubt that the countercultural revolution of the 1960s and 1970s influenced the life of the mind of the secular as well as of the sacred populace. In this period of philosophical perplexity, sentimentality trumped the rational and, in the name of love, sensation edged out logic. In this ethereal environment, experience dethroned *mere* knowledge and attempts at "escape from reality" catapulted the nation as a whole into relativistic, existential regions — a place where "feelings — nothing more than feelings" was the anthem, and empty-mindedness seemed synonymous with spirituality. In all of this, we no doubt received a booster vaccine against the life of the mind.

AND THE BEAT GOES ON . . .

The clear disregard for the life of the mind during the 1980s and 1990s alerted me to the fact that we had a serious problem. Until the mid – 1990s, I had invested little effort in seeking out our movement's historical attitude toward the intellect. I was mindful of the contemporary prejudice, but I did not necessarily view it as the fruit of our roots. I saw and heard evidence enough from the pew and pulpit, from students, professors, and Pentecostal – Charismatic publications, without having to awaken the ghosts of anti-intellectualism of Pentecost-past.

Within weeks of having come to Christ, well-meaning believers began to bury me with their favorite paperbacks. On one particular visit to the home of the "church grandma," I walked away with twelve slight volumes — doubling the store of Full Gospel fodder that awaited me on a makeshift shelf anchored beside my bed. Among the books dispatched into my possession was a lean leaflet penned in 1970 by Williard Cantelon, entitled *The Baptism of the Holy Spirit.* It's simply a short explanation and defense of its namesake. In this booklet, Cantelon's attitude replicated that of many others who wrote on the same subject. He informed the seeker (in a muddled fashion) that "two faculties, last to be surrendered, always are man's mind and his tongue"[10] (where does the "will" fit in?). He equates the blessing of being *filled* with the Spirit with the emptying of one's mind and asserts also that the mind must be handed over, claiming that it cannot be active or fruitful when one is spiritually baptized.

Like Brumback, Cantelon does what many seem to do when speaking against the power and need of logic or reason. He writes, "But, as would be *logically* expected, in spiritual Baptism one goes deeper than he does at the time of spiritual birth."[11] The problem here is that logic is an activity of the mind, so it's confusing to claim that one must *surrender* one's mind to experience what is logical. It's a bit like the man who, *while using English*, declares that he cannot speak a word of English, or the relativist who is *absolutely convinced* that absolute truth is a farce.

I received John Sherrill's popular treatise (hundreds of thousands in print), *They Speak With Other Tongues*, on the same day that Cantelon's book came my way. Though Sherrill's book assisted multitudes in their search for fullness in the Spirit, like Cantelon, his writing also courts a slant against things intellectual. Sherrill records a conversation he had with a seminary student just prior to his conversion. The student told him that Nicodemus (John 3) failed in his attempt to understand spiritual matters because he *reasoned*. He (the student) spun out his own "logic" by asserting, "Nicodemus' reason was a logical one; the very fact that he used logic kept him from succeeding in his search for the kingdom." "It isn't logic, but an experience, that lets us know who Christ is," was his closing argument.[12]

Sherrill recounts that the next morning his neighbor also gave him words of wisdom on the matter of salvation. She advised, "You're trying to approach Christianity through your mind; it simply cannot be done that way . . . you cannot come to it through *intellect*." Finally, she exclaimed, "It's just that which I'm hoping for you today . . . that *without understanding, without ever knowing why*, you say 'Yes' to Christ" (emphasis mine).[13] Welcome to modern evangelism!

Among the many books I own that are written by Full Gospel believers, few smack of boisterous anti-intellectualism. But many subtly warn against mixing matters of the mind with spiritual experience. It's this constant barrage of "not the mind," "not the head," "not logic," "not the intellect," but "the Spirit" that has deeply imbedded the seeds of this prejudice into the soil of the Spirit-filled soul. Remember, Jesus said "yes" to spirit *and* mind.

Another example of this intellectual prejudice is apparent in a book I picked up just weeks before writing this chapter. The book is *A Touch of Glory*, written by Lindell Cooley. In describing the "faces of revival" — that is, those who attended the services at Brownsville Assembly of God in Pensacola, Florida — Cooley distinguishes those who "look genuinely hungry" from those who have "intellectual faces." Now, there are humble-looking appearances, concerned expressions, desperate facial casts, and proud demeanors, but there is no category to determine one's intellect. Cooley probably means that some looked skeptical, quizzical, or doubtful. It's both unfortunate and strange that a high respect for the intellect or a leeriness of dupery is equated with a lack of hunger for spiritual things. But this attitude isn't as rare as we might hope.[14]

TRICKLE-DOWN ANTI-INTELLECTUALISM

There are many signposts of this problem in our movement, and they display themselves in so many different ways. I have talked with nearly two hundred pastors on the subject; many sense the same. I've surveyed almost 1,300 laypeople concerning reading habits, views on the mind, and knowledge of our own history; overall, they exhibited a consistent suspicion of intellectual pursuit. And in thirteen of the twenty-six countries that I've traveled to, leaders within the Pentecostal – Charismatic movement have voiced their concern over varying forms of anti-intellectualism.

In addition, there are indications that our movement still lags significantly behind in our pursuit of college-level education. Take, for example, the massive survey in 1993 in which 113,000 people were polled concerning their religious belief and level of education. Of the thirty religious groups included in the survey, Pentecostals ranked twenty-eighth. That is to say, only two other groups (one being the Jehovah's Witnesses) had fewer college graduates than did our movement. This may be hard to believe, but so is the fact that this is the first generation in American history whose children are less well educated than their parents.[15]

A 2000 national survey of 14,301 congregations demonstrates similar results. In the Assemblies of God (perhaps the most progressive and strongest Pentecostal-Charismatic promoter of higher learning) only 12.7 percent of their pastors possessed master's or doctor's level degrees. This is contrasted with 61 percent of pastors in the other forty denominations surveyed. When Assemblies of God churches were asked to rank those items most important to worship, Scripture received 76.4 percent, presence of the Holy Spirit got 22.9 percent, and human reason and understanding received one-third of 1 percent. In addition, over 14 percent of those polled believed that historic creeds and doctrine are of little or no importance.

Of all figures in the above survey, perhaps the most telling and most grave is the fact that one in six (17 percent) felt that reason and understanding is "of little or no importance" for people of faith; this speaks volumes! Combine this with the fact that (as the authors document) college graduates of the larger, more progressive churches were more likely to take the time to respond to the poll. If these are the results from the Assemblies of God, I wonder what the stats would look like if the *average* attendee of the *average* church in *all* Pentecostal denominations would respond?[16]

Our lack of interest in intellectual, artistic, social, political, philosophical, and scientific affairs speaks volumes. The lack of preaching or writing on the value of the life of the mind and our lack of teaching on apologetics and worldviews are further gauges measuring our intellectual biases. Furthermore, has a Pentecostal ever written a book on anti-intellectualism and the means whereby it can be remedied? And then there are the contemporary quotes from without *and* from within our own ranks that reveal a *growing awareness* of this problem in the Full Gospel world. In addition, how could it be that we have escaped the clutches of anti-intellectualism when men such as Sproul, Malik, Henry, Bloom, Noll, Guinness, Sire, Moreland, and other heavy-hitting analysts have sounded the alarm over mindlessness in our universities, in our evangelical churches, and in our nation as a whole? From the prophets of culture to the currents of thought and from laymen in the pew to spokesmen in the pulpit, there is evidence that our minds are endangered.

When pondering the ways that this problem has manifested itself in our midst, an acquaintance in ministry comes to mind, who has the habit of saying, "Now I'm not trying to get all theological on you," and, "Never mind, my mind is never right." And we've probably all heard the illustration of "the eighteen inches between the head and heart," or of those who speak of "heart knowledge" as obedience and "head knowledge" as hypocrisy. But remember, there is such a thing as "a wrong heart," that is, a heart with knowledge that chooses not to humble itself to God's decrees. Moreover, I've never heard of a functioning soul that didn't have a head!

Not only do these signs take place in "Podunk U.S.A.," but there are also many influential Full Gospel figures who seem oblivious to the dangers of promoting anti-intellectualism. There's the fellow who says that those who attempt to defend the faith are merely apologizing for truth. He also asserts that discussion of doctrinal precision is a total waste of time. Others warn that the mind will get you into spiritual trouble every time, that logic can never help you to find the kingdom of God, that God offends the mind in order to reveal the heart, and that believers are always at risk when led by common sense.[17]

These are the tributaries of anti-intellectualism that are cast into pop jargon, then trickle down incessantly through the decades, cascading into and lodging within the minds of the Pentecostal–Charismatic masses. Whether we are aware of it or not, this has affected the way we think about thinking and, in turn, has altered the way we live, minister, and worship God.

While writing this chapter, I received my father-in-law's monthly issue of *Charisma* magazine. Through the years, I've noted frequent anti-intellectual tendencies and numerous inconsistencies in logic in the "Letters" section of this publication. This copy was no different. In one letter, a respondent submitted that "God doesn't have to have a *reason* for doing something." In another note, a reader publicly criticized a particular Christian leader for publicly criticizing another Christian leader and argued that Christians shouldn't argue. In the end, this person made the argument that arguments are of no value when compared to experiences. O what a tangled web we weave.[18]

The same issue of *Charisma* contains an article entitled "New Gay Pentecostal Denomination Says Homosexuality Isn't Sinful." Understand first that the magazine itself isn't in favor of this "gay denomination." But herein lies the problem: The gay members of this "Pentecostal" group justify their position by way of *experience*, not doctrine. They claim to "experience the same lively worship and spiritual gifts enjoyed in the traditional Pentecostal denominations."[19] The short and the long of the matter is this: If "God doesn't have to have a *reason* for doing something" and if "we should enjoy *whatever* He [God] sends our way" (two direct quotes from the "Letters" section), or if our approach is that "others can have the argument, I'll take the experience" (also from "Letters"), where does that leave us? When dealing with issues such as "homosexual Pentecostals," we are left without an argument *for* biblical Christianity or *against* homosexual Pentecostalism. Lest we forget, ideas always have consequences!

BATTLING FOR THE BATTLEFIELD OF THE MIND

I wish to provide one last illustration of the battle we face when attempting to love God with our minds. The author of the best-selling book that I'll quote from is exceedingly popular in the contemporary Pentecostal–Charismatic arena. Personally, I believe that this person is so notable because of her no-nonsense, shooting straight-from-the-hip, challenging style. My family and I have helped to support her ministry by purchasing many of her tape series and books and have benefited from her excellent teaching. But I suspect that after bringing attention to some of her anti-intellectual statements, some will crave to shoot *at me* from the hip! Nevertheless, we need to consider this clear and contemporary example.

The teacher is Joyce Meyer, the book is *Battlefield of the Mind*, and her audience runs into the millions. It's ironic that these particular examples come from a work that speaks to the value of the mind. I initially bought this book in order to provide a positive example of how a Charismatic leader was endeavoring to help the life of the mind in our movement. Keep in mind that, in Meyer's own words, this is her "most powerful and most popular, best-selling book" (well over one million).[20]

I was mostly encouraged as I read the first nine chapters. It looked as if Meyer was challenging Full Gospel folk to begin to think about their thinking and to put to use their God-given reason. But as I worked my way through the chapter entitled "A Confused Mind," the tenor of the book seemed to change. Solomon tells us, "As a man thinketh in his heart, so shall he be." My heart began to think about Meyer's style of thinking. While discussing the reasons why God's people get confused, Meyer lists *reasoning* ("thinking logically") as a major culprit. She points out that this error occurs when a person tries to figure out why a teaching or event is true or logical, and she contends that if we do not fear the power of reason, then our heads will lead us, and Satan can easily rob us of God's will.[21]

Meyer goes on to explain that in light of the human mind's fondness for logic, order, and reason, the believer must not be tempted to invest excessive time in trying to understand everything that the Word of God says. In light of her addiction to reasoning, she writes of how God required her to give it up. She tells of how she could no longer tolerate the pain and labor of reasoning and that she came to understand that the normal condition in which God wants our minds to reside is *not* in reasoning. She suggests that anyone who is addicted to reasoning should likewise resolve to give it up, though "it is difficult for human beings to give up reasoning and simply trust God." She is convinced that in the long run, the Christian will be spared much deception and confusion, and that the pain that accompanies reasoning will eventually be replaced with discernment and revelation knowledge.[22]

In addition to reading these statements in her book, I heard Meyer speak on this subject on television. Referring to professors who had asked her about her theological studies, she stated, "All these people think they're so smart." After inquiring of her schooling, she replies to them with merriment, "I've got the most important degree of all; I've got a degree from the Holy Ghost." "I used to be a head person" she declares, "but realized you can't follow the leading of God and think too much" (at which time the crowd roars with applause).[23]

In practice, it is difficult to be consistent with these types of statements. While Meyer censures "reasoning" and "attempting to understand," she reasons and strives to understand. Though she says we shouldn't spend an "excessive" amount of time trying to understand what the Word says, she goes on to list and comment on hundreds of Scripture references in her book, attempting to *understand* what the Bible teaches on the topic of "the battle of the mind." Additionally, she says that it was only after she finally came to *understand* Paul's teaching on reasoning that she could be delivered from it. Finally, while gearing up to *prove* to her readers why they shouldn't trouble themselves with so many *reasons*, she states, "*Reasoning* is dangerous for many *reasons*" (emphasis added).[24]

Without a doubt, there is a place where the human mind stops in its tracks and where mystery begins. Our finite minds cannot begin to measure the length of eternity, the breath of space, where Christ's humanity met his deity, how three Persons compose the godhead, where God's sovereignty and human free will convene, or how everything can be created out of nothing! Our minds were simply not formed to comprehend all the details of such matters, for reason will never uncover what God has intended to stay hidden. Nevertheless, without the hard, long, and deep thought of the church fathers, who mined and hammered out the doctrines of the Trinity and true nature of Christ, we might never have enjoyed the beauty and richness of these teachings. There are many things that reason cannot do, but those things that it can do *must be done* — under the lordship of Christ. For example, reason aids us in reading Meyer's book, which offers many gems to assist us in managing our thought-life!

Ultimately, I think Meyer's intention is to deal with a certain type of reasoning rather than reasoning in general. In one place she writes of "carnal reasoning," which seems to be distinguished from "noncarnal" reasoning. Though this is more plausible, it's not what is conveyed throughout the chapter. I think (I'm not sure) that Meyer may mean "fear," "worry," "doubt," and "rationalization" when she says "logic," "reason," and "thinking." Rationalization is the enemy of faith, humility, honesty, and the supernatural; that is, the attempt to provide believable but untrue reasons. Furthermore, she is correct when she suggests that "the human *mind* likes *logic* and *order* and *reason*." Our God is a God who clearly exhibits these attributes, and since we are made in his image, we too, when reflecting his nature, are a people of logic, order, and reason.

An aspiring university student comes to mind as I ponder the strange relationship between faith and reason. He reasoned that a Pentecostal preacher might be able to help him with his faith, so he came to me. Reason led him to posit a host of provocative and important questions about the goodness of God and the origin of all that exists. His reason challenged him to seek out truth. In the end, he took a leap of faith — trusting in a belief system — not based on facts or evidence but based on "mere faith." In doing so, my friend chose to surrender to something that could not be proved — an atheistic strain of evolution!

The battle lines are not drawn between faith and reason, for reason that is pit against God's clear revelation is always wrong and faith in the revelation of God is always right. But it's also true that reason that is aligned with God's will is always right, and faith in whatever is not God's truth is always wrong. Those, like Meyer, Brumback, Sherrill, and others, who make negative statements about the nature of reason may not truly be anti-intellectual in their philosophy of the faith. And I hope that I have not misrepresented any of my brothers or sisters in the faith. Perhaps some of these could have explained better what they meant. But my point is simply that by making these statements, they tend to reinforce the bias against the value of reason in the mind of the reader or hearer. And this is what we must be careful *not* to do.

ONE SPECIES, MANY HYBRIDS

A small minority within Spirit-filled circles promotes balance between the experiential and intellectual aspects of the faith. I have met or read about many extraordinary men and women in our movement around the world who are acting as the avant-garde in the realm of academics, politics, the arts, and bringing about social change. Some have overcome the odds, cut against the grain, and though being misunderstood, have personally conquered the currents of anti-intellectualism. Others have been fortunate enough to belong to that diminutive contingency within our ranks that teaches that discipleship of the mind is an integral part of spiritual maturity. But this is, by far, the exception, not the rule.

There are prominent Pentecostal–Charismatic leaders who advocate *limited use* of the intellect in the spiritual life. Others *downgrade* the cognitive gifts to enemy status (all except the ones that their editors need to publish their books). A few point out the importance of the mind, yet are *extremely narrow* in their approach to the subject. These imagine that the "life of the mind" is limited to *what* one thinks, failing to recognize the incalculable worth of invigorating the intellectual life itself. Finally, there are those who give all kinds of *homespun definitions* to those elements relating to the mind (reason, logic, intellect, etc.), often borrowing the descriptions and analyses of the non-Christian world. As mentioned, these variations of the problem can make disentangling the snarls of anti-intellectualism complex. Moreover, when they dribble into the ranks of the laity, they produce even more exotic strains and hybrids of this irrational species.

In 1999, I took three surveys on "the life of the mind" to determine if what I thought I had consistently perceived was, in fact, the prevailing point of view. For the first survey, a total of two hundred churches (ranging from fifteen to fifteen hundred in attendance) received my questionnaire. What I had discovered to be true in fifteen years of ministry is, to a great degree, the case among the 1,296 respondents (approximately 4 percent responded). This survey simply listed sixteen subjects. The participants were asked to indicate, on a scale of "two to ten," the value they placed on the scrambled topics.

The bottom line of the survey showed that these Pentecostal–Charismatic believers considered *spiritual warfare, the heart, experience, tongues, demonology,* and *the gifts* as the most valued elements. These ranked an approximate average of 8.75 on the scale. On the other end of the gamut, there was *the intellect, reading classical literature, study of history, the head, apologetics, logic, theology,* and *reason.* Together, these topics ranked an average of 4.25. It's interesting that without the head, intellect, logic, and reason, one could not even comprehend the instructions of the survey itself, let alone delineate where each subject (in their assessment) fit on the scale! The findings of this survey confirmed to me *again* that this bias is real, consistent, and probably unnoticed by the average constituent of our movement.

The problem of bias against the intellect is all around us. If you listen closely, you'll hear it. Just in the couple of weeks before finishing this chapter, I've had the unfortunate opportunity to hear a pastor say that whenever he hears a preacher mention the need for higher education, he shuts out the voice of that preacher. I also heard a Sunday school teacher downgrade the church's library because there was so much "heady" theological material in it. When I recently asked a missionary, who plants schools in foreign countries, if apologetics is ever taught in their Christian schools, he said that, in his opinion, most people in other countries don't have the mental capability to deal with such complicated subjects. Finally, when I shared with a professor of evangelism that Jonathan Edwards was a philosopher in his own right, the fellow simply said that Edwards must have dabbled in philosophy before he came to Christ. By this, he was insinuating that one cannot be a revivalist and a philosopher simultaneously.

All four of these statements came from Pentecostals! The problem of downgrading the intellect or holding reason in suspicion is still around us; and it comes in as many shapes and sizes as one can imagine.

CONCLUSION

Unlike *most* of our critics, who are generally outside of our movement, I've gone to Brumback, Meyer, Gee, Bennett, Sherrill, *Charisma* magazine, and many of the others, not to criticize and dissect them but to inflame my faith. Though I point out Meyer's confusing chapter on "Confusion," in the past I have benefited from many of her tape series. I also quoted Lindell Cooley, but this isn't to say that I disagree with all, or even much, of his book. My family and I traveled 1,400 miles to stand in the protracted rows of hungry believers lingering outside of Brownsville Assembly of God in Pensacola, Florida. In each of the services we attended, my heart never failed to receive a challenge and a good measure of hope and enrichment, not only through the preached messages but through Lindell's music as well.

I have attempted to point out what seem to me like statements (made by some of my Spirit-filled brothers and sisters) that can embolden anti-intellectual convictions in the minds of the hearers or readers. As you have seen — and will continue to witness throughout this book — to those whom I have quoted as speaking or writing a questionable statement, I have also tried to give sincere compliments. It may not be the natural thing to do, but certainly it is the right thing!

When we offer corrective measures to our children, to a friend, or to a lost soul in need, we don't condemn everything they do. Rather, we help to guide them by isolating the trouble area of their life and by offering solutions — all the while loving them. Too often, we make the mistake of writing off a ministry or individual because of a disagreement we have with them in a couple of areas, because they've done something foolhardy or experienced an isolated failure. Millions have done this very thing to the Pentecostal – Charismatic movement. And we have done the same to the individuals and denominations or churches with which we have disagreed. This shouldn't be.

For far too long, Full Gospel people have been closed when approached on the subject matter of "the mind"; I think we call that close-minded. Our haste to put out the "mind on fire" is perhaps the very reason that in one hundred years of Pentecostal history, few, if any, have written a full-fledged volume on this subject. We have composed mountains of literature dealing with the importance of our physical being (i.e., healing), but few have written of our need to glorify God with our intellectual being. Bear in mind, it's not to the exclusion of experience that we are to entertain the intellect, nor are we called to augment our minds at the demise of emotion or piety. Balance is the bulls-eye at which we are to aim: loving God with body, spirit, *and* mind.

Earlier in this chapter we called on Donald Gee, inspecting engineer and metaphysician of the Pentecostal soul. We heard his heart's cry, calling Spirit-filled believers to come to grips with the unnatural dichotomy between enthusiasm and mental excellence. He challenged our preachers to offer edification steeped in study and urged our laypeople to trust less in weightless zeal and lean heavier on the refreshing zephyr breeze of God-given reason. I wonder what Gee — the Apostle of Balance — would say to our centenarian movement as we traverse the threshold of an unfamiliar millennium?

At the beginning of Chapter 5, I quoted a 1990 *Charisma* article wherein Pastor Jack Hayford challenged readers to be more open to the endeavors of those who take the risk of challenging us to reconsider one or more of our actions or beliefs. He shared with us that too many within the Pentecostal – Charismatic tradition automatically reject *much-needed* correction in the present because we have been the object of *unjust* criticism in the past. Finally, he challenged us to be open-minded, tolerant, and wise when asked to reconsider some of the things we have come to believe. My question is simply, "How have we done, in light of the two foregoing chapters?"

As Spirit-filled ambassadors to the twenty-first century, we must throw off our hesitation and love God with *all* of our minds, diligently sharpening and carefully utilizing our God-given intellects for his glory and thus becoming *Full* Gospel in every respect.

NOTES

1. Donald Gee, *The Pentecostal Movement: Including the Story of the War Years (1940 – 1947)* (London: Elim, 1949), 33 and 40ff.; idem, "Trophimus I Left Sick," 8 – 10 (this work was given to me in typewritten, hand-out form by my missions professor, Dr. Charles Greenaway, in 1986); idem, *Concerning Spiritual Gifts* (Springfield, MO: Gospel Publishing, 1994), 53.

2. Donald Gee, *Ministry Gifts of Christ*, 1930, as quoted in Womack's *Pentecostal Experience*, 179; Gee, *Concerning Spiritual Gifts*, 15.

3. Donald Gee, *Temptations of the Spirit-Filled Christ* (1966), as quoted in chapter 5 of Womack's *Pentecostal Experience*, 81, 84, 85, 89, 90, 91 respectively.

4. Donald Gee, *Concerning Spiritual Gifts*, 141; idem, *Temptations* and *Concerning*, as quoted in Womack's *Pentecostal Experience*, 92, 93, 123.

5. D. D. Bundy, "Donald Gee," in Burgess and McGee. *Dictionary of Pentecostal and Charismatic Movements*, 330; Synan, *Aspects of Pentecostal – Charismatic Origins*, 218; Menzies, *Anointed to Serve*, 171. Womack, *Wellsprings of the Pentecostal Movement*, 269; Blumhofer, *The Assemblies*, 1:48.

6. Carl Brumback, *What Meaneth This?* (Springfield, MO: Gospel Publishing, 1947).

7. D. J. Wilson, "Carl Brumback," in Burgess and McGee, *Dictionary of Pentecostal and Charismatic Movements*, 447; Donald Gee, *All With One Accord* (London, 1961), quoted in Womack, *Pentecostal Experience*, 235.

8. Brumback, *What Meaneth This?* 124 – 33.

9. Ibid., 344.

10. Williard Cantelon, *The Baptism of the Holy Spirit and Speaking with God in the Unknown Tongue* (Plainfield, NJ: Logos International, 1970), 17, 20, 52, 71.

11. Ibid., 77.

12. John Sherrill, *They Speak With Other Tongues* (Westwood, NJ: Spire, 1970), 10.

13. Ibid., 11.

14. Lindell Cooley, *A Touch of Glory* (Shippensburg, PA: Destiny Image, 1997), 161.

15. Barry Kosmin and Seymour Lachman, *One Nation under God* (Westminster, MD: Random House, 1993), 45; Charles Sykes, *Dumbing Down Our Kids* (Gordonsville, VA: St. Martin's, 1995), 121.

16. For other results relating to theology, doctrine, creeds, and congregational levels of education, see survey results at http://fact.hartsem.edu.

17. Paul Crouch, "Praise-a-Thon," Trinity Broadcasting Network (November 10, 1987); idem, "Praise-a-Thon," program on TBN (April 2, 1991); Steve Hill, in two messages at Brownsville Assembly of God, Pensacola, Florida, in 1998, and on television broadcast of "Awake America," from Minneapolis; Kenneth Hagin, 1985 Annual Hagin Camp meeting, Tulsa, Oklahoma; Jimmy Swaggart, Chapel service at Family Worship Center, Baton Rouge, LA (April 1986); John Arnott, *The Father's Blessing* (Orlando, FL: Creation House, 1995), 182; Kenneth Copeland, "The Force of Faith" (Fort Worth, TX: Kenneth Copeland Ministries), 10; idem, *Believer's Voice of Victory* (March 1982), 2.

18. "Letters," *Charisma* (January, 2000), 12.

19. "New Gay Pentecostal Denomination Says Homosexuality Isn't Sinful," *Charisma* (January, 2000), 20.

20. Joyce Meyer, "Life in the Word" program (January 3, 2000).

21. Meyer, *Battlefield of the Mind*, 11 – 12, 86, 89.

22. Ibid., 90, 91, 93.

23. Joyce Meyer, "Life in the Word" program (January 3, 2000).

24. Ibid., 90, 92.

7

Anti-Intellectual Roots in the Nineteenth Century

[They] tended to overemphasize immediate personal conversion to Christ instead of a studied period of reflection; emotional, simple, popular preaching instead of intellectually careful and doctrinally precise sermons; and personal feelings and relationship to Christ instead of a deep grasp of the nature of Christian teaching and ideas.

J. P. MORELAND, CHRISTIAN APOLOGIST

In 1740 America's leading intellectuals were clergymen.... In 1790 they were statesmen.

EDMUND S. MORGAN

Educated ministry and theological training are no longer an experiment. Other denominations have tried them, and they have proved to be a perfect failure.... Verily, we have fallen on evil times.

PETER CARTWRIGHT, 1810

The powerful fact about these protagonists is that, in relation to the accumulated wisdom of Protestant theology, they had few ideas and were little capable of cerebration. A religious revolution ... producing a distrust of calm preaching ... a type of justification by feeling rather than faith ... and an unnecessary division between head and heart.

PERRY MILLER, PULITZER PRIZE WINNER

While touring Israel in 1994, I had the opportunity to visit the site of Tell Megiddo. A "tell" is a mound that has resulted from successive layers of human occupation. As one civilization was conquered and vanquished, the next built their homes directly on the rubble of the former. Megiddo is the tell commanding the pass between the Sharon Plain and the Valley of Jezreel in north central Israel. Our guide explained to us that this stunning vantage point was one of the most strategic military locations in the country and that its lofty perch provides a bird's-eye view of the very site where many Christians believe that the "last battle" — Armageddon — will take place (Rev. 16:14 – 16).

As I perused the grassy slab below, it occurred to me that the view I was enjoying came directly from the peoples who had deposited themselves into the earthen monstrosity. Below my feet lay sandwiched together thousands of years of history, representing an accumulation of departed dynasties. For each of the twenty levels of civilization, the earlier one had functioned as the next one's foundation, and the angle at which each subsequent generation viewed the great battlefield below had been altered by the contributions of the preceding populace.

As with Tell Megiddo, earlier episodes of history provide the hidden keys to the view — the beliefs — that we moderns possess. When it comes to the roots of Pentecostalism's lack of concern for cultivating the life of the mind, we must go far below the level of her twenty-first-century manifestations. It is not by mistake that this movement arrived on the scene of an untouched century (1901) transporting a mother lode of anti-intellectual luggage. She was the religious-cultural consequence of ideological forces that had been forging their way steadily through the frontiers of American thought. Early Pentecostal believers possessed a pint-sized appetite for the liberal arts, the scientific method, and intellectual excellence primarily because the brand of spirituality that had nourished her was itself a by-product of a national mindset — one that had been brewing for well over a century.

Thus, if we want to identify and understand Pentecostal – Charismatic notions about mental discipline, cultural involvement, and critical thinking, we must excavate the data of preceding eras. Just as the nineteenth and twentieth centuries hold the keys that unlock the mysteries, misfortunes, and magnificence of the twenty-first, the late eighteenth century gives us insight into the underpinnings of the nineteenth. If we can sort out some of the philosophical sediments cemented into our making, we can understand better *why* we have come to think the *way* we think about the life of the mind.

THE SPIRIT OF DEMOCRACY IN AN AGE OF REVOLUTION

Although a liberal measure of individualism, the pioneering spirit, and an air of autonomy accompanied the Plymouth Rock pilgrims (1620), it took another 150 years for these deep-seated elements to erupt into a full-blown declaration of independence in the new world. This democratic spirit that mushroomed in the latter half of the eighteenth century forever defined the temper of a land occupied by the free and the brave.

Historians have designated the thirty-seven-year period from 1763 to 1800 as the "Revolutionary Era." It was during this interval that relationships deteriorated rapidly between Mother England and her far-flung stepchildren dwelling west of the Atlantic. Passions flared, wars raged, and reorganization as well as self-definition preoccupied the thoughts of the new American mind. This age of tumult set the stage for the ensuing century when, as one historian suggested, "the whole cosmos was in chaos." Cultural analyst W. R. Ward submits that this was not only a turbulent time but was "*the* most important single generation in the modern history not merely of English religion but of the whole Christian world."[1]

Meshed within the fiber of this fledgling "nation under God" were numerous hybrid images of freedom and equality. It was during these continental convulsions that philosophies, worldviews, and even the idea of truth itself were being weighed in the balance. And so were born a range of radically new perspectives on the status and nature of man, on God, Scripture, the church, human rights, government, history, theology, the mind, and the like.

In addition, eighteenth-century churches were facing their own particular array of challenges. The last quarter of that century saw a period of severe decline, diversion, and disruption for the American church as a whole. Even the revived churches of New England's First Great Awakening were severely affected by the distractions of America's revolution. In part, the waning was due to the fact that many of the local pastors were called into military service, leaving their congregations without an educated and disciplined ministry. Moreover, a myriad of ministers who held credentials from Oxford or Cambridge fled the country back to England in opposition to America's revolt. Wesley's equestrian emissaries (circuit riders) were acutely affected likewise. Of course, his loyalty was to England, and thus virtually every one of his ministers (with the exception of Francis Asbury, Wesley's protégé) took the fifty-four-day Atlantic trek back home.

The Anglican churches were hit the hardest during this religio-political tumult. More than 70,000 parishioners left the country, nearly all of their pastors exited, and their two schools, Kings (Columbia) and the University of Pennsylvania, made radical moves to separate from their Anglican origins. The impact was practically apocalyptic. In comparison to today's population, this would be like 7.2 million people exiting the borders of our country — in short order!

The heart of the educated clergy in America experienced an intellectual stroke, leaving it crippled and stumbling in the wake of a near deathblow. Yale, Harvard, Princeton, and other ministerial training schools were also encountering extreme trials. Many professors were summoned to soldiery and a high percentage of the students sauntered off into the clutches of deism. Historian Sidney Ahlstrom puts the matter bluntly: "The churches had little opportunity for recuperation; and even if they had, the intellectual climate was too debilitating." These issues, he argues, "disastrously affected the recruitment and training of a clergy."[2]

During these years of renovation, the tide of anti-intellectualism began to mount. The swells eventuated into a tidal wave that broadsided the nineteenth century with cataclysmic force. Up until the revolutionary years, ministry and mental discipline, revival and reason, the secular and the sacred, as well as the labels "pastor" and "intellectual" subsisted side by side. But attitudes toward politics, education, religion, and the partnership between things cerebral and things spiritual were changing rapidly and sweeping through the soul of the nation. One historian expresses it this way: "In 1740 America's leading intellectuals were clergymen, in 1790 they [leading intellectuals] were statesmen."[3]

In the estimation of George Marsden, scholar in American religious studies, the Great Awakening itself (1726 – 1756) had actually *prepared* the ground for the seeds of such sentiments. The colonies were mostly populated with those who had dissented from England. These, in turn, when jolted out of spiritual slumber in the Great Awakening, joined those churches that, in a strong sense, were opposed to the Anglican Church. In light of this, the independent inclinations of the dissenters were heightened.[4] As throngs of newly-awakened souls celebrated their emancipation from Anglicanism, they in turn fed, and fed off of, the burgeoning appetite for independence. Soon, all was washed in the blood of a revolutionary land. Suspicion of "learned men" and criticism of authority in general came into vogue. In short, the revolutionary years were a time when the idea of liberty and justice for all (African and Native Americans excepted) — a time when the idea that every man should do what was right in his own eyes — worked its way deep into the psyche of our nation, affecting every area of thought and life.

Ahlstrom writes that the church of America "reached a lower ebb of vitality" during the years 1780 – 1800 than at any other time in the country's history.[5] But if the American mind was impregnated with the seeds of anti-intellectualism in the movements towards autonomy from Anglicanism (1760 – 1775) — that is, if during the gestation period from 1775 to 1800 the New American was malnourished in a womb lacking intellectual nutrients — then it is to be expected that the birth of a feelings-based culture would occur full-term at the turn of the century. In some ways, the New Republic became a breeding ground for intellectual retardation, a nation where history had begun anew, where "liberty" was equated with anti-authority, and where her inhabitants worked to erase from their memory the premium once placed on intellectual spirituality. We were determined to compare ourselves only to ourselves — a new standard had been raised.

Thus, the margins of national anti-intellectualism were defined, and for the next hundred years (1800 – 1900), Christians of the revivalistic tradition broadened and deepened these into indomitable chasms. This period was marked by a suspicion of cultured clergy, an overemphasis on what the masses could accomplish by combining their might, and an unnecessary pitting of the common man against the learned. An increasing mistrust of reason, an escalating interest in enthusiastic, emotion-oriented religion, and an insurgent attitude toward authority all had their part in the transformation of the religious mind of the country. All of these elements combined created a distinctive and new-fangled variety of Christianity. These were the explosive ingredients, which, when mixed and lit, ignited the fury of an anti-intellectual inferno.[6]

INDEPENDENT RELIGION FOR AN INDEPENDENT NATION

While the First Great Awakening (1726 – 1756) was under way in New England, John Wesley had his "heart warming" experience in old England (1738). Thirty-three years later, in 1771, Wesley sent Francis Asbury, the "father of American Methodism," to help care for the 300 lay people accumulated in the previous two years. In 1816, their numbers had swelled to over 200,000; by 1856, the number of full-fledged members rose to over 1.5 million. For eighty years, from 1820 to 1900, the Methodist Church held the prestigious position of being the largest Protestant body in America. This is a vital statistic when evaluating the philosophical and psychological makeup of modern American Christianity.[7]

No other group prospered more in the American frontier than did the Methodists, primarily because there appears to have been a near-perfect match between the two. Many past and present historians have observed that Methodist thinking harmonized with the new mood in America much more than did the country's older denominations. Among the various characteristics that were shared by these two entities were criticism of the past, pleas for the simplistic, a penchant for the practical, a push for experience over dogma, and an emphasis on zeal above knowledge.[8]

In many ways, the "Kentucky Revival," centered at Cane Ridge, set the spiritual stage for many decades to come. It was here that immediate personal conversion, unshackled emotions, the simple gospel, primitive Christianity, the democratic spirit, and the common folk all seem to have converged. The first camp meeting held in conjunction with the revival was in July 1800, but the event that catapulted the meetings into notoriety took place on August 6, 1801. Started by the Presbyterians and continued by the Methodists and Baptists, the meetings drew upwards to 25,000 attendants per service. From this time forward, the "camp meeting" became a household word on the frontier.

When the eighteenth century lay buried in the ashes of revolution, many of its formerly-held religious convictions were crammed into the casket with it. Emphases on doctrine, authority, logic, and education were dwarfed considerably in popular evangelical circles. In many respects, cultivation of the intellect, efforts to connect all of life into a coherent Christian worldview, and the call for a learned clergy were left at the crossroads of these tumultuous times. A curtain of closure was cascading on Act One of the American saga. The dusk of a former era was encroaching rapidly — a time when revived, well-balanced, astute Christian leaders molded the minds of their spiritual disciples. The stage was set for Act Two. In large part, American Christianity had mutated, falling back into a primitivistic mode. This was an era when the value of the mind was notably overshadowed by emotion, and mentally disciplined religion was trumped by common-sense pragmatism.

One more factor that perhaps helped to retard the expanding evangelical movement's passion for intellectual improvement was the issue of the so-called "separation of church and state." Though much misunderstanding and complexity have surrounded the origin and meaning of this tide-turning affair, several things are clear. First, the document (a letter) referring to such a separation (written in 1802 by Jefferson as the Kentucky revival raged over the hills) simply confirmed that there would be no federal establishment of any one denomination over another.

Second, as time passed, other interpreters (Supreme Court justices) of the First Amendment suggested that religion should have no bearing on the government's business.

Third, the opposing camps continued to argue over whether this separation of church and state was meant to provide *freedom for religion* or *freedom from religion*. In this atmosphere, the gulf widened between religion and politics, public affairs and a private faith, the secular and the sacred, the spiritual and the intellectual. This provided a further impetus for the libertarian spirit that had ignited the American Revolution itself to persist in affecting the churches. Though these latter interpreters of "separation" had misled the people, the revived, free-spirited populace accepted it, and so came to resent "the establishment." Viewing the secular state as a restraining element, many nineteenth-century believers simply left the arena of politics and education to the book-learned elite. After all, what did the New Jerusalem (America: The City on a Hill) have to do with "Athenian" government anyway? All of these acted as ingredients in the making of an anti-intellectual culture — a culture that had only recently fought for the free expression of ideas and for the liberty to live out their ideals.

THE SLIPPERY SLOPE OF REVIVAL-*ISM*

Whereas the Puritan fathers, Wesley, and Edwards had conscientiously wedded "heart religion" and the mind, many within our otherwise indivisible nation under God felt at liberty to divide them. The nineteenth century saw many spiritual men and many an intellectual mind; however, to discover both attributes wrapped in the same skin was becoming increasingly infrequent. This is not surprising, considering that, as historian George Marsden puts it, "anti-intellectualism was a feature of American revivalism."[9]

The revived populace of the early 1800s viewed the events of 1801 in much the same way as the early Pentecostals later viewed the events of 1901 (i.e., as the new age of the Spirit). The Spirit had fallen anew on all flesh. Thus, those who were once specially equipped for ministry were now minorities among the Spirit-moved masses. Preachers popped up everywhere; and in many places, the only qualifications for pulpit ministry was a Christian testimony and passion. One commentator of the Kentucky Revival wrote: "Now all had equal privilege to minister the light which they received, in whatever way the Spirit directed."[10]

In the flurry of visions, prophecy, and healings, the implication was that a new age of the miraculous had dawned; God was shedding his grace on America in an extraordinary way. A new age had indeed dawned! It was marked by cogent conversions of multiplied thousands, by the revisitation of miracles, and by the sharing with *all* believers the otherwise private and often highbrow priesthood. The downside of this explosive revivalism, however, was that the animosity toward the mind that had been germinating in the eighteenth century came into full bloom with the dawning of liberated and frequently unbridled religion in the nineteenth century.

Religious historian Nathan Hatch says of this age, "Volatile aspects of popular religion, long held in check by the church, were recognized and encouraged from the pulpit."[11] Again, a veritable deluge of self-appointed prophets, preachers, leaders, and seers spilled into the mixture of American religion. Americans were weary of the tyranny wielded by one self-appointed king three thousand miles away; they opted instead for the rule of three thousand self-appointed kings one mile removed. Whereas a lone pontificating priest of Cambridge stock had previously stood to unravel the mysteries of the Holy Writ, now the learned priest, exiled to the hermeneutic hinterlands, was replaced by a whole kingdom of priests, each of whom, it seemed, created his own dogma, often based on mere opinion, internal leadings, superficial study, and popularity.

Again, there is no question that a tremendous amount of good came about as a result of the healing winds of God's gracious visitation. Equally, however, there is little doubt that the intellectual wound that we inflicted on ourselves during this era has haunted us for the next two hundred years. Orators with anti-tradition, anti-history, anti-creed, anti-organization, anti-clerical, and anti-authority predilections crafted their soap boxes during these blessed but chaotic times. Furthermore, the historical giants of the faith were cut down to size by the untutored masses who refused to believe that anybody was better suited than the next to "do theology," but supposed that all stood on level ground when it came to deciphering and elucidating God's Word. This may sound good, but have you ever tried to teach in this atmosphere?

One journalist, alarmed at the religious free-for-all, wrote in 1805: "No person is warranted from the word of God to publish to the world the discoveries of heaven or hell which he supposes he has had in a dream, or trance, or vision."[12] In 1808, Jonathan Edwards' grandson Timothy Dwight challenged seminary students everywhere to escape the onslaught of ignorance that was pervading the Christian landscape. He inquired that if a seven-year apprenticeship was demanded of wanna-be shoemakers, then why were so many preachers balking at the thought of equal preparation for dealing with men's hearts! Evidently, many believed that it took more learning and craft to work with the soles of shoes than it did to work with the souls of men. Others cried out that many doctrinal oddities were arising in the churches because the gospel was being peddled not only by men who couldn't read and write, but also by those who freely and frequently propagated a hatred for learning.[13]

During these times, the printed page was used to the maximum to spread the latest trends of popular religion in the New Republic. Hatch points out that many little-known members of the clergy were flippantly elevated to the status of the likes of Jonathan Edwards and Timothy Dwight through the rise of a democratic religious culture in print. Hofstadter indicates that it was the espousers of emotionalism and enthusiasm as well as the advocates of anti-intellectualism who flooded the religious literary markets in the early part of the nineteenth century.[14]

RELATIVISM, REVIVAL-*ISM*, AND SUBJECTIVE RELIGION

Since the liberated believer was encouraged to "minister in whatever way the Spirit directs," it should come as no surprise that the four major American cults were birthed during this nineteenth-century commotion. Mormonism had its debut in 1830, Adventism in 1844 (though today's Adventism has lost much of its cultlike characteristics and resembles contemporary evangelicalism), Christian Scientism in 1879, and the Jehovah

Witnesses in 1884. The leaders of all four movements were *self-taught*; all four believed that they were to restore *true* Christianity; all four claimed to be the *religion of the people and for the people*; and all four maintained that they were *privately and personally directed by God*. These cults were simply the extreme natural outworking of an anti-historical, anti-tradition, anti-creed, anti-theology, anti-intellectual mentality. Evangelical revivalism did not suffer in error to the same degree as the classical cults did, but because of a similar neglect of intellectual integrity they did suffer.

Though rationalism (reason without revelation) had been progressively creeping into the political, educational, and religious highbrow life of the nation, it did not succeed in penetrating the mainstream churches. The evangelical revival did, in fact, induce the masses to stand against the onslaught of rationalistic tendencies that could have quickly reduced the fabric of the New Republic into an ideological pile of rags, had it trickled down to the general populace. With this in mind, however, it's as if our back door was taken completely off its hinges while the front door was being barricaded. That is, rationalism could not march triumphantly into the church, but anti-intellectualism and relativism, her mutated next of kin, were allowed not only to enter but seemingly were heartily welcomed.

It's the age-old story of the log and the speck of dust, of the camel and the gnat, of the trees and the forest, of slaying the bandits followed by shooting oneself in the foot, or of Athenian victories and the Trojan horse. This subtle blunder is reminiscent of the fall of great warriors at the hands of a lover, or of a death of a great personality who, after fighting valiantly, is slain by a medicinal inoculation that was meant only for their good (like Jonathan Edwards, who sparked the Great Awakening but died of a smallpox vaccine). The evangelical revival of the nineteenth century had managed to sidestep the great plague of rationalism. Yet, simultaneously, she had volunteered to cohost a germ that eventually infiltrated the warp and woof of an entire nation.

One might have hoped that the leaders of the popular revival would have attempted to halt the rampant anti-intellectual avowals early on, but they did not. By the time various leaders of the Cane Ridge meetings voiced their conviction that reason and the rational had been recklessly cast to the wind, hundreds of thousands had been injected with a bias against the mind. Among those leaders who later repudiated the unreasonableness of various aspects of the revival were James M'Gready and Alexander Campbell. Earlier, both had fanned the flames firsthand at Cane Ridge. But within eight years, they saw that the movement had produced every manner of "schismatic preacher, entirely unhinged from every system of doctrine." These men discerned that "feeling, not thinking," had become the rule of far too many Christians.[15] M'Gready lamented that "the greatest divine and greatest Christian upon earth, if he have a calm, dispassionate address, cannot move [the crowd] any more than he could move leviathan."[16]

Like the great mound Megiddo, the substance of pop religion was concretized into the foundation of the fledgling republic. And like the multiplied layers of cultural litter strewn through the sands of time, so also many homegrown ideas were shuffled into the malleable minds of an adolescent nation. Pragmatism, experientialism, emotionalism, romanticism, individualism, and anti-intellectualism built up the knoll on which future decades and centuries have positioned themselves. From this theoretical and theological perch, the giants of nineteenth-century evangelicalism preached to the masses, witnessing the rebirth of hundreds of thousands of souls. As the lost were wooed down sawdust trails, they deposited their sins — *and often their intellects* — at the foot of the altar, returning to their seats with the two commodities most prized among American believers — *Jesus* and their *feelings.*

NOTES

1. Sydney Ahlstrom, *A Religious History of the American People,* 2 vols. (Garden City, NY: Image, 1975), 1:437; Stephen R. Graham, *Cosmos in the Chaos: Philip Schaff's Interpretation of Nineteenth-Century Religion* (Grand Rapids: Eerdmans, 1995); George S. Wood, as quoted in *The Democratization of American Christianity,* ed. Nathan O. Hatch (New Haven, CT: Yale Univ. Press, 1989), 220; W. R. Ward, "The Religion of the People and the Problem of Control, 1790 – 1830," in *Popular Belief and Practice,* ed. G. J. Cuming and Derek Baker (Cambridge: Cambridge Univ. Press, 1972), 237.

2. Ahlstrom, *A Religious History,* 1:443.

3. Edmund S. Morgan, "The American Revolution Considered as an Intellectual Movement," in *Paths of American Thought,* ed. Morton White and Arthur M. Schlesinger Jr. (Boston: Houghton Mifflin, 1963), 11.

4. George Marsden, *Religion and American Culture,* 29.

5. Ahlstrom, *A Religious History,* 1:442.

6. See Hatch, *Democratizaton*; John Woodbridge, Mark Noll, and Nathan Hatch, *The Gospel in America: Themes in the Story of America's Evangelicals* (Grand Rapids: Zondervan, 1979); Mark Noll, Nathan Hatch, and George Marsden, *The Search for Christian America* (Westchester, IL: Crossway, 1983), and Richard Hofstadter, *Anti-Intellectualism in American Life* (New York: Knopf, 1963), 81.

7. Hofstader, *Anti-Intellectualism,* 97; Ezra Squier Tipple, *Francis Asbury: Prophet of the Long Road* (New York: Methodist Book Concern, 1916), 191; Mark Noll, *A History of Christianity in the United States and Canada* (Grand Rapids: Eerdmans, 1992), 173; Dayton, *Theological Roots of Pentecostalism,* 63; Synan, *The Holiness-Pentecostal,* 218; Ahlstrom, *A Religious History,* 1:530.

8. Ahlstrom, *A Religious History,* 1:529; Ian H. Murray, *Revival and Revivalism: The Making and Marring of American Evangelicalism 1750 – 1858* (Edinburgh: Banner of Truth, 1994), 183, 187.

9. George Marsden, *Fundamentalism and American Culture* (New York: Oxford, 1980), 212.

10. Richard M'Nemar, *The Kentucky Revival, or, A Short History of the Late Extraordinary Outpouring of the Spirit of God* (New York, 1846), 31. Also see, Murray, *Revival and Revivalism,* 169.

11. Hatch, *Democratization,* 4, 10. Also see *The New York Times 1998 Almanac,* ed. John W Wright (New York: Penguin Putnam, 1997), 264 – 266.

12. See Richard Bushman, *Joseph Smith and the Beginnings of Mormonism* (Urbana, IL: Univ. of Illinois Press, 1984), 59.

13. Timothy Dwight, *A Sermon Preached at the Opening of the Theological Institution in Andover* (Boston, 1808), 7 – 8 (as quoted in Hatch, *Democratizaton,* 19). See also Lyman Beecher, *Address to the Charitable Society for the Education of Indigent Pious Young Men* (New Haven, CT: Yale Univ. Press, 1814), 5 – 8.

14. Hofstadter, *Anti-Intellectualism*, Part 2 ("Religion of the Heart"); Hatch, *Democratization*, 11.

15. Ian Murray, *Revival and Revivalism*, 189.

16. Report by M'Gready, "The Religious Intelligence," *Presbyterians in the South,* ed. Ernest T. Thompson (Richmond, VA: John Knox, 1963), 1:164 – 65.

8

Four Giants of Nineteenth-Century Evangelicalism

The nature of the evangelical spirit itself no doubt made the evangelical revival anti-intellectualist, but American conditions provided a particularly liberating milieu for its anti-intellectual impulse.

RICHARD HOFSTADTER, PULITZER PRIZE WINNER

I am obliged to say plainly that, in my judgment, we have among us neither the men nor the doctrines of the days gone by.... Once let the evangelical ministry return to the ways of the 1700's, and I firmly believe we should have as much success as before. We are where we are, because we have come short of our fathers.

J. C. RYLE, CHURCH LEADER, 1868

In the middle 1800's, however, things began to change dramatically ... emotional, simple, popular preaching instead of intellectually careful and doctrinally precise sermons; their overall effect was to emphasize ... personal feelings and relationship to Christ instead of a deep grasp of the nature of Christian teaching and ideas.

J. P. MORELAND, APOLOGIST

The Holiness movement and Pentecostalism shared certain outlooks ... by instinct and conviction, they reverted to those populist techniques that had characterized American popular religion for over a century.

NATHAN HATCH, HISTORIAN

THE CHANGING OF THE GUARD

An interesting yet tragic historical event illustrates well the war of values, thought, and religion that raged during the earliest days of our nation's establishment. When Thomas Jefferson, an avowed deist, became president in 1801, he chose Aaron Burr as his vice president. Interestingly enough, Burr was a grandson of Jonathan Edwards. In 1804, while another grandson (Timothy Dwight) was leading Yale in a phenomenal spiritual awakening, reviving dead souls *from* their figurative graves, Burr, who had totally rejected the faith, sent Alexander Hamilton, a passionate student of the Bible, to the grave — literally! As a result of a pistol duel sparked by Hamilton's attempts to block Burr's candidacy for New York governor, Hamilton died on July 12, 1804.[1]

In the span of five short years (1799–1804), the foundations of the nations were shaken. The atrocities of the French Revolution were airing, and Napoleon and his gang were prevailing over the world. George Washington passed on, Jefferson was inaugurated president, and the revival fires at Cane Ridge and Yale burned for hundreds of days. These were exciting times; but as we have seen, they were also transition times that set the centennial tone for the life of the mind.

The eighteenth-century advocates of blending experiential faith with intellectual cultivation — for the glory of God — were a dying breed. Francis Asbury died in 1816, and Timothy Dwight departed in 1817. From the dawn of Cane Ridge (1800) to the death of D. L. Moody (1899), the inhabitants of the greatest nation on earth experienced a self-induced famine of the mind. As calloused hands cultivated the frontier and as pragmatic pioneers fueled the Industrial Revolution, the evangelical mind was all but being treated to a sort of customized lobotomy. One diviner of the times has stated rather candidly, "The influence of the evangelical revival was intellectually retrograde."[2] Others said these were times of "narrow-mindedness," "extreme emotionalism," "guidance by feelings," "no interest in the arts and sciences," "a disdain for education," and "devotion akin to superstition."[3]

Of course, there were those evenhanded evangelicals who struggled in the midst of this ideological tug-of-war. But because they held to the benefits of both reason *and* revelation, they were regarded as unfortunate schizophrenics, lodged at the crux of conflicting worldviews. The rationalists viewed these sensible saints as superstitious *because* they naively accepted the Scriptures as God's truth. The revivalists, by contrast, regarded these evangelicals as prostitutes who slept with the archenemy, the goddess of reason, because these balanced believers also highly respected the power of the intellect. By the mid-1850s the rift in American Christianity between mind and emotion had widened so far that one concerned, well-known pastor cried out: "There is a general impression, that to be a clergyman with intellect is to be one deficient in piety, and that eminently pious ministers are deficient in intellect."[4]

THE GIANTS OF NINETEENTH-CENTURY POPULAR EVANGELICALISM

Between 1800 and 1900, four of the most notable players in the proliferation of revivalistic evangelicalism were Peter Cartwright (1785–1872), Charles Finney (1792–1875), Dwight L. Moody (1837–1899), and Billy Sunday (1862–1935). Together, they enjoyed 180 years of ministry in the nineteenth century. Each has been called the greatest in his own respect, each contributed to the anti-intellectual mood of their time, and each has also had an effect on the spirit and methodologies of Pentecostalism.[5]

Peter Cartwright

Cartwright has been labeled the most famed circuit rider of his era. During his sixty-nine years of ministry (1803–1871), he preached no less than 25,000 times and witnessed firsthand the exponential growth of Methodism in America. In the seven decades that coincided with his ministry, the Methodist movement grew from 65,000 to two million![6]

The intellectual metamorphosis that took place between Wesley's time and Cartwright's era (1790 – 1870) is staggering. What Wesley had fought for so valiantly (i.e., thinking Christianity) Cartwright appears to have abandoned almost wholesale — no intellectual bonanza here! Asbury (1745 – 1816), like Finney (1792 – 1875), was an intellectual hybrid of sorts. So, even though Cartwright had observed the high regard for the life of the mind in his mentor, Francis Asbury (as Asbury had witnessed in Wesley), he himself was twice-removed from the era when reason, science, literature, and logic were cherished among the clergy. That's to say, both were an interesting mix of the eighteenth- and nineteenth-century mindsets. Both were educated men, but each also had his feet firmly planted in the intellectual soils of two clashing time frames.

Asbury had been a voracious reader like his own mentor, John Wesley. He was bent on cultivating his mental capacities, consistently compounding his understanding of history, politics, and philosophy. It was his goal to read at least a hundred pages a day. By doing so, he taught himself Greek, Hebrew, and Latin. It is said of him that with ease and depth he could converse about Josephus, Herodotus, Louis XIV, Galileo, and Sir Isaac Newton (just to name a few). Just one more thing: Like Wesley, almost all of his studying was done on horseback!

After his death in 1816, Asbury's circuit-riding mantle was picked up by Cartwright, but the intellectual baton was dropped. From this time on, the band of galloping gospel Methodists who won the soul of America forgot Father Wesley's accent on the intellect. As a whole, the democratic aggregate depreciated the life of the mind, and Cartwright personified that depreciation.[7]

In his autobiography, Cartwright repetitively slammed theological training, the seminaries, book-learning, and preachers who spoke proper English. On one hand, his book — the chronicles of his ministry — is truly a remarkable volume, containing many exciting tales of God's presence on the great American frontier. On the other hand, it also contains a myriad of blatant anti-intellectual annotations. He says of himself and of other Methodist ministers: "We had little or no education; no books, and not time to read or study."[8] When this fist-fighting ruffian was converted at Cane Ridge, his style and methodology were all but predestined. With formidable frame, resolute jaw, piercing black eyes, and vociferous voice, this Christianized Kentuckian addressed crowds in every nook and cranny of the frontier. And everywhere he went, he spread two messages: *the lostness of man* and *the futility of mixing the intellect with faith.*

Every once in a while, he made a seeming gratuitous remark about education, such as, "I do not wish to undervalue education." But a "but" immediately followed. In this particular case, the "but" is followed by, "this educated ministry and theological training are no longer an experiment. Other denominations have tried them, and they have proved a perfect failure."[9] Evidently he did not realize, remember, or want to remember that his own heroes (Whitefield and the Wesleys) were themselves graduates of Oxford.

In the chapter of his autobiography entitled "The Mountain Preacher," Cartwright suggests that "from John Wesley down to the present day," the secret of success lay in a "baptismal fire of the Holy Ghost . . . not in learned theological knowledge."[10] It is true that Wesley stressed the sanctifying, preserving, and empowering Spirit, yet it was never at the expense of enrichment of the mind. Wesley was "Wesley" because he advocated and embodied both, a baptism of fire *and* a baptism of learning. Without *intellectual* width, you create a Cartwright, and without *experiential* depth, you foster a Pharisee. When *both are neglected*, you have a nominal Christian who has no idea why he believes what he has been told to believe. But then when you combine *both the experiential and the intellectual* dimensions of spirituality, you generate a Paul, Ambrose, Augustine, Aquinas, Luther, Calvin, Knox, Wesley, or Edwards.

Continuing through Cartwright's memoirs, one finds that he criticizes pastors for preaching "prepared sermons" (reminiscent of Finney), that he boasts of what God rendered through ministers without colleges and books (like Seymour later), and that he demeans pastors who regularly studied theology. He claimed that Methodists who sought education were "aping the world," and he says of himself, "When God knocked the scales from my eyes, this sinner could go without any theological training straightway to preach." In a later chapter, he simply says, "I will not condescend to stop and say that I am a friend to learning. . . . What has a learned ministry done for the world?" He might have found a proper answer to his question if he would have pondered further why he called himself a *Wesleyan Method-ist!*[11]

Apart from the paradox that wherever he went, he sold books to support his ministry, it seems that his love of books and desire for a better education was dismal. But there are those statements in the preface of his *Autobiography* showing ultimately that he had some regrets along these lines: "My abiding conviction is that I cannot write a book that will be respectable, or one that will be worth reading; I have no books to guide me." After sixty-nine years of discouraging an army of preachers from such futile practices, he laments, "I threw my manuscript journals to the moles and bats. This act of my life I have deeply regretted. If I had my ministerial life to live over again, my present conviction is that I would scrupulously keep a journal." By this time he had vented his negative thoughts on learning to millions.[12]

Having read Cartwright's autobiography, I highly recommend it to anyone who either *thinks* he or she has it rough in ministry or who is in quest of a spark to kindle an inferno in his or her soul *for* souls. Peter's missionary endeavors changed the eternal destiny of many lives; however, his commentary on the Christian's intellectual life discouraged multitudes of Americans from loving God with their minds. Cartwright is somewhat like those faithful soul-winning brothers who are outspoken against us Pentecostals and Charismatics; they do both a world of good *and* a world of hurt simultaneously.

Charles Finney

I have mentioned that Finney, like Asbury, was one who neither fit the mold of eighteenth-century intellectual Puritanism nor that of the endangered mind of nineteenth-century revivalism. Both Asbury and Finney looked to Wesley in their times of need, but the latter was much less likely to admit it. Asbury trumpeted the value of the teachers of days gone by, whereas Finney claimed more than once to need only the Bible and the philosophy of his own mind: "I had read nothing on theology except my Bible; I had nowhere to go but directly to the Bible."[13]

In his perennial classic, *Revivals of Religion*, Finney speaks of his disdain of the written sermon: "Every year's experience has ripened the conviction on my mind, that the man who writes least, may, if he pleases, think the most."[14] Finney and Cartwright were two of the most popular, outspoken critics of written messages; strangely enough, however, one can read their railings in their *Lectures*, *Memoirs*, and *Autobiographies*, respectively. Though today the art is almost nonexistent among those who call themselves "Full Gospel," we do well to remember that Luther, Latimer, Baxter, Chalmers, Payson, Davies, and Edwards are among the many major-leaguers who manuscripted their messages, and then *read* them from the pulpit. The results were profound; we refer to these results as The Great Reformation and The Great Awakening! Of course, there's no particular virtue to be found in reading one's sermons, but neither is there virtue in repeated generalities, trite monotonies, and emotional soapbox preaching.

In addition to Finney's loathing of written sermons, he detested most of the standard literary works of the day. He was curt on the matter: "Let me visit your chamber or parlor, or wherever you keep your books; What is here? Byron, Scott, Shakespeare, and a host of other triflers and blasphemers of God." Perhaps a particular volume housed in my library would have helped Finney to ward off this unnecessary prejudice against Shakespeare. A book that was around in Finney's day is entitled *Shakespeare's Knowledge and Use of the Bible*. In essence, it is a three hundred-page defense of Shakespeare's incredible comprehension of and commitment to the Holy Scriptures. Furthermore, Shakespeare's last will and testament opens with: "I commend my soul into the hands of God my Creator, believing through the merits of Jesus Christ, my Saviour, to be made partaker of life everlasting." Sadly, scores of nineteenth-century preachers assumed that if a work was not entirely "gospel," it must be anti-gospel. Though Finney didn't go this far, he came close to it. This is the legacy that later spilled into the Holiness and Pentecostalism movements.[15]

One encounters multiple anti-intellectual statements while reading through the writings of Finney. Various seminaries, theological training, learned ministers, and classical studies were added to his hit list. Upon ordination in the Presbyterian Church he admitted that he had never even read the most influential creedal standard for all Presbyterian affiliates — the Westminster Confession. The ministry of Charles Finney was, indeed, a strange mixture of old and new attitudes toward the life of the mind. He rejected the authority of men, yet led Oberlin College. He told ministers to throw away their notes, yet he published piles of his own. He claims to have had nowhere to go but directly to the Bible, yet at times admits to having diligently studied Wesley's writings. And he was convinced that revivals were *not* at all miracles, yet he employed a full-time prayer warrior (Father Nash) for the purpose of beseeching God for his manifest presence.

As explained, anti-intellectualism isn't confined to blatant comments against the value of the intellect; often it is simply an attitude or mindset. It is in this respect that Finney promoted anti-intellectualism. His ministry was marked by a pragmatic, audience-centered, individualistic, anti-authoritarian demeanor. Finney bolstered the anti-clerical, emotion-oriented disposition of the self-reliant masses, which, in turn, bred suspicion toward those who studied theology, philosophy, and the arts. Eventually, all this became backwash on Finney's evangelistic ministry, causing him to seriously reexamine his populist approach.[16]

Finney's constant insistence that "a revival is not a miracle, nor dependent on a miracle, in any sense" came back to haunt him. Highly emotional preaching to highly emotional, doctrinally illiterate people produced a rather odd strain of Christianity in America. Finney later described these masses as having experienced "temporary repentance and faith," yet "falling short of abiding in Him," and so "they would of course soon relapse into their former state."[17]

Much of what Finney accomplished was of tremendous value. He goaded preachers to speak straight, transparently, and passionately. Furthermore, he promoted the miraculous presence of God and stressed the need for intercessory prayer, radical immediate conversion, and violent repentance. These attributes were desperately needed and greatly appreciated by many. Yet in spite of this, his pragmatic techniques and emotion-centered evangelism left not only a host of backsliders in their wake, but also a horde of clergymen who proliferated his questionable methodologies.

Finney *has* been recognized as an intellectual of sorts; however, as one historian expressed it, while describing Finney and Mahan (Finney's right hand at Oberlin), "their culture was exceptionally narrow; their views of learning extremely instrumental; and instead of enlarging their intellectual inheritance, they steadily contracted [subtracted] it." It has been stated that "more than any other person, Finney molded the way people perceived revivalism in the middle third of the nineteenth century." Another has said of him, "Finney called for a Copernican *revolution* to make religious life audience-centered." The audience did, in fact, become the guiding force of the evangelical revival. They not only threw overboard what they viewed as the dead weight of the mind but almost abandoned the ship of the intellect altogether. Furthermore, that audience became the next generation of captains, who in turn steered the church and nation into the approaching century. Indeed, a revolution had come to pass.[18]

Dwight L. Moody

Dwight L. Moody is the third of four major players we are considering in popular nineteenth-century evangelical circles. I repeat — I believe that these men of God were greatly used for the advancement of the kingdom. Each was a phenomenal witness for the Lord Jesus, and each served the Master faithfully and fervently. In light of that, my personal prayer is that God will help us all to exhibit even a portion of the passion demonstrated by these senior brothers. The aim of this chapter, however, is *not* to delineate the admirable aspects of nineteenth-century evangelists. Rather, it is to display the downplaying of the life of the mind from 1800 – 1900 so that we, as Spirit-filled people, may see how we came by the anti-intellectual bias that we now possess.

Moody, too, was twice-removed from the era when reason *and* rationale were valued as God-given gifts, when the "Christian mind" was an essential component of the spiritual life, and when theological training was *not* optional. He fits squarely into the mold of his direct predecessors. One of Moody's biographers says, when referring to his evangelistic philosophy, "The evangelism, then, in whose tradition Dwight L. Moody stood, derived more from a Second Great Awakening in the early 1800's; and it was Charles Grandison Finney and Peter Cartwright, agents of 'muscular Christianity,' who typified this tradition."[19]

An example of his blithe attitude toward critical theological matters can be seen in his reactions to a Bible college student who had been wrestling over the authorship of the Pentateuch. Moody responded to the youth's query: "If a man has got the colic, what difference does it make to him where the mustard was grown that relieved him?" Or, after having been asked by a friend what were his thoughts on the controversy over the supposed dual authorship of Isaiah, Moody replied, "See here, it doesn't make much difference who wrote the book anyhow. God could have used half a dozen Isaiah's."[20] These may not seem like grave forfeitures of intellectual real estate; however, this was the very era when the foundations of the books of Genesis, Isaiah, and Daniel were being questioned and dismantled by rationalistic critics from across the Atlantic.

Moody's advice for those who were troubled by difficult Bible passages was to "look them full in the face and pass on, [for] the Bible was not made to understand." Furthermore, he counseled the saints to "be done with scholarship and colourless catechisms." While the secularists, romantics, and cult leaders were marketing their devastating doctrinal wares, Moody could be heard saying, "My Theology! I didn't know I had any. I wish you would tell me what my theology is." Thus, it should come as no surprise that, in his opinion, seminary-educated rascals were by far "the meanest of all rascals."[21]

By his own attestation, Moody read practically nothing apart from the Bible, and he regularly took potshots at science, literature, and culture. Learning, he believed, was often an encumbrance to the "man of spirit," making it plain that "we don't want intellect, but the power of God." It was this constant degrading of intellectual excellence and this perpetual pitting of zeal and spirit against knowledge and education that were transfixed in the minds of millions of Christians — Christians who, in part, formed the base of the Pentecostal Movement.[22]

Of course, just because Moody lacked a college education and made unsympathetic comments about higher culture did not mean that he was against basic training for ministers. Like Cartwright, who was instrumental in raising up McKendree College, and Finney, who headed Oberlin, Moody, too, set out to establish Moody Bible Institute. Some may think it strange that those who criticize intellectual endeavors would also found schools; it is not as strange as one might first think.

First of all, the fact that a learning institute is established says nothing of the content, aim, or methodology of its programs. I once saw a sign on a building that read "University of Modern Medicine." I was impressed by the sign, though the building was less than impressive. When I got to my speaking engagement in that town, I asked the pastor about the "university." He chuckled and said that a fellow from (I believe) Europe had set up the empire with a staff of two to teach chiropractic techniques and healing with herbal medicine. In other words, titles can be misleading.

Second, one may establish an excellent training center for preparing ministers, but this does not necessarily mean that an excellent and broad education is being offered. It is like the tech schools of today: They are proficient at training tomorrow's craftsmen, but they teach nothing about the political sciences, rhetoric, logic, philosophy, and the like. There has always been and always will be a need for learning establishments that teach the fundamentals of the Bible, prayer, evangelism, and pastoral ministry. But we must not confuse this narrow approach to practical ministry with the broad cultivation of Christian minds for optimum, lifelong learning in a world of complexity and change.

Third, the fact that a person has founded a school doesn't necessarily indicate what their thoughts are as to the relationship between faith and reason, a liberal education and Christianity, or theology and practical ministry. Remember Parham? He established "schools" in many locations, but he was the only teacher and he used only one textbook, the Bible. And then there are schools like Jimmy Swaggart Bible College and Seminary. Swaggart would rail against Catholics, psychology, and biblical criticism and then release his students from chapel to return to their classes to study the church fathers, psychology, and biblical criticism. Though he lampooned book learning and lambasted head knowledge, all the while preaching that all one needs is the power of the Holy Ghost, he built a 1,500-member Bible college student body in three short years!

Finally, just because great women or men of God make anti-intellectual statements doesn't necessarily mean that they are equally biased toward all of the components that make up the intellectual life. Practically every Pentecostal who speaks against the futility of "head knowledge" sends their kids to school every day for twelve years to acquire head knowledge. And most Full Gospel believers who make snide remarks about theology wish that they had a better grasp on how the Bible's themes fit together. Furthermore, many preachers, past and present, who have downgraded the mind wish they would have studied more in order to be better equipped to provide better answers to the difficult questions that they are now faced with. The bottom line is, regardless of where a Christian leader fits on the scale, if they make anti-intellectual statements, they unnecessarily fortify the anti-intellectual sentiments in the hearts of hearers.

Billy Sunday

Contemporary scholar George Marsden indicates that Billy Sunday exhibited most of the same characteristics of the great evangelists of previous eras — the commendable as well as the questionable. He suggests that Sunday, Finney, and Moody were basically all knit from the same yarn, pointing out that all three were more or less against, and operated as outsiders to, the established churches. It has been said that Sunday reflected Moody's disinterest in theological matters while combining the pragmatic, revivalistic techniques of Finney. Like Cartwright, Finney, and Moody, Billy Sunday was held in the highest esteem by American believers — so much so that, according to popular opinion at the turn of the century, he tied with Andrew Carnegie as the eighth greatest man in the United States.

Resembling the others discussed in this chapter in yet another way, Sunday also demonstrated a disregard for the intellectual life. Education was one target at which he loved to slash with poetic vindictiveness. For example, on one occasion he issued the following indictment: "The church in America would die of dry rot and sink forty-nine fathoms in hell if all members were millionaires or college graduates."[23]

Sunday believed that if children received schooling but didn't receive the Bible, they were much more apt to fall headlong into the depths of depravity than if they received neither. He went so far as to declare that learning gathered from the schoolhouse was "worse than useless" if it did not bring its beneficiaries to Christ. With passion he preached: "The road to the kingdom of God is not by the university." Thus, it is not surprising that he said something like the following to his enamored spectators: "Thousands of college graduates are going as fast as they can straight to hell. If I had a million dollars I'd give $999,999 to the church and $1 to education."[24]

Though he too raved about the worthlessness of written sermons, it has been said that upward to 75 percent of his sermons were "borrowed" from those who had taken the time to write them out. With shocking callousness he spoke of his desire to "sentence to death fifty popular writers" and of how "scholarship can go to hell" if it did not speak directly to the common understanding of common people. This view of scholarship matched his general opinion about doctrine, boasting, "Billy Sunday does not know any more about theology than a jack-rabbit knows about ping pong." Perhaps this is why, when he was asked fundamental questions about doctrine by his presbytery board, he answered, "That is too deep for me." Sunday was consistent in his views on learning; he not only spoke against theological erudition but also lived it.[25]

In addition to scholars, college graduates, classical authors, novelists, and other professional writers, Sunday had in his crosshairs those who peddled politics, flirted with philosophy, and stressed the importance of science and sociology. Remember, this is the man who, at one time, was considered by many as *the most popular Christian in America*. Pop religion has never had much time for the complicating matters of cultural cultivation and deep intellectual acumen. Rather, the pop Christian is satisfied with simple piety, peppered with a healthy measure of emotion, and infected by the latest entertainment epidemic. Though much good was wrought through this interesting but controversial servant of God, unfortunately, he stimulated further both the sensate nature and anti-intellectual inclinations of the American people. After Billy came to town, Sunday service would never be the same.

THE IMPACT OF THE FOUR

Men such as Finney and Moody did much good for the kingdom of God and for American society in general. They scrapped and struggled for the schooling of the poor and for women. They championed emancipation for slaves and fought vigorously for the abolition of alcoholic drink. They also showed a host of weary pilgrims how to locate the otherwise oblique gate that leads to the narrow path of eternal life. For their dogged industry in these areas we are to be thankful, but for their inattention (and sometimes aversion) towards teaching a nation to become thinking Christians, we cannot be as charitable. As T. S. Eliot noted about the nineteenth century, too many Christians were compelled to be merely pious, while too few were challenged to "think in Christian categories."[26] Varying degrees of social change did come about at the hand of the nineteenth-century church, but most seemed satisfied with personal piety and private religion while thinkers of less noble character set about transforming the mind of a nation.

When the audiences of Cartwright, Finney, Moody, and Sunday are added up, these men spoke into the hearts — the minds — of an inestimable number of nineteenth-century Christians. Sunday is said to have addressed hundreds of millions. In one particular set of meetings, the attendance was reckoned to be 1,443,000. Cartwright held camp meetings for fifty-two years with crowds up to 10,000 per gathering. Moody is attributed with having spoken to, perhaps, five hundred million hearers. In one cluster of convocations alone, he preached before one and a half million attendants. Finally, of the approximately ten million who sat under Finney's ministry, it is estimated that a half million souls sauntered down the sawdust trail to visit the celebrated "anxious seat."[27]

Think of it, a billion people sat under the tutelage of these four men. They were men through whom God was reconciling the world and who "shaped the Christianity of the American Republic."[28] But they were also men who championed emotion and utility, often at the expense of intellectual exercise and cognitive cultivation. These were the masters of the evangelical mind who all too frequently promoted oversimplistic, dogmatic formulas, boiling down evangelism into mere pragmatism and education into meager forms of indoctrination.

From 1801, when Cartwright was licensed to preach, up to 1899, the year of Moody's death, the war raged on. It wasn't so much a war between God lovers and God haters, but it was a battle to determine whether those who professed to love God would do so *with* or *without* their minds fully engaged. A new breed of Christian mindset had been forged in the furnace of a liberated yet susceptible nation. It was during this mind-bending, foundation-building interval that the Puritan ideal of thinking thoroughly and Christianly was surrendered for a mess of populist porridge. The contrived conflict between passionate piety and an elevated intellect ended in a disturbing separation of the two. The otherwise God-ordained marriage between mind and spirit was all but dashed — all but divorced.

CONCLUSION

The Spirit-filled forces of the early twentieth century seized on the popular Christianity of Cartwright, Finney, Moody, and Sunday. Historian Nathan Hatch notes that (among several other Christian groups listed) "the ... Holiness movement and Pentecostalism shared certain outlooks ... by instinct and conviction, they reverted to those populist techniques that had characterized American popular religion for over a century."[29]

Finney himself has been called "the second most important influence on early classical pentecostal belief."[30] According to theologian Fredrick Bruner, Finney was "the shaping influence on Methodist theology in the holiness churches" and the "major historical bridge between Wesleyanism and modern pentecostalism."[31] It was Finney's advancement of Wesley's "perfectionism" that sparked the propagation of "the baptism of the Holy Spirit" through the Holiness movement. Others recognize that most Pentecostal churches received their initial impulse from Methodism and the Holiness revival. Furthermore, in the realm of evangelistic technique, "American revivalism has been the most important formative influence on the modern pentecostal movement."[32]

As to Moody's effect on our movement, his revivalistic methodology has been important to the evangelical environment into which modern Pentecostalism was born. Moody was not only an advocate of the necessity of Spirit baptism, but he also preached the imminent return of Christ and believed in the New Testament gifts of the Spirit and in faith healing — all of which are central to Pentecostalism. Blumhofer mentions Moody as one figure to whom some Pentecostals trace their roots. This shouldn't be surprising, seeing that some of the earliest accounts of evangelical tongue-speaking rang out from his 1875 meetings in London. Finally, historian Vince Synan has summed up this connection by writing: "The religious experience of the pentecostals also bear a striking resemblance to the experiences of Wesley, Finney and Moody."[33]

NOTES

1. George Marsden, *Religion and American Culture*, 49; Tim La Haye, *Faith of Our Founding Fathers* (Brentwood, TN: Wolgemuth and Hyatt, 1987), 141; Noll, *The Search for Christian America*, 75 – 76.

2. Norman Sykes, *Church and State in England in the Eighteenth Century* (Cambridge: Cambridge Univ. Press, 1934), 398 – 99.

3. A. C. McGiffert, *Protestant Thought before Kant* (London: Duckworth, 1911), 175; S. M. Duvall, *The Methodist Episcopal Church and Education up to 1860* (New York: AMS Press, 1928), 5 – 8, 12.

4. Bela Bates Edwards, from his *Writings* (Boston, 1853), 2:497 – 98.

5. When comparing the disciplined preparation of those who prompted America's eighteenth-century revival with the leaders of nineteenth-century revivalism, one notices a glaring contrast. Whereas the most prominent leaders of the First Great Awakening had trained at Yale, Princeton, Dartmouth, Oxford, and Edinburgh, respectively, those spearheading the revivals of the nineteenth century almost completely sidestepped this phase of ministerial preparation. This doesn't mean everything, but I am confident that we will miss significant implications for the subject at hand if we simply rejoin "Can't God use men without degrees?" In other words, we must not purport that this divergence means nothing at all.

6. Ahlstrom, *A Religious History*, 1:531; Peter Marshall and David Manuel, *From Sea to Shining Sea* (Tarrytown, NY: Revell, 1986), 89.

7. Tipple, *Francis Asbury*, 90; Charles Ludwig, *Francis Asbury: God's Circuit Rider* (Milford, MI: Mott Media, 1984), 124.

8. Peter Cartwright, *The Autobiography of Peter Cartwright* (1856), 11. See Marshall and Manuel, *Sea to Shining Sea*, 85.

9. Cartwright, *Autobiography*, 64.

10. Ibid., 144.

11. Ibid., 145, 164, 204, 265 – 67.

12. Ibid., 11 – 13; see also 236, 315, 338.

13. Charles Grandison Finney, *Memoirs* (New York, 1876), 42, 45, 46, 54.

14. Charles Finney, *Revivals of Religion* (Virginia Beach, VA: CBN Univ. Press, 1978), 225 – 26.

15. Finney on literature, as quoted in William G. McLoughlin, *Modern Revivalism* (New York: Ronald Press, 1959), 118 – 20. See on Shakespeare, Charles Wordsworth, *On Shakespeare's Knowledge and Use of the Bible* (London: Smith, Elder, and Co., 1864); William Burgess, *The Bible in Shakespeare* (Chicago: Winona, 1903), xii.

16. See Hatch, *Democratization*, 196 – 201; Woodbridge, *The Gospel in America*, 145 – 46; Hofstadter, *Anti-Intellectualism*, 92 – 94; Marsden, *Religion and American Culture*, 49 – 55; and Murray, *Revival and Revivalism*, 223 – 74. See Benjamin B. Warfield, *Perfectionism* (Grand Rapids: Baker, 1981), 2:10, 21 – 28.

17. Finney, *Lectures*, 27; Warfield, *Perfectionism*, 2:24.

18. Hofstadter, *Anti-Intellectualism*, 91; Woodbridge, *The Gospel in America*, 145; Hatch, *Democratization*, 197.

19. James Findlay Jr., *Dwight L. Moody: American Evangelist* (Chicago: Univ. of Chicago Press, 1969), 3.

20. D. L. Moody, *Boston Evening Transcript*, January 5, 1897; *Boston Globe*, January 8, 1897, included in Findlay, *American Evangelist*, 410.

21. J. C. Pollock *Moody without Sankey* (London: Hodder and Stoughton, 1966), 58 – 61; McLoughlin, *Modern Revivalism*, 213, 273.

22. Gamaliel Bradford, *A Worker in Souls* (New York: George H. Doran, 1927), 24 – 26, 30 – 37, 64, 212.

23. Sydney E. Mead, *The Lively Experiment: Shaping of Christianity in America* (New York: Harper & Row, 1963), 114 – 15; Marsden, *Religion and American Culture*, 179; Hofstadter, *Anti-Intellectualism*, 115.

24. William B. McLoughlin, *Billy Sunday Was His Real Name* (Chicago: Univ. of Chicago Press, 1955), 138, 282 – 83.

25. Written sermons: McLoughlin, *Billy Sunday*, 26, 125, 132, 138, 164 – 70; Earle E. Cairns, *Endless Line of Splendor* (Wheaton, IL: Tyndale, 1986), 194; Hoftstadter, *Anti-Intellectualism*, 115, 122; Os Guiness, *Fit Bodies Fat Minds* (Grand Rapids, Baker, 1994), 38.

26. T. S. Eliot, *Christianity and Culture* (New York: Harcourt Brace, 1940), 22.

27. Elgin Moyer and Earle E. Cairns, *Wycliffe Biographical Dictionary of the Church* (Chicago: Moody, 1982), 143; J. D. Douglas, *The New International Dictionary of the Christian Church* (Grand Rapids: Zondervan, 1978), 940; Cairns, *Endless Line*, 159 – 60, 192.

28. Moyer and Cairns, *Wycliffe Biographical Dictionary*, 143.

29. Hatch, *Democratization*, 214.

30. Leonard Lovett, "Black Origins of the Pentecostal Movement," in *Aspects of Pentecostal Origins*, 128.

31. Fredrick Dale Bruner, *A Theology of the Holy Spirit* (Grand Rapids: Eerdmans, 1970),37.

32. William DeArteaga, *Quenching the Spirit* (Lake Mary, FL: Charisma, 1996), 109.

33. Menzies, *Anointed to Serve*, 26; Blumhofer, *The Assemblies*, 1:17, 381; Lovett, *Black Origins*, 128; Synan, *The Holiness-Pentecostal*, 99, 217 – 18.

9

Modern Culture, Anti-Intellectualism, and Pentecostal – Charismatic Beliefs

Anti-intellectualism gives rise to the most extreme form of sloth. It is to be found in persons for whom the ultimate objectives in life are the maximization of pleasure, money, fame, or power. It is almost as if they wished they did not have the burden of having intellects that might distract them from their fanatical devotion to nonintellectual aims.

MORTIMER ADLER, EDUCATOR–PHILOSOPHER

It is a monstrous thing to see one and the same heart at once so sensitive to minor things and so strangely insensitive to the greatest. It is an incomprehensible spell.

BLAISE PASCAL

Watchfulness is *especially* advisable in meetings when our spirits are *most likely* to become stirred: during powerful sermons, emotional prayers, or sentimental hymns or when others are exercising spiritual gifts. To *control our own spirits* is not to quench the Holy Spirit. It is *manifesting temperance.* (emphasis mine)

DONALD GEE, PENTECOSTAL LEADER

One month before my sixteenth birthday I witnessed the perfect storm. While working on top of a water tower at a catfish farm in north central Texas, a friend of mine and I spotted and then reported a tornado to the National Weather Service. Little did we know that twenty minutes later a twister, spawned from the same boiling clouds on that sweltering spring afternoon, would evolve into the infamous, sinister monster of "Black Tuesday." On April 10, 1979, at 6:00 p.m., what has been called the most damaging tornado ever recorded broadsided the Texas town affectionately known for over a century as "The Faith City" — Wichita Falls.

All of the conditions were ideal that day to produce a perfect storm. The barometric pressure, atmospheric humidity, and cold upper-air layer all converged on the outskirts of Wichita to breed a super-cell of unprecedented size, where five satellite funnels fed the parent tornado. This twister, which at times was one-and-one-half miles wide, was so low to the ground that it was wider than it was high and thus was mistaken by many as a mere thunderstorm. She cast her spell over The Faith City with 260 mph merciless force. She stayed on the ground for 47 minutes, destroying over one-fifth of our city of 100,000, leaving 52 dead and 1,700 injured Wichitans in her wicked wake.

On that dark, notorious day, the odds were against the city. You see, along the Texas-Oklahoma border lies the legendary "Tornado Alley," and at the heart of Tornado Alley sits Wichita Falls (my family's place was even named "Tornado Alley Game Farm"). To top it off, the city had sent the majority of her rescue units to two other cities that already had been devastated by twisters that day. So her circumstances, position, and all of the conditions were right; the deck was stacked against Wichita. All except this one thing — remember she is "The Faith City."

Wichitans rose valiantly to the occasion. Restoration was so speedy that more than one observer stated that the city's recovery was almost unbelievable. Within twenty-four months of this virtually apocalyptic storm, Wichita Falls was presented with the 1981 All-American-City Award. She not only gave hope to tornado victims everywhere, but became an international model for research and tornado safety because of the unique data collected after the twister.

For many years following that day, little faces — haunting reminders of nightmare winds — appeared in unsuspecting places. Hundreds of electric clock faces had been frozen in time in keeping with the particular moment when their current was cut by the killer storm. These clocks sat shuffled in with other mismatched items in rummage-sale boxes. Their blank stares that read 6:02, 6:03, 6:04, or 6:05 continued to rouse a disturbance in our minds.

COLLAPSE OF THE MIND

In this chapter, I would like to come full circle and discuss the disturbance of which we saw evidence in chapters 5 and 6. This disturbance — this storm — is the one that rages not only *in* the minds of many Pentecostal – Charismatic believers, but also *for* their minds. When confronted with issues of worldview, apologetics, philosophy, science, literature, theology, the arts, and history, our blank stares or trite responses betray the fact that, somewhere along the line, the current to our intellectual development was hindered.

The "life of the mind" was broadsided by the gales of anti-intellectualism at the turn of the century. For the many reasons that we considered in the two preceding chapters, the conditions were perfect to usher the twentieth century into the clutches of a feelings-based approach to all of life. But like the super-cell storm described above, which was fueled by other satellite funnels, the anti-intellectual attitude of many Spirit-filled people has been invigorated even further by elements housed within her distinctive historical and doctrinal makeup. These elements are *not ruinous in themselves*, but *when filtered through an already-present prejudice* against the intellect, they can become disastrous to the life of the mind.

In the last fifty years, a slender but unbroken stream of caveats have emanated from scholars about the demise of the intellect in the West, in the Americas, in the United States, in our primary and secondary schools as well as in our colleges and universities. Furthermore, every once in a while a critic here and a prophet there from among the Catholics, the

Reformed, or the evangelical wing gathers up the nerve to sound the alarm — to report a storm. The signs are all around us, but will we heed the warnings in time to prevent a cognitive catastrophe?[1]

It's one thing if we as a movement fail to see that anti-intellectualism is unbiblical (chapters 1 – 4). This is distinct from denying that there have been a myriad of signs of anti-intellectualism in the American church, spread over the last two centuries (thus the evidences of chapters 5 – 8). But it's another matter if we fail to see that certain elements within our history and doctrine can add further temptation to be anti-intellectual (i.e., this chapter). Moreover, it's a different issue altogether if we claim that *we* don't have a problem in the area of the life of the mind. This would be tantamount to saying that America, or the West, or our schools, or the evangelicals may be experiencing a crisis — a lack of first-rate thinking — but not us!

If you have not yet been convinced that there's a problem in our general culture with a lack of love for and pursuit of truth, or if you reject the idea that the church is failing to glorify God with all of her mind, then I doubt the rest of this book will convince you. But if you are a Spirit-filled believer who is seeing the influence as well as the propagation of anti-intellectualism in the Pentecostal – Charismatic movement, you are on your way to becoming a part of the solution. Before we can be a model to the world, we must first aid our nation. And before we can help the greater body of Christ in America, we must first *know* and *change* ourselves. To do this, it's necessary for us to become conscious of some of the factors in our movement that *can* reinforce the myth of anti-intellectualism — if we let them.

In the remainder of this chapter, my aim is to furnish a protracted index of factors that either have or still do foster an anti-intellectual bias in and "dumbing down" of the greater American culture. A list of beliefs held among American Christians that *can* or *have* encouraged intellectual passivity will also be rendered. After doing this, I will then point out those few features particularly within Pentecostalism that potentially act as extra-added stimuli, advancing our prejudice against the discipleship of the mind.

COMPONENTS OF WIDER CULTURE THAT *CAN* IMPOVERISH THE MIND

It's important to keep in mind four significant thoughts concerning the following lists. First, just because an element of our culture is listed below doesn't mean that, *by necessity*, it promotes anti-intellectualism.

Second, each of the factors manifests itself in varied ways. So without putting a "thinking cap" on, one may not immediately discern the manner in which these otherwise elusive factors display themselves.

Third, any *one* of the following factors, if strong enough in a person's philosophy of life, can in itself anchor one in the camp of anti-intellectualism.

Fourth, even though I categorize the following cultural tendencies into "General," "Christian," and "Pentecostal," they overlap considerably. These components are interrelated, play off of each other, bolster one another, and can even give rise to each other. Some are the energy behind anti-intellectualism, and some are the results of cerebral passivity.

Disposition of the Culture in General

Democratization	Noise pollution	Utilitarianism
Rationalism	Myriad distractions	Synthetic intelligence
Pragmatism	Hedonism	Youthism
Technologism	"God" of entertainment	Over-specialization
Microwaveable society	Self-centeredness	"Egghead" caricature
Fragmentation	Existentialism	Materialism
Dysfunctionalism	Culture of feelings	Divorce culture
Postmodernism	Subjectivity	Narcissism
Romanticism	Pluralism	Non-abstract thinking
Historical illiteracy	Use of clichés	Lack of discipline
Primitivism	Experience is everything	Relativism
Populism	Humanism	A-historicalism
Dumbed-down schools	Reductionism	Unthinking nationalism
Individualism	Therapy craze	Passivity
Busyness	Fadism	

Tendencies in American Christianity

Fideism	False definitions of	Positive thinking
Anti-clericalism	"spiritual"	Shallow literary diet
TV-gospel	Prosperity message	Polarization
Anti-theology	Emotionalism	Premillennialism
Lack of apologetics	Audience mentality	Philistinism
Volunteerism	Protectionism	Consumerism
Easy believism	Monasticism	Accomodation
The "simple" gospel	Bible-onlyism	Celebrity-ism
No Sabbath	The social gospel	Superstition
Compartmentalization	Revivalism	Sensationalism
Shorter messages	Neo-orthodoxy	Pragmatism
Mysticism	Higher criticism	Superstar mentality
	Liberalism	Entertainment mentality

Pitting of faith against reason

Overemphasis on temporal needs

False idea of what culture is

Giant-ism: "Big" is successful

False view of "inspiration"

Fragmentation of man's being

Pitting preaching *over* teaching

Seeker-sensitive format

Pitting knowledge against experience

Ignorance of church history

Prejudice against written sermons

False dichotomy drawn between "head" and "heart"

Lack of commitment to intense discipleship

Ignorance about roots of modern education and science

Subjective, private Bible interpretation

Failure to recognize the past intellectual giants of Christianity

Misunderstanding of Scriptures dealing with learning and wisdom

Failure to distinguish between reason, rationale, and rationalism

Belief in and expectation of "personal leadings"

Few leaders addressing the Christian's intellectual poverty

False definitions of "church," "faith," "revival," "reason," and other key concepts

Further Elements in Spirit-Filled Circles

Again, though our movement has aided millions in their search for spiritual health, latent within her genius are characteristics that make her *especially* vulnerable to the dangers of anti-intellectualism. Of course, one scant chapter cannot deal adequately with each of these in depth; this task would command a volume of its own. Because some will insist on misunderstanding the aim of this section, let me say it one more time: I do not view these factors as *fundamentally* anti-intellectual. Rather, they are only *prone* to being misjudged in relationship to the life of the mind; especially when not balanced out by other important building blocks, they stunt one's desire and/or ability to use his or her intellect for the advancement of the kingdom and the glory of God.

(1) **Many of the early Pentecostal leaders lacked education.** This, of course, did not disqualify them from laboring for the Master. It did, however, set the standard for those who became their followers, for seldom will a student rise above his or her tutor. In chapters 5 and 6 we saw that several early Pentecostal leaders spoke openly of their disdain for education. It shouldn't come as a surprise to us that most of these had little formal education themselves. It seems to be our nature (no matter how saintly we are) to place little value on what we do not possess.

What's more, the schools that were deemed "colleges," which some of these attended, were frequently little more than tiny institutions that offered courses only up to secondary school level. As we saw earlier, sometimes the curriculum was merely a loosely-knit program of indoctrination with proof texts. Pentecostal educator William Menzies states that one reason for general educational lack was the fact that these schools were more interested in "spiritual development rather than academic excellence."[2]

Historian Edith Blumhofer informs us that in the 1930s and 1940s, preparation for ministry through Bible school training was still held as suspect among many Full Gospel people. In addition, a high percentage of those who enrolled in Bible institutes "had not completed a high school education, and some had never begun one."[3] As if this combination isn't challenging enough within itself, there were problems finding educated Pentecostals to teach at the schools. Even as late as 1944 (forty-three years after Topeka's outpouring), the professors at our best Pentecostal colleges possessed only an average of 3.9 years of post-high school education, and many of these had been schooled in institutes much like the ones they now taught in.[4]

Again, I'm not suggesting that institutional higher education necessarily makes or breaks one's ministry. Nor am I signifying that attending establishments of higher learning deems one "pro-intellectual." It is common to find university students, and even professors, who are pro-education (perhaps "pro-information" is a better term), yet anti-intellectual (though I think it's impossible to find a person who is anti-education yet pro-intellectual). So, not only were many of our early leaders anti-educational, but also uneducated. This, in turn, shaped our movement in its embryonic years, steering it away from a deep respect for the life of the mind in general. The idea of educating the whole person was not foreign to the early Pentecostal movement but was severely dwarfed, and thus we still experience some of its influences today.

(2) **Some of the doctrines adhered to by Full Gospel believers afford special opportunity for the promotion of anti-intellectualism.** Here is a list of some beliefs that fall into this category: (a) the baptism of the Holy Spirit; (b) the verbal gifts; (c) the Rapture; (d) sanctification; and (e) altar theology. At first glance, these tenets may seem far removed from the issue at hand. With patience, I hope the reader will come to see my point.

(a) The idea that a "baptism by the Holy Spirit" is a type of cure-all is still somewhat common among our people, even though it was more prevalent in earlier days. One such aspect of this is apparent in our formative era when Parham taught that those baptized with the Holy Spirit, marching in God's last-days army, would help the body of Christ to avoid "wasting thousands of dollars, and often their lives in vain attempts to become conversant in almost impossible tongues which the Holy Ghost could so freely speak."[5] Few, if any, believe this today, yet related to this mentality is the concept that if the Holy Spirit "teaches all things," "leads into all truth," and delights in using "ignorant and unlearned men," then why unnecessarily put yourself through the rigors of mental and intellectual discipline?

Furthermore, as Pentecostals we have strong convictions about the priesthood of believers and its connection to "the baptism." One of the potential drawbacks that can accompany the vital doctrine of the lay priesthood is the belief that those who have been baptized in the Holy Ghost need not be concerned with earthly teachers. I once heard Billy Graham say, "The smallest package in the world is a person who is all wrapped up in himself." When Spirit-filled believers see themselves as the custodians of Full Gospel truth, a real temptation arises to overlook the vast reservoir of wisdom that God has deposited into other custodians. Thus, the blessing of the priesthood, instead of becoming a larger, richer gift to the world and the body, devolves into a pile of small independent packages all wrapped up in themselves!

Since Parham's day, many Spirit-filled believers seem to have used "the baptism" as a crutch to avoid engaging in demanding thought and study. As we have seen, Donald Gee addressed this issue numerous times over a span of forty years. Among the sundry statements made about this tendency is the following: "Many have a mistaken idea that the baptism in the Holy Spirit does away with all need of hard work, but it is not a labor-saving device. You might say, 'I suppose I won't need to study; I won't need to think; I won't need to pray now.'"[6]

A shallowness and sentimentality seem to accompany many who lean only on the Spirit for their intellectual nourishment. Of course, the issue is not whether the Holy Spirit can or cannot provide every need; it is whether he will or does. Is the baptism meant to merely substitute for, or to complement, intellectual training? Are the gift of intellect and the gift of the Holy Spirit at odds, or do they come from the same source? These are vital questions concerning this doctrine.

(b) The second doctrine of Pentecostals that may promote anti-intellectualism is that of "the verbal gifts": word of wisdom, tongues and interpretation, word of knowledge, and prophecy. The very idea that foreign languages, the future, deep insights, and information, all otherwise unknown, can be mainlined into the soul and then gush forth through the lips of a believer, can become a potent catalyst for anti-intellectualism.

One may think it frivolous, or even futile, to expend inordinate volumes of valuable time dissecting the twisted twines of history or forecasting the sociological trends of various mission fields if "revelation knowledge" falls from heaven like manna. Furthermore, Spirit-filled people can be dissuaded from burning the midnight oil in order to parse Hebrew verbs or poke around in heady hermeneutics if God freely grants his "informational gifts" of past, present, and future to the truly spiritual.

It's the teaching that these gifts bypass the intellect that *can* so easily promote an anti-intellectual bias. Think about it: It's tempting to forego meticulous intellectual exercise if God is inclined to provide the greatest of mysteries through disengaged minds. In fact, the very nature of this provocation is likened to the original temptation, which promised enlightenment, knowledge, and wisdom without participation in God's school of *lifelong* learning (Gen. 3:4 – 6).

I am not disputing that God is a God of supernatural revelation. He has revealed things to me that I would have otherwise never been able to uncover by studying. For these encounters, I am humbled and grateful. However, to assume that his supernatural gifts of revelation make the intellectual life obsolete is nonsense. None would dare pit a need for oxygen against a need for water. Both are of tremendous value, and one without the other creates major problems. When the language of pop-Pentecostalism is employed, such as "speaking in the Spirit" versus "speaking in the flesh," or knowledge filtrating through "the heart" versus "the head," the whole matter of the supremacy of "revelation knowl-edge" over "intellectual learning" is confused exponentially. But this seems to be the norm in the minds of many Full Gospel people.

As a case in point, consider the following statement by Charles Parham's sister-in-law upon speaking in tongues. She asserted that "floods of laughter came into my *heart*. I could no longer *think* words of praise, for my *mind* was sealed."[7] Elsewhere, when referring to his ability to preach prophetically with the anointing, Charles Parham said, "Our *minds* took no part, we became but interested listeners."[8] If this example seems antiquated, just flip back to chapter 6 or recall my opening illustration from the introduction.

Some may claim that the Bible itself uses the above terminology. In 1 Corinthians 14 Paul writes of "praying in a tongue" as praying with his spirit, and he refers to "praying with the mind" as praying in the learned language of one's present company. Paul does not, however, pit the human mind against the Spirit of God, as some assume. Nor does he even remotely suggest that speaking in tongues or any of the other verbal gifts are supe-rior to speaking in one's native language; actually, his emphasis is quite the opposite. He promotes the use of the mind in the public displays of the verbal gifts.[9]

At times, God has deposited a word of wisdom or word of knowledge into my mind, leaving it to me whether or not I shared this supernatural infusion with anyone else. These are humbling, sometimes troubling, sometimes exhilarating experiences. But we must be careful not to exchange rules for exceptions. That is to say, though God translated Elijah, we shouldn't quit our day job and wait for a blazing chariot. In like fashion, we must not evade the process of studying to show ourselves approved simply because God can and does give "revelation knowledge" and supernatural insight by way of his spiritual gifts. We are not apt to let a physician work on us if he claims to be led merely by revelation knowl-edge; we also demand that he possess some "old-fashion book-learnin'."

We seem to struggle with the idea that if something isn't logical, then it must be illogi-cal; or that if someone is not anti-intellectual, then he or she must be a rationalist; or that if a certain event is not of a rational nature, then by necessity it is irrational. This forced dichotomy has tinkered with our thinking about thinking in a myriad of ways. Question: Is laughing and crying rational, emotional, or intuitive? They seem to be all three, and not one at the expense of the others. Is our mind physical, spiritual, chemical, or ephemeral? It seems to be all of the above and more.

Just because something is physical ("using" the brain) doesn't indicate that it *cannot* be of a nonmaterial nature also. If we hurl our arm in front of our child when we hit the brakes while driving, we cannot say that this action is only physical; it also has to do with emotion, thinking, and instinct. In like fashion, we must be careful not to be so quick to argue that since spiritual gifts and other spiritual activities are not completely rational, they must not be rational at all. There is much work to be done in this area of concentration in order to help us to think better about the spiritual and intellectual dimensions of our faith walk, especially in the area of the verbal gifts.

To the five verbal gifts can be added our sometimes confusing approach and understanding of revelation, inspiration, and illumination. We have a tendency to juxtapose these three in a medley of arrangements. Add "the gifts" to this, and we get an interesting ad hoc mixture that, again, leans heavily toward minimizing the intellect. Sometimes I think that Plato is respected more than the apostle Paul. How so? In Plato's *Phaedrus*, he speaks of the dignity of "divine madness," wherein the god-given, enthusiastic state of being-beside-oneself is much preferred over the usual status of human reasonableness. He posits that while the ancient Greek prophetesses were speaking in ecstatic frenzy, they uttered so many amazing things; yet when they utilized their "mere minds," they were unable to say anything of great value. I think that more often than we realize, we entertain the same type of notion.[10]

(c) A third prominent Pentecostal doctrine that can lend itself toward anti-intellectualism is the belief in the "rapture" of the church. Now, it's not simply the biblical concept of a "catching away" of God's people that can promote detachment from cognitive endeavors. Rather, it's when one believes that this event will happen very soon and that time is running out. It's then that *tendencies toward* escapism can all too easily encroach. Rather than waste precious time preparing our minds, we must do the practical thing and just reach the lost.

In the end, this escapist way of thinking perpetuates not the Great Commission (for this is a mission of "making disciples," see Matt. 28:19), but only the winning of the lost, which is to be sure a great thing, but only a first step. Discipleship involves refashioning the whole person by way of disciplining the individual components of a new convert's life. This is difficult, if not impossible, for mentors to do if they themselves have not taken the time to adequately discipline their own spirit, body, and intellect. The case becomes even trickier if they attempt to focus on disciple-making while staring straight into the face of the eschatological clock.

"Jesus is coming soon" was, in many respects, *the* central theme of early Pentecostalism, and it no doubt was (and is) a very positive and vital biblical theme. Looking back on the Azusa Street meetings, a spokesman of the 1914 Hot Springs, Arkansas cooperative gatherings, stated, "Almost every city and community in civilization has heard of the ... prophecy which has been predominant in all this great outpouring, which is 'Jesus is coming soon.' "[11] One may naturally question whether or not it is worth dedicating oneself to long-term learning if he or she believes that this was the "last revival" and that only a short-term future awaits them.

In addition to the issue dealt with above, there is also a tendency to consider involvement in cultural affairs as a waste of time if the ship is sinking anyway. It has been put this way: "Why waste time and energy rearranging the chairs on the deck of the Titanic?" To a substantial degree, this was J. N. Darby's approach to the secular world. Darby (1800 – 1882) was chiefly responsible for reintroducing pretribulation theology and, in turn, heavily influenced the early Pentecostal movement. He believed that the rapture would take place soon and that the true church should not be involved in the "secular" affairs. In the "last days," the church was here, not to transform the world but to gather the lost quickly before God's wrath came on the apostate church. William De Arteaga says that for Darby, "the end times were so near that evangelization was no longer the chief thing, but the only thing. There was no time for the church to concern itself with social issues or even to teach the disciplines of the Christian life."[12]

Teaching on the rapture trickled into Pentecostalism's foundations, where it produced thoughts as to the lack of time to spare on relentless, private preparation and rigorous public debate. In 1908 William Seymour was snubbed by one of the more influential members of his congregation (Florence Crawford) for marrying, in light of the "fact" that the rapture was so close. In 1988, a family that I was personally acquainted with succeeded in discouraging their son from attending the state university in light of the 88 "facts"[13] pointing to the imminent rapture of the church. These are the same folks who let their horses run wild "that day" so that the animals wouldn't starve in the corral when the family was gone. The rapture did not take place, but a round-up of a different nature did. I believe that Christ will come at a moment we do not know, and I believe we will be caught up with him. I also believe, however, that until he comes, we must study to show ourselves approved and love the Lord God with all our minds.

(d) The fourth doctrine that may promote a prejudice against intellectual coherence is our particular bent on "sanctification." The idea that "the flesh," "the world," and "the devil" are to be avoided at all cost often causes one to treat "the world and all that is in it" as an enemy. That is, wider culture is to be ignored or despised. Furthermore, because "the world" despised our movement in its early beginnings, we can fall into the trap of despising "higher society" in the name of "sanctification." In light of this, we make the critical mistake of scorning higher culture, thinking of it and "the world" as one in the same, or by calling that which is not explicitly Christian "worldly."

Consistency in this vein is impossible. We would be forced to ask whether driving a car, learning to write, brushing one's teeth, or playing a game of volleyball is Christian or not. With this mentality, spiritual schizophrenia finds an ideal nesting ground. This false view of "the world" has caused many Full Gospel people to come out from among the secular universities, the realm of politics, the arts, humanities, technology, and the sciences. When "sanctification" or "holiness" is strained through this narrow filter, not only do the pools of societal and cultural thought suffer, but so does the aggregate of critical thought among those in Spirit-filled ranks.

(e) The fifth doctrine courted by Pentecostal–Charismatic believers and apt to entrench anti-intellectual biases is that of "altar theology." The idea that an *instantaneous* blessing of cleansing and power can be received by faith rather than by the arduous process of "seeking" was heavily promoted from the 1840s forward. Donald Dayton says of this doctrine, "This teaching tended to evaporate the spiritual struggle more characteristic of eighteenth-century Methodism and encouraged immediate appropriation of the experience."[14] This ideology carried over into twentieth-century Pentecostalism and has manifested itself in numerous ways.

Americans in general are almost unhesitatingly seduced by convenience, pragmatism, and instantaneous results. In short, we strive to become a thoroughly microwaveable society. Add to this the belief that "the baptism," healing, salvation, and deliverance can all take place by depositing the problem on the altar, and you have a philosophical structure that *can* easily lend itself to a "gain with no pain" mentality. Closely related to expectations of immediacy at the altar is the whole idea of casting Satan and his influence from an entire city or nation in one fell swoop. If this simple formula is viable, it seems that Jesus would have used it for his beloved Israel.

I do believe that God grants phenomenal blessings to the hearts of the humble who cast their care on him. He is the gracious Father who loves to give good things to his children. Certainly there are times when Jesus pours out a blessing on our needy souls that are nearly impossible to imagine or contain. God has ministered to me at the altar, in my closet, in my office, and at the front of the church building. God has also used me on occasion while ministering at the altar to cast out spirits. But these realities do not, by necessity, mean that resolute mental activity becomes obsolete. Nor does it mean that delayed results are inferior to those experiences that sometimes seem to be within an arm's reach at the altar. Just ask Eve, Abraham, Joseph, Moses, David, and the steadfast soldiers of the "hall of faith" in Hebrews 11.

There are several other beliefs we hold that, when combined with an already-present bias against the intellect, amplify the problem. I can only mention them here: circular reasoning based on "the Lord told me," modifying our theology to fit our experience, forcing current events into a last-days context, confusion over the exact use of the spiritual gifts, "if it feels right, it must be the Spirit," name-it-claim-it theology, and our avid appetite for miracles.

CONCLUSION

If we already tussle with the temptations of anti-intellectualism, then when the above-mentioned beliefs coalesce, they form a strong argument against the case for intellectual achievement, cultural cultivation, and critical thinking. As you can see, all of the conditions are right for our own "perfect storm." And though we have advanced in our fight against anti-intellectualism, we are coaxed again and again to engage in a type of mindless spirituality. But just as the people of Wichita Falls — "The Faith City" — rose up against the destructive monster of "Black Tuesday," so also we — the Pentecostal – Charismatic movement — can rise to the occasion.

The life of the Spirit surely finds even greater effectiveness as it dwells securely in the house of the intellect. With all that is within me, I state: If we would marry the power of the mind with the power of the Spirit, scholastic wit with heart-warming love, apologetics with the anointing, intellectual vigor with emotional vitality, and our contemplative capability with charismatic gifting, the positive impact that we could have on our culture and on the nations is beyond imagination! And we *can* rise to the occasion, for we, too, are a people of faith — "A City of Faith."

NOTES

1. In the 1940s and 1950s, C. S. Lewis began to alert the West of her intellectual wreckage — that her soul was dying. Others saw the calamity: Solzhenitsyn, Carl F. Henry, and even Mother Teresa. In the 1960s Richard Hofstadter presented *Anti-Intellectualism in American Life*, and in the 1970s, John Stott published *Your Mind Matters*. The 1980s brought Francis Schaffer's *The Great Evangelical Disaster* and Allan Bloom's *Closing of the American Mind*. And in the 1990s Mark Noll wrote *Scandal of the Evangelical Mind* and John Armstrong edited a volume entitled *The Coming Evangelical Crisis*.

2. Menzies, *Anointed to Serve*, 355.

3. Blumhofer, *The Assemblies*, 1:329.

4. Menzies, *Anointed to Serve*, 355; Anderson, *Vision of the Disinherited*, 101 – 2. In one study, only nine out of forty-five early prominent Pentecostal leaders were found to have had any formal education at all after their teenage years. This is only 20 percent, as compared to 60 percent among all other American clergymen. The same survey claims that whereas, 33 percent of *non*-Pentecostal preachers had graduated from college and went on to seminary, only an estimated 5 percent of Pentecostal leaders in the corresponding time frame could claim the same. Furthermore, it should be noted that this data compares *the most prominent Pentecostal leaders* of the era with the *average Protestant preacher*. If these statistics are even in the ballpark, they bear significance for the subject matter of this chapter.

5. Parham, *A Voice Crying in the Wilderness*, 28.

6. Womack, *Pentecostal Experience*, 71.

7. Parham, *The Life of Charles F. Parham*, 60 – 61.

8. Parham, *Voice*, 31.

9. One need only look at the key words and phrases to determine Paul's primary point: "no one *understands* him" (1 Cor. 14:2); "unless I bring you some revelation or *knowledge* or prophecy or word of *instruction*" (v. 6); "how will anyone *know*" and "*distinction* in the notes" (v. 7); "a *clear* call" (v. 8); "unless you speak *intelligible*" and "speaking into the air" (v. 9); "without *meaning*" (v. 10); and "grasp the *meaning*" (v. 11). Why is all of this so important? Because God desires that everyone in the assembly of believers understands with their minds! Further, Paul is not saying "use your minds sometimes and do not use your minds sometimes." He says if one speaks in a tongue, his mind is unfruitful. He then asks the rhetorical question, "So what shall I do?" (v. 15). His answer is, he will use his mind! Thereafter, Paul continues to emphasize the intellectual aspect of God's gifts: "Those who do not *understand*" (v. 16); "he does not *know*" (v. 16); "speak five *intelligible* words to *instruct*" (v. 19); and finally, "Brothers, stop *thinking* like children . . . in your *thinking* be adults" (v. 20). Tongues may not be rational per se, but neither are they irrational; instead, they are nonrational, but their interpretations must be rational to be of value to the hearer.

10. Plato, *Phaedrus* 244, 249, 265 (see his *Dialogues* (Princeton: Princeton, Univ. Press, 1961), 491, 492, 495, 496, 510, 511.

11. Assemblies of God, *Combined Minutes, lst General Council* (1914), 2.

12. DeArteaga, *Quenching the Spirit*, 104; cf. also Menzies, *Anointed to Serve*, 23.

13. Cf. Edgar C. Whisenant, "*88 Reasons Why the Rapture Is in 1988*" (self-published, 1988).

14. Dayton, *Theological Roots of Pentecostalism*, 69. For a brief but poignant study on altar theology or the rise of the altar call, see Iain Murray, *The Invitation System* (Carlisle, PA: Banner of Truth, 1967).

10

The Anatomy of Anti-Intellectualism

Anti-intellectualism is a disposition to discount the importance of truth
and the life of the mind. Living in a sensuous culture and increasingly
emotional democracy, American evangelicals in the last generation have
simultaneously toned up their bodies and dumbed down their minds.
Os Guinness, author and thinker

Even in the case of lifeless things that make sounds, such as the flute or harp, how
will anyone know what tune is being played unless there is a distinction in notes?
Again, if the trumpet does not sound a clear call, who will get ready for battle?
The apostle Paul, to the Corinthians

A woman who had recently started attending our church stood, walked to the platform, and began speaking to the congregation — at least she appeared to be speaking. As the music died down, I realized that though the woman was moving her lips, she was making no sound. As I questioned what she was doing, she answered, "I am giving a silent prophecy. Only those with ears to hear can hear what the Spirit is saying." I, for one, received the message — loud and clear! But it had nothing to do with what she thought and hoped that she was communicating. In her own mind, she was sharing exactly what she thought God wanted her to share. Yet through the confusing manner in which she shared her "gift," she was imparting, in fact, no message at all. Like the above-mentioned Scripture reference, her notes were not distinct, her sound was not clear, her call to battle was not understood.

At this stage in this book, I need to pause momentarily and ponder two questions: Have I played a distinct note — provided a clear picture — of what anti-intellectualism is all about? And has the reader — the hearer — heard a clear call? If the reader has not received my message, then who will get ready for battle? Before we move into the second half of this book, where we investigate the disciplines that can help the Pentecostal – Charismatic movement bolster the life of the mind, I want to make sure that I have not been misunderstood. It's important that we have a firm grasp on the nuances of anti-intellectualism as well as determine whether we have attempted to escape the grasp of its definition.

Many years ago, when my family was leaving town for a week, I gave instructions to two friends to watch after my loft of racing pigeons. When I returned, the manner in which the flock greeted me resembled a scene from a Hitchcock movie. I then noticed that the watering containers were dusty and that the feed bin was still brimming. Horror of horrors, my

124

thoroughbreds of the sky had been forced into a week-long fast! Both friends had nodded as I had given the directives how to take care of the birds, but each assumed that I was talking to the other.

How many times have we sat in the pew, heard a penetrating message, and with simplicity and smugness deflected the arrows of truth toward our spouse, our child, or sister So-in-So? I am like that, and you are like that, for we are all the children of Adam. It takes spiritual transparency and Christlike humility to approach the pastor after service and declare, "You were talking about me. I don't like it, but it's the truth. I want to be held accountable. Will you help me?" It's a happy day when the man of the cloth hears these words! But these days are few and far between because our nature is such that we each assume that the preacher was talking to someone else.

In all my years of speaking on the importance of the life of the mind and on the problem of anti-intellectual attitudes, I've never had one person to say: "I am an anti-intellectual," or "I think that education is of the devil" — never! Granted, many don't have a beef with mixing the intellect with the Spirit. But what about the hundreds that I have heard make carping comments against the mind? These somehow imagine that I must be speaking about other believers when referring to those with anti-intellectual tendencies.

Why is this? I think the answer lies in the fact that none of us wants to be labeled as prejudicial, for that is exactly what anti-intellectualism is all about. In light of this, I find it necessary to delve a bit deeper into the tones and shades of what prejudice against the intellect is all about. I have provided anecdotal evidence in the preceding chapters; now I will examine the very nature of the problem.

A BIAS AGAINST THE INTELLECT

As stated in chapter 2, anti-intellectualism can be defined as *a prejudice against the careful and deliberate use of one's intellect*. It is also a general attitude that reacts negatively to positive statements about the intellectual aspects of or involvement in the life of faith. It unnecessarily pits the intellect's worth against other equally important elements housed within the Christian experience.

Like worldliness, anti-intellectualism, more than anything else, is an attitude. Both of these manifestations exhibit themselves in a multitude of ways, but they are mere symptoms of the real problem. Some Christians claim they are not worldly because they do not use tobacco, drink alcohol, lie, or sport a spiked green hairdo. While straining at these symptomatic gnats, however, they may swallow a herd of camels in the form of gossip, materialism, pride, jealously, anger, greed, or prayerlessness. We may indeed be "worldly," but we finesse our way out of the clutch of our convenient, private interpretation of what worldliness is.

In like fashion, many Full Gospel folk maintain that they are not anti-intellectual because they have a measure of college education, use their minds on the job, study the Scriptures, or approve of Bible school training. Yet when asked about their view of the use of the intellect in spiritual matters, they often react negatively, quoting chapter and verse on the supposed animosity between man's mind and God's Spirit, between faith and reason, and between experience and intellect.

When such people are questioned about the value they place on the study of history, the importance of culture, the merit of logic in Christianity, the art of argumentation, the benefits of serious theological endeavor, or their knowledge of classical literature, the response intensifies. They often pull back the veil of modesty and explode with a barrage of reasons as to why these interests should be of little concern to the truly "Spirit-filled" believer or of how the intellect has led so many Christians astray.

INTELLECT VERSUS . . .

In the Pentecostal–Charismatic subculture, intellect is frequently pitted *against feeling*, for we often claim that a well-reasoned faith is incompatible with enthusiastic action or intimate emotion. Intellectual energies are often set *over against revelation*, because God's ways are not our ways, and so, we conjecture, our intense reasoning about deep spiritual matters can only be the result of our fallen nature. We also tend to contrast the intellectual with *the spiritual* or *the humble*, for many propose that those who are inclined toward the intellect become too clever for themselves and in the end resemble the lecturing serpent of Eden.

Furthermore, the *practical* is often judged as irreconcilable with the more intellectual aspects of life. We deem that unless we can see concrete and rather immediate results from our energy or activity, its worth must pale in contrast to those efforts that produce something tangible and instant. For many Pentecostals and Charismatics, the intellect also stands out against the beauty of "the priesthood of the believer" or the *so-called democracy* of the body of Christ. This prejudiced reasoning suggests that everyone's voice is equal in the kingdom of God; thus, those who are less educated, simple-minded, or not interested in intellectual matters are at no disadvantage. If this is true (they reason), then one must beware of those who claim to possess a better vantage point via their supposed superior aptitude for thinking or by their store of knowledge.

Like any other prejudice, anti-intellectualism is built solidly on myths. Like the person who takes offense at a certain race because of the color of their skin, so also those who spurn the intellect are in the business of fighting flimsy straw men of their own making. Their enemy exists in form but with little substance. Because there is little satisfaction in stabbing at straw-filled opponents, the prejudiced mind most often fights with emotion or with superficial rebuttals rather than with good logic, sound arguments, and consistent reasoning. Since prejudice is a preconceived hostile opinion without sufficient knowledge, anti-intellectualism, in a sense, is the mother of all prejudice — that is, of all irrational intolerance.

I'M NOT PREJUDICED, I'M JUST ...

Naturally, it's difficult for us to understand the nuances of prejudice until we ourselves have been on the receiving end of its venomous bite. When I was a child, I had an uncle who, in light of the fact that my mother had come from Hitler's war-torn Germany, found sport in calling me a "Nazi." And, with a name like "Nañez," it wasn't uncommon for kids on my bus to make jokes about "wetbacks" and "spics." Somehow, when my uncle or the bus kids said they were only kidding, I couldn't quite bring myself to believe that they were telling the whole truth.

As a Christian, a pastor, a missionary, and a seminary student, I, like many of you, have been the target of prejudiced statements having to do with these areas. When critics who do not know of our spiritual or professional stations in life degrade the religious right wing, lambaste money-grubbing preachers, or debase post-graduate theological studies, we recognize the brazen blade of prejudice, no matter how it's dressed up or explained away. Regardless of what a person says after these statements, it takes great effort to ignore comments made in this vein.

In addition, there is that whole world of bias with which Pentecostals are familiar. We've probably all felt the sting from preconceived notions and unfair remarks about "holy rollers" who swing from chandeliers, babble in tongues, and juggle snakes. We pick up on the slightest trace of bigotry when the target is something dear to our heart. Our first impression, when on the receiving end of such ridicule, is *not* that the critic probably possesses a small measure of love for Pentecostalism or that they most likely have good reasons for their seeming abhorrence toward our movement. Rather, our first thoughts are that they have not given us a reasonable chance, that they have been misinformed, that they are ignorant of our beliefs, that they are predisposed — that they have actually believed a myth! Mistaking a prejudice is not as easy as it may seem at first.

Furthermore, we as Pentecostals and Charismatics are quick to pick up on a skeptic's bias when it advances in the form of anti-supernaturalism.

- If we mention miracles — and an acquaintance automatically retorts, "Those TV preachers talk of miracles but their just in it for the money" — we do not have to deliberate on the meaning.
- When we refer to speaking in tongues and a family member immediately reacts with, "I once knew a person who claimed to speak in tongues and he went crazy," we don't ask ourselves, "I wonder how they feel about tongues."
- When we share with a coworker how we were physically healed by the Lord Jesus and she states, "Believe what you will, but the Scriptures teach that those gifts passed away with the apostles," you suspect that a prejudice lurks in the shadows.
- We get wearied by people responding to our experiential faith with, "Well, you have to be careful. You know, you can get unbalanced and all messed up with emotions."

- When a person feels that he or she has to respond to your interest in a demonstrative, emotive faith by pointing to radicals, extremists, exceptions, and unbalanced weirdoes, you know that they have a grudge against what you shared with them.

In all such instances, you may wonder *why* a person is touchy or seemingly anti-experiential, but of one thing you are certain: They are apprehensive about joining your enthusiasm and perhaps are even out-and-out antagonistic toward to the topic. A person may claim not to have antipathy toward Pentecostalism, but if the first thing that comes out of his or her mouth on the subject is negative, what else are we to think?

I once had a neighbor who harbored a deep dislike for foreigners (all expect Norwegians; his mother was from Norway). Any time I made reference to an African American, an Asian, or a Middle Easterner, his face reddened as he spewed contempt. One day I asked him why he was so prejudiced. In response, he performed every manner of linguistic gymnastic to try to convince me that he was not prejudiced. In the end, he simply stated that he was not anti-foreigner, he just didn't want one living next to him!

It's like a person who puts nepotism into practice; he says, "I'm not nepotistic, it's just that the only qualified workers in my city have the name Vankennedyeiser." Or what of the male chauvinist who states, "I'm not prejudice against women, I think every man ought to own one"? My point is, whether or not people admit to being chauvinistic, nepotistic, anti-Semitic, anti-Pentecostal, or anti-intellectual, out of the abundance of their heart, their mouth speaks!

I'M NOT ANTI-INTELLECTUAL, I'M JUST ...

So, what are we to think when so many Pentecostals and Charismatics respond negatively to the mention of the intellect, when they could have just as easily responded with a positive comment? What are Full Gospel believers really saying when, if I point out to them the value of theology or apologetics, they respond, "OK, but our faith is a heart thing, not a head thing"? Why do so many Spirit-filled advocates instantly point out Scriptures about "ignorant and unlearned men" and the dangers of "wisdom of this world" when the value of education is championed? What is the difference between a skeptic of emotion saying, "Yeah, an emotional approach to the faith will lead you down the wrong path" and a skeptic of the intellect saying, "Yeah, an intellectual approach to the faith will lead you down the wrong path"?

When people are passionate about a topic, they do not sit idly by when an opportunity presents itself for them to voice their passion. This is exactly why so many Spirit-filled (and evangelical) believers are prepared to joust when the importance of the life of the mind is referenced. They are prejudiced against what they deem as an enemy to the faith. They feel that they have a spiritual responsibility to keep the intellect in its proper place — in the outer court, where strangers mingle with those of lesser faith.

The ways that some of our people portray the intellect as a villain are numerous. There are those who have knee-jerk reactions to the very word "intellect," as if the word itself is cause to throw down the gauntlet. There are those who read voraciously, yet speak of the dangers of reading. They can feel justified in their attack because all that they read are books that they already agree with. Some have college educations, but warn of those who seek "too much education," whatever this means. And there are those who teach — even professors — who are narrow in their outlook and who merely indoctrinate their students.

What we need to understand is that anti-intellectual attitudes are not limited to those who have little education. If we view the problem in this way, then we can all claim that we are not carriers of this prejudice; which is what many seem to do. Some say things like: "Pastor Smith is not anti-intellectual, he went to Bible school"; "Clara is not anti-intellectual, why she's a school teacher"; or, "Bob, he's not against the intellect, I see him reading all the time."

I have met men who say they love their mothers, wives, and daughters but who take every opportunity to speak of women as sex objects or second-class citizens created to fold their underwear and fix dinner. I have met business owners who employ minorities, but who get a kick out of telling minority jokes, which usually paint them as ignorant and lazy. What of some who contribute to charity but who are forever down-talking those in poverty — at the same time, their poor parents worked three jobs a piece to put them through law school? Remember, even Hitler may have carried Jewish blood.

The bottom line is, prejudice comes in all stripes and measures; and for a person to exhibit prejudice does not require that they avoid contact with or refuse to use the thing that they are prejudiced against. Thus, a person may claim not to be prejudiced, or a believer may claim not to be anti-intellectual; but as we listen to the pressure valve of their heart — the mouth — we know otherwise. We may ask how this can be. There are as many reasons that a person holds a bias as there are biased persons.

WHY DO WE STRUGGLE WITH ANTI-INTELLECTUALISM?

As we discussed earlier in this work, many have simply been told that the Bible teaches that the mind is at enmity with God's Spirit and that reason is the opposite of faith. But we all read the same Bible; so why do some accept this notion and some not? There are underlying causes that tempt some to *want to* cultivate an anti-intellectual bent. When the rubber of the heart meets the road of prejudice, it is the "want not" or "want to" that makes the difference.

Some *are afraid* of exposing their beliefs to scrutiny, to logic, or to alternative opinions. Perhaps at one time they were deeply rattled in their faith because of the heavy-duty data presented by an evolutionist, a Muslim, or an atheist. Instead of preparing to give excellent reasons for the faith they hold dear, they coddle their faith and thus accuse intellectual bantering of being dangerous.

Some have had a *bad experience* with intellectual but impractical professors, worldly seminary students, or arrogant scholars. In light of this, instead of setting out to demonstrate that we can be both intellectual and spiritual, they simply choose to stereotype those who seek higher learning as talking eggheads without a walk.

Others bash reason, logic, philosophy, or reading widely because they feel *intimidated* or *jealous.* These feelings turn into a sort of reverse prejudice. It's like the high school student who still takes the bus to school while his friends are cruising in a shiny, four-door sedan. Instead of taking a job sweeping floors in order to purchase his own "ride," he downplays or criticizes the other person's pride and joy to make himself feel better. The one harboring anti-intellectual sentiments says, "Yea, but the intellect isn't everything." That is, they would rather criticize the guy who has worked for his knowledge than to admit that they would like to possess the same.

This latter point brings up the simple fact of *laziness.* There are people who desire the breath of thought, length of reasoning, and depth of knowledge but who are not willing to work for it. This shallow approach is consistent with their cry, "It's not practical." Many in this category would rather manicure their lawn one more time to impress their neighbors, rent ten more videos for their viewing pleasure, watch the pigskin thrown around by people they'll never meet, or squeeze in one more fishing excursion before it gets too cold.

Often, our practicality quickly degenerates into hedonism, materialism, or laziness. As a guy who fell far short in his first semester of college and who struggled for many years with reading comprehension, I understand all too well the battle of keeping distractions at bay in order to shore up the mind and cultivate the intellect. A man who is too lazy to take a day job will criticize the man who prepared to sculpt a career. Often the one who argues against intellectual acumen is guilty of the same.

Though I want to be extremely careful about how I state this point, I think that it is a viable consideration. Perhaps some nurture an antipathy toward the life of the mind because of *the influence of the enemy.* Is it possible? As Pentecostals and Charismatics, we are especially keen to the idea that demons or evil spirits influence societal trends, religious propaganda, and individuals' thoughts, do we not?

If a person denies that Jesus is the Son of God, deeming him a liar, we are not bashful about attributing this view to Satan. If a person believes that they can live in adultery and serve Christ as well, we are not slow to think that the father of lies has infiltrated this person's judgment. Furthermore, I've heard it said on many occasions that those who refuse to believe that the apostolic-spiritual gifts are for today have been blinded by the enemy. Why do we think this way? Simply because we believe that the Scriptures teach that Jesus is the Son of God, adultery is sin, and that the *charismata* are for today.

The Scriptures teach that we should be wise as serpents, prepare our minds for action, love God with all of our minds, seek understanding, hammer out doctrine, train in order to give good reasons for our faith, argue, debate, and provide proofs to the lost. If these are God's truths, and yet believers fight against them when brought up in conversation, then is it possible that the enemy of our soul is attempting to keep us from these truths? As I mentioned in the beginning of this book: If our minds are the image of God in us and yet we see our head/mind as an enemy to our heart/faith, then we are sinning when we hold a prejudice against things intellectual.

Of course, there's always the question about those who cannot be "intellectuals" — those who do not have the mental capability to plumb the depths of Van Til's presuppositional apologetics or to argue about the eschatological significance of Jewish apocalyptic literature according to Paul's realized eschatology. Please note that this book is not about becoming an "intellectual." Rather, it is about *not* harboring anti-intellectual attitudes in our hearts and about marrying the life of the mind with the life of the Spirit.

Second, anyone who asks the question about those incapable of serious study usually does not feel that he or she is one of those with limited mental abilities. Most simply use it as a smokescreen for self-justification, like those who say, "I have a problem with God's judgment on the unsaved. What about those poor heathen who have never heard?" If they were truly concerned about the heathen, they would submit their lives to Christ and become a missionary to the unreached masses!

Third, if God commands us all to love him with all our minds, then we have to take the question up with God. No doubt, God does not expect the impossible. He would not say of invalids that they are "worse than infidels" because they didn't hold a day job. He would not condemn a barren woman because she could not "be fruitful and multiply." And he would not criticize a brain-damaged accident victim because he didn't become a brain surgeon.

In the same way, God has created us all with different levels of intellectual abilities. He only expects us to do our best with what he has given us. Now, we must be careful when standing before God and telling him that we have stretched to our capacity. He may remind us of Milton and Homer, for each wrote their *magnum opus* while blind; of Beethoven, who scored his Fifth when deaf; of the man who climbed Mount Everest without legs; or of someone like my father-in-law, who cooked, drove, started his own business, and led worship at a Pentecostal church for many years, even though he was confined to a wheelchair for half a century!

I must honestly ask myself the question: "Am I preparing to defend my faith, explain my doctrine, understand my neighbor, and vie for cultural change by reading widely, learning to use good logic, and feasting on the great minds of antiquity?" If *I* am, then I'm on my way to loving God with my mind and, thus, am pleasing him by obedience to his call and his command. For those who are grooming their minds for action and for those who are not but long to sharpen their intellectual iron, we now turn to some of the instruments that can aid in that significant and stimulating process.

PART 2

AMMUNITION FOR THE FULL-GOSPEL MIND

11

The Fine Art of Thinking: Reason and Logic

We must use our best reason to know which are the true Canonical Scriptures,
to expand the text, to translate it truly, to gather just and certain inferences
from Scripture assertions; to apply in matters of doctrine, and worship.
RICHARD BAXTER, PURITAN LEADER

Every Sabbath he [Paul] reasoned in the synagogue,
trying to persuade both Jews and Greeks.
LUKE, ABOUT THE APOSTLE PAUL

It can't be repeated too often, Braintwister: Never try to use
reason to tempt them. Reason is our enemy. Get them to think of
reason itself as unfeeling, or old-fashioned, or even Eurocentric.
SNAKEBITE TO HIS TRAINEE, BRAINTWISTER; *THE SNAKEBITE LETTERS*

In other words, do not rely on reasoning. Reasoning opens the
door for deception and brings much confusion.... Reasoning and
confusion go together.... Reasoning is dangerous for many reasons.
JOYCE MEYER, CHARISMATIC LEADER

The trickle-down effects of our cerebral scantiness are not only widespread but also come in a vast variety of flavors. Many believers in Full Gospel fellowships are prone to promote feel-good preaching, a consumer audience mentality, and hackneyed hermeneutics. Fascination with Christian celebrity-ism, self-centered praise, and emotionalism, as well as a cultivation of sensational and marginal beliefs, are all further indicators that many Full Gospel people have cast reflective thought to the periphery of their faith life.

In our revolt against reason, we have mutated the "faith which was once delivered unto the saints" (Jude 3 KJV) and failed to equip ourselves to defend this faith. Though reason, logic, and critical thought are by no means our only tools, without them we will be inclined toward misconstruing God's Word, possessing zeal without knowledge, and almost certainly misusing his heavenly gifts. The life lived by faith should not be devoid of good thinking; rather, especially as Christians, we are charged with the responsibility of faithfully managing those few cubic centimeters of gray matter inside our skull. By preparing our minds for action (1 Peter 1:13), we make ourselves ready for the day of battle;

and by improving our minds, we become a kingdom of thinkers, thus bringing honor and glory to our God.

FAITH AND REASON

The comments of one of the most popular "Full Gospel" preachers of the 1990s exemplify the common dilemma of pitting faith against reason. She posits: "It is difficult for human beings to give up reasoning and simply trust God."[1] Those who see faith as the antithesis of reason are hard-pressed to explain how we can believe something that the mind *knows* is untrue, or how we can trust in something if we entertain doubts about its validity. Furthermore, how can we determine if something is true unless we have put to use our God-given reason? The heart surely cannot rejoice in what the intellect has deemed inaccurate.

Biblical knowledge itself is comprehended by the gift of reason; thus, it is nonsensical to suggest that faith and knowledge, or faith and reason, are hostile to one another. It is true that *faith in my opinion* (when different from Scripture) and *faith in God's Word* are incompatible, just as *reason* that denies God's truth is an enemy to *reason* that embraces his will. In other words, wrong reasoning is the opposite of right reasoning and faith in the correct data is contrary to faith in faulty data. This, then, is where the battle lines should be drawn.

When I used to skydive, I would vault from the single-engine Piper by faith. That is, I trusted that I would free fall in rapturous transport and live to tell of it. Though I leaped by faith, I did so with faith *in* gravity, faith *in* my parachute, faith *in* my judgment and timing — *faith in my knowledge* of this data. Likewise, when I fell headlong into the arms of God, I did so by faith. That is, faith *that* he loved me, faith *that* he forgave me, faith *that* he would not wring my neck — faith *that* he was true to what he had promised. Faith, in the biblical sense, is faith *in* or faith *that*. Anything less is simply sentimentality, superstition, mysticism, or wishful thinking, which, in the final analysis, is not thinking at all.

Now, for those who might claim that reason is our all-in-all, it is important to point out that, by itself, human reason can never find its way to heaven. One cannot gradually climb the ladder of wisdom, eventually discover the door of the kingdom, and by persistent intellectual battering, break down the barrier between human thoughts about God and God's revealed thoughts to humans. Without God's gracious gift of his written self-revelation, we as humans, by reason, would never have known our true spiritual condition or God's cure for that condition.

On the flipside, many confuse rationalism with reason. Whereas rationalism is the belief system suggesting that there is no such thing as revelation, reason is a God-granted commodity. Thus, the answer to rationalism is not *ir*rationality, the antidote for anti-intellectualism is not intellectual*ism*, and by no means is mysticism the solution to the misuse of reason. God's invitation still holds: "Come now, let us *reason* together" (Isa. 1:18); his beckoning call still resonates to "present your bodies a living sacrifice . . . this is your *reasonable* [*logikos*] service" (Rom. 12:1, personal trans.); and his command is yet contemporary, "Be ready always to give an answer to every man that asks of you a *reason* of the hope that is in you" (1 Peter 3:15).

REASON, FAITH, AND FEELINGS

Waves of romanticism, relativism, individualism, and New Age teaching have unleashed a rising emphasis on feelings over thinking, emotions over doctrine, and experience over intellect. Wherever these find an inroad, it comes at the expense of casting away our rational rudders. In turn, this steers many believers into the currents of waywardness — into the vast sea of subjectivity, where the drizzling clouds of mysticism dictate their spiritual journey.

When this takes place, the turbulent winds of half-truth blow the helpless castaways into the vicious crags of confusion and mindless spirituality. It's unfortunate that so few Pentecostal – Charismatic authors have written on the nature and dangers of mysticism and subjective intuition. By this absence, we seem to be saying that either the problem is rare in our ranks or that it is widespread, yet insignificant. If this is truly what we are declaring, then we probably need more help than what I have suspected.

Mysticism is generally that way of judging truth and reality whereby feelings, impressions, and personal experiences formulate one's view of life and dictate one's decisions. Those who approach their spiritual life in this way often claim that they "know that they know," and so they place themselves beyond the scrutiny of reason and good advice. Even when the "truth" they received *doesn't* come to pass, they tend to rationalize away why it didn't, or they alter their "truth" so as to fit what *has* taken place. In their estimation, the impression that they intercept is authoritative because it has come from within; and because it has come from within, it must have been the Holy Spirit; and because it was the Holy Spirit, the voice cannot lie. This type of circular reasoning not only damages a Christian's testimonies but causes untold heartache for friends, family, and congregations who are held hostage by such silliness.

All of us can probably recall numerous odd incidences that we have witnessed as a result of questionable strong impressions, personal leadings, and inner voices. My point is not to inundate the reader with examples but simply to allude to the type of craziness that *can* result from a casting away of reason. I'm reminded of a man who lost his good-paying job because he "knew" that he was to speak in tongues in front of his non-Christian fellow workers. His only defense was that he could not tell God to shut up. Gossip, greed, laziness, fornication, and a host of other activities have been blamed on God, in the name of "being led" and in the absence of using reason.

Nor can we forget about the multitudes who feel strongly led toward a certain church, only to fail to get involved so that at their convenience, they can "feel led" to escape it for another fellowship only a few weeks later. Or what of the many pastoral victims who have been voted into a congregation? The democratic voice and the voice of the Spirit said "yes" to the candidate, but only weeks or months later the same Spirit is telling the same demo-crats that he is *not* their man. We all make mistakes — but let's call them what they are. You and I both know that the list could go on and on ...

THE LEADING OF THE HOLY SPIRIT

Now, having said this, it's vitally important for the reader to understand that I am totally convinced that the Holy Spirit still speaks to his body and that a genuine personal lead-ing is *one* method whereby God directs his children. If a person quenches the power and presence of the Holy Spirit by being *overly* critical, he or she will inevitably miss out on some of God's special events that he desires to involve that person in. There is something wrong with us if we are not exhilarated over the thought of being led by the Spirit of God. However, there is also something wrong if we jettison our minds, confusing every potent inner notion with the voice of God, and thus basing our system of belief on phenomena (real or imagined).

Certainly, we must be open to unusual occurrences, but we must believe only what is clearly taught in Scripture. Test every spirit, prove all things, and by all means, avoid being weird just to be weird, because most often this is simply old-fashioned pride! We need to be careful not to follow every inner unction (especially when self-serving!), not to be bent on *seeking* signs and wonders, and not to cast off logic and reason as if they were enemies of the supernatural.

The two great borders between which we must seek to operate are those of *quench-ing the Spirit* on the one extreme and *sensationalism* on the other. It seems as if there's always that closed-minded crowd who automatically cry "foul" when anything outside of the realm of *their* personal experience is purported. Then there are those who are always chomping at the bit to champion the newest and strangest manifestation. Whether we are guilty of gullibility because of our fear of quenching the Spirit, or we err in *actually* quench-ing the Spirit by way of fear of presumption, we must seek to know our own weaknesses and tendencies in order to bring balance to our spiritual life. Without openness to other views and honesty with one's own prejudices, a person can never hope to find that balance.

Much could and needs to be said about the Pentecostal – Charismatic mind. There's a vast amount of work to be done in order to adequately assist Full Gospel people in living out a fully conscious and examined life in our tricky and bewildered society. One of the first steps toward this goal is simply to help our people to see that reason and faith are not mortal enemies. Second, adherents of our movement need to confine their doctrinal convictions to the realm of explicitly biblical teaching. Third, we are obliged to emphasize, learn, and teach the value and art of logic.

THE LOGIC OF GOD

Logic is often treated as a rebellious stepchild by those who are devoted to Christ. But like many of the other topics discussed in this book, logic too should be championed, *especially* by soldiers of the cross. Those who are interested in truth really need to be concerned about good thinking, and those who know that their thoughts about God, Scripture, and life are of the utmost significance should be intimately familiar with logic. Believers who supposedly object to the idea of mixing logic with Christianity make at least one of two mistakes.

First, when so-called antagonists speak against logic, they inevitably provide reasons or arguments as to why they consider logic dangerous for the person of faith. Of course, they want the hearer to accept what they say as logical. In this way, they reveal that in order to present their case, they must utilize the very thing that they presumably reject. The second mistake is intimately linked to the former; it is to err *by definition*. Such people define logic as a fallen faculty that lies beyond repair, or they claim that logic is the art of explaining away the supernatural. Let's now reason together and see why logic is actually our friend.

Logic, as Webster defines it, is "the science of the formal principles of reasoning." In short, logic is the study or practice of thinking correctly. Logic is following rules of thought and reality in order to reach legitimate conclusions — the process of putting one's thoughts into order. Logic is the opposite of confused thought and dislocated explanations. Its proper use reveals inconsistencies, destroys prejudice, and untangles complex issues. When logic is applied to science, politics, religion, art, music, philosophy, moral issues, or any other discipline, it not only examines the method one uses in judging facts, but it also tests each link in the chain of argumentation and their relationship to each other. In this way, logic plays the part of a policeman, blowing the whistle when one of the laws of correct reasoning is violated.

In light of the fact that everybody thinks, and assuming that everybody *wants to* think correctly, the exercise of logic is of extreme importance. At least the early church fathers, the medieval scholastics, the Reformers, the Puritans, and the Great Awakeners believed so. Even the great fire-brand Wesley taught logic at Oxford and penned a 247-page book on reason![2]

"IN THE BEGINNING WAS THE LOGIC"

In his slender volume *Logic*, Christian philosopher Gordon Clark took the bold and acceptable step in translating the prologue to John's Gospel, "In the beginning was Logic, and Logic was with God, and Logic was God" (John 1:1). Viewing Christ, the Word (*Logos*), in this way helps us to understand why the laws of logic are embedded within the fiber of all creation (after all, through the *Logos* all things were made, John 1:4) and why in the end nothing makes ultimate sense without taking Christ into consideration. Clark actually took the same step that many of the earliest church fathers took nearly 2,000 years ago. One need only glance at the indexes of any Ante-Nicene or Nicene church fathers set in order to witness their keen interest in the *logos*.[3]

Athenagoras says that the Logos is "the understanding and Reason of the Father." Irenaeus defines the Logos as "the principle that thinks." Origen's definition of the same is "reason," opting for this synonym because in his understanding, "he [Christ] takes away from us all that is irrational and makes us truly reasonable." Why is it so strange that we should think of Jesus as Reason Incarnate? Do we not readily accept the fact that he is the living Word? Is the word "Word" more personal than "Logic" or "Reason"? Actually, a word is the result of thought, for it is out of the abundance of the heart (mind) that the mouth speaks.[4]

ARGUING LIKE A CHRISTIAN SHOULD: REASON, LOGIC, AND ARGUMENTATION

I had known the Lord for only three years when I was fortunate enough to stumble on a dusty copy of A. G. Sertillanges' *The Intellectual Life*, a perennial classic among pensive minds. Throughout this cerebral-spiritual goldmine, the author awakens, provokes, and inspires adventurous souls to lend their minds to Christ for *his* work. In doing so, he mentions the call to occupy oneself in "the Living Logic." He explains that this is the principle of participating passionately in the life-long development of the intellect, where the human mind, radical intellectual exploration, and the mind of God meet in the sanctuary of truth.[5]

If we desire to think like Christ about created *and* eternal things, we must walk in the Living Logic — so that the Living Logos can work through us. To think accurately, we must be able to detect when incorrect methods or illogical conclusions creep into our minds. Moreover, as we seek to discover sound theology (*theo-logos*), we will need to employ sound logic, for theology is nothing less than rational discourse about God based on his revealed mind. Since Christians are commanded to demolish invalid arguments and take captive every thought that contradicts Christ (the Logos; see 2 Cor. 10:4 – 5), we must know how to argue properly.

One evening many years ago, a fellow visited our church while I was teaching on the value of apologetics and preparing a good defense. In the midst of my teaching, he stood up to declare that it was sinful for Christians to argue. After attempting to clarify further to him the value of a valid argument, he exploded into a tirade, going on and on about why quarreling never benefits the kingdom of God. He not only mangled his definitions of arguing and quarreling, but he ended up doing exactly what he claimed was taboo for Christians. This brother had equated brawling with providing arguments and quarreled with me out of emotion rather than reason, storming out, never to return. Here was a case where a person verbally denigrated logic, yet tried to use logic and reason to do so. Ever tried to put out a fire with gas?

This misguided man made the mistake that many believers seem to make: He had wrongly defined the nature of an argument. An argument is "a series of reasons which one uses to prove the truth of what one wishes to assert,"[6] or more simply put, a group of statements with evidences and a conclusion. Those who provide reasons in order to support their case may furnish or build an argument, but they do not have to be argumentative.

In fact, I have found that the person with the *fewest* good reasons for his case is usually the most argumentative. Those whose explanations lack content seem more likely to get defensive, emotional, and louder than those who are well-prepared for the discussion.

Christians shouldn't shun arguments but welcome them, because they are the basis of correct thinking and logical explanations. Furthermore, it's impossible to know *why* we believe *what* we believe without having formulated an argument in our mind. Though there are many settings where a good discussion is of great value, an argument doesn't have to be verbalized in order to be an argument! But whether spoken or simply thought, an argument needs to be valid. Here is where the hinge of logic meets the door of debate, and here is where we benefit from being acquainted with the most common errors while presenting an argument.

RECOGNIZING AN ILLOGICAL ARGUMENT

If you are like me, you have probably been in discussions where you disagreed with someone but didn't know how to express your disagreement. And you have most likely experienced the frustration of knowing that another person's argument was faulty but didn't know exactly where that person went wrong in their explanation. Finally, we have also been the architect of arguments that we ourselves have struggled to follow but continued in them because of our inability to discern precisely where we strayed off of the patent path of logic.

Making blunders in our reasoning process is as prevalent as sin, but knowing where the error lies and what to do about botched logic seems almost as rare as hen's teeth. Whether we are discussing the gifts of the Spirit, presidential debates, public schools, or flavors of ice cream, knowing the common fallacies that plague human thinking is of incalculable benefit.

Since this book is of a nontechnical nature, I will not deal with *formal* fallacies (having to do with the *form* of arguments). It is in the realm of *informal* fallacy that most of us fail or with which we are accosted. Informal fallacies are mistakes in clarity or in soundness of the reasoning process. They range from unintentional vagueness to the deliberate misleading of one's hearers, and from incorrect grammar to evasion. Regardless of which fallacy is our favorite to use or the one by which we are most often abused, they can cause us to embrace wrong conclusions for inadequate reasons or even right conclusions for wrong reasons.

In the following list of informal fallacies, I will not attempt to provide the technical labels of these common fallacies but will simply furnish brief explanations of some of most widespread ways that we rupture the rules of good reasoning.

- Appealing to people's emotions rather than to facts
- Evading a question and moving on to what one wants to say
- Arguing that the ends justify the means

- Shifting the burden of proof to your opponent in order to cover up ignorance
- Using exceptions to make a rule
- Posing an either/or choice when, in reality, there are many more than two options
- Using unfounded, popular clichés instead of a series of tightly knit statements
- Parroting technical language in order to impress the hearer or to confuse an opponent
- Acting as if there are no problems with our view, all the while cataloging the problems of an opposing view
- Suppressing relevant but unfavorable evidence
- Dismissing another's view without a logical response
- Using false analogies that break down on closer scrutiny
- Misquoting another, using a different tone than the original speaker did, or placing an accent on words that were previously unaccented
- Attacking the arguer's character rather than the argument
- Claiming that something is right because so many do it or because it has been done for so long
- Using incorrect definitions of words or concepts
- Trying to prove fact by feeling or intuition
- Parroting back the same response again and again even if evidence to the contrary is mounting
- Attempting to prove a rival wrong by referring to other unrelated areas where the person may be wrong
- Making claims that are impossible to verify
- Bringing up a totally different subject because you're running out of evidence
- Fighting symptoms of a problem rather than the problem itself
- Asking too many questions without giving the hearer opportunity to answer
- Answering another's questions only with questions *in order to* keep the burden of proof off of oneself
- Raising one's voice when content is waning and so appearing to increase authority
- Misrepresenting an opposing view (superficially) and then destroying it
- Overusing all-encompassing words, such as *never, all, always, constantly*, and the like
- Using sarcastic false humility: "Yes, I'm all wrong, everything I said is all wrong, and everything you said is right."

Though there are undoubtedly other *informal* fallacies and then many *formal* fallacies, the above list should give a fair indication of the keen reflection that is needed in order to reason logically. Failure to understand the prevailing pitfalls of bad thinking has held the masses in bondage to superficial views about many important topics. In particular, we as Christians should be very concerned about the process by which we come to accept something as true or false. Furthermore, as agents of truth and ambassadors of Christ, we must know how to best persuade the lost of their erroneous and disastrous views of life and eternity. When we know this, we will be prepared to join the likes of Paul, "arguing persuasively," "vigorously refuting," and "publicly debating" (Acts 18:28; 19:8 – 9) for God's glory.

CONCLUSION

In his letters to the Spirit-filled believers of Corinth, Paul challenged the readers to take captive every thought until it lined up with the truth of Christ (2 Cor. 10:4 – 5). He also enjoined them to become better thinkers, writing, "Stop thinking like children ... in your thinking be adults" (1 Cor. 14:20). By following these directives, we as God's modern-day, Spirit-filled children can become adept at outwitting Satan in his *il*logical schemes (2 Cor. 2:11). And as we fortify our aptitude for good thinking, we will magnify the image of God in us, bringing glory to the One who has sent his one and only Son, Jesus — the living *Logos* — into our lives. If there is a principal habitation on this earth for the laws of logic and for superb reasoning, surely it's in the hearts of those who are called by his name.

NOTES

1. Joyce Meyer, *Battlefield of the Mind*, 91.
2. John Wesley, *The Works of John Wesley* (Grand Rapids: Baker, 1996 reprint), 14:1, 12, 33, 78, 147, 161, 319, 345; 8:1 – 247; *The Journals of John Wesley*, ed. N. Curnock (London: Epworth, 1916), 1:110 – 12, 133 – 34, 209 – 10, 237 – 38, 278, 295, 299, 300, 354; 3:320; *A Compendium of Logic*; *Reason and Religion*; *Primitive Physics*; *A Compendium of Natural Philosophy*; 4:190; 5:247; Oden, *John Wesley's*, 67; Telford, *Letters*, 4:123, 166; 5:176, 342; Bonamy Dobree, *John Wesley* (Folcroft, PA: Folcroft Library editions, 1974), 23.
3. Gordon H. Clark, *Logic* (Jefferson, MD: Trinity Foundation, 1988), 117 – 31.
4. Athenagoras, *Ante-Nicene Fathers* (Schaff ed.), 2:133; Irenaeus, *Ante-Nicene Fathers*, (Schaff ed.), 1:400; Origen, *Ante-Nicene Fathers* (Schaff ed.), 9:319 – 20.
5. A. G. Sertillanges, *The Intellectual Life: Its Spirit, Conditions and Methods* (Washington, D. C.: Catholic Univ. of America Press, 1987).
6. Ibid., 1.

12

The Molding of the Human Mind: Education

The end then of learning is to repair the ruins of our first parents by regaining to know God aright, and out of that knowledge to love him, to imitate him to be like him.
JOHN MILTON, AUTHOR OF *PARADISE LOST*

Education is killing Christianity. . . . Head knowledge gets into religion . . . . It makes our young people question the virgin birth. The less education, the more easily you can accept salvation.
EARLY PENTECOSTAL LEADER

We are not against others having an education, but we want to keep it out of our organization. Don't mix up the Bible school with the intellectual trends of the world today. We want to keep our organization pure and holy and simple.
ERNEST SUMRALL, PENTECOSTAL LEADER

For several decades now, education has been lambasted in the arena of pop culture. From sitcoms portraying the professorial-type as an abstract egghead to cherished songs depicting learning as impractical and dangerous, the opinions of the masses concerning higher learning have been voiced. Take, for example, a popular song from the 1960s, which is still played daily on "oldies" stations. The artist proudly proclaims that he doesn't know much about geography, algebra, history, biology, and so on, but the one thing he does know is that he loves and is loved by his girl. His synopsis of life is "what a wonderful world it could be" if everyone were like him.[1] In the early 1980s, a smash cult-hit recorded by Pink Floyd and turned into a movie, the repetitive message is, "We don't need no education, we don't need no thoughts-control," and then, "Teachers, leave those kids alone."[2]

Many similar examples could be noted, but perhaps it will suffice to add one by a Christian artist. The Rev. Dan Smith has recorded a snapping blues ditty regarding his lack of learning. In the song, he pits seminary against Calvary over and over again. Woven throughout this latter fancy is the declaration: "I don't have no education, as you may readily see. Well, I'm not an intellectual, nor have I tried to be. I never won a diploma, I never earned a degree." The purpose for pointing out all of this is that he got all that he needed from Calvary.[3]

These slams and confusion about higher education are accompanied by the widely-held notion that anyone who sits in classes long enough, ipso facto, becomes an educated person, irrespective of *what* they have studied and *how* they have studied it. Related to this is the ever-present enigma of indoctrination, the practice of spoon-feeding a set of dogmatic beliefs. This approach sadly presupposes that the student is unable to decipher truth from among an array of competing views. In due time, this cheap approach to education (from pulpit and classroom alike) births a colony of religious automatons fully armed with dull clichés and aped answers.

Although a person may become puffed up in his or her knowledge, the remedy for *pride in one's learning* is by no means ignorance, any more than the remedy for gluttony is starvation or the cure for greed is poverty. Moreover, the medicine for ill-formed minds, uneducated hearts, and fragmented thinking is not intellectual escapism but *true* education — education that widens our minds and aids in the endeavor to harmonize our love for God with our procured knowledge.

TRUE RELIGION AND TRUE EDUCATION

From the Old Testament to New Testament Christianity and throughout the earliest centuries of the Christian era, education played an important role in the expression and spread of the gospel message. The ancient Jews were a highly literate people. This shouldn't surprise us, seeing that their Maker communicated the truth of reality to them through a book, the Hebrew Scriptures. It's worth noting that as early as 180 B.C., schools for Jewish boys existed, and by 100 B.C., Jewish elementary schools were not uncommon. Beyond any doubt, Jesus himself learned to read (Luke 4:16) and write (John 8:6b).

Moreover, Jesus was referred to as a teacher over fifty times, and although he did not attend the most noteworthy academies of the great rabbis (John 7:15), at age twelve he sat among Jerusalem's teachers and astounded them with his remarkable questions and his "understanding and his answers" (Luke 2:46 – 47). The apostle Paul taught in the lecture hall of Tyrannus in Ephesus for two years. He also knew Greek philosophy and literature (Acts 17:27 – 28; Titus 1:13), quoted ancient poets, spoke with refined rhetorical techniques, and wrote with an intricate and profound ability in the discipline of debate.

When one peruses the book of Proverbs, one recognizes that this "student manual" for the youth of Israel is not child's play. Its broad borders encompass teaching on personalities, logic, temptations, labor, faith, love, materialism, integrity, generosity, sex, mental discipline, the nuances of pride, the principles of friendship, and many other challenging topics. Furthermore, this collection of wisdom not only tells the readers *what* to think but truly sharpens their intellectual iron (cf. Prov. 27:17), teaching them *how* to think and *why* to think this *way*.

The New Testament is relatively silent on the issue of the formal education of children. We find no specific mentions of elementary schools or universities. But this should not bother us, for neither do we find the mention of church buildings, the use of instruments in Sabbath praise, a choir director, church buses, Sunday school, or children and youth pastors. They didn't even have Bibles! But we do know that instruction was primarily the responsibility of the family (Eph. 6:4; 2 Tim. 1:5; 3:15), as it should be today, even though we have other institutions to aid us in the process.

One of the reasons that "Christian" schools are not mentioned in the New Testament is that the early church was packed with Jews; thus, their children would naturally be trained in the same fashion that they were previously. Remember, the church was viewed as a sect within Judaism for the larger portion of the first century. All this changed, however, when Judaism relinquished all ties with Christianity and when the Roman Empire sought to persecute specifically those who named the name of Christ. Thereafter, Christians began to establish schools in every corner of the empire.

SAINTS, SCHOLARS, AND SCHOOLS

As we venture into the second century and beyond, we see that Christianity's leading figures were not only widely read but passionately pursued education on all levels. Many of the early church fathers were men of notable learning and thinkers of the highest order. That is to say, they not only possessed voluminous bits of information but understood something of the nature of fitting those bits together.

These giants of the faith laid hold of the fact that all truth is God's truth, realizing that Christianity had powerful implications not only for a narrowly-defined religious life, but for all of life — especially the life of the mind. For them, Jesus was the Eternal Logic, who brought together the splinters of reality that had become fragmented and scattered through the Fall. This view enabled them to see the merit in what might otherwise be termed "secular" learning.

As these godly mentors taught a myriad of converts in the early Christian era, they challenged them to a high educational standard. Their goal was not to merely fill the hearer's brains with data but to condition their *way* of thinking. Listen to the thoughts of one of Christianity's greatest teachers of the second century, Clement of Alexandria, as he exhorts believers toward excellence in education:

> The spiritual man applies himself to the subjects that provide training for knowledge. He takes from each branch of study its contribution to the truth. So he studies the proportion of harmonies in music. In arithmetic, he notes the increasing and decreasing of numbers and their relations to one another. . . . Studying geometry, which is abstract logic, he comprehends a continuous distance and an unchanging essence that is different from these bodies. And through astronomy, he is mentally raised from the earth.[4]

Most likely, within fifty years of the death of John the apostle, catechetical schools were being established where "seekers" and converts sat under the tutelage of renowned Christian teachers. By approximately A.D. 225, there were well-developed institutions in Alexandria, Rome, Antioch, and other significant population centers. The saints gathered there to have their understandings sharpened and souls stretched. In the course of their attendance, they studied geometry, physiology, science, logic, philosophy, ancient poetry, ethics, grammar, and theology. The early creeds were dissected and expounded upon, doctrinal issues were hammered out, and expository sermons were provided from the Old and New Testament books alike.[5]

With this type of education, the students' thinking was elevated in clarity, their moral convictions were buttressed, and their minds grasped the meaning and power of God's written Word. Because the early church fathers viewed Christianity as a *reasonable* service, they sought to educate the spirit *as well as* the mind. It is evident from their writings that they believed that all of the discoveries, chronicles, and fortunes of learning were available to be freely utilized by those who had become yoked with Christ. They understood where the laws of nature came from; they knew the origin of the principles of mathematics, logic, and thought. They were keenly aware that their Redeemer is the One "in whom are hidden all the treasures of wisdom and knowledge" (Col. 2:3). Beginning with these inaugural impulses, God's people became the major impetus behind founding the great learning institutions of antiquity and beyond.

Wherever the message of Christ has penetrated, methodical education has been one of the direct results. From mission movements of remote times to modern-day endeavors to formulate alphabets and translate the Bible for unreached cultures, the need for and participation in intellectual cultivation has served to spread the cause of Christ. Thus, the relationship between Christianity and education is twofold. It seems safe to say that education both *advances* the kingdom and is *advanced by* the kingdom once established in a particular group.

An emphasis on learning, especially when radiating from a deep reverence for God, has served humankind again and again. For hundreds of years, the monks of Europe preserved the texts of Scripture, the writings of the church fathers, and classical literature. In the embryonic stages of the Reformation, Wycliffe, Tyndale, Coverdale, Calvin, and Luther fought for the education of the masses and for the translation of Scriptures into the language of the common man. And during the golden age of Puritanism, the classrooms of Cambridge and Oxford were crowded with the men who, through intellectual sweat and passionate devotion, set their part of the world ablaze for Jesus.

Though England had emphasized learning for centuries, when the Puritans gained power, the number of schools actually doubled in number! The Puritans maintained a remarkable abhorrence toward mental laziness, intellectual passivity, and willful ignorance — a conviction that followed them from the cradle to the casket, from prison to parliament, from college to cathedral, and from the Westminster Confession to the colonization of the new world of the West.

When it came to the raising up of settlements in North America, the same ardor for sanctimony and schooling accompanied the vision of New England's brave hearts. The Puritans set the principle of godly learning on the pinnacle of their newfound "City on a Hill." As a case in point, Harvard College was established in 1636, only six years after the first large exodus of Puritans from England to the new continent. In their own words, Harvard's founding was motivated by their "dreading to have an illiterate Ministry to the Churches, when our present Ministers shall lie in the Dust." And so, Harvard, along with Yale and Princeton, were responsible for populating vacant pulpits and destitute mission fields for over a century.[6]

These universities influenced many of the optimal Christian leaders in American history, including "the last great Puritan," Jonathan Edwards. Edwards, who spearheaded the First Great Awakening, was a graduate of and tutor at Yale and later become the president of Princeton. The mammoth revival that took place under his ministry was ignited while Edwards served at a church in Northampton where his grandfather, Solomon Stoddard, had pastored for fifty-seven years. Stoddard himself was a graduate of and librarian at Harvard. Edwards' grandson Timothy Dwight was a graduate of Yale, with honorary doctorates from Princeton and Harvard. Carrying the anointing cloak of his grandfather and of his great great grandfather, Dwight helped to lead our nation into the Second Great Awakening, which commenced in 1801 while he was president of Yale.

The Pilgrim fathers not only emphasized higher education but also primary education. In 1647 they proceeded with what was referred to as the "Old Deluder Satan Act," requiring each and every town to hire and pay school teachers. The bill acquired its name from the idea that Satan more easily guides those whose minds have not been formed to think efficiently.[7] They took seriously the biblical injunction to "prepare your minds for action" (1 Peter 1:13). We too must withstand the temptation to keep the spiritual life in one corner and the intellectual life in another. We must rejoin what the cream of God's crop have historically wedded: God's Spirit and the human mind.

THE STATUS OF TODAY'S SECULAR AND SACRED EDUCATION

Lying at the root of many of our frustrations concerning today's education are two basic but conflicting ideas. One school of thought supposes that education primarily has to do with getting information into the mind; the other sees education as the process whereby the mind is formed. At the heart, it is an issue of *information* versus *formation*. The difference is between telling a learner *what to think* versus teaching him *how to think*. It can be compared to the old adage of *handing a man a fish* or teaching him *how to fish*. A fish in the hand will suffice for the day, yet leaves one without a means whereby he can fish for himself tomorrow.

The difference can also be likened to a preacher telling people *what* to believe versus demonstrating *why* they should believe what they're told they should believe. The first produces passive, slothful minds, bored by explanations, addicted to entertainment, and afraid of the pain that accompanies real thinking. The latter type of instruction transforms the mind as the hearer actively engages in the logical sequence of the message and labors to think, as opposed to merely hearing the words or remembering information. There is a vast contrast between the two — one that can be seen clearly on the countenances and in the lives of those who experience them.

Many within the church have been tarnished by indoctrination, a spectator mentality, and so-called leisurely learning. All three promote intellectual laziness as well as confusion over what education is all about. These impostors of education fail to train minds how to think; thus, in the end they only prepare us to parrot out conditioned responses. In turn, we find ourselves at a loss when interrogated over a slightly-altered aspect of the subject that we thought we knew. Indoctrination itself breeds in us an overprotective attitude, which in turn suffocates creative thought, cultivates close-mindedness, and bolsters arrogance — it can even *diminish* one's faith!

Walking hand in hand with indoctrination is the myth of *pain-free learning.* The average Christian knows full well that getting into shape physically will likely cost them big time. They also take it for granted that to be good at a hobby, favorite sport, or occupation, they must continuously exert great volumes of effort and even experience pain. But when it comes to understanding the Bible, concentrating on their pastor's words, or sitting in a classroom, many of these same people expect the benefits to come without cost. We know that osmosis didn't work when we tried sleeping on our geometry book on Sunday night for Monday morning's exam. What makes us think that it will work when our eyes are open but our minds are asleep while listening to teaching from God's Book on Sunday morning?

Whether in our public institutions or Sunday schools, it seems we have come to believe that the atmosphere must be filled with as much fun and as little discipline as possible. We devise elaborate programs in order to make learning as effortless as watching our favorite TV game show. Somehow we have come to suppose that though everything else in life that is worth obtaining calls for sacrifice and struggle, the intellectual endeavors of life should come to us as easily as possible. Short sermons, voluminous jokes, cute or tear-jerking stories, and fast-paced, simple, pragmatic presentations rule many of our church platforms. As a result, the ideas of mental strain, logical labor, and intellectual taxation have become nearly foreign in the realm of education in general and in spiritual education in particular.

Our bent toward *materialism* tells us that our lawn, new roof, or engine problem requires immediate attention, sweat, money, and thinking. Our *hedonistic* view dictates that hard-earned overtime pay, strategic planning, and a careful comparison of brand names and models must accompany our purchase of a new plaything to park in the garage. Our *religious* view speaks loudly of the ultimate sacrifice that Another had to pay in order for us to become recipients of eternal life. Our *vocational* philosophy says that we must be ever ready to troubleshoot, plan our retirement, and fight as hard as necessary to keep our job. Our *intellectual* outlook, however, assumes that education is something that we got back in school, and to dedicate quality time and effort to cultivate our minds now has little practical value, especially when pain is involved.

As twenty-first-century teachers/preachers, we struggle with promoting passive hearing; we fear teaching over the heads of the hearers, often failing to realize that passivity advances hypocrisy and that nothing can elevate the mind unless it's "over one's head." So we calculate the lowest common intellectual denominator in a group and then strike at its center. In doing so, we leave the average mind as average and bring the above-average down a notch. We then claim that the hearers have received education or teaching; whereas most have merely heard the sound of the teacher's voice diffusing unrelated facts or opinions into common breathing space.

In the pulpit we do the same by preaching to death "the simple gospel," trite generalities, or our denomination's pet themes, wearing narrow but deep grooves into the easily-satisfied, desensitized minds of the tithe payers. Furthermore, we tend to avoid complicated sermons either because it will demand of us too much mental rigor and pain or because it will take away from the busy work that begets immediate results — which, in turn, helps us to feel useful. Some of us sidestep difficult issues and dumb down our messages because the crowd may dwindle if we insist on intellectual excellence in the spiritual life. If our audience begins to seek out the sermon of least resistance elsewhere, we may then find that our fragile self-worth (based on attendance and budget) begins to crumble, and this brings on a new species of pain.

True education can only take place when hearers are taught *how* to think for themselves. Naturally, educators must seek to teach *what* is right, but this comes only through knowing *how* to think and by being self-critical. Learning that takes place outside of these parameters is less than true education. Education without critical thought, creative inquiry, and logical rigor is really not education at all; it is merely the sharing of information and, at best, the storage of data.

A LIBERAL EDUCATION

When Christians hear the word "liberal" today, most probably associate it with left-wing looseness. That's to say, we imagine that it has something to do with liberal-*ism*. We live in an age when Christian parents are concerned about the federal government's over-involvement in rocking the cradle of our kindergartens. We are alarmed about the aims of Outcome Based Education and frustrated over the relativistic instruction that is so common in many of the nation's schools. In this type of climate, the idea of "liberal education" may smack of atheistic meddling in the minds of our offspring. On the contrary, a truly liberal education plays the opposite role. It *liberates* the learner by *generously* providing the intellectual ammunition needed to set free the minds of those who are otherwise held captive to false worldviews.

A good education is never the result of merely cramming as much information as is possible, about as many unrelated subjects as possible, into a pupil's cranium. Rather, its aim is to unfetter the learner's mind from faulty thinking, to bring precision to their judgment, and to assist the Christian in understanding the human experience as a whole.

This, in turn, helps them to think excellently enough to affect the temporal world for the honor of their Maker.

The perennial problem of viewing life in a fragmented manner (even more striking today) seems to be good evidence that the Fall has affected every aspect of our lives. We struggle to connect facts and faith, history and the contemporary, culture and Christ, fads and philosophy, theology and practicality, prayer and manpower, works and grace, the laws of nature and supernatural intervention, the heart, head, mind, and soul, and so on. A liberal education can help to bring back into coordination all of these and myriads of the other diversified strata of life, helping us to see everything in the human experience through the eyes of faith.

It may be argued that education by itself cannot bring cohesiveness back to the broken image of the human experience. It is true that when education is disassociated from God's revelation, life becomes broad but lacks ultimate meaning. An informed life may be interesting and charming, yet in the end it is a deformed life because it lacks context. It is also true that when revelation is disconnected from education, life is full of meaning yet narrow and shallow — meaningful yet limited. When *true*, liberal education takes place, the truth of God in Christ is included in its pool of instruction and thus brings breadth, depth, width, and meaning.

Liberal education is built on the *liberal arts*. These are termed "arts" because they aim to shape or generate a certain kind of mind — a liberated mind. Like an exquisite carving chiseled from a cold slab of granite, the mind that is forged and fine-tuned by these arts is set free from its bondage of prejudice and narrowness. This does not mean, however, that we are free to determine our own "truths," devise our own worldviews, and define new theological frontiers. Rather, we are liberated — freed — to be productive and imaginative *within* the bounds of God's truth. We are like horses that have been set free from the dark, boring, walls of a confining stable into the breezy, open meadow; a meadow with fences! Though the liberal arts do, in fact, aid in liberating our minds, we must not lose sight of the fact that in this liberty we are to remain captive to Christ — hemmed in by the fences of his truth.

Many have leaped into the realm of higher education, forgetting to attend closely to their faith, to weigh consistently their motives, and to scrutinize the multiplicity of ideas that fly at them from every direction. Thus, like boats that pull anchor and drift with the current, these people gradually lose their way and shipwreck their faith. The sirens of secularism call from the deep. In other words, Christians who choose the route of university training must prepare to fight the fight of faith in the arena of conflicting worldviews. If we abandon this arena, we abandon the chance to influence millions of pliable minds who are searching for truth, and we forfeit the opportunity to prepare intellectually so that we might curtail the continuing upsurge of secular trends in society at large.

A distracted mind is endangered wherever it may happen to be, but it is all the more vulnerable in the college or university setting. If one begins to imagine that education is some kind of cure-all or fails to remember that intellectual cultivation addresses only one component of the human being, that soul will inevitably begin its journey down the slippery, dark slope of arrogance and lost-ness. The development of the mind *must* take place under the lordship of Christ. Though mindless emotionalism, syrupy sentimentalism, ignorant faith in the name of simple faith, mystic superstition, and sectarianism are all evidences of a warped Christian life, a well-educated, religious person who has lost the faith to secularism is a deformation of life itself!

We must seek to mingle a good measure of humility with the liberal arts, and though we may shuffle paper and pursue scholarship, we can never let these be substitutes for purposeful sacrifice and Christlike service. If we don't think through the truths that we discover, we will not *truly* know if they are true. And if we do not passionately demonstrate what we know to be truth, we really don't know it at all. So, let us use our brains to explore all of God's truths, wherever they may be found; but let us do so with humility, care, sincerity, and, above all, with brains that are baptized in the Holy Spirit!

EACH ART A DISTINCT TOOL

The traditional liberal arts include grammar, rhetoric, logic, arithmetic, geometry, music, and astronomy — the first three serving as a foundation for the latter four. Each of these taught *properly* serves to provide the mind with the tools to appraise wisely, inquire accurately, and express eloquently. *Logic* helps the learner think in a consistent and reasonable manner; *rhetoric* enables the thinker to speak thoughts in a precise fashion; and *grammar* aids in arranging and writing out those otherwise undomesticated, hazy thoughts.[8]

From the first century through the Middle Ages and reaching to the Renaissance, the liberal arts served as the platform from which all other disciplines were studied. Up until the nineteenth century, most notable Christian leaders championed the value of the liberal arts. While defending education, Luther referred to those who avoided the liberal arts as "blockheads, unable to converse properly on any subject."[9] And it was Wesley's firm belief that even his circuit riders, who went forth to reach the lowly and uneducated, must have "first, a good understanding, a clear apprehension, a sound judgment, and a capacity of reasoning with some closeness." He went on to explain that these aptitudes come only from studying the liberal arts.[10]

The study of *logic* and *mathematics* aids the mind in reasoning in an authentic fashion. The subject of *language* assists one in communicating their reasoned thoughts. The natural and social *sciences* sharpens one's ability to ask the right questions. The *humanities* (literature, the fine arts, philosophy, and ethics) discipline the imagination and train the mind to discern which of many answers most likely is superlative. Studying *philosophy, history*, and *theology* empowers the student to notice trends of thought and trace out these trends through time and geography. Possessing a historical perspective is invaluable as a corrective for small-mindedness and prejudice. Exposure to the ins and outs of philosophy will help a person demonstrate the interrelationship between different systems of thought. This in turn helps to show *why* others believe *what* they believe and *why* they may balk at the offer of the gospel.

Not only do these disciplines provide the student with the ability to think consistently, understand the interconnectedness of life, and acquire knowledge, but they aid the Christian in the walk of faith. With these attributes, the believer is better equipped to refute bad philosophy, defend the faith with integrity and clarity, interpret the Scripture more carefully, and thus be in a more suitable position to understand *why* one thinks the *way* one does.

Finally, the above instruments of intellectual extension serve to challenge our deeply-held, yet sometimes wrong ideas. With good thinking and a measure of humility, the liberal arts enable us to reassess our beliefs. Only then will we be equipped to reconfigure half-baked ideas, reject false notions, reform half truths, or rejoice because we are able to firmly retain what has been tested fully. For those who love truth, this is a genuinely liberating experience!

CONCLUSION

Next to the bounty of salvation, the human mind is the greatest benefit bestowed on us. Of course, without minds we wouldn't possess the equipment required to communicate with our Creator, read his revelation, practice his presence, or even identify his existence. Our mind is a reflection of God's mind, and our desire to understand the universe of ideas that God has disseminated into his creation is a manifestation of our relationship to him.

In addition, our endeavor to become premium thinkers prepares us to live the most effective lives possible as we subdue and rule the earth (Gen. 1:28). As we personally and corporately strive to form our intellects through learning, we will inevitably permeate our society with a flaming faith housed in minds afire. And with this God-ordained union, at last we will exhibit to a lost world what it means to be a people with renewed and educated minds — *minds molded for the Maker*!

NOTES

1. Sam Cook, "Wonderful World."
2. Pink Floyd, "The Wall."
3. Dan Smith, "I've Been to Calvary."
4. Clement of Alexandria, *Ante-Nicene Fathers* (Schaff ed.), 2:484.
5. Charles Bigg, *The Christian Platonists of Alexandria* (Oxford: Clarendon, 1888), 41, 42, 50.
6. Ahlstrom, *A Religious History*, 1:198; Leland Ryken, *Worldly Saints: The Puritans as They Really Were* (Grand Rapids: Zondervan, 1986), 186; Peter Toon, "John Harvard," in *The New International Dictionary of the Christian Church*, 453.
7. Samuel Blumenfeld, *Is Public Education Necessary?* (Boise, ID: Paradigm, 1985), 10.
8. Gilbert Highet, *Paideia* (New York: Oxford Univ. Press, 1945), 1:314.
9. Martin Luther, *Works of Martin Luther* (Philadelphia: Holman, 1915), 4:122; 5:298.
10. Wesley, *Works* (Baker ed.), 10:480 – 500.

13

Defining the Faith: Theology

Truly spiritual people do not quibble over points of doctrine.
CHARLES PARHAM, FOUNDER OF PENTECOSTALISM

My theology! I didn't know I had any. I wish you would tell me what my theology is.
DWIGHT L. MOODY

It is important to note that theology did not arise out of speculative interests. Theology arose out of the very practical needs of the early church as it sought to put its beliefs into teachable form for instructing new believers, refuting heresies, and for the persuasion of outsiders.
HAROLD H. DITMANSON, CHRISTIAN EDUCATOR

It is scarcely an exaggeration to say that during the nineteenth century and well into the twentieth century, religion prospered while theology slowly went bankrupt.
HENRY COMMAGER, HISTORIAN

One Sunday morning a young man picked our congregation to be his experimental choice for that particular week. He had been rummaging round about the region, searching for a church that could adequately satisfy his deep appetite for inspired preaching. At that time I was engaged a verse-by-verse expedition down Paul's Roman road. I had worked my way through the first three chapters of the book when our friend came to visit. After the message, he approached me with "words of encouragement." He communicated that he had been challenged by the exposition of the text and that the congregants were some of the friendliest people he had met lately. I braced myself, bearing in mind such accolades might precede words of criticism.

Sure enough, the other shoe dropped. Dogging his enchanting affirmations were critical comments about the lack of the Spirit's presence in my sermon and in the worship service in general. He enlightened me on the dangers of "dry doctrine," on the fine art of releasing the Spirit, and on the things he had experienced that would be hard for me to fathom. This fellow left, and I did not see him at our worship services again.

About a year later, as I was making my way into the twelfth chapter of Paul's *magnum opus*, we had another visitor. After the service I conversed with this man about his family and occupation. Subsequent to the chit chat, he began lecturing me about "dead theology," informing me of the lack of practical teaching in our churches. He viewed any instruction that couldn't be applied immediately as mere mortar for hypocrisy. In his estimation, the only viable teaching was "practical" teaching.

Little did I know until I was collating old visitor lists that the latter guest was actually the father of the former. In a sense, this quirky connection serves to illustrate two attitudes toward theology that many of us have had to deal with on a regular basis. Both derive from our evangelical roots in the nineteenth century, where the two chief adversaries of theological erudition were experientialism and pragmatism. These egocentric twin daughters of individualism are perpetually interested in answers to questions like: What will it do for *me*? Can *I* use it immediately? How will it make *me* feel? Is it simple?

THEO*LOGIC*AL BEINGS WITHOUT *LOGIC*

A crisis has spread over the landscape of modern Christianity; its tentacles have reached into the recesses of much of evangelicalism and of the Pentecostal–Charismatic movement. The crisis is that of the undervaluation of and disregard for theology. A penchant for the spectacular, for emotional manipulation, and for superficial discipleship often displace the rewarding practice of forging out an orthodox belief system — that is, a system that can shield us from heresy, help us to articulate the tenets of our faith, move us from narrow prejudices, and aid us in reaching a world confused by the clamor of a million muddied opinions.

Because of our quasi-democratic approach to Bible exposition, many Spirit-filled devotees claim their truth *is* truth whether or not their discovery meshes with the tried and true principles of biblical interpretation. These augment the ranks of religious relativists who have little need for the hermeneutical hands of the body of Christ. These become architects of their own "orthodoxy," having trivialized two thousand years of arduous theological thinking. As a result, some who screech the loudest against popish authoritarianism, in turn, *become* a kingdom of popes speaking *ex cathedra*, denigrating any who question their private interpretation.

In the midst of this doctrinal free-for-all, a host of half truths reign supreme; for who can err in an atmosphere permeated with the unspoken credos: "It works for me"; "That's what it means to me"; and "God told me"? Surely, the dams of historical theology have been smashed by the pressures of popularity, where technique trumps truth, methods overshadow the message, the practical outshines thought-provoking preaching, and the "feel goods" dethrone conviction.

When the rich reservoirs of theology are neglected, the superficialities of pop religion rise up to claim front and center, and the doctrinal divines of a more reflective era are replaced by Hollywood-type personalities. Without a passion for fertile doctrine, the body can so easily become a sterile hybrid — unable to generate vibrant offspring, often settling for growth that is composed of little more than recycled believers who have been bartered for at the table of convenience and immediate gratification. Such is the state of a church that sheds a deep doctrinal heritage, the state of affairs in a number of sectors of the evangelical and Pentecostal traditions.

ANTI-THEOLOGICAL ROOTS

The parallels between the earliest days of nineteenth-century evangelicalism (1801 – 1825) and the initial stages of the Pentecostal movement (1901 – 1925) are remarkable. Both claimed to be sovereign forces raised up by God as protests against the unspiritual churches surrounding them. Both lambasted ministers who invested their minds in secular and/or graduate theological studies. The two movements also claimed that their creed was the Bible alone and that doctrinal systems were often complicated counterfeits of God's simple Word. Instead of consulting mere human books, both sought heaven for their theology. As early as 1800, individualistic intuition played an important role in the establishment of revivalism. One particular leader of the movement stated, "I could say in truth that the gospel that was preached by me, was not after man; for I neither received it of man, neither was I taught it by man, but by Jesus Christ, through the medium of the Holy Spirit."[1]

The notion that one needed no special training in order to interpret plain Scripture was prevalent among both the early revivalists and the Pentecostal proponents. Both claimed no obligation to consult or connect with others, for they had no use for systems of belief. As one preacher proudly put it, "I shut myself up, prayed to God to lead me into truth, and not suffer me to embrace any error; I laid myself open to believe whatsoever the Lord revealed."[2] Strange that this method of discerning "plain and simple" Bible texts produced (and continues to produce) dozens of contradictory results, spawning a bizarre collage of marginal, sectarian, and even cultic beliefs.

While the evangelicals were busy erecting beautiful structures to house the saints, Darwin (1809 – 1882) and Wellhausen (1844 – 1918) were deconstructing the foundations of the book of Genesis — one through speculative "science," the other through discoveries made in higher criticism. While revived souls were competing against "First Church" down the street and ladies were picketing saloons, Marx (1818 – 1883) and Nietzsche (1844 – 1900) were plotting the "death of God," and Friedrich Hegel (1770 – 1831) and William James (1842 – 1910) were haggling over how relative was so-called ultimate truth. In the midst of Freud's (1856 – 1939) and Dewey's (1859 – 1952) schemes to mesmerize the psyche of the masses, many popular preachers were preoccupied with the cause of the democratic message. The believers, however, did not ignore all of the fanciful philosophies afloat; along with the "saint of rationalism" (as John Stuart Mill has been christened), the saints of revivalism bought hook, line, and sinker into the theory of pragmatism. Threatening challenges from around the world were knocking at our door, but was anyone home?

This same lack of mental alertness that allowed the above-mentioned ideologies to take root also gave rise to a garden variety of cults. This brief window of time witnessed Joseph Smith (1805 – 1844) and Brigham Young (1801 – 1877) breeding latter-day little gods by the thousands, while Miller (1782 – 1849) and his followers were camping on a mountain-top waiting for the Second Advent. In the meantime, Mary Baker-Glover-Patterson-Eddy (1821 – 1910) was busy arranging a marriage between pantheism, gnosticism, and Christianity. At virtually the same time, Russell and Rutherford were hard at work, making banquet reservations for the 144,000 who had witnessed their way into the halls of the Kingdom.

All of this transpired while the *leaders* of popular, conservative Christianity insisted on downplaying the importance of engaging in the life of the mind through theological excellence. Their cry was, "It is not the intellect we need; it is only the Spirit!"

DEFINING "THEOLOGY"

As is the case with the terms "logic," "spirituality," "worship" "holiness," and a host of other wide-arching topics, everyone seems to have an arm-chair definition of what *theology* is all about. Theology, in its unadorned sense, is the combination of two Greek words: *theos*, which means "God," and *logos*, which denotes "thought, reason, discourse, logic, word." Thus, theology is "thought that deals with the nature of God and his relationship to creation." In turn, this thought can be dissected into dozens of subtopics. Thus, *doing* theology is the orderly arranging of the teachings (i.e., doctrines) found in the Bible, showing how they relate to one another. From this interrelationship, believers seek to understand how doctrine is to be lived out for the glory of God. In a nutshell, *doing* theology is the act of loving the one true God with all one's mind for the sake of magnifying him (i.e., making him large) in everyday life.

Theology: Why Not?

Given these nuances, one may wonder how any Christian could ever neglect, or even degrade, the act of devoting oneself to theology. I suggest several reasons. First, many may be simply too lazy to consecrate the time needed to cultivate the theological gardens of their hearts. Paul instructs Timothy to devote himself to the public preaching and teaching of doctrine (1 Tim. 4:13), and he warns him, "Watch your life and doctrine *closely*" (4:16). In a later letter, Paul charges his son in the faith, "Do your best to present yourself to God as one approved, a workman who does not need to be ashamed and who correctly handles the word of truth" (2 Tim. 2:15). Though the fields of theology are ripe and the rewards are ready for harvest, few seem inclined to invest the interest, time, and perspiration needed to reap their bounty.

Second, many may avoid wading into the depths of doctrinal investigation because of their misunderstanding of the nature of theology. They think of it as elective rather than necessary, as peripheral rather than central. They point to those who have been used of God even though they lacked penetrating theological savvy; they claim that as proof that they don't need to apply themselves to doctrinal studies in order to be an instrument of

God's purpose. Such people ignore the rule of church history and latch on to the exceptions. Furthermore, they seldom exhibit the passion for prayer, extraordinary evangelistic fervor, or sacrificial lifestyle for which their reputed heroes lived and died. The pragmatic lenses through which they peer cause them to deem theology optional, and so they opt out of the amplifying adventure that could have broadened their tunnel vision.

I should note that those who say that they can get to heaven without garnering great measures of theological knowledge betray themselves by how they act in other areas of their lives. In their jobs, marriages, tech courses, and so on, most don't have the I-can-get-by-without-much-knowledge attitude. Neither do college students refuse to pay $500 for a boring class, taught by a monotone "prof" in a cold lecture hall, while perched on hard seats to boot! They are fully aware that the better the grade, the better the job, and the better the job, the better the pay. In light of the monetary payoff, detailed knowledge of supposedly unimportant facts all of a sudden warrant the investment of long hours and lots of strong coffee. So, in light of this double standard, how should we view the Christian who courts an aversion toward intellectual toil when it comes to lifelong theological investigation and doctrinal excellence?

A third reason that many in our tradition pay only minor attention to theological reflection may be its slow recompense. Whereas we may become elated over a prized nugget of *instant* doctrinal insight, it's more likely that the process will resemble the steady tick of the clock. Like the patient pupil of music seeking mastery over Rachmaninoff's *The Bells*, the student of divinity whose quest leads him or her into the complexities and sublimities of theological thought must pay the price with time, practice, skill, prayer — and did I mention time? — thus postponing heartfelt satisfaction.

Fourth, many sidestep the subject of theology simply because they fear it. They believe that *learning about* God and *loving* God are planets apart. They forget that it's impossible to love someone unless you first *know* that someone, and that it's not likely that you will get to know a person until you know *about* him or her. To know someone, you must know what they have done in their lives and how they think. Whether we set out to build a relationship with a friend, our spouse, or our God, we must first *know* who this person is before we can love them *for* who he or she is. True, to know about God doesn't require knowing or loving him, but to love him *does* require knowing *about* him. Some, however, fear that by learning more *about* God, they will grow cold in their love toward him.

I suggest that when believers grow cold toward their Savior, whether while dedicating themselves to doctrinal debate, collecting Beanie Babies, or running marathons, it's because they are experiencing a longing for deeper intimacy with God but choose not to go to him to satisfy that need. Thus, they fill the gap (which had already emerged) with whatever is at hand. When we see this happen to a person who is on the golf course four days a week, we wonder what has transpired in his life to pull him away from his one-time fervent faith. When we witness the same in the life of one who studies theology every night until the cows come home, we lament that too much theological "head knowledge" has snuffed out his numinous candle. Prejudices die hard, but we must strive to be humble, consistent, and honest about these matters.

Temptations to Theological Pride

Though I have met many more Christians who boast over their burgeoning church, spirituality, pretty pinky rings, spiritual gift, self-righteousness, or sleek luxury vehicle, it's true that theological knowledge *can*, indeed, lead to the sin of pride. When we believe that our knowledge of God sets us above the wider community of saints, we have started to take on the characteristics of an adversary of God in contrast to the traits of his children. When we use theological acumen to belittle, embarrass, or manipulate those made in the image of God, we are playing a dangerous, self-defeating game and must repent.

As the contemplative writer Thomas Merton puts it, "Our destiny is to live out what we think; unless we live what we know, we do not even know it. It is only by making our knowledge part of ourselves, through action, that we enter into the reality signified by our concepts."[3] To be on guard against the above-mentioned pitfall, we must keep the following essential guidelines in mind. First, we *must* handle doctrine with hands and hearts of prayer. Studying theology is a spiritual act and should be superintended by the Holy Spirit. As we pray earnestly and with the right motives, the Holy Spirit will keep our hearts humble and our minds pliable.

Second, we need to appropriate our God-given reason as we study theology. In Job 38:36, we read that God gives "understanding to the mind." Pascal is right: "Man is only a reed, the weakest in nature, but he is a thinking reed."[4] When we jettison reason, we invite heresy, and if we disdain logic in theo*logic*al matters, we opt to proceed foolishly. God has chosen to reveal his treasures to us through rational means. The human race has fallen, but we still carry God's image in our reasoning capabilities. Theology, though spiritual, is also a genuinely intellectual procedure. It is through the rational medium of written language that God has spoken to us, and it is through our thinking heart that we understand the language of his "love letter."

Third, respect for the spiritual giants of yesteryear provides a quantum leap for those who wish to enter history's theological adventure. By consulting those whom God has appointed as teaching guides in the past, we will find plenty of opportunity to practice the virtue of humility. That is, as we behold the insight, richness, wisdom, and discretion of our spiritual brothers and sisters from yesteryear, we will walk humbly and more softly through the electrifying yet sometimes thorny labyrinth of theology.

THE BENEFITS OF THEOLOGY

While I was talking about the importance of thinking and theology to a group of students in a foreign seminary, one young woman piped up, "The Christian faith is about a person, not about theological controversies." This type of objection is all too common among modern-day believers, and they are right to a certain extent. But what they do not take into account is the fact that persons are about deeds, events, and ideas. If these elements do not exist, then neither does the person — including the person of Jesus Christ. He does exist in time and in eternity, in reference to who he is, what he has said, what he did, and what his words mean.

Since all Christians automatically "do" theology (have thoughts about God), the initial objective is to render *sound* rather than defective theology. This leads to the subsequent goal of knowing God as truly as any mortal can, which in the end yields the ultimate aim of theological toil — the glory of God. No benefits can surpass these; but just as a person whose goal it is to live longer secures many intermediate benefits by following a schedule of diet and exercise, so also Christians, whose supreme goal it is to glorify God by participating in theological study, accumulate many benefits along the way.

Theology aids us in becoming better disciples, because by nature it establishes our lives in biblical truth. We live in a world unlike that of any other era in history, where it's increasingly easier to become exposed to deceptive tutoring. Just consider how simple it is for believers to be caught in the confusing internet of ideas as their susceptible minds surf the turbulent waters of cyberspace! Mooring oneself to the tethers woven by great theologians and to the tried and true methods of biblical interpretation will keep one from being "blown here and there by every wind of teaching and by the cunning and craftiness of men in their deceitful scheming" (Eph. 4:14).

In regards to this preventive measure, there is no substitute. Neither dreams nor visions, neither intuition nor gut feelings, not even prayer can guarantee that you will escape the decoys of deceptive doctrines. Even many forefathers of the renowned cults stumbled in their devilish duplicity *while seeking truth in the closet of prayer.* Peter, who himself was at times inclined to think the thoughts of Satan (Matt. 16:22 – 23), wrote of the command to grow in the knowledge of Jesus lest one distort the Scriptures out of ignorance and instability (2 Peter 3:16 – 18). Good theology functions as a map, leading God's pilgrims down old proven paths and setting them free to run the race with excellence and certainty in an otherwise mediocre and bewildering land.

Second, the consistent enterprise of building theological foundations adorns our very life. We cannot help but be changed when we dine steadfastly on a diet of holy doctrine. It will do us well to remember that it was the doctrinal addresses of Ambrose that punctured Augustine's pride, and the lofty theological treatises of Augustine brought Luther to the end of his legalistic rope. In turn, Luther's well-known commentary on Galatians wrestled Charles Wesley to repentance, and his exegetical treatment of the book of Romans brought a holy heartwarming to the more famous Wesley — John. Wesley's comments on the commentary of Luther then struck a fire within the soul of the roving reverend who galloped tirelessly through America's hinterlands. Francis Asbury himself not only voraciously consumed thousands of pages of theology, but untiringly exhorted a thousand more circuit riders to do the same.

It's a grave mistake to deem doctrinal studies as a dry, dusty undertaking that merely swell up one's brain cells. Mr. "Mere Christianity" himself held a strong conviction that to avoid abstract theological works was to cheat oneself out of a sublime blessing. C. S. Lewis states:

> For my own part, I tend to find the doctrinal books often more helpful in devotion than the devotional books, and I rather suspect, I believe, that many who find that "nothing happens" when they sit down or kneel to a book of devotion, would find that the heart sings unbidden while they are working their way through a tough bit of theology.[5]

In respect to changing a Christian's life, theology also informs believers of who they are and what privileges they possess as children of God. When we know better how to pray and learn why we are here, we are more likely to love God in deeper dimensions, offering ourselves in greater service to him and following in more resolute discipleship. In turn, these by-products of theological study counteract the pervading shallowness that typifies our endangered society.

The third major benefit of devout doctrinal thought is that of being able to articulate one's tenets of faith. We have probably all struggled with frustration in trying to inform another individual of our beliefs but found ourselves incapable of putting them into words. When this happens, it's not only disconcerting to the speaker but baffling to the hearer. Dedication, then, to doctrinal contemplation helps to untangle our otherwise confused thoughts about life and God. Poor expression of one's beliefs is more often than not the outgrowth of confused thought, which, in turn, is the hallmark of laziness in theological investigation. In the reverse, studying theology will help *us* to understand distinctly what we are trying to communicate to others.

When we apprehend better the meaning of the gospel, we become better-qualified messengers to those in danger of losing their soul. If for no other reason, Christians should study to show themselves approved in order that they may best relate the message of reality to those held captive to sin. Many Christians claim they know enough to get along or have no time to invest in the impractical amusements of theology. We must never think that the study of theology is purely for the fortification of *our own* lives. In this matter, we must also consider the lost.

Fourth, theological study helps to turn the tide of homiletic mischief. That is, as shepherds mine the marrow of theology, they in turn provide theological sustenance for their flocks. As the sheep dine on the marrow, they begin to crave a diet of doctrine. Superficial sermons that are theologically threadbare are a dime a dozen. These makeshift messages composed of cute illustrations, borrowed material, mere Scripture texts, and simplistic answers tend to amplify the theological anemia found in their hearers.

"How to" sermons, while evoking short-term commitments, are often void of the careful theological reflection needed to establish God's army in the trenches of everyday warfare. When we seek only to apply truth without defining, explaining, and defending its worth, we merely hack at the symptoms of greater problems and thus are forever straining at gnats and devouring camels. A vast majority of pulpits and pews alike have come to believe that sloppy doctrine is forgivable but lengthy theological preaching is not. This is one reason why many pastors have adopted the credo of a popular preacher who wrote, "People, I've discovered, will forgive even poor theology as long as they get out before noon."[6] Tell that to Jesus!

Last, but by no means least, when Christians participate in history's theological conversation — with an honest soul and hungry heart — they begin to move out of their narrow and often intolerant views. As they become dissatisfied with their present level of understanding, they will exchange their borrowed beliefs — which often have been accepted by mere blind faith — for truth that has been mined by the labor of love. As anti-intellectual dogmatism dissolves, the practice of mature reflection, solid argumentation, and doctrinal modification will become an integral part of the believer's spiritual life. When this transpires, we will have learned much about the art of living, moving, and having our being in our *Theos* through his *Logos*!

NOTES

1. Caleb Rich, "A Narrative of Caleb Rich," *Candid Examiner* 2 (1827): 205 – 8.
2. Elhanan Winchester, *The Universal Restoration* (London), xvii – xviii; Elias Smith, *The Life, Conversion, Preaching, Travels, and Sufferings of Elias Smith* (Portsmouth, NH: Beck & Foster, 1816), 257 – 58. All of these references are cited by Hatch, *Democratization*, 40 – 43.
3. Thomas Merton, *Thoughts in Solitude* (London: Burns and Oates, 1958), 67.
4. Blaise Pascal, *Pensées* (New York: Penguin Books, 1975), 95.
5. C. S. Lewis, "On the Reading of Old Books," *God in the Dock* (Grand Rapids: Eerdmans, 1970), 205.
6. See Douglas Webster, *Selling Jesus* (Downer's Grove, IL: InterVarsity Press, 1992), 82ff., for comments on the problem with abbreviated "how to" sermons.

14

Defending the Truth: Apologetics

Always be prepared to give an answer to everyone who asks
you to give the reason for the hope that you have.
THE APOSTLE PETER

As his custom was, Paul went into the synagogue, and on three
Sabbath days he reasoned with them from the Scriptures, explaining
and proving that Christ had to suffer and rise from the dead.
LUKE, WRITING ACTS 17

There are those who spend a lifetime—we call them apologists—
they spend their whole lives apologizing for the Scripture.
PENTECOSTAL–CHARISMATIC LEADER

If Christianity is not worth defending, what then is?
EDWARD JOHN CARNELL, APOLOGIST

I was wrestling on the floor with my friends' kids when I glanced out the picture window and saw a black column of smoke spiraling above a cluster of scraggly trees a mile or so away. I supposed it to be a bonfire but thought I would double-check. When my older son and I arrived on the scene, we found that we were the first to appear at the site of a monstrous farm fire. A bewildered boy stood by, seemingly too petrified to rescue dozens of milk cows, calves, and show horses that were housed in the barns that blazed with staggering heat. He had stayed behind that afternoon as his parents had driven into town for supper.

As my son and I entered the inferno, we saw that scores of calves were anchored to their posts. One by one we snatched the helpless and bewildered beasts from the fire, leading them to safety. After several trips, there was a devastating explosion, blowing out the south end of the facility. Between the billowing smoke and bellowing calves, chaos reigned, but through it all most of the livestock survived. By the time it was over, five fire departments and over a hundred spectators dotted the scorched landscape of this family farm. I was proud of my son that day for taking a brave risk, for sacrificing, for being prepared — in and out of season. On that otherwise lazy afternoon, we had contended for what was right and had defended the innocent.

Though we didn't know it at the time, another fire would occur at this same residence only a few months later. This time the house was engulfed by the flames — the flames of an arsonist, the same bewildered boy who had set the barn on fire. At first, I was bothered that the reckless idiocy of this boy's family feud had brought risk to my own family. Nevertheless, I recognized that regardless of the evil motives behind the tragedy, my son and I had the opportunity to contend for what was right and defend the innocent victims. Mixing mercy with fear, we had snatched some of God's creatures from a deadly fire.

Jude, the half brother of our Lord, had originally intended to write a letter about the common salvation he shared with his recipients. Instead, he felt compelled to draft a memo urging Christians to fight for the faith against those who were distorting the authentic message of Jesus Christ and to aid those who were drifting into spiritual oblivion. Jude writes of unreasoning men who have rejected authority, arrogant money-grubbers, self-seeking drifters with no roots, boasters, scoffers, doubters, and flatterers (Jude 8, 10 – 12, 16, 18, 22). His positive instructions were to contend for the truth, answer the skeptics, defend the doubters, and snatch others from the fire and save them. Contention for the faith (polemics) and a defense of the faith (apologetics) were invariably near and dear to God's apostolic army.

I originally intended for this book to be a manual of apologetics for Pentecostal – Charismatic believers. As I pondered that undertaking, I realized that though some within our movement might be ready for a Pentecostal handbook as such, the majority might not have even grappled with the validity of the subject. Then I was disquieted by a subsequent realization that beyond the necessity of providing a defense for apologetics, I had to lay the groundwork first by defending the intellectual life. Thus, the inspiration arose for the volume you now hold in your hand. The importance of the life of the mind is the key to accepting the validity of apologetics. If one seriously questions the merit of reason, logic, argumentation, philosophy, science, and theology in the life of the believer, there is little need to demonstrate how to utilize these in defending the faith.

Thus, like Jude (minus the canonical inspiration), I write: Beloved, when I gave all diligence to write to you of the way of apologetics, it became needful for me to write to you and exhort you that you should consider the advantage of reason, theology, education, and the intellect that was once delivered to, but has been neglected by, many of the saints.

DEFINING APOLOGETICS

Contrary to our common use of the word "apology," which indicates an admission of error or an expression of regret, an "apology" in the biblical sense is *a rational defense of the Christian faith.* Paul, in his letter to the Philippians, speaks of himself as having been brought to Rome "for the *defense* of the gospel" (Phil. 1:7, 16). Peter too urged those who found themselves in hostile territory to prepare "to give a *defense* to everyone who asks" (1 Peter 3:15, NKJV). In both of these cases, the word "defense" is the English translation of the Greek term *apologia*, which means "a speech in defense of something"; thus, Christian apologetics means to provide responses for the essential question, "Is Christianity rationally defensible?"[1]

As we have seen, the task of theology is to outline the content of the Bible's teaching on various matters relating to God and humankind. The task of apologetics, then, is to demonstrate the truthfulness of these teachings. As with all intellectual effort dedicated to explaining the faith, so also *apologetics is an act of spiritual warfare*. It takes little effort to offer trite replies to our skeptics or to claim to have cast down a multitude of menacing spirits. But preparing to skillfully supply answers to excellent questions about our faith takes much study, discipline, and patience. Because modern-day believers tend toward quick-fix measures, competency in apologetics is relatively rare in our movement. Warfare for human souls is not supposed to be easy. Thus, as people of Spirit and power, we must hear what the Spirit says about defending the faith and trust God for the *power to deny ourselves* as we prepare to give great answers to those who ask weighty questions.

DEFENDING THE DEFENSE OF THE FAITH

If God is big enough to defend himself, if believers possess the power of Christ, if our Father will give words to speak when they are needed, and if many come to Christ without the aid of apologetics — then why consecrate our precious time to come up with rational replies to queries dealing with Christianity? The clearest answer is that *God commands that we do*. Though there may be numerous other reasons, this should settle the matter. Yet for many this doesn't suffice. These, then, must take up the foreboding task of arguing with God about why he demands that we engage with lost human beings concerning his demands on them. I find it somewhat puzzling that many who refuse to prepare to defend their faith nevertheless expect the apologist to give several good and rational answers for exercising apologetic adeptness. In keeping with the spirit of apologetics, I will supply the reasons why every Christian should be prepared to defend the faith.

(1) In the Old Testament, Moses and the prophets put to use measures of defense when confronting an unbelieving world. The revelation of God resided as a solitary island of truth in a tumultuous sea of pagan thought. It has been pointed out that Genesis 1:1 is perhaps the epitome of biblical examples of the apologetic technique. In one fell swoop this verse rebutted all of the prevailing pagan and heretical views of the origin of life in the ancient world.[2] Even today, atheism, polytheism, naturalism, humanism, and evolutionism are all challenged by this one verse. In a sense, the next 1,400 pages of the Bible act as the proofs that validate this master proposition.

In addition, the prophets repeatedly appeal to the facts of history, prophecy, creation, careful logic, and providence in order to reason with the other nations. Tightly reasoned arguments are scattered throughout the Pentateuch, Psalms, and Prophets, pointing to God's existence and marking out humanity's accountability to his Maker. The protracted Socratic-style argument presented by God himself to Job's objections (Job 38 – 41) is a prime example of hemming in a skeptical mind via the piercing arrows of logic.

(2) Jesus was a master thinker, who used a multitude of apologetic strategies. By performing miracles and through logic and debate, he turned interrogators on their heads. The gospels also reveal a Messiah who was thoroughly acquainted with the philosophical and doctrinal misnomers of the Pharisees and Sadducees. Thus, he was able to work circles around their inaccuracies, showing them not only *that* they were wrong but *where* they erred (see Matt. 21:23 – 27; 22:15 – 46; Luke 13:10 – 16; 18:2 – 8; John 5; 7:21 – 23; 8). He also used compelling rationale in his parables, proving his case so well that his enemies often became frustrated and infuriated. His skill in argumentation, his emphasis on the mind, and his desire as well as ability to provide good answers to difficult and controversial questions are summed up well in the gospel narratives that record the discussions between Jesus, the Pharisees, the Herodians, and the Sadducees. Note this example:

> One of the teachers of the law came and heard them [Jesus and the Sadducees] *debating.* Noticing that *Jesus had given them a good answer,* he asked him, "Of all the commandments, which is the most important?"
>
> "The most important one," answered Jesus, is this: '... Love the Lord your God with all your heart and with all your soul and *with all your mind* and with all your strength.'" (emphasis added)

(3) Paul's letters are packed with illustrations, rational arguments, historical examples, and reasonable retorts aimed at the accusations, doubts, and false reasoning of skeptics. A quick glance at the book of Acts will testify to his apologetic missionary methods. Luke writes that it was Paul's *custom* to *reason with, explain, prove, debate, persuade, defend, refute, argue,* and *discuss* as he endeavored to evangelize the cynical, rebel sheep of Israel as well as the cerebrally-bent, though skeptical Greeks (Acts 17:2 – 4; 11 – 12, 16 – 34; 18:4 – 13, 19, 28; 19:8 – 10; 22:1; 25:16).

Wherever falsehood had "poisoned [human] minds" (Acts 14:2), Paul set the record straight with penetrating reason. Wherever inquisitive intellects "examined the Scriptures daily" to determine whether what Paul said was true (17:11), the apostle came alongside to affirm the harmony of the Old and New Testaments. Wherever cynics sought to discredit the gospel of Christ, Paul sought, in return, to demolish their lies with iron-cutting arguments. No doubt, he recognized the peculiar connection between lost souls, the fear of death, the power of God, and the employment of persuasion. As he put it in 2 Corinthians 5:11, "Since, then, we know what it is to fear the Lord, we *try to persuade* men."

(4) The New Testament writings instruct believers to defend the faith. In his second letter to the charismatic church at Corinth, Paul challenges the Corinthians to wage spiritual warfare by demolishing arguments and to deal with false allegations opposed to scriptural teaching. The warfare Paul refers to takes place in the realm of thought and speech (2 Cor. 10:4 – 5). As believers in every age furnish honorable answers to calculating critics and seeking souls, they undoubtedly follow Paul, just as Paul followed Christ (1 Cor. 11:1).

In Titus 1:9, Paul uses apologetic terminology to instruct church leaders how to "*refute* those who oppose*" sound doctrine. The word "refute" (*elencho*) means simply "to convince." Paul performed this very task for two years in the Ephesian lecture hall of Tyrannus, where he refuted the obstinate and mentored the malleable to such a degree that all who lived in the province of Asia heard the message and its defense (Acts 19:9 – 10).

(5) The best-known biblical endorsement of apologetics is found in 1 Peter 3:15. In this passage, Peter commands Christians to *be ready* also to furnish *answers* or a *defense* when asked by seekers or skeptics what their *reason* or logical explanation is for their belief that Christianity is true. The verb "ask" (*aiteo*) indicates that these questions occur in normal everyday conversation, not in a formal court of law. The key words "always" and "to everyone" indicate the scope of time and influence for apologetic activity. In other words, *all* Christians are to prepare to answer *all* questions asked by *any* person at *any* time and under *any* circumstance. Most important, this is to be done with gentleness and respect!

(6) The early church fathers assumed the role of apologetics from the apostles and New Testament writers. In fact, the second century A.D. has been called "The Age of the Apologists."[3] As Christianity spilled forth from the borders of Palestine into the uttermost parts of the Roman Empire, it encountered all manners of opposition. False philosophies, pagan religions, humanistic thought, imperial edicts, oddities of culture, and constraints of every kind confronted the fledgling church. In response, the patristic "warrior prophets" who clung to the coattails of the apostles rose up to defend Christianity against the unjust accusations that had led to persecution and martyrdom.

Quadratus (A.D. 120) wrote to Emperor Hadrian, arguing for the superiority of the Christian faith, contrasting it with Jewish and pagan worship. Aristides (c. 130) described the one true God and showed how Chaldean, Greek, and Egyptian notions of deity were inferior to that of Christianity. Justin Martyr (c. 100 – 165) wrote *Against Heresies*, wherein he combated hedonism and gnosticism. Athenagoras defended the resurrection of Christ, Tatian (110 – 172) demonstrated the harmony of the gospels, and Origen (185 – 254) championed creation's cause over the inadequacies of alternative cosmologies. Others contended for the deity of Christ and the inspiration of the Scriptures. They scrapped with atheism, confronted polytheism, and answered the allegations of contradiction in both Old and New Testament books. Like their senior brothers in the faith, the second-century saints prepared to answer those who attempted to maliciously thrust their swords of criticism into the breastplate of the righteous, and they provided intellectual and spiritual satisfaction to many who probed for reasonable resolutions to their haunting doubts.[4]

(7) Human beings have been created in the image of their reasoning God. When we reason, explain, prove, debate, and give good arguments, we exhibit attributes granted by our Creator. What better way to put to use the divine gift of reason than by providing satisfactory accounts of Christ's truthfulness? Contrary to popular Christian dogma, faith *does not* transpire in an empty head, and reason and knowledge are not the opposites of faith

and experience; they are allies, not rivals. They stand *together* against irrational thought, mere feelings, superstition, and prejudice.

Faith in the gospel message is not meant to be absent of reason, and the Holy Spirit does not convert the soul without data. Thus, a gospel emptied of its contents teeters on the brink of irrational mysticism, producing not only "another gospel" but hybrid believers whose faith is rooted firmly in thin air! Because the gospel makes sense, not *non*sense, believers are called upon to use apologetic reasoning, which in turn reflects the character of their God.

(8) Christians are obliged to participate in apologetics because unbelievers have some very good questions. An inquisitor may merely be looking for loopholes, using a smokescreen, or challenging Christianity for sport, or he may be sincerely seeking for relief from agonizing doubt. Regardless of the motive for asking, Christians should be able to provide fair and competent answers. Though apologetics can win adherents over to Christianity, its chief design is to give good answers to good questions.

(9) Apologetics can help eliminate barriers to faith and so assist unbelievers in welcoming the message of Jesus Christ. Of course, apologetics doesn't produce conversion; only the Holy Spirit through the shared Word can accomplish that. But by demolishing objections (not objectors), the way can be cleared for a person to consider the gospel. God is not helpless without apologists; but he has chosen to use us to make ready the soil of men's souls in the same way that he uses us to share the message of Christ itself. Without a preacher, none will hear the gospel (Rom. 10:14 – 15). Without apologists many will hear, but some will be incapable of swallowing the truth because of intellectual and cultural barricades. These are the ones to whom God refers as needing good answers for placing one's hope in Christ.

If the technique of apologetics seems too mundane or carnal, consider the fact that God uses our testimonies, a special song, or acts of everyday kindness to crush the pride and perforate the otherwise sealed-up souls of hell-bound humanity. It's not unheard that God makes use of deeds such as baking a pie for a lonely neighbor, mowing a lawn for a rude skeptic, or babysitting for a single mom in distress. God has used each of these pre-evangelistic acts of love to eliminate hostility and open the way for sharing the love of Jesus. If God can use these ordinary means, then he can certainly make use of the extraordinary instrument of apologetics.

(10) Preparing to defend the faith can encourage Christians by giving them fortitude and certitude. It not only helps them to see that their faith can stand the test against critics, but it also aids them in moving forward into the otherwise intimidating arena of public and private witnessing. Furthermore, when in times of testing and doubt, when feelings are fickle and circumstances are grave, the believer can ward off the personal invasion of schemes rooted in satanic uncertainty. This produces a consistent source of boldness for life and ministry.

(11) Apologetics is needed because we live in a day and age when various breeds of newfangled concepts are disputing the uniqueness of Christianity. Postmodernism, when

mixed with secularism, is perhaps our most severe contemporary challenge, for it hazes the senses and shatters the sanity of many within our culture. Though not evil within itself, postmodernism is a carrier of many potent and disturbing concepts, for she often accommodates a lack of belief in objective truth.

For postmodernists, independent and constant reality is discarded, descriptive language is relative, self-awareness and self-esteem are ultimate, and religion, myth, and science are all tossed in the same philosophical hat. In years past (1780s – 1960s), the Western mind has sought for truth in reason apart from revelation, but the tide has turned. Chaotic, irrational thought is now in vogue, which essentially means that everyone is free to interpret life according to the whim of the moment. As an intuitively-led people, we must also take heed, guarding our minds against the subjective, relativistic tempest of postmodern thought.

Moreover, if the present-day church is not careful, she will fail to take advantage of the unique evangelistic opportunity being afforded to her because of the postmodern syndrome. In a culture of religious pluralism and moral relativism, the standard and hope of an eternal Christ *can become* remarkably attractive. Whereas confusion, disheartenment, and meaninglessness ooze from the grim darkness of humanistic postmodernism, in their place order, encouragement, and significance radiate from Jesus Christ. When the darkness gets darker, the light shines more brilliantly. The day is upon us. Toss your bushels to the wind, prepare to probe the hearts of the postmodern masses, and allow your apologetic light to shine in a progressively darkened culture!

(12) Practicing apologetics is also valuable because it *has* helped many to enter into the kingdom of God. Beginning with the early church, you can find a consistent trail of otherwise restless and rambling souls who, through the apologetic endeavors of faithful witnesses, placed their hope in God's Son. From Justin Martyr in A.D. 130 to Frank Morison in 1930, many who have sought truth point to apologetics as the schoolmaster that led them to conversion.

Consider the following men of faith who have surrendered to Christ after having their objections to Christianity demolished.

- C. S. Lewis yielded his life to God after reading Chesterton's defense of Christ's uniqueness in *The Everlasting Man*.
- Chuck Colson, soon after the Watergate scandal, submitted to the Lord as a consequence of reading Lewis's apologetic work *Mere Christianity*.
- Viggo Olson, M.D., launched into a detailed study of Christianity with the design of dismantling her scaffolding. After combing through countless volumes of apologetic works, both he and his wife bowed their hearts to the living Savior.
- Lee Strobel, author of *The Case for Christ*, was converted as a result of attempting to dethrone Christ's claims.[5]
- John Warwick Montgomery, apologist and professor of law, was led to Christ through the relentless witness of a college roommate. He had fed Montgomery a healthy diet of the best and latest apologetic material available.

- Frank Morison, who penned the classic volume *Who Moved the Stone?* set out to prove that Christ's resurrection was nothing but a myth. His scrutiny, however, led him to an ironclad faith.
- Finally, Josh McDowell, one of the most distinguished modern defenders of the faith, like Olson, Morison, and Strobel, was determined to demonstrate Christianity's error. In the course of his venture he became persuaded that the Scriptures were trustworthy and surrendered his one-time skeptical heart to the One whom he had discovered was more than just a carpenter.[6]

These examples should come as no surprise to those who are familiar with the book of Acts. In Thessalonica Paul *reasoned with the Thessalonians from the Scriptures, explaining and proving* the reality and significance of Christ's death and resurrection (Acts 17:2 – 5). The Bereans, too, *weighed the evidence* before them (17:11 – 12). In Athens, Paul quoted Greek philosophers and poets and provided arguments on creation, the brotherhood of man, religious longings, and the resurrection. (17:16 – 34). In Corinth he preached, testified, *persuaded*, and *reasoned* with its inhabitants (18:4, 5, 8, 13, 19). In each of these cases, we see many souls relinquishing the rule of their life to Jesus Christ as a result of apologetic-enriched ministry.

DO WE HAVE ANSWERS?

Allow me to hurl before you a handful of questions that need provocative apologetic discourse today:

- How do you know truth exists?
- How do you know there is a God?
- If God is so good, then why did he make the devil and people who are so bad?
- If God is good, how can he send people to hell forever?
- If God knows the future, then why does he not change it?
- If human beings wrote the Bible, then how can we be certain that they made no mistakes?
- If God chose which books were to be in the Bible, how do we know that *he* chose them?
- I have a book showing thousands of mistakes in the Bible; what do you say to that?
- If Jesus was God and he died, did God die?
- Why has the Bible changed so much throughout history?
- Can God give new revelation today; if so, is it equal to Scripture?
- If God wants everyone to be saved, then is God still in control if he doesn't get what he wants?
- If there are hundreds of interpretations of the Bible, how can we tell which is the right one?

Get the picture? There are hundreds of good questions that are asked, not only by skeptics and critics but also by thinking Christians. The creation-evolution debate alone yields a multitude of intriguing inquiries. Each heresy, difficult saying in the Bible, and alleged discrepancy also provides abundant ammunition for the cultist or honest doubter. Pragmatism, pluralism, secularism, and postmodernism all render their own legion of brain-twisting, soul-searching controversies. And when one takes into consideration the newest problem areas in the realm of medicine, science, technology, cyberspace, and bioethics, the arena expands exponentially.

In such a complicated atmosphere, we must be scrupulous about our facts, attitudes, and responses. Many who claim to have answers merely revert to circular reasoning or offer nothing more than worn-out, simplistic comebacks, which fall far short of qualifying as satisfactory solutions. But self-protectionism, dogmatic but untested beliefs, and emotional responses are not suitable for the soldier of Christ. We are called to demolish arguments, gird up the loins of our minds, study to show ourselves approved, and prepare to provide *superb* answers to great questions. As we function in this capacity with humility, compassion, and gentleness, we will not only enter into obedience to our Master's apologetic call, but we will glorify our God by reflecting his mind, love, and wisdom before those who are desperately in need of a Savior.

NOTES

1. Colin Brown, *New International Dictionary of New Testament Theology*, 1:51.

2. Henry Morris, *The Genesis Record* (Grand Rapids: Baker, 1976), 37 – 38.

3. F. F. Bruce, *The Defense of the Gospel in the New Testament* (Leicester, Eng.: InterVarsity Press, 1977), vii.

4. Robert Grant, *Greek Apologists of the Second Century* (Philadelphia, PA: Westminster, 1988), 34 – 175; David W. Bercot, *A Dictionary of Early Christian Beliefs* (Peabody, MA: Hendrikson, 1998), 265.

5. Viggo Olsen, *Daktar: Diplomat in Bangladesh* (Grand Rapids: Kregel, 1996); Lee Strobel, in the "Foreword" of R. C. Sproul's *Reason to Believe* (Grand Rapids: Zondervan, 1978), 6 – 7; idem, *The Case for Christ* (Grand Rapids: Zondervan, 1998), 13 – 15. Zondervan has numerous letters on file of people who have come to salvation in Jesus Christ as a result of reading *The Case for Christ*.

6. John Warwick Montgomery, *Evidence for Faith* (Dallas, TX: Probe Books, 1991), 9 – 11; Frank Morison, *Who Moved the Stone?* (London: Faber and Faber, 1972), back cover; Josh McDowell, *The Best of Josh McDowell* (Nashville: Nelson, 1993), 13 – 19.

15

Thinking about Reality: Philosophy

Good philosophy must exist, if for no other reason,
because bad philosophy needs to be answered.
C. S. Lewis

I understand the philosophical quest as an existential experience centered in the core of
the human mind, a spontaneous, urgent, inescapable stirring of a person's innermost life.
Josef Pieper, philosopher

For several years, while my brother and I travelled on foot, our manner was for him
that walked behind to read aloud some book of history, poetry, or philosophy.
John Wesley

During the years 1985 – 1988, I spent many of my sultry southern Louisiana evenings beside the soggy banks of the Mississippi. My wife and I lived only a mile from this famed mud-tinted waterway. Thus, in the evenings I jogged down to the levee, wove my way through the swampy gardens of moss-laden live oaks, and prayed to my Father in secret while pondering the beauty of his creation. In the Algonquin Native American tongue, this enormous causeway was named "Misi-Sipi," literally meaning "Big Water."

Often I sat mesmerized beside this gargantuan continental artery, imagining the plight through which its ripe contents passed on its way toward the Gulf Coast. I would mentally map out its most northern navigation from St. Paul, Minnesota, where crystal clear streams converged, to its convulsive clashings with the miry Missouri and Ohio Rivers. I was intrigued that what I witnessed waltzing southward was an ad hoc mixture of elements absorbed from thirty-one states and two Canadian provinces. Along its 2,350-mile journey, this meandering river had sifted sediment from the glacial sluiceways of Wisconsin, from the lowlands of the interior and Great Plains, and even from the august Appalachians — a river vital to tens of millions within the United States.

One could easily imagine that in some mysterious way, because of its power and might, this powerful stream was dependent directly and purely on the Creator. But God often uses that which already exists in order to "create" what appears new. In regards to the Misi-Sipi, she would be but a mere winding bed of dust if it wasn't for the ungrudging donations of a 1.2 million square-mile delicate drainage system. The mighty Mississippi was comprised of thousands of sacrificial tributaries. In a similar vein, the waterways of Christian theology, methodology, and practice are likewise, in many respects, the results of ideological streams and rivulets. Christianity through the ages has been shaped and directed by the cultural currents and philosophical sediments that have gone before her.

Why this geography lesson? Simply because we are prone to forget that great natural and even supernatural events, formations, and movements result from things that have preceded them. God used catastrophic waters and debris to carve out Colorado's grandiose canyon; he maneuvered the coming of Messiah through the genes of at least forty-two generations of Jews; and he brings to fruition the fountains of revival fires through preparing a people. Sometimes, this process can stretch from the promises of Pethuel's prophet, Joel, to the fulfillment found at Pentecost under the prophet Peter. Who we are, what we think, and how we act are all based on the ideas of those who have gone before us. The philosophical forces of each age have not only stimulated Christian thought, but have helped believers to make their faith relevant to the society in which they live.

Throughout the church age, the relationship between philosophy and Christianity has been one of strain, competition, and at times out-and-out hostility. Discussion over the part that philosophy plays in developing the mind, the origin of its discipline, and the values or dangers of delving into its subject matter has been an integral part of the ebb and flow of church history.

As to explicit mention of *philosophy* in the Bible, there is but one, and this one seems to warn believers about dabbling in philosophical thought. Upon closer scrutiny, however, the text merely cautions the Colossian Christians to eschew a *certain type* of philosophy. Specifically, Paul warns the Colossians to avoid the kind of philosophy that is "hollow and deceptive" (Col. 2:8). The culprit here is not philosophy per se, any more than faith is the felon in James 2:14 – 26, signs and wisdom are the issue in 1 Corinthians 1:22, or prayer is the problem in Matthew 6:7. To be more precise, these cautions have to do with *dead* faith, *empty* praise, *repetitious* prayer, sign-*seeking*, *pride in* knowledge, *false* knowledge (1 Tim. 6:20), and *deceptive or hollow* philosophy.

In the Old Testament the actual word "philosophy" never appears; however, it does point repeatedly to wisdom that lies outside of the realm of God's commonwealth. Egypt (Isa. 19:11 – 13), Esau's descendants (Jer. 49:7), the Phoenician culture (Zech. 9:2), and many others knew much about the world in which they lived. Moses himself "was educated in all the wisdom of the Egyptians and was powerful in speech and action" (Acts 7:22).[1] We are informed in Scripture that God is a God of knowledge and that believers are to passionately pursue knowledge, to love God with *all* their mind, and to do their best to show themselves approved of God (Prov. 1:7; 13:16; Matt. 22:37; 2 Tim. 2:15). These are implicit indicators of God's desire that we should seek wisdom wherever it may be found.

Philosophy in itself is never condemned in Scripture. The idea of a love for or study of wisdom (the term *philosophy* literally means "to love" [*phileo*] "wisdom" [*sophia*]) not only escapes divine denunciation but actually rings true of that which God approves. One need only browse the contents of Proverbs to observe that in twenty-three of its thirty-one chapters, the writer pleads for the reader to search for, attain, and cherish wisdom. Furthermore, any casual survey of Proverbs will certify that a healthy portion of its contents does not deal with what might otherwise be termed as "religious knowledge." Proverbs, as well as Ecclesiastes, Job, and many other smaller segments of Scripture, bears a distinct philosophical bent.

What, then, should the Christian make of the war of ideas that often pits the speculations of philosophy against the so-called simple, conspicuous teachings of the Bible? Does philosophy have any place in the life of faith, or is it merely a meddling pseudo-religion that seeks to beguile its unsuspecting victims with half truths? Are these disciplines friends or foes of Christianity? Are they archrivals or amiable associates belonging to a common family of truth?

ALL TRUTH IS GOD'S TRUTH

When asked the question "What is truth?" many Christians respond with some form of the cliché, "Why, Jesus is truth," or, "The Bible, this is truth." No doubt this is true; however, what this snappy superficial comeback fails to address is the issue of truth outside of the Bible. The simple fact is, we all believe there is truth outside of the words of Scripture, though most are not quick to state this for fear that someone might suspect that they are too "progressive" or even relativistic. The reason we think this way is because we have dedicated little time to the enterprise of thinking about *how* we think and *why* we think *what* we think. Any Christian who has walked with God for an extended period of time must have realized already that not everything in the Bible is truth and that there is truth outside of the realm of the Old and New Testament.

Before the reader prematurely slams this book shut, let me explain. When Satan said to Eve, "You will not surely die" (Gen. 3:4), he was lying; but this lie is found in the Scriptures. When Peter, speaking to the servant girl, maintained that he didn't even know this person called Jesus, he too was fibbing. Yet there it is, right toward the beginning of the New Testament — a prophet *not* telling the truth. So what gives? Someone might say (as I have heard it argued): "Yes, but Peter didn't 'have' the Holy Spirit yet." We don't have time to probe this in depth right now, but I will say that we must be careful with this line of thinking; we can easily work ourselves into a corner when we realize that Peter also recognized Jesus as "the Son of the living God" (Matt. 16:16) before he "had" the Holy Spirit.

So, yes, Peter was waiting for the outpouring and indwelling at Pentecost *just like all of the Old Testament prophets*! Nevertheless, we trust that the Old Testament architects, from Moses to Malachi, were led by the Holy Sprit, do we not? At least Peter thought so (2 Peter 1:21). Ultimately, it doesn't matter on which side of Pentecost Peter stood; he lied. So, whether the example is the serpent in the Garden of Eden speaking to the first Adam — "you surely will not die" — or the serpent at Caesarea Philippi, speaking to the last Adam through Peter — "you surely will not die" (Matt. 16:22) — lies are not truth, even if they are found in the Bible. In a similar vein, truth is not falsehood, even if it is *not* found in the Bible. Augustine vied that all truth is God's truth, wherever it may be found. He stated: "We must show our Scriptures not to be in conflict with whatever [our critics] can demonstrate the nature of things from reliable sources."[2]

So, let's return to the suggestion that all Christians believe in truth outside of the Bible. Though we trust that "2 + 2 = 4" is absolute truth 100 percent of the time, how do we explain the fact that it's found nowhere in the Holy Writ? We also believe that two things cannot simultaneously, in the exact same way, be precisely the same and exactly the opposite. Another truth held universally by Christians is that, if A = B, and B = C, then by unqualified necessity, A = C. Of course, not everyone would readily acknowledge the above postulates; however, when it comes to everyday life, it seems that even relativists abide by the laws of noncontradiction. For example, as apologist Ravi Zacharias points out, even though Hindus may claim that something can be *both* true *and* untrue concurrently, they, too, look both ways when crossing a road, for they know it will *either* be the bus *or* them that survive an unsolicited collision.[3]

If indubitable mathematical maxims, unwavering laws of noncontradiction, and the pristine principles of logic are all true, yet are not spelled out in our leather-bound Authorized King James Version, how then do we explain that truth resides outside of Scripture? Again, the answer is that *all truth is God's truth*, whether found in a history book, compendium of logic, scientific treatise, psychological evaluation, philosophical formula, or fictional literary masterpiece.

In keeping with Augustine's above-mentioned adage, Clement of Alexandria suggests that knowledge is of special value to Christians and that they are to take from each branch of study its contributions to truth. Wesley too held that it is perilous for Christians to court the notion that only believers can teach them. He was convinced it is a grave mistake *to think this way for even a moment*. I am persuaded that because Full Gospel devotees often lack this comprehensive view, they enter handicapped into the stadium of thought where the battles of ideas transpire and the war of worldviews is waged.[4]

When Christianity is misunderstood strictly as a religious system, when "spirituality" is narrowed down to that which concerns only devotional matters, or when the so-called secular issues of life are moderately divorced from so-called sacred affairs, *Christianity has missed her mark*. When our faith is viewed as such, an essence of disconnectedness pervades every sphere of our lives. This hinders us from regarding the world, everything in the world, and the activities of human beings and their minds as an integrated, comprehensive, and consistent system of truth. But studying philosophy can help us to see the awe-inspiring, coherent mosaic of maximum reality.

WHAT IS PHILOSOPHY?

As noted above, philosophy is, in general, the practice of loving wisdom. Here, wisdom is tantamount to *reality*, and the passion with which we seek to comprehend this reality is called *love*. Those who participate in philosophy are endeavoring to think hard about the various facets of the origin, nature, purpose, struggles, and relationship of the human race to all that exists. Philosophers examine not only their own lives but seek to know how all of reality *fits together*. They seek to understand the world that they live in and desire to determine how they can *know* that their particular understanding is true. In light of this, the student of philosophy peruses history's landscape in order to witness and understand how others have grappled with the questions of life.[5]

At various times everyone philosophizes, and so to a lesser or greater extent, everyone is a philosopher. In addition, everyone drinks in the philosophy of others on a regular basis. Even though many Christians would nearly faint at the thought, the fact is that whenever we watch television, whether in the form of sitcoms, documentaries, or commercials, we listen to philosophy. That is, we give ear to others' thoughts as to what is important and what is worth owning, knowing, or fighting for. We are reinforced, manipulated, or moved as to the things over which we are willing to cry, laugh, or get angry. Special interest crusades, views of morality, and political issues are hung out on the radio- and TV-waves for all to entertain. This exposure to *casual* philosophy or worldviews challenges and changes us more than what we might be willing to admit.

The art or practice of philosophizing is meant to lead us away from superficial answers and into a more detailed deliberation on *why* we believe *what* we claim to believe. In this way, philosophy is intimately related to logic, theology, and apologetics. All of these disciplines are concerned with the clarity, consistency, and the coherence of the ideas that we profess to hold dearly.

When we fail to engage in serious contemplation of life's dominant issues, we place ourselves and our entire society in a precarious position. This is true because by relinquishing these reins, we bestow on less noble minds the privilege of constructing a worldview for which *we must all pay the consequences*. C. S. Lewis points out somewhere that each person must participate in the philosophical currents of one's culture, if for no other reason than to ward them off; and if one does not have a good philosophy, he or she will inevitably fall prey to bad philosophy.

So, what is philosophy? Simply put, it is the set of assumed ideas through which a person views all of life, or it is the study of those ideas. Because everyone has ideas, all of us have a philosophy of life. And because our ideas have a direct impact on how we live our lives, our philosophy of life is not only extremely practical but also very important. As to whether a person's philosophy is good, consistent, coherent, clear, virtuous, tested, or twisted — this is quite another issue.

CHRISTIANITY AND PHILOSOPHY

In the Old Testament, the prophets of God repeatedly made use of the natural and moral order of the world to defend the religion of Israel. For example, arguing against the false gods of the pagans, they pointed out that something as large as the world could not have been fashioned by something as small as a wooden idol (Isa. 44 – 45). This is philosophical reasoning.

In the New Testament, Jesus (the *Logos*) steadfastly employed the power of logical acuteness to bring hearers to the place of facing God's holiness and their sinfulness. Jesus argued by using analogies (John 7:21 – 23), he reasoned from empirical evidence (John 5), he participated in complex debates (John 7 – 8), and he used what we would term the Socratic method — answering his questioners by asking them questions. Furthermore, he astonished teachers with his understanding and amazed the common folk with his strategic use of the natural order and human nature. All of these are the marks of philosophical acumen par excellence.

The apostles also put to use philosophical argumentation and intricate reasoning in order to expound the gospel to a lost world. Paul especially sought to apply his knowledge of the Greek philosophers so that the philosophically-minded citizens of the empire might understand better the message of Christ. It is a well-known fact that Paul quoted the philosopher Epimenides in at least two instances (Acts 17:28a; Titus 1:12) and Aratus once (Acts 17:28b). Others have suggested that Paul also drew on popular Hellenistic theology (see Rom. 1:20).[6]

In Athens and Corinth, Paul encountered Epicureans and Stoics, and in Colosse he was forced to deal with gnostic-type notions. Each of these brought about unique challenges to the truth of God's revelation. In keeping with these various philosophies, Paul sought not only to detect the common ground between believers and unbelievers, but also to answer the critics in accordance with their particular errors. Paul could not have done this unless he first knew their philosophies well enough to understand where his hearers were coming from. This is one of the great benefits of studying philosophy — knowing why others believe what they say they believe *in order to* help them discern inconsistencies in their thought.

Then, of course, there is John and his use of the Greek word *logos*. Heraclitus (524 – 475 B.C., during Zechariah the prophet's ministry) first used the term to signify the harmony and patterns evident in a world of change. Several hundred years later, Philo, the Jewish philosopher from Alexandria, identified this *logos* with the *wisdom* of Hebrew literature. John uses the same term to describe the eternal Word (Logic or Reason), who is incarnated in Jesus Christ, Sustainer of all things. According to tradition, John wrote his gospel while in Ephesus — interestingly enough, the ancient home of Heraclitus.

In the second century and following, many of the great church fathers were astute in handling the intricate nuances of primitive and contemporary philosophy. Justin Martyr (c. 100 – 165), who was born about the time that the apostle John died, believed that philosophy was a type of handmaiden to the gospel and that Christianity was, in fact, the greatest of all philosophies. Clement of Alexandria (150 – 215) conjectured that "perhaps, too, philosophy was given to the Greeks directly and primarily until the Lord would call the Greeks." In another work, he explicitly states that philosophy is "the work of God." Many of the church fathers concurred.[7]

Throughout the church age, many men of spiritual notoriety implemented ancient philosophy, and many became known as philosophers in their own right. Augustine, Thomas Aquinas, Anselm, Blaise Pascal, Gottfried Leibnitz, and Jonathan Edwards are among the many who had deep relationships with Jesus Christ and affected the kingdom of God in marvelous ways, and they are also considered by many as *the greatest philosophers of their age*. Even the fireball evangelist John Wesley, who delighted in "dipping into Plato for relaxation," wrote philosophical treatises, including an entire compendium of natural philosophy.[8]

Not only did Wesley require his circuit riders to study philosophy with regularity, but he also saw the importance of exposing the minds of school-age children to a veritable smorgasbord of philosophical thought. In his *Short Account of the School in Kingswood*, he spelled out the aim and design of the education provided there. Amidst the enormous list of necessary texts, one finds works of such philosophers as Plato, Erasmus, Caesar, Virgil, Ovid, Juvenal, Homer, Paterculus, Locke, Hume, Euclid, Newton, Livy, Suetonius, Pascal, Epictetus, Marcus Antoninus, and Xenophon. For Wesley (whom some deem as "the father of Pentecostalism"), conquering the world for Christ included stirring, awakening, and converting men's minds. In order to accomplish this, he was persuaded that the mind must be baptized with the great philosophical ideas of history. Following this directive he prepared a virtual army, and with this army he reformed a nation.[9]

If anyone questions the philosophical erudition of the early church fathers, the medieval keepers of the faith, or (some of) the Great Awakening heroes, they need simply to go to the indexes of their works and view the litany of references to the giants of philosophy. There are good reasons why the prominent champions of Christianity have purposed to know the minds of the philosophers. These humble, hungry minds were aware that just maybe, they didn't have a corner on truth and could learn from some of God's other minds. In contrast to this, the glaring fact that few leaders (let alone laity) within the Holiness and Pentecostal – Charismatic traditions have cared to study and write philosophy — this speaks volumes.

In addition, philosophy can serve us by reminding us of the common ground we share with pagan cultures. It is always of special interest, especially to missionaries, when the philosophy of their targeted culture provides bridges across which they can share the gospel message in a more meaningful way. The discipline of philosophical rigor is also of incalculable assistance to the science of Bible interpretation. The intellectual exercise alone, which arises as a result of jousting with divergent perspectives, proves to sharpen one's sensitivity to subtle shades of meaning and cultural innuendos. Moreover, philosophical thought, when it leads to major discoveries or developments, such as the earth's shape, the sun's centrality, geometry, calculus, or biological classification, can benefit the church by revealing truth about God's creation.

It is also true that practicing philosophy and studying the philosophy of others helps us form our ideas about particular matters for which the Bible does not provide *particular* answers. It is here that the practicalities of personal philosophies come home to roost.

Ideas have consequences (just ask the Jews of Auschwitz, or the mishandled masses under Marx's brainchild Stalin), and the ideas we cherish, whether rooted in a cultural, family, ancient, or community philosophy, rule our daily life. Finally, in many instances our philosophy can even dictate how we view Scripture as a whole and how we interpret individual passages.

Some of our solutions to life's problems come as a result of belonging to "the West"; others come to us by way of the media. Still others are the by-product of our Greco-Roman, Judeo-Christian, European, Puritan, pioneering, Southern, or Northern roots. Some of our convictions on these matters are due to an American philosophy, and some are held simply in keeping with mere superstitions. Regardless of their roots, our philosophies become the filter through which we work out and walk out the nuances of our everyday existence.

It is by dipping into the deep reservoir of our philosophy of life that we approach and reply to so many of life's questions. But the *value* of our philosophy depends on its consistency, coherence, and clarity. Added value comes to our system of thought when we actually live out that philosophy, when it appears to line up with reality, and especially when it's in accord with the principles written in the revelation of God. Though everybody has a philosophy of life, not everyone has a good one. Some have a narrow, stunted, bigoted, or inharmonious philosophy. Others talk a good philosophy but don't live it. Still others own an admirable philosophy and live it but don't know how to explain it or defend it. Finally, there are those who, by dedicating themselves to the study of great minds, have a solid philosophy of life, embody it, *and* are able to express why they believe what they believe. Ultimately, these become the most proficient at helping others to ascertain where they have gone wrong in their thinking.

HOW PHILOSOPHICAL ARE OUR BELIEFS?

At this juncture, some readers may still be asking how their beliefs are affected by philosophical forces. For one, when we say that we have to take a Scripture portion in context, take the culture into consideration, or say "times were different then," to some degree, we are talking philosophy. Furthermore, our very view of how the Scriptures are inspired is philosophical, for we step outside of the Bible to determine if the Bible is true. If any Christian era is at variance from any other Christian era, if the Christianity of any modern-day society is dissimilar from the Christianity of another society, or if one Christian family differs from another Christian family down the street, be assured that somewhere along the line, philosophical differences lie at the root of these variations.

Our views on childrearing, economic security, retirement, vocational aspirations, political biases, and views about science — these are all philosophical in nature. Philosophical thought is behind our outlook on marriage laws, lawsuits, gluttony, men's earrings, war, Social Security, art, what constitutes swearing, the use of icons, and methodology of birth control. There are literally hundreds of questions that can be posed to us that will help us to see that we rely on more than clear-cut Bible verses to form our understanding of everyday life. For example:

Q: If we have no record of church buildings being built in the New Testament, is it right for us to build?

Q: Was Paul the apostle or Abraham Lincoln right about slavery?

Q: Was Paul or early Pentecostals correct in their view about women speaking in the church?

Q: When is the age of accountability for a child and where do we get our evidence?

Q: Is the United States of America a blessed or cursed nation? Why?

Q: Is it right to make an unprovoked military strike on a foreign land?

Q: How do we measure materialism or worldliness?

Q: Should a man marry his cousin?

Q: Is dancing wrong? What kind of dancing?

Q: Are mind-altering drugs wrong? What if prescribed by a doctor for a terminally ill patient?

Q: Are curse words still curse words if they are found in the Bible?

Q: Should our children read everything in the Bible, including the explicitly sexual passages (e.g., Ezek. 23)?

Q: Would it be wrong to lie in order to save the lives of our children?

Q: Was it wrong to lie in order to save Jews in Nazi Europe?

Q: Is cannibalism wrong under all circumstances?

Q: Did our souls exist before we were born?

Q: How much TV should our kids watch?

Q: Can God's will for a particular person be thwarted? What of aborted persons?

Q: At what age should a person be allowed to marry? Go to war? Drive?

Q: How much education is needed?

Q: Is God in favor of sending our kids to public schools?

Q: What is progress? Success?

Q: How old is the earth?

Q: How much money should a person make?

Q: What of arranged marriages?

Q: Does playing the stock market constitute gambling?

Q: Are natural disasters God's doing?

Q: Was it wrong for Cain to marry his sisters? For Abraham to marry his half-sister?

Q: What about God's building the nation of Israel on Jacob's polygamy?

Q: Should common-law marriage be recognized by the church?

Q: What constitutes suicide? Is it suicide to request that life support be withheld?

Q: What about living wills?

Q: Does God cause what He permits?

Q: Was America ever a Christian nation?

Q: How does God view the habitual sin of gluttony in the life of Christians?

Q: Is casting lots a viable way to determine God's will?

Q: Was Paul right to condone "dictatorships," or are we right to dethrone them?

To a certain degree, these are all philosophical questions. If you take a stab at answering them, you are providing solutions that are an ad hoc mixture of theology, culture, and philosophy. And if you do not make an honest attempt at answering these, you are allowing another person's philosophy to dictate your life. So, how philosophical are our beliefs?

FURTHER BENEFITS OF PHILOSOPHY IN A CONFUSED AGE

We live in an age of irrationality, where feelings, pleasure, pragmatism, and material gain often dictate what we christen as "right." Christians, too, have fallen for the "god of entertainment," situational ethics, materialism, and postmodern relativism. Radical skepticism pervades large sectors of our society, and anti-intellectualism has found its way into the nooks and crannies of the university classroom and sanctuary pew alike. Moreover, a new multitude of religious charlatans has joined the growing ranks of those advocating Eastern (New Age) thought, the Islamic faith, the cults, and pop astrology. And, of course, with the new "information super highway" we are more vulnerable than ever to *bad* philosophy.

The answer to bad philosophy is good philosophy, and the route to developing a good philosophy is by rubbing *our* minds against *greater* minds. As we contemplate the philosophical systems of the greatest intellects of history, we will begin to jostle our otherwise padlocked minds and augment our mental agility. In turn, we will become more self-critical and reflective. As our intellects are exercised, we will work to refine our own ideas, learn to express them in better ways, and winnow some of the weak or naïve notions that we have tenaciously held on to. Our ability to recognize invalid arguments and present valid ones will aid us in defending the gospel of Jesus Christ and in leading those with bad philosophy into the love of the true *Logos*.

A healthy reflection on philosophy can also help us to understand the impulses behind those movements within Christianity that swerve too far to the left or right. It will become clearer to the student of philosophy why and how the forces of gnosticism, mysticism, and pietism gained ground in the kingdom when they did. Likewise, the powers of scholasticism, deism, fundamentalism, and the likes will make all the more sense to those who investigate the history of ideas. The alternative to this approach is exactly what we witness: a shallow understanding of the forces that have shaped the lost world *and* the kingdom of God on earth.

As mentioned, philosophy and theology have so shaped each other that becoming familiar with philosophy can greatly benefit one's theological savvy. We can better articulate the doctrines of creation, the Trinity, the Incarnation, bodily resurrection, the inspiration of Scripture, and many more when utilizing some of the language and concepts of philosophy. When we struggle to put our ideas about God into words, it's often due either to our neglect of thinking long and hard about the issues or to our lack of reading those who have already thought long and hard about them. Reading the accumulated results of lifelong thinkers is often the catalyst that can provide a much needed intellectual quantum leap for those who labor intensely to express themselves.

Apart from the litany of above-mentioned reasons for participating in the study of ideas, there is the sheer adventure of exploring the way the human mind thinks. There is also the refreshing and amusing phenomenon of bumping into clusters of thought that we ourselves have deliberated on, yet have never articulated to ourselves or shared with others. When we find a "great" mind that has contemplated kindred notions and dreams, we realize that the brotherhood of humanity fishes in a common pool of speculation and wonder. Detecting a bit of brilliance may not convince us of our own genius, but it's likely to stimulate us toward better thinking.

Finally, it is simply fascinating to sense a smidgen of Seneca or Cicero in Paul the apostle, and equally peculiar and humbling to hear Plato describe something near to the Christian concept of the Fall and of redemption in *Republic* (505 – 18) and of creation in *Timeaus* (27 – 53). To catch sight of the faint shadows of our Maker in Aristotle's "Unmoved Mover" (*Metaphysics* 13.6 – 10), to behold hints of Christ in Philo's *Logos*, and to witness from the sagacity of Socrates human utterance via a divine spirit (*Phaedrus*; 240 – 49, 265) — all of this is strange and exciting!

This process is not only entertaining, it's beneficial as well. It is beneficial to read the treatises of Descartes that deal with the existence of God and awareness of one's being (*Meditations* 1 – 3), the works of David Hume on the historicity of Christianity (*Essays Concerning Human Understanding*, 2.1 – 3), and the dissertations of Søren Kierkegaard addressing a human being's passionate quest for God. All of these serve to challenge our presuppositions, inspire the soul, and spark the mind.

CONCLUSION

Philosophy is the quest for right ideas and the ideal. And because intense ideas eventually leave a wake of consequences in their path, philosophy directly affects everyday life. Despite the fact that the Scriptures speak generally to scores of issues and explicitly to some, there is that multitude of matters for which the Holy Writ does not give detailed resolutions. Modern notions on democracy, sexuality, citizenry, diplomacy, economy, family, psychology, public policy, industry, and technology, as well as the educational, political, and ethical mores of today's world, are all to some degree constructs of the theoretical energies of pensive minds.

We have all been crafted in the image of God and infused with the aptitude for reflective and innovative thought. As creatures belonging to the community of God, we have heard his call *to love him with all our mind*. As kindred spirits of the human race, we are invited to partake in the ongoing symposium of thought where the constant conversation of inquisitive intellects speak to and shape our world. It is incumbent on us, then, to offer to this great pool of thought that distinct sliver of God's mind that he has deposited into each of us. In doing so, not only will we exercise his image in us, but perhaps even change our world!

NOTES

1. As any "Bible background commentary" indicates, there are numerous reflections of the wisdom of the ancient world in passages of the Bible as God's people interacted with their neighbors; see, e.g., John Walton, Victor Matthews, and Mark Chavalas, *The IVP Bible Background Commentary: Old Testament* (Downers Grove, IL: InterVarsity Press, 2000).

2. Augustine, *The Beginning of Truth*, in *Nicene and Post-Nicene Fathers* (Schaff ed.), 1:21.

3. Ravi Zacharias gives this cute but true illustration on his tape entitled "Answering Relativism," side 1.

4. Clement of Alexandria, *Ante-Nicene Fathers* (Schaff ed.), 2:498; Wesley, "Christian Perfection," in *Works* (Baker edition), 7:428.

5. J. P. Moreland, "Philosophy," in Beck's *Opening of the American Mind*, 49.

6. F. F. Bruce, *The Defense of the Gospel in the New Testament* (Grand Rapids: Eerdmans, 1977), 44–45; Christopher Stead, *Philosophy in Christian Antiquity* (Gateshead, UK: Athenaeum, 1995), 115.

7. See Edwin Hatch, *The Influence of Greek Ideas and Usages on the Christian Church* (Peabody, MA: Hendrickson, repr. 1995); H. A. Wolfson, *The Philosophy of the Church Fathers* (Cambridge, MA: Harvard Univ. Press, 1970). See also Justin Martyr, *The Ante-Nicene Fathers* (The Ages Digital Library ed.), 1:287, 360, 613; Clement of Alexandria, *The Ante-Nicene Fathers* (The Ages Digital Library ed.), 2:597, 1043 (*Books for the Ages* [AGES Software, Albany, OR: Version 1.0, 1997]).

8. Wesley, *The Works of John Wesley* (Baker ed.), 14:300ff.; cf. *A Life of Wesley* (Albany, OR: AGES Software, 1998).

9. Wesley, *The Works of John Wesley* (Baker ed.), 13:283–89.

16

Discovering the Realities of Nature: Science

When I consider your heavens,
    the work of your fingers,
the moon and the stars,
    which you have set in place,
what is man that you are mindful of him,
    the son of man that you care for him? ...
You made him ruler over the works of your hands;
    you put everything under his feet.
PSALM 8.3 – 4, 6

Truth comes from God, wheresoever we find it, and it is ours, it is the church's. We must
not make an idol of these things, but truth, wheresoever we find it, is the church's.
RICHARD SIBBES, PURITAN PASTOR

God did not want scholars and clever persons. He had
no need of science. All he wanted was pure hearts.
EARLY PENTECOSTAL, 1907

I saw a distressing and haunting act when I was about ten years old. Many weekends
of my childhood were spent at the cockfighting pits of Oklahoma. So on this particular night, it wasn't strange that I saw a magnificent creature — a gamecock — slashed to
death by the iron weapons fixed to the feet of his foe and spilling his lifeblood onto the red
dirt floor before a howling crowd; I had seen that thousands of times. But on this occasion, as I leaned on the pasty white boards wrapped with wire, which formed the fence
around the cockfighting arena, I saw a beautiful red rooster being prepped for the fight.
As his opponent entered, a fellow close to me hollered out that you couldn't tell one cock
from the other, that they looked just alike. At that moment, the owner of one of the birds
replied, "They should, they're brothers." For a few moments that night, time stood still ...
two brothers, nurtured by the same mother, pitted against each other ... to the death ...
perplexing, distressing, and haunting.

It's no secret that science and religion, or more specifically modern science and Christianity, have had their share of disagreements. John Draper's book *The Conflict between
Religion and Science* (1876), Andrew White's monumental study, *A History of the Warfare
of Science with Theology in Christendom* (1896), and Henry Morris's work, *The Long War*

184

against God: The History and Impact of the Creation/Evolution Conflict (1989)[1] are representative of the ongoing strained relationship in which science and faith exist. That these two realms of knowledge have their differences is not a question; yet how they differ, how they are related, and why these two brothers are in conflict are issues as large as the cosmos itself.

Rarely have the convictions of the saints and the conventions of science failed to sharpen each other's iron. At times they have fought side by side against a common foe. At other times, in mortal combat, they have slung armor-penetrating words toward each other, as heavy and as deadly as any sword. Whether the controversy has been the Copernican Revolution, Darwinian evolution, partial birth abortion, genetic manipulation, life-support systems, euthanasia, nuclear weapons, or one of a hundred other issues, the church finds herself again and again caught in turbulent and tricky crossroads where Scripture and science, and theology and technology, meet.

Though the church was in error when condemning Galileo's heliocentric theory, the majority at that time commended the religious hierarchy for their stand. By contrast, many condemned the church when she failed to link up with the daring young Darwin in his quest for our elusive origins. One can readily see that by her very nature, the church has to maneuver through difficult and delicate philosophical and scientific waters. She is comprised of imperfect human beings and thus possesses the intrinsic capacity to err. Thus, at times she plays the tragic role of the sleeping giant in a land of pygmies and at times that of the raging bull in a kingdom of crystal. Nonetheless, in other seasons she is the sagacious handmaiden diffusing wisdom and reality on all within her reach, championing true science and censuring false science that only masquerades as truth.

MODERN SCIENCE AND THE CHRISTIAN FAITH

As I have pointed out again and again, one of the great lies that Christians have bought into is that of divorcing the intellect from the spiritual life. Another closely related prevailing myth embraced by many Christians is that modern science was hatched in the steely minds of cold, theoretical, unbelieving laboratory technicians. One of modern Christianity's best-kept secrets is that modern science was birthed in the bosoms of God-fearing, devout believers.

Dozens of experts in various fields of science admit to Christianity's major role in the modern scientific age. The Nobel Prize-winning biochemist Melvin Calvin emphasized that because the ancient Hebrews viewed the universe as governed by a single God and because Christians inherited this conception, the historical foundation for modern science is to be found in *monotheism*. In like fashion, the noted nineteenth/twentieth-century philosopher Alfred North Whitehead believed that *Christianity* is the mother of science because of the medieval insistence on the rationality of God. Writing about the character of modern science in the celebrated English periodical *Mind*, M. B. Foster posits that the answer lies in the Christian revelation and the Christian doctrine of creation. English professor James Moore went a step further to propose that there is obvious evidence that *Protestantism* gave rise to modern science. The distinguished twentieth-century Christian philosopher Francis Schaeffer concedes the same, repeatedly mentioning throughout his works the Christian roots of modern science.[2]

Many other prominent scholars recognize the close connection between Christian spirituality and science, God's Word and God's world, the Reformation and the modern scientific revolution, the Puritan age and the age of scientific experimentation. There are good reasons why the other great religions and cultures of antiquity each failed to develop scientific research as we know it today. For example, though the Arabs had a deep knowledge of the world, little science evolved from their knowledge, primarily because the Islamic mind entertains a fatalistic bent (life follows a predetermined destiny); if fate rules, then the rules for God's handiwork are set and invincible to human manipulation. The Chinese system of thought also restrained scientific progress because of its lack of confidence that the code of nature's laws could be unveiled and read. The key ingredient that a divine being, even more rational than themselves, had formulated such a code capable of being read was all but missing.[3]

The Greeks, no doubt, provided important intellectual elements that helped to set the stage for the sixteenth-century explosion of scientific investigation. However, as some have indicated, the Greeks defaulted in actually producing the likes of modern science because of their lack of interest in hands-on experimentation. Since to them created things were mere forms of eternal realities, they did not seek to trace out the causes of these *mere* forms. For the Greek mind, the elements were something to be pondered and speculated about, not something to be experimented with and then used for the advancement of society. Others have drawn attention to the science-defeating views of Hinduism, noting that Hindus believe that the material world is not a "real" world at all. What then is the value of investigating that which does not really exist? The Hindu faith also thwarts scientific inquiry because of a belief that a *multi*plicity of gods rule the so-called *uni*verse. This is a monstrous contradiction in itself, which in turn destroys the idea of coherent continuity in the material realm, making science dubious.[4]

One observer goes so far as to say that "modern science could not even have risen in our modern culture because modern man believes that life is irrational and illogical."[5] Of all these worldviews, the Judeo-Christian faith alone looks at the natural world according to its comprehensive reality. Thus, in the fullness of time, the adherents of this outlook put their hearts, heads, and hands to work for the glory of God, for the appreciation of his creation, and for the love and aid of humankind.

GOD'S TWO BOOKS: THE BIBLE AND CREATION

Francis Bacon (1561 – 1626), "the major prophet of the Scientific Revolution," as Francis Schaeffer calls him, set a modern precedent for the Christian's interest in scientific research when he wrote: "There are two books laid before us to study, to prevent our falling into error; first, the volume of the Scriptures, and then the volume of the Creatures."[6] In articulating this, Bacon was attesting not only to fact that God is the Author of all things created (Col. 1:16), but that what can be known about God and his power is revealed in Scripture *as well as* in creation. For, as the apostle Paul declares, "God's invisible qualities — his eternal power and divine nature — have been clearly seen, being understood from what has been made" (Rom. 1:20). The psalmist too communicates the truth of God's revelation in nature: "The heavens declare the glory of God; and the firmament shows His handiwork" (Ps. 19:1 NKJV).

It is true, of course, that only God's revelation in Scripture adequately divulges his mind on the matters of the origin of the human race, sin, moral accountability, judgment, redemption, and grace. Our first responsibility, then, is to surrender to his authoritative will concerning these unfeigned realities. But it is also true that the creative, rational God, who originated the universe, also created humankind in his image, and thus his principal creature on this planet is able to appreciate as well as understand the physical world, at least in part. No doubt, before humanity's plunge into waywardness, we were better equipped to participate in God's thoughts. Nevertheless, even though we have fallen, wounding our reasoning aptitude, the psalmist still declares: "Great are the works of the Lord, they are pondered by all who delight in them" (Ps. 111:2). The mandate to exercise dominion (investigation and administration) over creation is still intact (Gen. 1:28), and this includes the scientific enterprise.

Although in theory Christians have always held to these maxims in general, they became an integral part, in particular, of the seventeenth-century Puritan worldview. The Puritans believed that all areas of life and of nature were to be placed under the dominion of God and utilized for the benefit of the children of God, who, in turn, would bring glory to God. It shouldn't come as too much of a shock, then, when one discovers that many look to Puritanism as a major impetus to modern science. As historian Robert Frank Jr. points out, "The predominant forms of scientific activity during England's Puritan decades can be shown to be a direct outgrowth of a Puritan ideology."[7]

It is truly amazing that upward of 70 percent of the scientists who formed the nucleus of the Royal Society of London (a society established in 1660 to advance the cause of science) were Puritans, and this was at a time when Puritans were a minute minority of England's populace. Because these other-worldly, yet practical pilgrims trusted that the human mind was adorned and invested with venerable gifts from the Creator, they left their indelible stamp on the scientific mission that was beginning to take hold across Western Europe. This keen but balanced interest in methodical inquiry and experimentation was passed on to the next generation.[8]

In a nutshell, the Puritans' confidence in God's rationality convinced them that involvement in the scientific venture was valid. They believed that human beings were made in God's image, that God created a rationally knowable world, and that believers should view their Creator as a God of order. In turn, order is evidenced by patterns, and patterns are discernable by those who can think the thoughts of the One doing the ordering. This set the stage for involvement in the process of experimentation, seeing that God's creation has an inbred consistency and harmony. The laws of nature find their origin in the very nature of God, and since we are created in his image, we are capable of tapping into those laws. That is, we possess the curiosity to know, the capacity to know, and the ability to put to use that knowing.[9]

The word *science* comes from the Latin term *scientia*, which simply means "knowledge." Knowledge is that which is knowable, and God is all-knowing. Consequently, as we penetrate the laws of nature, we gain knowledge of that which God knew first and infused into the working universe. Though there is much debate over the ultimate nature and definition of science, in the strictest sense, science is the discipline of discerning and using the laws of God found in nature. Of course, that brings up an even more controversial issue: To what purpose are we to use these laws? Thus enters the sticky subject of ethics, the subject of another book.[10]

FROM THE MOUTHS OF THE PIONEERS OF MODERN SCIENCE

The principal players in the modern scientific revolution were Nicholas Copernicus (1473 – 1543), Francis Bacon (1561 – 1626), Galileo Galilei (1564 – 1642), Johannes Kepler (1571 – 1630), Robert Boyle (1627 – 1691), and Sir Isaac Newton (1642 – 1727). Each of these held strong convictions that the key to understanding the natural world was to be found in anchoring one's trust in the one true God.

Copernicus, for example, was responsible for initially presenting the case of heliocentricity (i.e., the sun is the center of the solar system rather than the earth). He was convinced that the universe was "wrought for us by a supremely good and orderly Creator."[11] He also believed that God had imposed order and harmony on his creation and that its patterns were disclosed through mathematics. His reverence for God (and fear for his life) is also seen in the dedication of his groundbreaking work, *The Revolutions of the Heavenly Bodies*. There he speaks of his responsibility before God to avoid unnecessary controversy and to use his God-given reason to refrain from unorthodox theories. As with each of those who followed in his revolutionary footsteps, he recklessly abandoned himself to the trustworthiness of his Creator.[12]

Francis Bacon, the father of the scientific method, found it strange that though much knowledge of the natural world was available, it had not been utilized by Christians to restore the dominion that had been lost in humanity's fall. As noted above, in his assessment God had provided two essential bodies of revelation knowledge: "the Scriptures, which reveal the will of God, and the creation, which expresses his power."[13] Furthermore, he was convinced that these two divine deposits of wisdom were provided for humankind so that after having fallen "from his state of innocency and from his dominion over creation . . . religion and faith" would restore to him the first, and "the arts and sciences could aid [him] in repairing the latter."[14]

Galileo, who defended the Copernican model, became the lightening rod of the earliest major conflict between Christianity and modern science. For supposedly teaching heresy (that the sun was the center of the solar system), he was placed under house arrest by the Inquisition for the last ten years of his life. Though he was accused and found guilty of holding views contrary to supposedly clear teaching of the Bible, he was a man of God whose life and work were profoundly influenced by the Scriptures. It is significant that he was also a devout reader of Augustine. As the Reformation was gaining speed throughout Europe, primarily a result of the voice, labors, and guts of an Augustinian monk, the scientific revolution was brewing in Italy, a result in part of Galileo's meditation on Augustine. Luther had been spurred on by Augustine's accent on justification by faith; Galileo had been helped along by Augustine's linear view of history, submitting that progression to goals was a valid enterprise for human beings.[15]

Galileo illustrates his trust in the Bible in writing the following: "Holy Scripture could never lie or err, its decrees are of absolute inviolable truth ... nevertheless some of its interpreters may sometimes err in various ways."[16] He conceived of God not only as the source of the Holy Writ, but also as "a Divine Craftsman or Architect Who created the world as an intricate mechanism," which should be studied for God's glory and for the practical benefit of man.[17]

The great astronomer *Johannes Kepler* also pointed repeatedly to the Scriptures as his gauge for life and guide for science. Throughout his writings, you can find dozens of references to his love and appreciation for the things of God as well as his keen awareness of the power of prayer. While at the University of Tübingen, Kepler wrote, "My wish is that I may perceive the God whom I find everywhere in the external world in like manner within me."[18] Many times thereafter he attested to the fact that his wish had come to pass. For example, later in life he states, "My life is only and alone in the service of Jesus Christ. In Him is all refuge, all solace."[19]

As the founder of physical astronomy, Kepler was certainly not one who would have gotten bent out of shape over the proposition of science and religion walking hand in hand. Unlike Darwin, who sought to study theology and then turned to a life of displeasure with God, Kepler desired at one time to give himself to theology, but instead studied the God of the heavens by studying the heavens of God. In the twilight of his towering life he was able to say, "I had the intention of becoming a theologian ... but now I see how God is, by my endeavors, also glorified in astronomy, for 'the heavens declare the glory of God.'"[20]

Robert Boyle, the trailblazer for modern chemistry, was "particularly concerned ... with demonstrating that science and religion were not only reconcilable but in fact integrally related."[21] He not only wrote books on chemistry, but dedicated much time to translating works on the gospel and to penning impressive volumes on apologetics. In addition, he left a substantial sum of his life earnings to be used for the defense of the gospel.[22]

Sir Isaac Newton, like Boyle, wrote penetrating books on the veracity of Christianity. In his later years, this man, who is considered one of the greatest mathematicians ever to live, invested much time in the study of biblical prophecy. Some even ridiculed him for his inordinate devotion to the latter interests, accusing him of squandering so much time on biblical investigation that he neglected his scientific endeavors. But as Schaeffer points out, "If Newton and others had not had a biblical base, they would have had no base for their science at all."[23]

Though Newton, like his contemporaries Pascal and Leibnitz, contributed much to the realm of mathematics, he, also like these two, believed that "to truly know the Creator one must study the natural scheme of things — original ordering of matter and the laws that govern its composition and motion."[24] He knew well the gravity of straddling the spheres of science and religion, but it seems, perhaps by providence, that he was to become one of the choice apples of God's eye; for he was a man of God, knowing the heart of his Master through his Word and further discovering the mind of God through his world.

Space doesn't permit me to deal with each of the great scientific minds that also possessed great faith. In view of this, I will provide just a quick chart of the more prominent pioneers of modern science who were also outspoken about their confidence in the God.

Scientist	Date	Discipline founded or invention
Blaise Pascal	1623 – 1662	Hydrostatics, barometer
John Ray	1627 – 1705	Natural history
Nicolas Steno	1631 – 1686	Stratigraphy
John Woodward	1665 – 1728	Paleontology
Carolus Linneaus	1707 – 1778	Biological classification
Richard Kirwan	1733 – 1812	Mineralogy
William Herschel	1738 – 1822	Galactic astronomy
John Dalton	1766 – 1844	Atomic theory
Georges Cuvier	1769 – 1832	Comparative anatomy
Humphrey Davy	1778 – 1829	Thermokinetics
Michael Faraday	1791 – 1867	Electromagnetics
Samuel Morse	1791 – 1872	Telegraph
Charles Babbage	1792 – 1871	Computer science
Matthew Maury	1806 – 1873	Oceanography
James Simpson	1811 – 1870	Anesthesiology
James Joule	1818 – 1889	Thermodynamics
Rudolph Virchow	1821 – 1902	Pathology
Louis Pasteur	1822 – 1895	Bacteriology; biochemistry
Gregor Mendel	1822 – 1884	Genetics
Joseph Lister	1827 – 1887	Antiseptic surgery

Scientist	Date	Discipline founded or invention
Joseph Clerk Maxwell	1831 – 1879	Electrodynamics
John A. Fleming	1849 – 1945	Electronics
Wilbur Wright	1867 – 1912	Aviation
Orville Wright	1871 – 1948	Aviation

This much-abbreviated list is representative of the multiplied dozens of God-loving individuals who have helped pave the way of early modern science. I have included in this roster only those whose specialties are somewhat recognizable to the average person.[25]

CHRISTIANS TODAY AND SCIENCE TODAY

When science becomes scientism (worship of knowledge), or when the study of nature degenerates into naturalism (nature is ultimate), true science becomes deified and thus defies God. Obviously, when in the minds of human beings science takes on the attributes of *a* god, *the* God of science is displeased (Rom. 1:21 – 32). Thus, it's only natural that Christians also become displeased when secular humanists bend the rules, furnish fraudulent data, or accuse Christianity of being superstitious. By contrast, when naïve, close-minded Christians ignore, misinterpret, or warp scientific findings, advocates of true science are naturally peeved as well. Whereas many in this latter camp have indeed rejected Christianity, there's no justification for Christians to return the favor and snub science. Instead, we should help to redeem science for the glory of God.

In order to help direct science, we must first become involved in the scientific enterprise by girding up the loins of our minds (1 Peter 1:13), rolling up our sleeves, and exercising our God-given creativity and rationality in the realm of scientific research. It will not do to hold to the unbiblical, fragmented, and oversimplistic view that the uncomplicated life of prayer and piety will bring the creation under our dominion and ward off atheistic misuses of God's laws in nature. I am not suggesting that Restorationism (that we build our heaven on earth *in order to* usher in Christ's second coming) should be our aim. Rather, the motivation for our intimate involvement with the world of science should be connected with the two great commands: Love God with all your heart, soul, and mind, and love your neighbor as yourself.

It is incumbent on us to wrangle with the mind-twisting controversial issues such as genetic engineering, medical research, space travel, euthanasia, the use of technology, the environment, the evolution-creation debate, and the like. In addition, we must contribute our pool of thought to groundbreaking research and to do apologetic business in the arena of debate. We must find our voice and let that voice be heard on the issues that, with or without our involvement, are affecting and will continue to affect the lives of billions.

We know that the Christian doctrine of creation teaches that nature is not divine but that it is God's handiwork delegated to human responsibility for its care and protection.

We also know that science, without the aid of biblical revelation, can never truly define ultimate reality. Neither can science prove wrong what is *clearly* revealed in Scripture. Still, I think that we also know that religion divorced from scientific investigation can never concoct cancer cures or cubed ice, produce polio vaccines or pictures of great grandma for our photo album. Leukemia research and laptops, anesthesia and automobiles — they all belong to the realm of the scientific enterprise. None of these will spontaneously generate if we fast and pray and sing enough.

In light of the fact that almost every Christian I know appreciates ice, anesthesia, and photos, it seems strange that we often speak of scientific advancement as a necessary evil. We should be careful not to hem ourselves into the position of a young man who argued with me that animal fur shouldn't be used for clothing. We were on pretty even ground until I noticed his shoes; they were Hush Puppies, fashioned from cow skins. Or what of the Amish man who once explained to me why he wouldn't own a mechanized vehicle. He did so from the back seat of a passenger van. Surely, it's unsuitable for Christians to allow the ringmasters of modern science to lead them around by the snout. But it's also inappropriate for God's people to speak ill of the scientific endeavor and yet thank God for increasing their store of things produced by science. This is hemming oneself into a position unbecoming of a Christian.

CONCLUSION

When Enlightenment humanists deemed their era as "the Age of Reason," the Christian masses reacted befittingly by castigating the false "goddess of reason"; but they *over*reacted by nurturing an unfounded prejudice against the God of reason by questioning his gift of rationality to the human race. In like fashion, when secular naturalists deemed that the Genesis account of creation was fraudulent and that, for all intents and purposes, God was dead, Christians reacted violently against this atheistic brand of science. But we as Christians also made a mistake in handing over the science of God to those who had maligned the God of science. In doing so, reticent romantics, passive pessimists, evangelical revivalists, and the vast majority within the Holiness movement have slighted the importance of the Christian's involvement in scientific endeavors. Modern-day evangelicals, fundamentalists, and Pentecostals inherited this predisposition and still, to a notable degree, fail to see the tremendous responsibility and value of the believer's active interest in science.

Of course, scientific research, discovery, and applications run parallel to, or are interwoven with, a multitude of life-and-death issues. So naturally our participation is vital. But aside from these concerns and apart from the material benefits that come our way as a result of science, there are other advantages to our involvement. Through embracing the scientific mission our worldview is refined, our critical faculties are exercised, and our investigative powers are vitalized. When we survey the beauty, immensity, and depth of creation, our passion for learning is increased, our hearts are humbled, our curiosity is aroused, our sense of wonder is amplified, our minds are awakened, and our appreciation for and estimation of God are broadened and enriched.

Because the theme of "science and faith" is so astronomical in proportion, prudence deems that in this succinct section one can only deal with elemental rather than peripheral points. This isn't to say that discussions on quantum physics, quarks, quasars, and a thousand other subsidiary subjects are insignificant; they are vital, but the space allowed here doesn't permit use to delve into them. And though tempted to elaborate on scientific quackery before closing out this chapter, there's room only to mention the famed hoaxes such as those surrounding Piltdown Man, Java Man, Rhodesian Man, Peking Man, Nebraska Man, and the likes.[26] But these frauds and the host of others that have been peddled in the halls of science pale in light of the illustrious myth that science and Christianity are essentially foes rather than friends.

There are *two* books laid before us to study, to prevent our falling into error — the volume of Scripture and the volume of creation. One is the Word and one is the world created by the Word. There are *two* laws laid before us — the laws of God carved on the tables of our hearts and the laws of God indelibly stamped into nature. There are *two* men. Of the one it is said, "All things were created by him and for him" (Col. 1:16), and "in him all things hold together" (1:17). He is the sustainer of all of creation and has reconciled all things on earth and heaven to himself (1:20). And the second man? He is you and I — the man of whom it was said, "You have made him ruler over the works of your hands; you put everything under his feet" (Ps. 8:6; Heb. 2:6 – 8). And, the First Man — the Creator, the Lawmaker, the Sustainer — dwells within us.

NOTES

1. John Draper, *The Conflict between Religion and Science* (London: Henry King, 1876); Andrew White, *A History of the Warfare of Science and Theology in Christendom* (New York: Braziller, 1955); Henry Morris, *The Long War against God* (Grand Rapids: Baker, 1989).

2. Melvin Calvin, *Chemical Evolution* (Oxford: Clarendon, 1969), 258; Francis Schaeffer, *How Then Shall We Live?* in *The Complete Works of Francis Schaeffer*, (Westchester, IL: Crossway, 1982), 5:157 – 61 (see also 1:225, 309, 328; 4:6, 9, 79; 5:27); Beck, *Opening of the American Mind*, 155; Tim Dowley, ed., *The History of Christianity* (Oxford: Lion Publishing, 1977), 48.

3. Ian Barbour, *Religion in an Age of Science* (San Francisco: Harper & Row, 1990), 3 – 30; Schaeffer, "The Rise of Modern Science," in *Complete Works*, 5:155 – 56; Joseph Needham, *The Grand Titration: Science and Society in East and West* (Toronto: Univ. of Toronto Press, 1969), 327.

4. Arthur Holmes, *The Making of a Christian Mind* (Downer's Grove, IL: Intervarsity Press, 1985), 63; D. James Kennedy and Jerry Newcombe, *What If Jesus Had Never Been Born?* (Nashville: Nelson, 2005), 95.

5. D. James Kennedy and Jerry Newcombe, *What If the Bible Had Never Been Written?* (Nashville: Nelson, 1998), 101.

6. Francis Schaeffer, *How Then Should We Live?* in *The Complete Works*, 5:159; quoted in Henry Morris, *Men of Science — Men of God* (San Diego: Master Books, 1988), 15. This twofold revelation of God was taught earlier in the writings of the Reformed branch of the Protestant Reformation; see, e.g., *The Belgic Confession*, Art. 2, written by Guido de Bres in 1561.

7. Holmes, *The Making of a Christian Mind*, 66; Gregory Miller, "Voices From the Past," in *Elements of a Christian Worldview*, ed. Michael Palmer (Springfield, MO: Logion, 1998), 134 – 35; Robert G. Grank Jr., review of *The Great Instauration*, by Charles Webster, *Science* (January 28, 1977), 386.

8. For dozens of direct quotes from the Puritans on the subject of science, one may wish to peruse the monumental two-volume work of Perry Miller, *The New England Mind: The Seventeenth Century* (Cambridge, MA: Belknap, 1982 print of the 1939 edition); idem, *The New England Mind: From Colony to Province* (Cambridge, MA: Belknap, 1998 print of the 1953 edition); R. J. Hooykaas, *Religion and the Rise of Modern Science* (Edinburgh: Scottish Academic Press, 1972), 130 – 49; idem, *The Principle of Uniformity in Geology, Biology, and Theology* (Leiden: Free Univ. Press, 1959), 211, 225; idem, *Science and Theology in the Middle Ages* (Leiden: Free Univ. Press, 1954), paragraphs 6, 7, 8, 12, 13; Robert K. Merton. *Science, Technology, and Society in Seventeenth Century England* (New York: H. Fertig, 1970).

9. See Francis Schaeffer, *Complete Works*, 5:27, 157 – 59.

10. J. P. Moreland, "The Definition of Science," in *Christianity and the Nature of Science: A Philosophical Investigation* (Grand Rapids: Baker, 1989), 17 – 58.

11. Pearcey and Thaxton, *The Soul of Science*, 25.

12. Lawrence McHargue, "The Christian and Natural Science," in Palmer, *Elements of a Christian Worldview*; Nicolaus Copernicus, *Famous Prefaces*, vol. 39 of the Harvard Classics.

13. McHargue, in *Elements of a Christian Worldview*, 158; Morris, *Men of Science*, 15.

14. Francis Bacon, *The New Organon*, ed. Anderson (New York: Bobs-Merrill, 1960), 119; Pearcey and Thaxton, *The Soul of Science*, 36.

15. See Jerome Langford, *Galileo, Science, and the Church* (Ann Arbor, MI: Univ. of Michigan Press, Ann Arbor Paperbacks, 1971), 137 – 58; Giorgio de Santillana, *The Crime of Galileo* (Chicago: Chicago Univ. Press, 1955), 317 – 48. Augustine's view was set in opposition to the cyclical or circular view held by the Greek world. The latter hindered scientific discovery, for if the world began anew with each cycle, there was no hope of real progress.

16. In Stillman Drake, *Galileo at Work: Scientific Biography* (Chicago: Univ. of Chicago Press, 1978), 224.

17. Pearcey and Thaxton, *The Soul of Science*, 71; Hooykaas, *Religion and the Rise*, 124 – 26.

18. Kepler, quoted in Will Durant, *The Age of Reason Begins* (New York: Simon & Schuster, 1960), 600.

19. J. H. Tiner, *Johannes Kepler: Giant of Faith and Science* (Milford, MI: Mott Media, 1977), 193.

20. See Kennedy and Newcombe, *What If the Bible Had Never Been Written?* 105 – 6; Beck, *Opening of the American Mind*, 164 – 65; Ann Lamont, *21 Great Scientists Who Believed the Bible* (Brisbane, Australia: Creation Science Foundation, 1995), 14 – 23; Morris, *Men of God*, 11 – 12; Pearcey and Thaxton, *The Soul of Science*, 23.

21. *McGraw-Hill Encyclopedia of World Biography* (New York: Mcgraw-Hill, 1973), 2:125.

22. Kennedy and Newcombe, *What If the Bible Had Never Been Written?* 104; Morris, *Men of Science*, 16.

23. Schaeffer, *How Should We Then Live*, in *Complete Works*, 5:160; Morris, *Men of Science*, 26; Kennedy and Newcombe, *What If Jesus Had Never Been Born?* 100.

24. Gale Christianson, *In the Presence of the Creator: Isaac Newton and His Times* (New York: Free Press, 1984), 41.

25. For various lists that catalog many more God-fearing scientists, see Roy Varghese, *The Intellectuals Speak about God* (Chicago: Regnery Gateway, 1984); Henry Morris, *Men of Science*; Ann Lamont, *21 Great Scientists*.

26. For explanations of how these famed "ape men" were only figments of dishonest imaginations, see Marvin Lubenow, *Bones of Contention* (Grand Rapids: Baker, 1992), 59–112; Scott Huse, *The Collapse of Evolution* (Grand Rapids: Baker, 1983), 96–103; Ian Taylor, *In the Minds of Men* (Grand Rapids: Baker, 1988), 204–56; William Broad, *Betrayers of Truth*: *Fraud and Deceit in the Halls of Science* (New York: Simon & Schuster, 1982), 119–22.

17

Enlarging the Mind: Reading

What has exceedingly hurt you ... is the want of reading.... Your preaching is
lively, but not deep, there is little variety; there is no compass of thought.
Reading only can supply this, with daily prayer. You wrong yourself by
omitting reading. You can never be a deep preacher without it any more than a
thorough Christian. Whether you like it or no, read. It is for your life; there is no
other way; else you will be a trifler all your days, and a pretty superficial preacher.
JOHN WESLEY, *LETTERS*

Because readers exert the most influence in a society, however the
masses amuse themselves, Christians may find themselves once again
the thinkers and leaders in society. Something similar happened 1500 years
ago in the first Dark Age when the Vandals trashed a civilization based on
law and learning.... The Vandal aesthetic may be coming back in the
anti-intellectualism of the mass culture and in the Postmodern nihilism of the
high culture. Christians may be the last readers. If so, they need to be in training.
GENE EDWARD VEITH JR.

Those who succumbed to being bookworms ... He [God] gently steered toward
quiet, shallow waters where we lost sight of them. They could be satisfied with
less, so less they got! Why? Because books are in themselves only dead things.
HOWARD GOSS, EARLY PENTECOSTAL LEADER

A book-burning time such as is described in Acts 19:19 would be a blessing to our land.
Our government would do to follow the Nazi government in at least one respect.
PENTECOSTAL EVANGEL, 1935

The story is told of a man who spoke with the Lord about heaven and hell. The Lord said
to him, "Come, and I will show you hell." They entered a room where a group of people
sat around a huge pot of stew. Everyone was famished, desperate, and emaciated. Each
held a spoon that reached the pot, but the spoons had handles so much longer than their
arms that they couldn't be used to get the stew into one's own mouth. The frustration and
suffering was horrifying.

The Lord said after a while. "Come now, and I'll show you heaven," They entered
another room, identical to the first — the pot of stew, the group of people, the same long-

handled spoons; but there everyone was happy and well nourished. "I don't understand," said the man. "Why are they so happy here when they were so terribly miserable in the other room; everything is the same?" The Lord smiled. "Ah, it's simple; here they've learned how to feed one another."

Church history is crowded with men and women who have bent their hearts toward heaven, receiving insight into things eternal. Often these servant subjects of the kingdom have written down these treasures to aid other toiling travelers along the King's highway. With their conversation, they beckon us latter-day pilgrims to listen to their more ancient wisdom. Yet sometimes we court the Corinthian attitude saying, "I don't need you" (1 Cor. 12:21). In doing so, we tragically forfeit the nourishing grace that could otherwise bring us enhanced ability, scope, joy, and balance. We desperately need the sustenance found in the brimming, long-handled spoons of other souls. Sometimes these spoons come in the form of books, and sometimes their handles are centuries-long, providing revitalizing vintage porridge for our famished soul. This chapter is about books and how reading can expand the life of the mind.

READING AND FULL GOSPEL PEOPLE

Though the bias is nowhere as acute as in our earlier years, there is still a mentality within some Pentecostal circles that hangs on to the notion that "books are dead things."[1] These people deem most books as lifeless pocket-sized corpses comfortably resting in little leather-hinged coffins. As I have pointed out several times, courting a prejudice usually doesn't mean that a person blatantly expresses his or her bias. The same can be said about anti-literary sentiments. This problem manifests itself in several ways. Reading very little, reading only what one agrees with, or reading only contemporary literature are three of the most common symptoms of the problem.

After the 1820s, the popular preachers of the "people's religion" were virtually silent on the importance of examining the great literary works of antiquity. Instead, men such as Finney, Cartwright, Moody, Sunday, and others not only lambasted the renowned classics but failed to support the reading of the church fathers, scholastics, Reformers, Puritans, and the likes. Something dreadful happened in revivalistic religion in the New Republic; in large measure, fellowship with the mammoth minds and brilliant Christian leaders of the past was severed.

With the added thrust of the mid- and latter-nineteenth-century Holiness movement, the treasured tomes of prior times became twice-removed from the interest of popular Christian circles. And when Pentecostalism was launched at the headwaters of the ensuing century, the "people of the Spirit" assumed that they had little need for antiquated books scrawled by pre-Pentecostal Protestants and for the musty volumes of cloistered Catholic mystics.

It is no secret that most of the leaders in Full Gospel movements have failed to champion the cause of the great books of the ages. Think about it for a moment. When is the last time a book written before 1900 was recommended to you? Can we recall ten or five or even one article in our preferred Full Gospel periodical heralding the praises of Dante, Donne, Doddridge, or Dostoevsky, Baxter, Boston, or Brooks, Augustine or Anselm, Law or Lancelot Andrews, Sertillanges or St. Thomas, Temple or Jeremy Taylor? Or how many hands do we need to count on to calculate the times that our favorite preacher has referred to Flavel, Fenelon, Frost, Plutarch, Pascal, Pound, Woolman or Watts? Furthermore, is it any wonder that few if any Pentecostals have taken possession of prominent positions in the literary world during the last one hundred years?

When comparing the prescribed reading lists of Edwards, Wesley, Spurgeon, Lewis, Sanders, Lloyd-Jones, and Tozer with the reading habits of contemporary Full Gospel people, there is much to be desired. The gulf between the great literature of yesteryear and what is popular today is wide and ever increasing. In addition to the hundreds of pastors and laity that I have spoken with about their reading habits, and above and beyond the numerous church and pastoral libraries I have perused, I have also performed various surveys regarding the same.

On three occasions, I have collected data from Full Gospel lay leaders and pastors. One question on the surveys asked that the participants name the most effectual Christian classic that they had read. Among those listed the most often were: *The Left Behind* series, *My Utmost for His Highest*, *The Cross and the Switchblade*, *In His Steps*, *The Pursuit of God*, *Hinds Feet in High Places*, *The Late Great Planet Earth*, and *Piercing the Darkness*. One-third of those polled could not think of one work that they considered a "classic." In addition, an overwhelming 96 percent attested to exclusively reading volumes written in the twentieth century. Among the most commonly mentioned, all-time favorite Christian authors were Chuck Swindoll, Janette Oke, Max Lucado, Frank Peretti, Watchman Nee, John Maxwell, James Dobson, Neil Anderson, and Tim LaHaye. Each of these writers offer aid to today's Christian; however, I would suspect that many of them would point to authors of antiquity as their cerebral and spiritual meat and drink. Why?

It is truly tragic that none of the premium theological or devotional literature of the church's first 1,800 years showed up anywhere on the surveys of "Pentecostal Reading Habits." If Spirit-filled believers herald their Full Gospel status, they should at least be compelled to show an interest in the way that God has deposited his truth, via the fullness of his Body, throughout the eons of past Christian centuries.

To be Full Gospel means to fully trust that God is capable and willing, in *every* era, to perform all that was carried out in the apostolic age. This has direct implications on how Pentecostals should view God's great writers of today and from antiquity. The Full Gospel disciple professes to believe that God still opts to bestow heavenly wisdom through his imperfect, earthly images (word of wisdom, word of knowledge, tongues and interpretation, prophecy, etc.). Of all people, we have confidence that, as Francis Schaeffer put it, "he is there and he is not silent." In view of this, doesn't it seem that Pentecostal believers should be not only among the greatest of writers, but also among the most astute of readers? But this does not seem to be the case.[2]

A quick illustration will confirm the lack of interest that we often have toward good reading material. A few years ago, a flyer was sent out to Pentecostal pastors in a certain region that indicated that a collection of between 5,000 and 10,000 Christian books was to be given away. After traveling almost two hundred miles to partake in what I figured would be a dream too good to be true, I was astonished to find that not a single pastor showed up until I had rummaged about the book bonanza for nearly two hours. Like a whirlwind, I had clutched a handful of 110-year old classic works of Spurgeon, a number of vintage Puritan volumes, firmly fitted a few stacks of reference works into one box, and began to handpick a harvest of Schaeffer, Ryle, Murray, Luther, and the like. The garnering netted, among others, volumes by Muggeridge, Manton, Boston, Bacon, Waugh, Weil, Sayers, Solzhenitsyn, Dodd, Dostoyevsky, Chesterton, and Chekhov — a veritable fortune of literary treasures.

Not only did the second benefactor arrive two hours late, but only ten total showed up the whole day. As the browsers entered the little apartment that was plastered with wall-to-wall print, they'd ask if anyone had spied out their favorites. One spoke up for first dibs on anything by Kenneth Copeland, another laid claim to the works of Billy Graham; others hunted feverishly for Max Lucado, Chuck Swindoll, Oral Roberts, David Wilkerson, and James Dobson. I glanced at the stacks that some of the others had put aside; most were books on pop psychology, daily devotionals, sermon illustrations, church growth, and charismatic paperbacks. I was saddened as I gazed at the books stacked up in columns awaiting their new homes in the studies of those who just arrived to adopt them. I was saddened even more by the neglect of those ignored altogether.

It is almost inconceivable that the rich theological, devotional, and philosophical works that nourished the spiritual giants of bygone ages teeter on the brink of extinction in the Pentecostal – Charismatic subculture. But we are not alone. As is the case with practically every dilemma dealt with in this book, there is also a neglect of good reading among Christians in general in our culture. Whether in Pentecostalism, fundamentalism, or evangelicalism, the weighty works of old remain on the severely-endangered-literature-list. Pulpit and pew, clergy and laity alike, appear to have forfeited the lush literary treasures of their inheritance.

In order to arrest the progressing tide, we must be willing to mine out the collective spiritual and intellectual wealth — the hard-earned fortunes — of the great cloud of teachers, scholars, mystics, and prophets through the books they have written. The simple combination needed to unlock their treasures is: hunger + humility + willingness + sacrifice of time. As we spill over the threshold of a new millennium, we must grasp the bounty of great lives housed in the volumes of lore, that we may become more balanced and more thoroughly prepared to carve a new course into the next chapter of *His*-story.

READING AND THE AMERICAN MIND

Because our Christian ethos is to some degree a product of the greater culture in which we have been nurtured, one shouldn't be surprised that America in general struggles with reading. To a great extent, this is the very defect that impedes our aspiration and aptitude toward recovering a national life of the mind. Among those who *do* read and desire to be hoisted into the realm of intellectual excellence, many face a colossal battle when attempting to apprehend and assimilate information in a proficient and satisfying manner. Something has changed drastically in the way we think and grasp ideas. Our very ability to capture thoughts through print has deteriorated at an alarming rate.

The modern-day mind seems sluggish, settling for superficial explanations rather than opting for rigorous combat in the arena of ideas, arguments, logic, polemics, and superior thinking. True reading is thinking at its best; testing each proposition, line upon line, precept upon precept, in order to determine whether or not the *thinker behind the words* has struck a balance between honesty and wisdom. Comparing facts, opinions, and ideas sharpens our intellectual iron, moving us one step closer to becoming an "original thinker," who can contribute to the ongoing, universal, historical dialogue that explains and defends what is reality. But again, we seem not to be up to the task.

As I have chatted with others over the contents of this chapter, some have questioned the validity of my argument. There are also those who view themselves as astute readers, yet inadvertently confirm that they too suffer from the same problem as does the majority. Needless to say, when some of the reading habits of our nation are disclosed, most are stunned. For example, at the end of the twentieth century, it has been reported that 23,000,000 Americans in the work force are functionally illiterate; 80 percent of the books read in the United States are read by 10 percent of the population; and 90 percent read less than five minutes a day. In 1987 the former assistant secretary of education discovered that a mere 5 percent of American seventeen-year-olds could read with enough proficiency to comprehend a literary essay or major historical work. Another study shows that 50 percent of those entering into a community college read below the ninth-grade level; over 80 percent of these believed they were *very good* readers. In addition, there are twenty-three countries that sell more books per capita to their people than does the United States; and in 1983 we ranked forty-ninth in literacy out of the 158 members of the United Nations. Later reports rank us fifty-fifth and sixty-first respectively.[3]

In one Philadelphia high school, 85 percent of the graduates were reported to be functionally illiterate. Add to this the fact that in some cities, upward of 42 percent (Washington, D.C.) and 43 percent (Boston) of high school students dropped out before they could even qualify to participate in this type of survey! Even as recently as May 2000, one entire Midwestern district deemed their schools as "unfit to be called centers of education," admitting to graduating less than 50 percent of their students. In large part, low reading skills was to blame for the districts' demise. Less than one in ten within the system could read on a level in keeping with their age. Finally, when the reading acumen of the twenty most "advanced" countries on the planet was tested, American high school students scored last or next to last in every category. It is statistics of this magnitude that provoked a Christian social critic to lament, "We are rapidly becoming a nation of illiterates, with a greater number of non-readers than almost any other industrialized nation."[4]

The reasons for our degeneration are numerous. Among the most notable are as follows:

- the revolutionary shift to visually-oriented communication
- the fast-pace flood of images in our society
- the peddled glut of context-free information
- the common use of the "sound byte"
- an insatiable appetite for sensationalism
- the fostering of short attention spans
- mindless trite advertising
- the general redefinition of leisure
- dwindling of public debate
- power of spectatorship entertainment
- expectation of immediate results
- an overwhelming emphasis on "the practical"
- the loss of classical education.[5]

The invasion of these cultural-philosophical forces has aided in altering our former mastery of digesting the printed page. We struggle with understanding concepts, interpreting complex data, and following compound sentences (tried Shakespeare, Irving, or John Owen lately?). Analytic reasoning skills and creative expression suffers — generalities reign supreme ("Like, have ya listened to, like, the limited hollow lingo-stuff and things that are, like, prominent among our nation's youth?"). In this frustrating and debilitating atmosphere, following logical sequences in order to solve word problems becomes more foreboding than the actual problems themselves. We face difficulties in drawing inferences beyond simple facts, and following as well as providing multilevel arguments are fatiguing for our microwave mentalities.

In short, our mental organization and intellectual discipline have taken a nosedive, and yet many are oblivious to this phenomenon. Others are aware but seem unconcerned about its barbarian implications. Whoever takes the lead to bring back to our culture the marriage of intellectual excellence with spiritual fervor will be afforded an opportunity of arresting magnitude! But, mark it down, whoever thinks that they are up to this challenge must first deal with the crippling effects of functional illiteracy and the overall dissipation of cognitive skills related to reading.

THE READING OF GOOD BOOKS

Quicker than almost any other practice, a passion for the reading of good books can move one into the vanguard of the critical present-day conflict for the dominion of the human mind. It is not by coincidence that the foremost Christian leaders of ages past, who have aided in reviving, reinvigorating, and reforming the straying church, have, almost to the man, been voracious readers. But they have not only read, they have also voiced their conviction that reading is *the* way to broaden the mind, exercise the intellect, and bring better focus to one's image of reality.

Through the years, I have collected over a hundred statements from the most notable Christian figures of the past on the value of reading good literature. When I ponder this consistent and convincing testimony, I am dismayed that the modern American church has seemingly ignored this lesson in wholesale fashion. Either we suspect that these leaders are telling the truth but we refuse to pay the necessary price, or we refuse to see their wisdom altogether. Perhaps we have simply failed to recognize their admonishment to read the great spiritual and classical works because we have not taken the time, or had the interest, to read their thoughts about reading.[6]

By indulging in exceptional writings, a reader can embellish his speaking abilities; learn from others' mistakes; enhance his depth of conversation — that is, become a more interesting person! Readers are inclined to become enlightened as to how much they *do not* know and so hopefully experience depth of humility. Furthermore, in consuming the great literary works, the reader vicariously joins the great adventurers of the world in experiences otherwise unknown. Books bring fertile friendship and provide rich entertainment and much more.

Consumption of the printed word can reveal to us who we really are and make known to us that there are many others who think the thoughts we think and ask the questions we pose. Reading keeps us company in times of otherwise loneliness, gives insight into others' cultures, brings ideas to life, and alarms us to the nature of and seriousness of the problems surrounding us. Wrestling with and ingesting the ideas of God's other minds explodes our prejudices, obliterates narrow-mindedness, slaughters sectarianism, broadens our horizons, and refines our sympathies. Excellent, challenging books educate the mind, enhance our writing ability, enlarge our vocabularies, spark impulses to service, fine-tune our intellects, shake us from complacency, prick us from passivity, shock us out of indifference, and try our consciences. Associating with good books transforms us into better-balanced, better-informed, better persons.

To be captivated by the works of literary renown, one must at least flirt with their text. Only after the reader has tasted of the past masters of prose and poetry will they be in a position to truly gauge the quality of more recent works. Feast on Cicero or Calvin, digest a helping of Dickens, Dillard, or Dr. Johnson, break bread with Buechner or Burroughs, sample Tolstoy or Newman, Carnell or Merton, O'Connor or Chesterton. It doesn't take long to discern a remarkable profundity in these authors, recognizing the significant expanse separating today's pop-Christian literature from the spiritual and cognitive concentrate of yesteryear's plumes.

TAKING TIME TO READ

One distinguished pastor, who wrote often on the value of good books, profiled the enemies of reading: sloth, excessive sleep, spending too much time on the body, inordinate amounts of entertainment, idle talk, time with undisciplined friends, inordinate recreation and sports, the pursuit of material gain, and maintaining one's material goods. Someone may retort, "We live in a busy world, unlike those bookworms of former days who had little more to do than make their way through the pages of leather-bound manuscripts." Oh, I failed to mention that the above distinguished pastor was the Puritan Richard Baxter. And he wrote of these thieves of reading in the 1600s, when men exhausted themselves by cutting firewood, plowing by hand, lugging water from the creek, grinding grain, and carrying coal, along with a hundred other daunting duties for upwards of eighteen hours a day! Before we can become proficient readers, we must first carve out both adequate *and* quality time to do so. Others have faced the same challenge. If they made room in their foreboding schedules, so must we.[7]

The "Father of Modern Missions," William Carey, educated himself by propping books up while making shoes. Abraham Lincoln cultivated the soil of his mind while cultivating the soil of the earth, binding books to the crossbar of his plow. The Wesleys read the great Greek poets and philosophers for leisure and picked up Spanish and French while trekking the trails of England, equestrian style. Likewise, Francis Asbury, the greatest of the circuit riders, became a cultured man by reading nearly 60,000 pages per year *while on horseback*! Though often in danger, weary, and buffeted by weather, he made it his goal to read a minimum of a hundred pages per day. Of course, things were much different for him; he didn't have to contend with all the conveniences we enjoy two hundred years later. Nevertheless, if we aspire to do so, we too can triumph over the tyranny of busyness, materialism, and hedonism, making place and time to feed our minds.[8]

We would all have more time to read if we turned off our TVs or computers, had fewer "things" to maintain, worked fewer optional overtime hours, and incorporated more reading into our social, recreational, family, and leisure time. We would also be more apt to make these changes if we enjoyed reading more, and we would enjoy reading more if we tasted of its grand benefits. Perhaps we would be more apt to taste of these benefits if we better understood the nature of books, for they are, in their basic essence, the deposit and pool of the best and worst recorded thoughts of the human race.

Reading what an author says is like listening to a conversation. Books are, in a sense, the immortal part of humanity's earthly experience, the most enduring part of his personality. If good, they are oracles of wisdom and truth, trickling down from the Father of lights, sifted through the soul of one made in his image, and delivered in printed language on a page for all to read, contemplate, absorb, and then apply — or simply jettison. But books provide much more! Many who have dared to invite excellent literature into the chambers of their inner soul have gotten more than they bargained for. They were looking for recreation, relaxation, casual consideration, or mere mental titillation, but instead they came face-to-face with spiritual transformation!

LOST SOULS AND LIVING PAGES

When wading through the chronicles of conversion history, I have almost been overwhelmed by the sum of saints who came to Christ or were propelled into new levels of spiritual maturity through the reading of influential literature. I am not able to provide a protracted list here, but I think it's important to mention a few of those who were brought nearer to Christ through books. In addition, it's interesting to discover that oftentimes, celebrated souls have been nourished by the same famous founts, confirming that greatness begets greatness.

Consider the cases of A. B. Simpson, A. J. Gordon, and R. A. Torrey. All three were instrumental in the nineteenth-century Holiness movement; all three were, in some respect, forerunners to Pentecostalism; and all three came to Christ as a result of pondering books written over a hundred years before their births. David Livingstone read *Philosophy of a Future State*, Hudson Taylor read "a little booklet," George Mueller perused a written sermon, Mrs. Adoniram Judson was touched by *True Religion*, and Adoniram Judson studied an old booklet. All resulted in the conversions of these great soldiers of Christ who, in turn, would shake their worlds for him.

In salvation history, you also have the sublime and fascinating sequences where movers and shakers in the faith were connected to one another via good books — like Augustine, who was first provoked to pray for God's revelation through the reading of Cicero's *Hortensius*. Martin Luther set his sights on Augustine's writings and so was drawn to his Savior. John Wesley listened to a layman read Luther's preface to his commentary on Romans, and Charles Wesley pined upon Luther's commentary on Galatians — both surrendered their lives to Christ as a result. In turn, Francis Asbury's heart was unlocked by the challenge he received in *Wesley's Journals*.

The great Puritan pastor Richard Baxter admits that his soul was awakened to power in Christ through reading Dr. Sibbes' *The Bruised Reed*. John Janeway acknowledged that Baxter's *Saints Everlasting Rest* was the instrument of his conversion. David Brainerd got a hold of Janeway's book *Token for Children* and bent his knee to heaven as a result. Jonathan Edwards penned *The Life of Brainerd*, a volume that provoked William Carey to lead the Protestant world out of their own little world of private religion into the entire world — into a vigorous, explosive, missionary endeavor; a revolution that continues to this day.

There are many more examples. Phillip Doddridge was greatly influenced by Baxter's works. William Wilberforce (the abolitionist) attested that Doddridge's writings toppled his intellectual barriers to the faith. Teresa of Avila read Augustine's *Confessions* and turned to God and Thomas à Kempis, an Augustinian monk, leaned heavily on his mentor's counsel while fashioning his *Imitation of Christ.* In turn, Teresa of Lisieux as well as John Newton, author of "Amazing Grace," attributed their salvation experiences to reading *Imitation of Christ.* The literary genius G. K. Chesterton had feasted on Aquinas for spiritual nourishment. And C. S. Lewis ascribed the climax of his spiritual search to the reading of Chesterton's work *The Everlasting Man.* Chuck Colson came to a saving knowledge of Christ while examining Lewis's *Mere Christianity.* And the president of Decker Communications, Bert Decker, discloses that while reading Colson's *Born Again*, he himself was born again.

How incredible and how beautiful is this connectedness by books. This aspect of the "world of books" is not only fascinating but is truly where the rubber-of-life meets the road-of-reading. Books change lives! Surely, whoever said that books were only dead things wasn't too familiar with salvation history! In a sense, as it has been put, "books are people," and "books once were men."[9] Again, these paperbound treasure chests are the dim reflections of the Creator's mind, filtered through the secondary gifts of reason and creativity of those made in his likeness. They pour forth thought to describe, make sense of, and illustrate God's primary gift to humanity called the experience of *life.* Books are rivers where the mind is fed and fortified, where the barren intellect is whetted and irrigated. Books serve as mentors — mentors who demand time.

Our Father has stationed master spirits like sentinels through the centuries, making available to us these fellow sojourners who possess enlarged intellects, gigantic hearts, and broad insight. These represent the aggregate of wisdom and learning of the ages; not "dead men entombed," as some uninformed soul put it. John Milton — the puritan divine and author of those great epic poems *Paradise Lost* and *Paradise Regained* — would object to this superstitious notion by declaring, "Books are not dead things, but do contain a potency of life in them to be as active as the soul whose progeny they are; they preserve, as in a vial, the purest efficacy and extraction of that living intellect that bred them. God be thanked for books!"[10]

There are so many other aspects of books and reading that should be dealt with here, but again, space limits elaboration. Thus, in a future volume I hope to flesh out the philosophy of reading, examine the whole issue of God's choice in communicating with us through word and print, elaborate on the nature of "the classics," and put in plain words how we can better promote the reading of first-rate literature. The importance of knowing authors and studying prefaces, of reading "Christianly," of building a library, of varying genres, of reading plans, and of the volumes suggested by the spiritual giants — all of these can serve us in becoming Spirit-filled readers who know how to free our minds, discipline our minds, feed our minds, bolster the "life of the mind," and mine truth from the world's treasured tomes.

CONCLUSION

I close this leg of our journey with two illustrations about two books that I ran across in two different libraries, both of which embody our reluctance to invest in reading good literature. The first book was entitled *Rediscovering the Great Ideas*. It had to do with the significance of ideas of antiquity that the author perceived as being tragically neglected. The book, which was written in 1874, had been donated to the university library in 1922, and it had been checked out for the first and only time in 1924. When I disengaged the volume from its long-forgotten tomb, it had been seventy-three years since it rubbed shoulders with society at large. If, as a culture, we are this ill-mannered toward the great ideas of a century twice-removed from ours, we should not be shocked if we find people in the twenty-first century exclaiming, "Look here, I've invented a revolutionary mechanism that will indeed transform life as we know it, I think I'll call it 'The Wheel.'"

The second book was written by C. S. Lewis. I discovered it at a local library sale in 1996. The book was in mint condition — no dog-eared pages, no underlining or scribbling, not even a pocket wherein a checkout card was to be lodged. There were only two marks on the book. One mark was in the rear, indicating the date that it was put into service (January 20, 1965). The other mark was in the front of the book, simply reading in bold red letters "DISCARD." This volume was a first edition, 1964 copy of Lewis's defense of medieval and renaissance literature. In this book he argues for the importance of reading works of antiquity and highlights the negative influence on the mind when neglecting the classics. The title of this brilliant little volume, which was never checked out in thirty-two years and was now marked DISCARD, ironically is entitled: *The Discarded Image: Medieval and Renaissance Literature*.[11]

By our sheer numbers alone (600 – 700 million planet-wide), we in the Pentecostal – Charismatic movement can make a tremendous difference in a culture where image-plastered screens mesmerize the minds of millions and where the general populace has forgotten the power of the written word. Spirit-filled believers, if they desire to, can rise to become the avant-garde in the realm of reading. The opportunities that are before a well-read, Full Gospel, deep-thinking people are unfathomable. But in an increasingly dumbed-down, illiterate, sensate, and secular society, the window of opportunity may be closing sooner than one might imagine. If we close ourselves off, if we ignore the handwriting on the walls of history, and if we insist on pontificating behind the veil of protectionism, we will only aid in advancing the problem and thus facilitate something that resembles a new "dark age." However, as men and women who choose to become agents of light and loving God with *all* of our minds, we can help to repel the barbarian attacks of anti-intellectualism by working while it is yet day, regaining the paradise of great reading that is woefully on the verge of becoming lost.

NOTES

1. Howard Goss was the successor of Charles Parham, "Father of Pentecostalism."

2. Francis Schaeffer, *He Is There and He Is Not Silent* (Westchester, IL: Crossway, 1982), part 3 in vol. 1 of *The Complete Works of Francis A. Schaeffer: A Christian Worldview*.

3. K. Barrow, "Achievement and the Three R's: A Synopsis of National Assessment Finding in Reading, Writing, and Mathematics," NAEP-SY-RWM, 50, 1982 (ED 223 658); Diane Ravitch and Chester E. Finn Jr., *What Do Our 17-Year Olds Know?* (New York: Harper & Row, 1987); K. Reed, "Expectation vs. Ability: Junior College Reading Skills." *Journal of Reading* (March 1989); J. Kozol, *Illiterate America* (New York: NAL, 1986). As quoted in Jane Healy, *Endangered Minds* (New York: Simon & Schuster, 1990), 24.; Stephen Graubard, *Reading in the 1980's* (New York: Bowker, 1983), 13.

4. As reported by the district superintendent of the St. Louis School District on *ABC Nightly News* (May 2, 2000); see also James Dobson and Gary Bauer, *Children at Risk* (Dallas: Word, 1990), 30.

5. Neil Postman, *Amusing Ourselves to Death* (New York: Penguin, 1985); Gene Edward Veith Jr., *Reading between the Lines: A Christian Guide to Literature* (Wheaton, IL: Crossway, 1990); Earnest Dimnet, *The Art of Thinking* (Greenwich, CT: Premier, 1963).

6. Among the many who talked about the importance of reading great books are Augustine, Martin Luther, John Angells, Richard Baxter, Charles Spurgeon, Oswald Sanders, Thomas Aquinas, C. S. Lewis, John Wesley, A. W. Tozer, Isaac Watts, A. G. Sertillanges, and Martyn Lloyd-Jones.

7. Richard Baxter, *The Practical Works of Richard Baxter: Select Treatises* (Grand Rapids: Baker, 1963).

8. John D. Woodbridge, *Great Leaders of the Christian Church* (Chicago: Moody, 1988), 306–12; Douglas, *The New International Dictionary*, 192; Tipple, *Prophet of the Long Road*, 90; Dobree, *The Biography of John Wesley*, 82; Sam Wellman, *Abraham Lincoln* (Uhrichsville, OH: Barbour, 1985), 48, 54, 78, 90.

9. George McCutcheon, *Books Were Men* (New York: Dodd, 1931); Ethel Sawyer, *Books Are People* (Denver: Alan Swallow, 1951).

10. John Milton, as quoted in James Baldwin, *The Book-Lover* (Chicago: McClurg, 1892), 12.

11. C. S. Lewis, *The Discarded Image: Medieval and Renaissance Literature* (Cambridge: Cambridge Univ. Press, 1964).

18

Pondering the Great Minds of God

Step one generation away from the New Testament writers to meet the men who were discipled by the apostles and you find treatises, apologies, and circular letters of stunning intelligence from those intensely devoted Church Fathers.

DAVID HAZARD, CHRISTIAN EDUCATOR

When it was to his [Paul's] purpose, he cited Greek authors just as he at other times employed the subtle rabbinic lines of reasoning.... Ambrose, Jerome, and Augustine, following Paul, learned to appreciate and utilize classical learning.

FRANCIS SCHAEFFER, CHRISTIAN PHILOSOPHER

Despite dynamic success at a popular level, modern American evangelicals have failed notably in sustaining serious intellectual life. The historical situation is ... curious. Modern evangelicals are the spiritual descendants of leaders and movements distinguished by probing creative, fruitful attention to the mind.

MARK NOLL, CHURCH HISTORIAN

Maybe you have heard of the young man who noticed that his newlywed wife had cut off the end of the Easter ham while preparing it for the holiday. When he inquired why she trimmed the meat in this fashion, she responded, "This is the way my mother always did it; for some reason it invariably makes the ham much better." With a bit of suspicion he suggested that his wife call her mom and ask about the mysterious practice. When the daughter asked why she was always insistent on slicing off the end of the holiday ham, she retorted, "Oh, the meat is always better when it's been trimmed in this manner; mother never cooked one any other way."

At this, the young man prompted his wife to phone Grandma in order to get to the bottom of this riddle; his skepticism prevailed. When Grandma was asked about the family's secret cooking tradition, she laughed and replied, "When I was growing up, my mom always cooked the ham whole; but when I married your grandpa, we were so poor that we only had one pan. Because the ham was too big for the pan, we'd slice off the end until it would fit. We just got used to baking in the same ole pan; it had nothing to do with improving the flavor!"

Just because things are the way they are doesn't mean that they have always been that way. And just because we assume we know *why* we do what we do doesn't necessarily indicate that we truly know. The modern dilemma of the lack of a Christian mind is a bit like the "shortened ham story." Because for two hundred years so many fine Christian leaders have shortened their intellectual scope, making it fit into a dumbed-down culture ruled by pragmatism, opinion, and experience, the believing masses assume that it has always been this way. What's more, they think that somehow the flavor of Christianity will be harmed if it's expanded to encompass the "life of the mind." In other words, many still fear what a well-meaning Pentecostal leader conjectured many years ago by asking: "Is our movement branching from experience to intellect? This is the rock of stumbling which has brought about decline in every other denomination's ministry."[1]

What many Pentecostal–Charismatic believers seem unaware of is that before the nineteenth century, it wasn't uncommon for the most-esteemed Christian figures to both highly cultivate their minds *and* experience profound passionate devotion. From the early church fathers (A.D. 100) to the earliest days of the Second Great Awakening (1800), it wasn't unusual to discover a fondness for emotion and experience, philosophical and scientific inquiry, spiritual intimacy and deep thinking all in the same heart. But, as I have explained in foregoing chapters, for modern believers this model of Christianity has been out of sight for so long that it's also out of mind.

In a setting like this, we have only the legroom to take a cursory jaunt through the historical halls of faith, highlighting a few of those leaders who were head and shoulders above their contemporaries. In an upcoming work, I hope to extend the scope and depth to at least seventy-five giants of faith, each of whom displayed a striking balance of reason and faith. But for now, let's take that stroll, observing along the way that whenever optimum and lasting results are found in the saga of sacred history, they almost inevitably follow in the wake of a balanced personality who not only valued experience and God's supernatural manifestations, but also cherished intellectual cultivation and excellence in thinking.

THE FIRST CENTURY

If there remains a skeptical reader this late in the game, that reader must still deal with the apostle *Paul*. Here we have a missionary, a man of potent prayer and multiplied miracles, who also possessed an incredible mind and challenged others to use their reasoning abilities. Paul was abreast of the false philosophies and half-cocked religions of his day, yet he knew how to call on his God for power. He quoted celebrated thinkers and poets, he debated, defended, proved, argued, persuaded, lectured, and reasoned; and yet he spoke in tongues with ease and regularity.

This man of great learning, who entertained God-sent dreams and visions, also challenged believers to pray in the Spirit on all occasions and to demolish strongholds with good arguments. He visited the third heaven, cast out demons, and raised the dead, but he also commanded you and me to study to show ourselves approved, defend the faith, and carve out sound doctrine. He gave the directive to be filled with the Spirit and, at the same time, charged us to prepare to teach, to recognize false science, to identify Satan's schemes, to discern slipshod philosophy, and to be transformed by the renewing of our minds. This is Paul — the first "Christian mind on fire!"

THE SECOND CENTURY

This was the age when believers rose to the occasion of defending their faith in the face of spreading persecution and encroaching heresies. In a culture saturated with Greek popular philosophy, educated Christians commended their faith with finely-tuned apologies (defenses), turning the heads of those in both low and high places and even capturing the attention of emperors.

Athenagoras (c. 140 – 190) was among the most-celebrated saints of the second century. He is described as "a Christian philosopher of Athens," who addressed the emperors Marcus Aurelius and Commodus. He wrote in exquisite classical style in order to defend the historicity of Christ's resurrection and exonerate Christians from the charge of atheism. He was a grammarian and theologian who passionately supported the gift of prophecy and the spiritual gifts, and he developed the first explicit teaching of the Trinity. Athenagoras placed notable weight on the mind, teaching that a reasoning faith is the hallmark of the Christian. He taught that "the Son of God is the Logos of the Father, in idea and in operation," and that "the Understanding and Reason of the Father is the Son of God." This valiant follower of Jesus also used his knowledge of the works of Homer, Pythagoras, Herodotus, and Plato, as well as Jewish literature, art history, Egyptian religion, and much more to open the minds of those hostile to the faith.[2]

THE THIRD CENTURY

Tertullian (c. 160 – 220) came from a high-ranking family in the Roman imperial army and was schooled in literary artistry, rhetoric, law, philosophy, ancient literature, and medicine. Putting his erudition to use, he wrote more than forty volumes concerning the faith. He beckoned Christians to commit all to Christ, laid important groundwork for the doctrine of the Trinity, disputed with heretics, and called the pagan world to repentance. He wrote fluently in Greek and Latin, making his mark as "the first significant Christian author to write in both languages." His works, along with Augustine's, were instrumental in stirring the hearts of those who led the Reformation. Interestingly enough, Tertullian's Apology was one of the first books ever to be published in moveable type — by Gutenburg himself (1483).[3]

Tertullian is said to have delivered a devastating attack on the most dangerous heresy of his time — gnosticism. Many believe that this false religion posed the real threat of extinguishing the Christian faith altogether. But it was works produced by the likes of Tertullian that curbed the assault of this deadly cult and advanced the cause of Christ.

In addition, this "father of Latin theology" penned the most-developed arguments for the Trinity (up to his time), wrote powerful treatises on the healthy relationship between faith and reason and between Christianity and culture, and defended the place of the Holy Spirit's ongoing activity in the body of Christ. It's critical to note that Tertullian joined the Montanist movement, a group that practiced prophecy, miracle-working, and speaking in tongues. Here is a man who saw no contradiction in ecstatic speech, miraculous encounters, intellectual pursuits, theological expertise, and a deep devotional life.

THE FOURTH CENTURY

From the beginning of the third century (202) to the early days of the fourth century (311), the storms of persecution pelted the church of Jesus Christ, but those days were coming to a close. By 325 Emperor Constantine himself sat with the church fathers as they hammered out the original drafts of the Nicene Creed. It's interesting that whether the church was the object of ridicule and torture or the recipient of imperial admiration, the leaders in the body of Christ sought to maintain high intellectual standards. Critical thought, doctrinal precision, mental discipline, cultural awareness, philosophical shrewdness, and apologetic debate continued to share a respectable partnership with a concentrated missions effort, fervent devotion, and participation in the manifest presence of God.

It was the fourth century that gave rise to *Eusebius* (c. 263 – 339), the father of church history; *Athanasius* (c. 296 – 373), who was at one time almost the sole defender of Trinitarian theology; *John Chrysostom* (c. 374 – 407), christened "golden mouth" because he was considered the greatest preacher of the ancient church; and *Jerome* (c. 345 – 420), the architect of the Latin translation of the Bible (the Vulgate). In many ways, the light shined the brightest in these 165 years between the heydays of Diocletian's dominion (303 – 311) and the Dark Ages, which officially commenced in A.D. 476 with the termination of the Western Roman Empire.

Hilary of Poitiers (c. 291 – 371), too, was among those who possessed an admirable mixture of piety, power, and rationality. As a youth, he procured a superb education in philosophy and the classics, yet like all of the church fathers mentioned, he passionately sought out lifelong learning. At age fifty, for example, Hilary taught himself Greek so that he might drink in the wisdom of the earlier church fathers. His main work was that of defending the doctrine of the Trinity, but he also delighted in composing a host of great hymns. Jerome, a contemporary, tells of the mighty wonders that followed in Hilary's wake: healings, miracles, and expulsion of demons. Jerome writes, "There would not be time if I wanted to tell you all the signs and wonders performed by Hilarion."[4]

Two more remarkable figures of this era were *Basil* (c. 329 – 379) and *Gregory of Nyssa* (c. 330 – 397). These two men were brothers. Their father had served as a presbyter and both became presbyters themselves. They were known for their oratory, poetry, theological vividness, practical Christianity, self-sacrificial lifestyles, and great learning. Basil's concentrated studies were in philosophy, literature, and rhetoric; his passion was unity and "body life." Gregory's strong suits were theology and philosophy, which he used in combination with a demonstration of power to reach the lost and combat heretics. Many of Gregory's writings also centered on the Holy Spirit and holiness.

In addition to their healthy interest in the life of devotion, both of these men had multiple occasions to personally witness the power of healing. In one instance it was Gregory's own daughter who was supernaturally raised up. Gregory of Nazianus, another church father and a friend to these brothers, writes of Basil's frequent demonstrations of wonder-working powers.[5]

THE FIFTH CENTURY

As one can see from the following statements, it is next to impossible to overemphasize the importance of *Augustine* (354 – 430) in the realm of Christian thought. Bible teacher and philosopher R. C. Sproul says of Augustine:

> Certainly it would not be an overstatement to say that no one in the first one thousand years of Church history had such a formative influence on Christian thinking as this man did. He is the greatest theologian, at least, of the first millennium of Christianity, if not in the entire history of the Church.[6]

Other conservative theologians have dubbed him as "one of the most important thinkers of history" and have said of his writings that they have "influenced almost every sphere of Western thought throughout the centuries."[7]

This humble servant of immense intellectual capability never allowed his peculiar power of reason to squelch his reverence for the sovereign and supernatural intervention of the Spirit. Augustine was thrilled to recount the details of many phenomenal happenings that took place in his presence. One needs only look to chapter 28 of book 22 in *The City of God* to witness his high valuation of God's direct intervention in the lives of the saints. After cataloging dozens of healings, visions, and other supernatural occurrences, he writes, "If I limited myself to those [miracles] that happened here at Hippo and Calama, I should have to fill several volumes." He writes elsewhere, "It is a simple fact that there is no lack of miracles even in our day."

Augustine was a man of the Spirit who prayed fervently, a man of learning and a master intellect who composed thousands of pages of theology, a deep devotional man, and an ardent lover of souls, who has stirred hungry hearts for 1,600 years. He is a true archetype of God's Great Minds![8]

THE SIXTH CENTURY

Gregory of Tours (c. 538 – 594) was a highly educated French historian who was born of a noble Roman family and was promoted to the office of bishop at the age of thirty-five. He spoke multiple languages, had knowledge of astronomy, was schooled in logic and rhetoric, and was well-read in the ancient classics. He was a prolific writer, producing ten volumes on history, a book on the lives of the church fathers, works on offices in the church, and a variety of commentaries on numerous books of the Bible. He not only penned works on theology and history but wrote seven books on confirmed miraculous occurrences in the lives of believers.

In his *Dialogues* Gregory talks about his close friend Eleutherius, who prayed over a dead man, raising him to life. He also chronicles an episode of demons being cast from a boy and of his own healing from a physical malady. Gregory is man who, following in the footsteps of the early church fathers, was not only committed to first-rate scholarship for the Savior but was also sold on the Christ's supernatural intervention.[9]

THE SEVENTH AND EIGHTH CENTURIES

Bede (c. 673 – 735) was an English-born Saxon, who personified the beautiful balance between intimate spirituality and ardent intellectual activity. The combination of rich Celtic tradition and passion for reading accounts for his rare mixture of evangelical truth, elevated education, and experience-based faith. Bede is known as the most important scholar and writer between the age of the church fathers and the Carolingian revival of learning (c. A.D. 800). He excelled in geography, theology, history, religious education, and biography. He was also a tremendous Bible expositor and teacher of ethics. This doctor-divine also delighted in hymn-writing, in singing, and in extended seasons of prayer.[10]

One more thing about Bede — you guessed it, like the other aforementioned personalities, he too possessed a keen interest in the "moving of the Spirit." He makes abundant mention of supernatural happenings throughout his classic work *Ecclesiastical History of England*. He records accounts of the blind seeing, the dumb speaking, would-be martyrs delivered, people suffering from demon possession set free, and the dead being raised. To this scholarly, spiritual saint, God was the author of history, the grantor of knowledge, and the source of supernatural gifts.[11]

THE THIRTEENTH CENTURY

Bonaventure (1217 – 1274) is known mostly for his sublime devotional classics on piety, humility, and creation. What many seem to forget is that this saintly brother was also a master theologian and heavy-duty thinker. Though by modern devotees he is referred to as "The Prince of Mystics," to his contemporaries he was "The Seraphic Doctor," denoting his excellence in learning. Through his profound communion with God and his belief that attaining and applying knowledge were to God's glory, he produced one of the richest syntheses of Christian spirituality known.

Bonaventure was schooled in Paris, receiving his master's degree in theology and later entering into leadership at the Franciscan school in the same city. He wrote voluminously, cranking out over 18,000 pages of scholastic treatises, theological works, devotionals, and commentaries, as well as doing landmark work in textual criticism. It is said of his writings that they "are replete with analytic and logical techniques" and "were utilized by learned men of all stripes in his day."[12]

Bonaventure also had a special interest in the supernatural healing power of Christ. It seems that as a child, he was miraculously snatched from the jaws of death by the intercession of Francis of Assisi. In his two outstanding biographies on Francis, he often conveys his experience with the gift of prophecy, word of knowledge, healing ministry, and the Spirit's anointing. Here is another great man who saw the gifts of the Spirit (penning *The Seven Gifts of the Holy Spirit*), seriousness of study, and mental discipline as complimenting, not opposing, each other.[13]

It's interesting to witness how this master soul integrates the high call to learning and philosophy with the power and blessedness of the Holy Spirit. He often mentions the gifts and liberality of the Spirit in one sentence, followed by a reference to logic or rationality in the next. He saw no conflict between rigorous learning and Franciscan simplicity, nor did he view the mastering of theology and rhetoric as a contradiction to the life of humility. Bonaventure truly epitomized the new and blessed breed of medieval leaders who faithfully served as tributaries of light, as God prepared the church for a river of raging reformation.[14]

The men who acted as the avant-garde for religious transformation voluntarily deposited their lives on God's altar, daring to go into battle against what had become a worldly, tyrannical church. The warfare they waged took place in the realm of prayer, thinking, theology, doctrine, debate, scholarship, and self-sacrifice. In the spirit of the Renaissance, they possessed revived minds; in the Spirit of Christ, they possessed hearts ablaze for souls. By God's grace, they had captured the truth that, as philosopher Arthur Holmes puts it, "dynamic Christian movements exerting a long-lasting influence have always involved the evangelization of the mind."[15]

THE FIFTEENTH CENTURY

One of the most fascinating forerunners of the Reformation was *Girolamo Savonarola* (1452 – 1498), the fiery preacher of Florence, who preached to audiences in excess of ten thousand. He not only studied medicine and wrote philosophy but also mastered Hebrew and Greek. Though, like Chrysostom, he is known for his eloquent yet hot-blooded exhortations on heaven and hell, like Aquinas he was also given to visions and dreams; he was similar to Montanus in his predictive prophecies and resembled Augustine in his devotional writings (*Miserere* and *Triumph of the Cross*). Ironically, this "renaissance man," who cried aloud for Christ in the very cradle of the Renaissance itself (Florence), was hanged and burned for preaching the message of "rebirth" and "the regeneration of the church" in that selfsame city.[16]

Savonarola had no clue that within sixteen years of his death, all five of the great Reformers would be born in their respective corners of Europe. These were the men who would build on the sweat, tears, and blood of the pre-reformers (Wycliffe, Tyndale, Coverdale, Bradwardine, Huss, etc.), ushering in an age of spiritual renewal and ecclesiastical revision, of which the forerunners could have only dreamed. The "morning stars," as the pre-reformers have been affectionately called, had faded but the bright day of the Reformation had dawned.

THE SIXTEENTH CENTURY

It is said of *Martin Luther* (1483 – 1546) that "more books have been written about him than any other figure in history, excepting Jesus of Nazareth."[17] Luther is known as a monk, professor, theologian, hymn-writer, translator, revolutionary, reformer of education, political figure, and mystic. However he may be labeled, all agree that he was a man who changed the world. Simply put, his mission was that of liberating the minds of the masses from the stranglehold of a man-made, hybrid gospel, which had become anything but good news.

Luther attended the University of Erfurt and then Wittenberg University, where he earned the degree of Doctor of Divinity. He invested the rest of his life (thirty-four years) lecturing in the classrooms of the latter. Though he was critical of an overemphasis on the intellect, as should any balanced believer, he did value greatly the use of reason, logic, philosophy, the classics, theology, history, and all other components of the life of the mind. Luther was a master linguist and political reformer; he dabbled in astronomy (not astrology) and mathematics and greeted the "new science" (except for Copernicus's heliocentric theory) with enthusiasm. It was his aim that a solid education be mandatory for the children of all peasants, leading civilians, and clergyman alike (Luther broke the mold of compulsory celibacy).[18]

Though some attempt to claim Luther as a tongue-talking ancestor, there seems to be no evidence from his writings that this is the case. Nevertheless, Luther believed in divine healing, spoke frequently on the need for and might of the Holy Spirit, and declared over and over again the significant place and power of prayer in the believer's life. He also included over 4,500 references to the Holy Spirit in his writings. Luther was definitely not afraid to proclaim the believer's dependence on the Holy Spirit in everyday life.[19]

It is significant that though Luther did appear at times to advocate a cessationist view (i.e., that the spiritual gifts passed with the apostolic age), his personal correspondence and private prayer life reveals differently. One citation from Luther's writings, which exhibits his belief in the ongoing supernatural intervention of God, comes from a personal letter written to friends. Here he counsels them to call on the "power of Christ with the prayer of faith" in order to counteract the "affliction that comes from the devil." He encourages them to do as James 5:14 – 15 indicates, taking two or three deacons or "good men" from the church, telling them to "lay your hands upon him," and pray. He then challenges them to "graciously deign to free this man from all evil, and put to nought the work that Satan has done in him." Before leaving the habitation of the indisposed man, Luther instructs, "Lay your hand upon the man again and say, 'These signs shall follow them that believe; they shall lay hands on the sick, and they shall recover.' "[20]

One also finds several favorable mentions of the gift of prophecy tucked away in his writings. He asserts that the gift of prophecy was still present in his day, though not as conspicuously as in the days of the apostles; and that Christians could receive predictive knowledge. He draws the line, however, when the prophet purports revelation that is set in contradistinction to the revealed word of faith in Scripture. He was not only a brilliant scholar and enduring intellectual but was a man of powerful prayer who leaned heavily on the abiding presence of the Holy Spirit. Surely, he was a man for all seasons, another example of a mind on fire for Christ.[21]

THE EIGHTEENTH CENTURY

One may ask how a master mind who penned penetrating scientific treatises at age eleven and who had a working knowledge of Latin, Greek, and Hebrew by age thirteen could have spearheaded one of the premier spiritual awakenings in the world's history.[22] It's really quite elementary; *Jonathan Edwards* (1703 – 1758) was convinced that the human mind was to be a reflection of the all-knowing God. He saw all truth as God's truth and so refused to pit scientific and philosophical reality — of which the mind is capable of grasping — against religious and experiential reality, of which the spirit and senses are fitted to lay hold. In a nutshell, Edwards simply sought to earnestly love God will all his spirit, soul, mind, and strength.

Edwards was often accused of being an enthusiast; one who promoted emotionalism and mindless religion. But nothing could be further from the truth. Edwards was indeed a man of passion, but his intellectual strengths are what set him apart from most others who, though passionate, fail to fastidiously love God with their mind. As biographer Perry Miller has put the matter, "The real life of Jonathan Edwards was the life of his mind."[23]

Edwards was a remarkable scholar, curious scientist, deep-thinking theologian, loving pastor, university president, humble missionary, prolific writer, and premier evangelist. Although he was plagued with physical weakness, he invested a minimum of thirteen hours a day in his study. And although he leaned on his pulpit, reading his manuscripted messages often in a dull monotonous voice, he acted as the flint that sparked the move of God, which became the Great Awakening of the American colonies. This, in turn, has incited inspiration for all who have sought true revival thereafter.[24]

This giant of the faith has been lauded as "the greatest philosopher-theologian ever to grace the American scene" and as one who "came closer to ascertaining the mind of God in the realm of rational reflection and biblical investigation than any other person."

Eighteenth-century evangelist Samuel Davies stated that he was "the profoundest reasoner, and the greatest divine that America ever produced."[25]

Though Edwards was an intellect extraordinaire, he also wrote abundantly on the supernatural manifestations of Holy Spirit revival, maintaining that when the Spirit visits his people in extraordinary ways, all manners of phenomena are likely to accompany the outpouring. His defense of physical manifestations in revival, incessant mention of the Spirit, euphoric devotional writings, and expectation of "the church's latter-day glory" led many to view Edwards as a sentimentalist and dangerous fanatic or mystic. These thought it was deplorable that this brilliant man allowed his heart to run away with his head.

The truth of the matter is that those who have helped to bring about the foremost positive changes in the history of the church have, almost to the man, been accused of being too "heady" or intellectual by some, and too mystical or spiritual by others. But the greats themselves never see a contradiction between applying their intellects for the glory of God and participating in the unfeigned experiential aspects of the faith. This explains why they have often been viewed in such contrasting and conflicting ways.[26]

This remarkable metaphysician of the soul saw clearly that neither the intellect nor the emotions were to be deemed as ends unto themselves. More accurately, he viewed them as being instrumental — that is, as means to an end. For Edwards, that end was always the glory of God, via our veneration and enjoyment of him. Echoing Augustine's famous dictum on the matter, Edwards affirmed that "the enjoyment of God is the only happiness with which our souls can be satisfied."[27] All else (including the intellect, emotions, and supernatural occurrences) are but the avenues by which we travel to — or from — the soul's meeting place with God.

CONCLUSION

Though there is no room in this chapter to deal with the countless others who call from the past for us fragmented moderns to bring faith and reason back into partnership, there must be room in our hearts. I would love to devout a bit of time to Aristides and Aquinas, Pascal and the Puritans, Bradwardine and Bernard of Clairvaux, Origen and the Orthodox fathers, Wycliffe and especially Wesley; but here I cannot. No doubt, Wesley is an important figure for the Pentecostal – Charismatic movement, and he is a perfect example of what this chapter is all about. But since I have already mentioned him in foregoing chapters, I'll withstand the temptation to summarize his stunning synthesis of "the life of faith" and "the life of the mind."

Since the early 1800s, a new sort of "dark age" has been slinking out of the shadows and sinking slowly into the vacated minds of American Christians. The late church fathers faced the Vandals; we too are encountering the barbaric hordes (Eastern religion). The Scholastics met with Muslim raids; we too must deal with Islamic encroachment. As the opiate of ignorance dulled and darkened the minds of a medieval age, so also the mind of America has become numb through the self-induced anesthetic of materialism and pleasure. As pre-reformers faced the plague and as Reformers encountered revolutionary backlash, we too have plundering pestilence (AIDS) and cultural confrontations that we must cope with.

In the midst of all this, we have foolishly cast off the church fathers, sneered at the Scholastics, ripped up our Reformation roots, untied the tethers of the Great Awakening, and rerouted our ancient Puritan paths. The head has been separated from the heart, the intellectual has been isolated from the spiritual, and we wander — we stagger — in the darkness. How dark will our darkness become? How long will our "dark age" last? Only we can determine that.

Thus, the call to the contemporary church is not to engage in a choice between either a Spirit-filled life or a knowledge-filled life; rather, we are summoned to reconcile the two. Unless we rescind the unnatural divorce between mind and emotion, experience and intellect, faith and reason, we will most certainly be guilty of keeping asunder what God in his sovereignty intends to be joined together!

NOTES

1. Blumhofer, *The Assemblies of God*, 2:117.

2. Robert Grant, *Greek Apologists of the Second Century* (Philadelphia, PA: Westminster, 1988), 102 – 9.

3. John Wimber, *A Brief Sketch of Signs and Wonders through the Church Age* (Placentia, CA: Vineyard Christian Fellowship), 9; Walton, *Charts*, 6; Ferguson, *Encyclopedia of Early Christianity*, 883.

4. Joseph Deferrari, *Early Christian Biographies* (Fathers of the Church, v. 15; Washington, D.C.: Catholic Univ. of America Press, 1964), 262 – 63; Ferguson, *Encyclopedia of Early Christianity*, 425 – 26.

5. *Nicene and Post-Nicene Fathers* (Schaff ed.), 1/7:243, 263, 264, 412; Wimber, *A Brief Sketch of Signs and Wonders*, 14; Elgin S. Moyer, *Who Was Who in Church History* (New Canaan, CT: Keats, 1962), 32, 171.

6. R. C. Sproul, "Augustine," in the cassette series *The Consequences of Ideas*, vol. 2, tape AP 12.9/10, side #2.

7. Alister McGrath, *A Cloud of Witnesses: Ten Great Christian Thinkers* (Grand Rapids: Zondervan, 1990), 27; Ron Nash, "Augustine of Hippo," *Great Leaders of the Christian Church*, 85; Wright, "Augustine," *New International Dictionary of the Christian Church*, 88.

8. Augustine, *Nicene and Post-Nicene Fathers* (Schaff ed.), 1/2:486 – 489. Moyer, *Who Was Who in Church History*, 22; Ferguson, *Encyclopedia of Early Christianity*, 121, 489 – 90; also see Augustine, *Confessions* 9.7.16, for comments on healings, visions, and the casting out of demons.

9. Moyer, *The Wycliffe Biographical*, 171; *Who Was Who*, 175 – 76; Ferguson, *Encyclopedia of Early Christianity*, 402 – 3; Wimber, *A Brief Sketch of Signs and Wonders*, 21 – 22.

10. Philip Schaff, *History of the Christian Church*, Vol. 4 of Books for the Ages (Albany, OR: AGES Software; Version 1.0, 1997), 532 – 537

11. John Giles, editor, *The Venerable Bede's Ecclesiastical History of England* (London: Bohn , 1845), 1:13 – 15, 26 – 28, 30 – 34; 2:68 – 69; 3:128 – 34; 5:235 – 44; A. H. Thompson, *Bede: His Life, Times, and Writings* (Oxford: Clarendon, 1969), 201 – 29.

12. Ewert Cousins, ed., *The Soul's Journey into God* (New York: Paulist, 1978), 4 – 9; Douglas, *New International Dictionary of the Christian Church*, 140.

13. Bonaventure, *Major and Minor Life of St. Francis*, ed. Benen Fahy (Chicago: Franciscan Herald, 1973); for other references to prophecy, healing, miracles, and gifts, see Ewert Cousins, ed., *Bonaventure: The Soul's Journey into God* (New York: Paulist, 1978), 4–9, 85, 113, 163, 164, 174, 184, 195, 196, 225–38, 247–50, 267, 277–81, 295–309.

14. For examples of this delicate blending, see especially: Bonaventure's *The Soul's Journey into God*.

15. Holmes, *The Making of a Christian Mind*, 30.

16. Kepler, *Fellowship of the Saints*, 247–52; Schaff, *History of the Church*, 6:684–90.

17. Carl S. Meyer, "Luther, Martin," in Douglas, *New International Dictionary of the Christian Church*, 611.

18. Scott H. Hendrix, "Luther's Communities," in *Leaders of the Reformation*, ed. Richard De Molen (London: Susquehanna Univ. Press, 1984), 48; Geoffrey Hanks, *Seventy Great Christians* (Bristol, UK: Christian Focus, 1992), 104–5; Moyer, *Wycliffe Biographical*, 250–251. See also F. Painter, *Luther on Education* (St. Louis: Concordia, 1889), chs. 4–8, 10.

19. Thomas Zimmerman, "Pleas for the Pentecostals," *Christianity Today* 7 (January 4, 1963): 12; Jerry Jensen, *Baptists and the Baptism of the Holy Spirit* (Los Angeles: Full Gospel Businessmen's Fellowship International, 1963), 2.2; Carl Brumback, *What Meaneth This*, 91–92; Williard Cantelon, *The Baptism of the Holy Spirit*, 72. See also Luther, *Works*, 55:141–43, 256 (index volume); *Works*, 24:366ff., 413; 40:50, 53, 55, 59, 70, 83; 48:365ff.; E. G. Rupp, *Patterns of Reformation* (Epworth: Epworth, 1969), 100, 112, 186.

20. Luther, *Luther: Letters of Spiritual Counsel*, ed. Theodore Tappert (Library of Christian Classics v. 18; Philadelphia, Westminster, 1955), 52.

21. Luther, *Works*, 24:366; *Works: Lectures in Romans*, 444–51. See also Luther, *Sermons of Luther*, ed. John N. Lenker (Grand Rapids: Baker, 1983), 1:5.

22. C. H. Faust, "Edwards as Scientist," *American Literature* (New York: American Books, 1930), 1:393–404; Winslow, *Jonathan Edwards: Basic Writings*, 31; Douglas, *New International Dictionary of the Christian Church*, 334.

23. Perry Miller, *Jonathan Edwards* (New York: Sloane Associates, 1949), xi.

24. Charles Chauncy (1705–1787) vehemently fought against Edwards, traveling three hundred miles to collect data in order to "prove" Edwards wrong. His conviction was that Edwards was leading the region into religious chaos via emotion and unrestrained enthusiasm. For discussion of this account, see Keith Hardman, *Issues in American Christianity* (Grand Rapids: Baker, 1993), 44–46; Iain Murray, *Jonathan Edwards* (Carlisle, PA: Banner of Truth, 1987), 204–8, 244–46, 252–54, 281–83. On Edwards' study and writing habits, see Serono Dwight, "Memoirs," in *The Works of Jonathan Edwards*, ed. Ed Hickman, 2 vols. (Carlisle, PA: Banner of Truth, 1987), 1:xxii, xxxvi; Edwards, "True Excellency," in idem, 2:957.

25. Sam Davies from *Sermons on Important Subjects*, 456; Sang Hyun Lee, *Edwards in Our Time* (Grand Rapids: Eerdmans, 1999), vii; Miller, *Jonathan Edwards*; John Gerstner, *Jonathan Edwards: A Mini-Theology* (Wheaton: Tyndale, 1987), 11; G. Whitfield, *Journals* (Edinburgh: Banner of Truth, 1960), 476, 486, 517, 567.

26. Jonathan Edwards, a letter to William McCulloch, *The Works of Edwards*, ed. C. C. Goen (New Haven, CN: Yale Univ. Press, 1972), 4:560; John Opie, *Jonathan Edwards and the Enlightenment* (Lexington, MA: Heath, 1969), 33; Chauncy, quoted in Murray, *Jonathan Edwards*, xxiii.

27. Edwards, "Dissertation concerning the End for Which God Created the World," in *Works*, 1:94–121; "The Christian Pilgrim," *Works*, 2:224.

19

Challenges and Caveats

Orthodoxy means not thinking, not needing to think, Orthodoxy is unconsciousness....
It wasn't the man's brain that was speaking; it was his larynx.... Already we are
breaking down the habits of thought which have survived from before the Revolution....
Don't you see, the whole aim is to narrow the range of thought?... Every year fewer
and fewer words, and the range of consciousness always a little smaller.... But,
they need only to rise up and shake themselves like a horse shaking off flies.
GEORGE ORWELL; EXCERPTS FROM *1984*

Knowledge without zeal is not true knowledge, and zeal without knowledge is only
wild-fire.... The preaching that hath most commanded my heart is that which most
illumined my mind.... To study the nature and course and use of all God's works is a duty
imposed by God on all men.... Not only my spiritual life, but all the life I live in this world
is by the faith of the Son of God: he exempts no part of life from the agency of his faith.
JOHN COTTON, PURITAN PASTOR

WHEN TRUTH HIDES

There it was, pressed into a corner with twenty more modern books piled on top of it, and
with another hundred volumes heaped around that stack. Through the years, paperback
patrons had moseyed right past it, oblivious to its presence. It was there all along — but
it was hidden — until one day the bibliomaniac within provoked me to dismantle the
mountain of literature that smothered this little book, written on the topic of "knowing
the truth." It was a 1657 edition of John Cotton's comments on the first epistle of John.
This seventeenth-century, leather-bound treasure not only preserved the words of the first
pastor of Boston's Congregational Church, but possessed handwritten notes by the very
voyager who had procured it in England and transported it to New England.

On the inside of the cowhide-wrapped cover, the proud Puritan owner had jotted notes
about pilgrims and strangers. He and subsequent owners scribbled down their vision for
the future and the Scripture references on which they stood. The last hand-scrawled entry
was made about 1800 — almost two hundred years ago. I have many questions about this
curious, old volume. Did the original custodian see his dreams come to pass? What would
he think of America and her church today? How did this book come to be buried beneath
a muddled mess of literary junk food in a dark corner of a secondhand store? Even more
haunting: How could such an intriguing chronicle of New World history be hidden for
nearly two hundred years?

220

I have suggested throughout this book that views toward the mind's involvement in the life of faith changed radically somewhere around the end of the eighteenth and the beginning of the nineteenth centuries. Thus, while writing this book, more than one inquisitor asked me, "If the neglect of the intellect has been so serious for two hundred years, why have so few mentioned it?" By saying this, some imply that "the life of the mind" isn't very important, while others suggest that it is important but that we have probably done just fine in this endeavor; otherwise many others would have called attention to it.

Lest we forget, the biblical truth of "justification by faith" lay in a corner, covered by the cobwebs of tradition for over a thousand years. Note too that our position as Pentecostals and Charismatics in general is that the use of "the gifts of the Spirit" and doctrine of "the baptism in the Holy Spirit" virtually plunged into oblivion for the better part of sixteen centuries. Thus, the crown jewels of Protestantism and Pentecostalism are both snatched from our possession in one fell swoop if we suppose that an idea must be suspect if it has been neglected for so long. Surely we are thankful that Luther, Calvin, and Knox did not think this way, and no doubt we are glad that early Pentecostals weren't daunted by such thought.

Thinking people know that truths can vanish as quickly as they emerge. Let us not forget that the Holocaust transpired in the one-time hallowed haunts of Luther's Germany, that Islam has now become a stifling mantle over Augustine's North Africa, and that Patrick's Ireland and Wesley's England are but transient ghosts of Christian-past. To recall how fast the tide can turn, it is also helpful to remember the blotting out of the Herculean first-century church of Ephesus or Thessalonica, the faded glory of the fourth-century believers of imperial Rome, and the slaughter of tens of millions of unborn babies in a land where all people are supposedly created equal and where tens of millions of born-again believers live out their happy, and oftentimes, passive faith.

Our culture is in trouble. The collective "life of the mind" in today's America seems to be little more than a ramshackle ad hoc system, soldered together at its mismatched joints by materialism, dislocated data bits, superstition, and relativism. She is an adolescent empire that may be teetering on the brink of her twilight; a heedless juvenile who has flirted too long with the self-defeating forces of hedonism and irrationalism. Forgetting how to think, she has forgotten how to live. It seems that her occupants are almost completely unacquainted with the fact that their civilization has not yet exited her adolescent years, and that she is making many of the same fatal mistakes that her elder sister did in more ancient times:

> *Like the Roman Empire, we've focused on ourselves;*
> *avarice in the forefront, introspection on the shelf.*
> *We're enchanted with our privileges,*
> *and defined by whims and whines.*
> *While crisscrossing private Rubicons*
> *we've turned our collective backs to the Rhine.*

We say we fret over Vandals,
engineering plane attacks;
but we raise herds of homegrown Visigoths,
who dismantle our cultural walls —
Thus, as we gaze at Rome's twin towers,
our intellects are sacked.
"Do not be alarmed" cries Christendom.
"We've neither fallen nor declined."
And then nay-saying prophets proph —
"Don't you hear the hordes of barbari at the gates of
your hearts and minds?"

RICK M. NAÑEZ

SALVAGING A CULTURE FROM INTELLECTUAL SAVAGERY

There are many cultural forecasters who warn that impending darkness looms nearby. Whether on par or overstated, many point out our flabbiness of thought, lethargy in theological matters, and the failure to meet head-on the lies of failed philosophical systems. When reading the more senior works of Gibbon or Toynbee, one could easily mistake their descriptions of those civilizations that have declined in history's dust for *our* own nation in *our* own time. The classical signs indicating that a society is careening into cultural corrosion seem to be dawdling at our doorstep. The secular squeeze is intensifying, and buckling under its feel-good, materialistic pressures not only invites the darkness to smother us but accelerates its advent.

Mindless busyness, declining educational standards, heightened superstition, and personal debt are chief indicators of crumbling cultures. The burgeoning of nontraditional religions, a lack of self-restraint, concentration on material acquisition, devaluation of human life, disregard for history, and intellectual apathy are all pointed out by diviners of culture-wide conditions as aiding in the dismantling of great empires. We are a culture of endangered minds.[1]

From our kindergarten classes to our Ph.D. programs and riding on the airwaves of our mass media, one can detect a malaise of the mind. Infiltrating the warp and woof of the entertainment industry, the world of publishing, the realm of drama, and the arena of politics, and hidden within the job descriptions of a host of popular careers is a dumbing-down process that is taking place with alarming velocity. Theologian Carl F. Henry once told me that in his opinion, there has never been a time in the history of human thought that has seen such rapid and radical change of standards and ideas as in the latter part of the twentieth century. Former Lebanese ambassador Charles Malik saw anti-intellectualism as the greatest of many threats to American Christianity. Christian teacher and philosopher R.C. Sproul suggests that the twentieth century may be the most anti-intellectual in all of history.[2]

We willfully worship at the seductive altar of self-servitude. The ideological makeup of entertainment, education, religion, and paganism have been blended and mutated, producing all manners of hybrid behavior. Edu-tainment, info-mercials, virtual reality, cyberspace, death metal, and the likes litter our oxymoronic cultural landscape. We are mindlessly addicted to hollow heroes who themselves are addicted to the opiate of their choice — icons who too often obliterate their own minds with a drug overdose or .357-magnum. We mourn the passing of yesterday's celebrities while remaining oblivious to yesteryear's true heroes.

We live in a civilization where the trivialization of relationships is common fare, where the lure of leisure is found in its escapist qualities, and where advertising propaganda leads a distracted army of material gluttons by the rings in their calloused snouts. Market moguls cash in on our animal passions, preparing us for tomorrow's pursuit of disposable possessions by creating new values and inciting dormant desires. In this environment, it's easy to blur the lines between temporal goods and the eternal God, information and wisdom, spectatorship and action.

The West is facing the struggle of her life. Her relativistic and resigned worldview has domesticated her one-time fervor for prudence and honor. Passivity reigns supreme; our badge is so-called tolerance. Instead of character, "image" has become her driving force. We are a culture that works harder at fun than at work, unless working harder at work becomes the means whereby we can enjoy a greater variety of temporal pleasures. And our radically-altered definition of success, instead of conveying the venerable gist of commitment, consistency, patience, and integrity, has been reduced to popularity, possessions, and position.

Whether we want to admit it or not, in many ways the ideological fabric of our dearly-loved country is being worn down, becoming a mere threadbare philosophical rag. The truth is that human beings struggle, nations are comprised of humans, and God is involved in the rising and falling of nations. Does this then mean that we are beyond repair?

I once heard Chuck Colson say that there has probably never been another interval in all of history when *so many* Christians have been *so ineffectual* in shaping the culture in which they live. Thus, the answer is that we are not beyond repair, but the church must first rise up and shake herself off like a horse shaking off flies; we must repair her morality, refocus on her mission, and reawaken her mind. Before we can change our nation, we must defend ourselves against the savagery of thoughtlessness.

COMING OUT FROM AMONG THEM

The American church is not doing its best at penetrating the society she inhabits. Within her ranks, it seems that her lack of disciplined thought is not too much different from the masses of zombie-like refugees in our greater preoccupied land. Like the surrounding narcissistic culture, she flirts with amusing herself into oblivion, often too busy to expand her intellectual real estate. The faithfulness, integrity, and commitment (i.e., the "permanent things") that once peppered our religious landscape have been short-circuited by the allure of selfishness and materialism. We dwell in a plastic society, where virtue is as thin as the cosmetically-altered faces behind which it hides and where the domination of consumerism too often dictates at which church the redeemed choose to shop. Perfect ability in the exterior shell at the expense of the interior life has always been a hallmark of a struggling soul.

In order to be distinct from the intellectually-passive populace, we must invite teaching that, though over our heads, will prompt us to stretch our necks; avoiding the sitcom, channel-surfing, attention-deficit-prone ways of a restless audience mentality. Pastors must again imbue their messages with logical sequence, theological meat, and cerebral challenges, perhaps even elongating their sermonic delivery if the content is capable of justifying the protraction.

The false, self-imposed breach between "the secular" and "the sacred" has kept so many American Christians at arms-length distance from the concentrated combat of worldviews. We wage war for men's souls but ignore the battle for men's minds. In doing so, we not only lose cultural ground but forfeit a host of first-rate minds. When the church teaches her people *what* to think but fails to instruct them on *how* to think, she may enjoy short-term success but set herself up for long-term failure. On varying levels, that's exactly what she seems to be doing!

THE SPIRIT-FILLED CHURCH IN AMERICA

That the body of Christ in America would follow a lost culture into acute mindlessness is perplexing, but it's even more of a riddle that we who profess to be *full* of the Holy Spirit would forfeit the intellectual life. The word "holy" carries the meaning of "otherness" or "set aside for." This being the case, those purporting to possess a greater measure of the Holy Spirit should exhibit a life that is set aside for God in greater measure than by those who don't claim to be filled with the Spirit. If the Holy Spirit pervades our life, then our intellect also should be set aside for kingdom use. This takes place as we participate in altering the culture, not only by evangelizing but also by becoming disciplined thinkers, defending the gospel, and sharing in the constant conversation of great ideas through the ages, for again, ideas have consequences.

The worship of worship, a penchant for short sermons, the demand for signs and wonders in the sanctuary, and an addiction to the "feel-goods" demonstrate that many Full Gospel people are grasping at Eden in much the same way as does the rest of our society. Our fascination with fame and fads and our disdain for doctrine-packed teaching also indicate that we possess an undersized intellectual appetite. Moreover, we must desist from blaming sin and misfortune on demons, resist embellishment of testimonials, and forfeit shamanistic name-it-claim-it prayer techniques. The commonly held beliefs that "bigger is better" and "whatever works is right" must go; only uncritical, undiscerning minds fall for such pragmatism.

Furthermore, all too frequently we confuse the ends of Pentecostal power, assuming that this power is almost synonymous with "control" while voluntarily forgetting that the supernatural power of the Spirit has much to do with power to deny ourselves. There is nothing as powerful — as supernatural — as fallen human beings willfully denying themselves for the sake of raising up those around them. Shouldn't those who are filled with the Spirit of Christ also be filled with the humility of Christ?

In addition, shouldn't those baptized with the Holy Spirit be extra sensitive to the contrast between their preferences and God's will? Much too often and with frightening casualness, we substitute the voice of our conscience for the voice of the Creator, using whichever serves best our preconceived plans. Too many within our ranks use the all-powerful trump card of "God told me" or "God showed me" as a way of wielding power or dodging responsibility. For each of these, dozens of other struggles could be added. Of course, good thinking without God-consciousness and cerebral excellence without the fruit of the Spirit advance our cause little. However, anointing without intellectual balance and charisma without mental fidelity lead to a host of problems that affect every area of individual and communal faith.

We have a monumental task before us! Within Full Gospel circles we must think well, more exactly and more deeply, about issues surrounding fullness, fellowship, and faith. With minds afire, we must hammer out issues of doctrine, devotion, demons, and discipleship. With open hearts, we must revisit again and again the matters of miracles, missions and mysticism, holiness and healing, culture and cultivating the mind. And without the mask of protectionism, we have the intellectual obligation to talk openly about legalism, nepotism, bureaucracy, and the like. Questionable techniques surrounding fundraising, leading believers into Spirit baptism, and bringing unbelievers to Christ, as well as the hot topics of seeker-sensitivity, postmodernism, and relativism, must each repeatedly find their turn in the roundtable of discussion.

Trying to convince the lost that Jesus is "worth trying" because of the practical benefits that accompany salvation is closer to the sales methodologies of modern hedonists than it is to the evangelistic mandate of the Master. And if we base our faith on bizarre experiences, personal prosperity, or emotional blessings, we play directly into the hands of the menacing, relativistic mindset that pervades our confused culture. In the end, we are left without a distinctive defense when those whom we are attempting to win to Christ claim that they too possess truth based on *their* experiences, *their* prosperity, or *their* emotional well-being.

The prevailing philosophy of relativism will find little resistance from the Full Gospel realm if we persist in our anti-intellectual posture. We tend to defeat the aim of proliferating truth when peddling *our* interpretations and *our* directives "from the Spirit" — that is, *our* feelings-oriented faith. Though we don't use the fashionable phrase, "so it's true for me and not true for you," we opt for other perilous terminology: "God told me this is true, whether he told anyone else or not." When we choose to snub rational discernment and instead pursue truth by way of private interpretation, fleeces, and feelings, truth is crowded out and mere human opinion reigns supreme. Clearly, it will be impossible for us to rescue a world that prostitutes truth via relativism if we ourselves flirt with her elusive sisters — mysticism, individualism, and sensationalism.

As people who claim to have been transformed by the renewing of our minds, we must abandon our conformity to the world's thinking. This includes resisting emotional manipulation, refusing to emphasize praise over preaching, and forsaking the ways of Hollywood where stars mesmerize their fans and where picture-perfect people are hallowed as gods. The gospel of good looks and show biz should have no place among Spirit-filled devotees.

Last of all, there is the whole matter of our general attitude toward men and women who place a high premium on first-rate thinking. Indications are that we have lost many good minds to other movements because of our suspicion of intellectual matters. These often view themselves as alien intellects in hostile territory, thinkers who have been offered a left hand of fellowship for doing what they were specially created to do — think! I wonder how many have been plagued by the pressure of holding to intellectual integrity or casting critical thinking aside for the sake of unthinking unity.

It seems odd to me that a movement that promotes individuality and liberty through distinctive gifts would pressure those *gifted* with innovative intellects. One's exploration of cutting-edge thought, one's penchant for questioning superficial answers, or one's interest in thinking through the issues should demonstrate further, rather than diminish, one's aptitude for *Full Gospel* service — wouldn't you think?

NOTES

1. See Carl F. Henry, *The Christian Mindset in a Secular Society* (Portland, OR: Multnomah, 1978); Jacques Barzum, *The Culture We Deserve* (Middletown, CT: Wesleyan Univ. Press, 1989); Herman Dooyeweerd, *In The Twilight of Western Thought* (Nurley, NJ: Craig, 1965); Christopher Lasch, *The Culture of Narcissism* (New York: Norton, 1978); Neil Postman, *Amusing Ourselves to Death* (New York: Penguin, 1985); Charles Colson, *Against the Night* (Ann Arbor, MI: Servant, 1989); Richard Weaver, *Ideas Have Consequences* (Chicago: Univ. of Chicago Press, 1948); Harold Brown, *The Sensate Culture* (Dallas: Word, 1996); Michael E. Jones, *Degenerate Moderns* (San Francisco: Ignatius, 1993); Arnold Toynbee, *A Study of History* (New York: American Heritage, 1972); Edward Gibbon, *The Decline and Fall of the Roman Empire* (New York: Dutton, 1978); Jim Black, *When Nations Die* (Wheaton, IL: Tyndale, 1994); James Burnham, *The Suicide of the West* (Washington, D.C.: Regnery Gateway, 1985); Shep Clough, *The Rise and Fall of Civilization* (New York: Columbia Univ. Press, 1951); Sam Einstadt, *The Decline of Empires* (Englewood, NJ: Prentice, 1967).

2. Sproul, "Burning Hearts, Empty Minds," *Christianity Today* (Sept. 3, 1982), 100; see also Charles H. Malik, *The Two Tasks* (Westchester, IL.: Cornerstone, 1980), 33.

20

Conclusion and Practical Helps

As I began my introduction, so I commence this last chapter. It had been almost twenty years since I sat mesmerized by the strange words spoken at the camp meeting by the world-renown Full Gospel preacher. Since my earliest years in the faith, my ears have bore witness to thousands of comments that seemed to convey the same message: The mind is a second-rate participant in the life of faith, a constituent to be held in suspicion.

One afternoon not long ago, I was chatting with a department head from one of our Charismatic Bible colleges when he suggested to me that, perhaps, we no longer had a heart/head problem in the Pentecostal – Charismatic movement, that it was a thing of the past. We bantered for another twenty or thirty minutes and concluded our conversation. Within an hour of that exchange, I went to the TV and turned it to a religious station. It couldn't have been more than five minutes before the preacher (who claims an audience of millions) began to instruct his spectators to reach out to God. It had been twenty years, and it had been the voice of another Spirit-filled celebrant, but the message was exactly the same! The preacher simply instructed the people to listen to God, to listen closely, but to be certain *not* to listen with their natural minds. He coached them to resist thinking and to replace their thinking with Holy Ghost communication. After a minute or so, he led the people in thanking God for all truth that he had revealed to the unthinking crowd. I feel safe to say, I'm certain that our confusion over the life of faith and the life of the mind *is not a thing of the past*!

DOING *GOOD*, DOING *BETTER*, DOING OUR *BEST*

In spite of all that has been said in this book about our relationship with and view of the intellect, we find ourselves afforded — perhaps — an unprecedented opportunity in the history of the world. One author has written recently on the theme of how, in their passion for combining faith and learning, the Irish salvaged civilization during the barbaric assaults on medieval Europe.[1] As a growing, major influence in today's global neighborhood, Pentecostal – Charismatic residents may find the occasion to take part in a similar cultural experiment. We can, *if we will*, become an army of change-agents for the salvaging of a multitude of twenty-first-century souls *and* minds. But we must first see where we are and where we need to be.

I am well aware that our movement has come a long way. I know that even in our embryonic stage, we were host to a modest number of keen minds. I know that we are beginning to dot the literary landscape with a few first-rate works of theology. A small number of Pentecostal politicians, Full Gospel philosophers, Charismatic culture changers, and Spirit-filled scientists are emerging to take their battle positions in the struggle for the sanctity and sanity of humankind. Our liberal arts schools are laboring to sculpt the minds of thousands, and a handful of pastors are beginning to see the value of training their people to think in terms of worldview and of priming them for polemics and apologetics. And, of course, we have burgeoned into a worldwide force of roughly six hundred million, which brings us to a vital point in this whole issue of success and change.

As briefly mentioned, during the writing of this book some have asked me why we need this challenge if we have been so successful in numerical growth. Others wonder why we really need correction if we can point to those among us who blend the spiritual and intellectual life. First of all, to my knowledge, no one has ever taken the time to pen a book on the matter of anti-intellectualism in our movement — especially not someone from within our ranks. Second, quantity doesn't prove quality. Third, just because we are strong in some areas doesn't mean that we are strong in every area of biblical truth. Fourth, if there's a scriptural mandate to "love God with our mind," then no amount of encouragement is too much. Fifth, those in our midst who have mingled their passion for the supernatural with a passion for intellectual excellence are a tiny minority. We cannot justify our passivity toward the subject by merely pointing out the exceptions among us. Finally, if we are doing well, then we can do even better.

Some Full Gospel believers are alarmed that upwards of 35 percent of their fellow constituents haven't experienced the classical signs of being filled with the Spirit. Why? Many pastors are concerned that 90 percent of their people have never led another to Christ and properly discipled them. Why? And who is not concerned that 45 percent of marriages among Christians fail the test of time? We don't say that we're doing just fine because 65 percent of our people are baptized in the Holy Spirit. We are not satisfied that 10 to 20 percent share their faith and are engaged in discipling others. No, we write books to challenge our people, in spite of the fact that a small fraction is faithful to the Great Commission. And do we feel successful because 55 percent of Christian marriages survive "till death do them part"? No, we are horrified! Get the picture?

Let's say that a hundred thousand or even a million within our ranks have learned to marry reason and faith, possess apologetic acumen and pray in the Spirit, and are just as concerned about the intellectual life as they are about the life of experience. One million — that would be approximately one-sixth of one percent of the Pentecostal–Charismatic movement. Even if 50 percent of our people appreciated theology and classical literature, studied logic and church history, could debate worldviews, had an interest in culture, and surveyed the liberal arts, what of the other half who harbor a prejudice against the mind?

Furthermore, dozens of times I have heard Pentecostal believers suggest that the greats — Luther, Edwards, Spurgeon, Billy Graham, and others — could have accomplished so much more if they had been "filled with the Spirit." We won't go there now; but I will say that we make statements like this because, though we know that these men achieved amazing things for God, we also believe that those who do well can do better when combining all of the spiritual resources that are available to us.

ON RUNNING WELL

At age eleven I learned a big lesson about what I possessed and what I lacked. I learned that I had the ability to run well and run far. I had entered a twenty-mile walk/run for the March of Dimes. The night before the event, I got the kind of Forrest Gump-notion into my head that I'd try to run the whole race. So the next morning, I did just that. Of the thousands of participants, only twenty finished before me, and I was first in my age-category. I learned that I could run. I also learned on that day that I went into the race unnecessarily handicapped; I just didn't know any better. No one had told me.

No one told me to use running shoes, so I wore tennis shoes. No one told me to wear shorts, so I wore corduroy pants. No one told me that there would be refreshments along the way, so I took bags of salted peanuts, starburst candies, and a thermos of lemonade. What a strange sight I must have been, toting that tattered beige bag over my shoulder and clipping along in my brown corduroys. That day I discovered that I had a gift, but also found that by combining my gift with a little knowledge I could avoid needless hindrances and cover more ground in less time. I had run well, but I learned to run better.

In many respects, the Pentecostal – Charismatic movement has run very well. She has led millions in rediscovering the language of the heart, away from the contagion of ice-cold religion. Her focus has been on our human needs and our ability to enjoy a direct experience with God. An expectation of his sustaining presence and empowering gifts and an anticipation of his supernatural intervention have been promoted with persistence and fervor. In these ways, our movement has run quite well. Yet like the boy who sported slacks in a marathon, we too entertain self-induced hindrances and thus haven't run the race as well as we otherwise could have.

In a sense, our movement resembles a peculiar edifice I once saw while traveling in Central America. I got a glimpse of a row of pristine pillars lining the courtyard of what must have been a rather impressive home. But as I rounded the corner, I realized that the magnificent columns were surrounding a less impressive structure. The powerful and stunning pillars held up only a portico attached to a home — a windowless home made of tarnished and mangled sheet metal! One aspect of this building had been heavily invested in and thus profoundly accentuated. The other part had been constructed out of mere scraps — leftovers. For whatever reason, the owners hadn't calculated in such a way as to erect a house of symmetry, where the strength and beauty of one part would complement the other. Though our movement possesses its own pristine pillars, for whatever reasons, as a whole it hasn't built symmetrically.

Of course, as discussed throughout this book, there are reasons for our lack. Many of us have simply *never been told* that by steadfastly cultivating the life of the mind, we may enjoy a richer, more creative and productive walk and ministry — that is, that we can cover more ground in less time or erect a better-balanced spiritual house. Others have never seriously pondered that we can glorify our Lord by reflecting his image through our rational faculties and so fulfill a deeper obedience to his supreme command to love him with all of our heart, soul, *and* mind. For those who have failed to realize these facts, the foregoing pages have hopefully aided in revealing these truths.

Some within our ranks *have been* challenged in the intellectual dimension of their faith, finding it refreshing and intriguing. But many of these have also discovered that it can be a rather lonely endeavor to relish an inflamed intellect wrapped in a Full Gospel faith. These can now be encouraged that they are not without companionship. And there are those who are *thoroughly excited over the task* of cultivating the gardens of their intellects, yet have desired a sort of manual in hand to inform and challenge those around them who still court a prejudice against "the head." These now have such a handbook at their fingertips.

In 1947, beloved Pentecostal theologian Stanley Horton, who in many ways exemplifies the balance between Spirit, mind, scholarship and devotion, wrote of the acute lack of teaching in Christian circles on the subject of the Holy Spirit.[2] One of Dr. Horton's own professors had asked many years earlier how many students in the class had heard a sermon on the Holy Spirit in the last five years. Roughly 95 percent had not. Since this time, the message of the Holy Spirit has proliferated in a marvelous way. For this we praise the Lord Jesus!

In the past several years, I have traveled to almost thirty countries. I have asked students on four continents whether or not they had ever heard a sermon on the importance of the intellectual life. On most occasions, not a single hand was raised, and I cannot recall more than one hand to rise in the affirmative on any one occasion. The time is now that we must seek to add knowledge to our zeal, truth to our worship in Spirit, and the act of loving God with our minds to our efforts of loving him with our emotions. Perhaps in twenty or thirty years, another can write of the marvelous way and painstaking fashion in which we have spread the message of the need to cultivate the intellectual dimensions of our Pentecostal faith.

PRACTICAL HELPS FOR BUILDING UP THE MIND

The second half of this book contains many areas of study which, when pursued and applied, can help to awaken our slumbering minds, aid us in correcting our mental mistakes, and blend a healthy life of the mind with the more experiential, emotional, and devotional aspects of our faith. There are, of course, hundreds of ways to better develop the mind so that it may be used for the glory of God. In the following pages I propose just a few of those ways.

(1) As I've mentioned elsewhere, *reading* is, perhaps, the optimum way to exercise the mind — stretching it, facilitating its ability to see things it has never seen before, and rethinking factors that it has taken for granted for far too long. But for us to benefit from reading, we must read "outside the lines." That is, we must read *widely* and dare to read the provocative authors who break track with our more narrow train of thought. We must read the "thinkers;" and if we are not familiar with those who think with ink, we can always ask someone who is informed. One way that I've been led to some of the most fla-vorsome food for thought is by *perusing the bibliographies* of the books that have shaken my complacency, stretched my imagination, and irrigated the shallow wells of my mind.

We must also read "*worldviewishly,*" with thinking caps on! With our intellects fully engaged, we should ask "why," "what," "how," and "if;" and we should banter with the author's line of thought, philosophical assumptions, and believability of conclusions. Ask such questions as:

Is he or she being fair as they write?

Am I being fair with the author as I read?

What does their background have to do with their conclusions?

Who have *they* read?

What worldview do they hold?

What are the implications if I accept the author's truth *as* truth?

Deliberately force your mind to make a case *for* or *against* the author's mind. In many ways, this is intellectual exercise at its best!

(2) A second way to embolden and refine our intellects is to participate in *continuing education.* This is much like the above suggestion, especially when it comes in the form of nonformal education. University classes can be of tremendous value (depending on the approach of the teacher and the application of the student), but what I want to underscore here is the merit of *lifelong learning.* In a real sense, high school and college courses are only meant to help a person pursue a life of continuing intellectual growth. That is, these controlled settings are meant to teach us "how" to study and think, not just "what" to study and think.

As I've spoken on the intellectual life as a spiritual calling, many have responded with statements like: "I never went to university," "I don't have the time to go back to college," or "I don't have the schooling that you have." Let me say it clearly: *I do not believe that a person has to have a college degree to be well-educated.* Though I have invested in several years of institutional learning, I don't believe that this *necessarily* means anything in itself (except that I spent a ton of money, warmed a lot of cold seats, and was on several schools' enrollment lists). I'm in favor of working for degrees and attending established institutes of learning, but I also believe that being a lifelong student who works to keep the mind flexible and strong far outweighs the few short years of making grades to earn degrees!

Because of narrow conceptions about the nature of the intellectual life and loving God with one's mind, many have mistakenly assumed that my message can be boiled down into: "More institutional learning!" This is far from my intent. *Excellent thinking for the sake of discerning truth, defending truth, reaching lost souls, and glorifying the Maker of our souls is the heart of what my message is all about.* One way to participate in this endeavor is to engage in lifelong learning — in a classroom, under the tutelage of living college professors, or in your living room in the counsel of a multitude of mentors in the form of professors-become-print.

(3) I have often dreamed of *the local church becoming somewhat of a university* in itself. The very word "university" indicates *uni*-ty in di-*versity* or "many in the one." The Scriptures teach us that "the body is a unit, though it is made up of many parts.... So it is with Christ" (1 Cor. 12:12). If in Christ "are hidden all the treasures of wisdom and knowledge" (Col. 2:3), and if you as a believer are reminded of this "so that no one may deceive you by fine-sounding [but untrue] arguments" (2:4), then what of the idea of the church, even the local church, combining its "parts" of knowledge in order to possess more completely the wisdom and knowledge of Christ?

To take it a step further, what if ten, twenty, or fifty believers from a local church each chose and dedicated himself or herself to one area of study for which they had a specific interest and passion? A substantial starter library on any particular topic would cost, perhaps, the price of a dozen golf games, a new electronic tool, ten Sunday brunches for the family, or fifteen new CDs. Just think of how the congregation and the community would benefit from having an army of prepared "specialists" on dozens of worthy, crucial topics. For example, Christian perspectives on:

ethics	worldviews	science
biology	astronomy	vocation
finances	civilizations	philosophy
the arts	history	language
leisure	psychology	education
world religions	the cults	sociology
architecture	debate	economics
the media	archaeology	politics
anthropology	physics	chemistry
literature	poverty	war
technology	friendship	sex
medicine	courtship	sports

Others could carve out time to study and thus be the go-to person on subjects such as:

Bible difficulties	hard sayings in the Bible	polemics
apologetics	church history	revivals
Christian classics	great biographies	marriage
biblical languages	death and grieving	parenting
women in ministry	Bible study methods	covenants
hermeneutics	Christian music	

Wouldn't it be incredible to know that there's a person in the congregation who has devoted hundreds of hours to the study of Mormonism or marriage, creationism or the covenants, finances, the fine arts, or one of a myriad of other issues? If you needed answers to pressing questions from seekers, skeptics, neighbors, teachers, family members, or workmates, you would have a body-member of your unit in whom you could confide and from whom you could gather condensed assistance. Or how exciting would it be to offer various eight-week courses on how to think Christianly about dozens of helpful, interesting, and vital subjects? I believe that this type of diverse study within the unified local body is not only within reach, but is perhaps *the* key to preparing the church to give good answers to the good questions that are asked of her and of shoring up the intellectual foundations of the body of Christ.

(4) In conjunction with the above, in the church setting, we can offer *apologetic and worldview classes* for those who are preparing for or involved in college life. Libraries can be built, housing an array of classical *and* cutting-edge materials dealing with every dimension of intellectual fortification. And books of particular interest that challenge the mind can be mentioned from the pulpit, highlighted in the bulletin, and displayed in the foyer.

Of course, the pastor has much to do with the intellectual climate of his congregation. If the shepherd is easily intimidated by sheep who know more about certain spiritual matters or biblical topics than he does, then he will not do well at preparing the saints for works of service, whether they be devotional, evangelistic, or intellectual works. But if the pastor truly wishes to participate in helping his people to refine their thinking, invigorate their intellects, and love God with all of their minds, there are many ways he can do so.

The pastor can practice *verse-by-verse* (expository) *preaching*, working his way through each chapter of a book of the Bible. This helps the believer to think systematically, logically, and coherently. Books of the Bible can also be preached in the style in which they were written. For example, at various times, I have preached from Job using a Socratic style, communicated messages from Isaiah in poetic form, or presented epistles in the first-person. Also, for sixty-six Wednesday evenings, I introduced the books of the Bible. I gave the thematic, geographic, archaeological, sociological, theological, cultural, apologetic, and historical background on each. Then I showed how the message of the book was important for today.

A church can *form debate groups*, assigning panels to contemporary topics and controversial issues for organized discussion. At times, groups from our Christian education class have debated the existence of God, creationism versus evolution, the deity of Christ, the cults, and the like. We have also performed evangelistic skits, where skeptics and critics challenged the believer to provide excellent answers for first-rate questions. Outlines, handouts, and, at times, even homework suggestions for application of the message were provided for these events.

Once I set aside Wednesday evenings for the presentation of great Christian authors, presenting a biographical sketch and a list of the writer's best works. And, as strange as it may sound, more than once I even preached a two-week series on "The Importance of Introductions." That is, I wanted our people to be able to think through the body of a message *with me, in light of* the purposeful introduction that I had prepared. Closely related to this, about every three or four years I preached a four-week series on "How to Hear a Sermon." It seems odd to me that we think it peculiar to preach this type of message. But it seems even more peculiar to me that we seldom talk to the people about how they can proficiently do what they have come to do: to listen — truly listen — to a message from the Word of God!

(5) Finally, and most important, we must seek to clarify fuzzy thinking, arrange befuddled ideas, increase our breadth of perspective, and stimulate our intellects by way of *prayer*. It will do us well to remember that the prayer life is not contrary to the life of the mind, that prayer is most often an intellectual act, and that the intellectual dimension of our faith is also spiritual! Jesus is concerned about what we think, how we think, what we know, why we believe, and how we use our minds for our own sake and for the Father's glory.

We pray for physical healing, traveling safety, financial help, trigonometry tests, noble attitudes, and job interviews. We approach the throne of God to ask for blessings on our hamburgers and our neighbor's pet, and to withhold the farmer's rains in order to provide good weather at the church picnic. If we come to God for all of these and more, we should also consider approaching him over the element without which we could not pray at all — the mind!

We can pray for *humility*, so that we will not be proud in our secure but close-minded approach to the ideas of others. We also need humility so that when we do open our minds, we will not think of ourselves as something special. Rather, we will keep in mind that Jesus was the smartest human that ever lived and yet, at the same time, the most humble! We can pray for *flexibility* to change, *meekness* to admit error, and *boldness*, so that we will not allow the fear of error to hinder us from pursuing truth wherever it may be found.

To these we can add petitions for *openness, willingness, steadfastness*, and *passion* as we strive to "think christianly." And, of course, we must always pray for the Spirit's abiding *protection* from the penetration of perilous ideas. The Father desires that we be led by the wisdom of Christ and power of the Holy Spirit in order to think aright. He wants to be involved in the formation, sanctification, and fortification of our minds. For, as Sertillanges put it, he who seeks to develop his intellect is "not self-begotten; he is the son of the Idea, of the Truth of the creative Word, the Life-giver immanent in His creation. When the thinker thinks rightly, he follows God step by step."[3]

We can also *pray the Scriptures*, asking the Father to help us to love him with our entire mind (Matt. 22:37), to aid us in preparing our minds for action (1 Pet. 1:13), and to become mature in our thinking (1 Cor. 14:20). In keeping with his will, we are invited to ask for his help, that we may find the discipline in order to be able to give superb answers to everyone who asks us the reason for our hope in Christ (1 Peter 3:15), that we will be eager to contend for the faith (Jude 3), and that we will exercise care and skill as we develop and watch our doctrine (1 Tim. 4:16).

We sing the song, declaring that when the Spirit of the Lord moves on our hearts, we will sing and dance like David sang and danced (1 Chron. 15:29). Surely it would also be fitting for us to pray for the Spirit of the Lord to move on our hearts that we might debate, prove, explain, reason, argue, and persuade like Paul (Acts 17 – 19) — that is, to follow Paul as he followed Christ (1 Cor. 4:16; 11:1). Finally, we can pray that the eyes of our minds may be enlightened (Eph. 1.18) and that the Lord will open our minds (Luke 24:45), so that we can possess the mind of the Maker — the mind of Christ (1 Cor. 2:16)!

Raise up an army, O God – an army of Spirit-filled, awakened minds!

NOTES

1. Thomas Cahill, *How the Irish Saved Civilization* (New York: Doubleday, 1995).

2. Stanley Horton, *The Holy Spirit*, (Springfield, MO: Gospel Publishing, 1947), introduction.

3. Sertillanges, *The Intellectual Life*, viii.

Selected Bibliography

BOOKS

Adams, Henry. *The Education of Henry Adams*. Boston: Houghton Mifflin, 1918.

Adler, Mortimer J. *Philosopher at Large: An Intellectual Autobiography*. New York: Macmillan, 1977.

_____. *How to Think about God*. New York: Macmillan, 1980.

_____. *Reforming Education: The Opening of the American Mind*. New York: Collier, 1990.

Ahlstrom, Sydney. *A Religious History of the American People*. 2 vols. Garden City, NY: Image, 1975.

À Kempis, Thomas. *The Imitation of Christ*. Chicago: Moody Press, 1980.

Allen, Diogenes. *Three Outsiders*. Cambridge, MA.: Cowley, 1983.

_____. *Philosophy for Understanding Theology*. Atlanta: John Knox, 1985.

Ames, William. *The Marrow of Theology*. Boston: Pilgrim, 1968 reprint.

Anderson, Gordon. "Questions, Problems, Challenges;" side one of Tape #1 in the cassette series, "Pentecostals at the End of the 20th Century."

_____. "Doctrines" and "Problems, Evaluation, and Conclusion;" on Tape #4 in the cassette series, "The Prophecy Movement."

Anderson, Paul. *Professors Who Believe*. Downer's Grove, IL: InterVarsity Press, 1998.

Anderson, Robert. *Vision of the Disinherited*. New York: Oxford Univ. Press, 1979.

Ante-Nicene Fathers, ed. Philip Schaff. Grand Rapids: Eerdmans, 1989.

Armstrong, Ben. *The Electric Church*. Nashville: Nelson, 1979.

Armstrong, John, ed. *The Coming Evangelical Crisis*. Chicago: Moody Press, 1996.

_____. *The Compromised Church*. Wheaton, IL: Crossway, 1998.

Arnott, John. *The Father's Blessing*. Orlando, FL: Creation House, 1995.

Asbury, Francis. *The Journal of the Reverend Francis Asbury*. New York, 1821.

Atter, Gordon F. *"The Third Force"*: A Pentecostal Answer to the Question . . . Peterborough, ON: College Press, 1962.

Augustine, Saint. *The Confessions of Saint Augustine*. Chicago: Moody Press, 1981.

_____. *Concerning the Teacher*. New York: Appleton, 1938.

Bacon, Francis. *The New Organon*. Ed. F. H. Anderson. New York: Bobbs-Merrill, 1960.

_____. *The Advancement of Learning*. Oxford: Clarendon, 1876.

Bahnsen, Greg. *Always Ready*. Atlanta, GA: American Vision, 1996.

Baldwin, James. *The Book-Lover*. Chicago: McClurg, 1892.

Barbour, Ian. *Religion in an Age of Science*. San Francisco: Harper & Row, 1990.

Barrett, David, ed. *World Christian Encyclopedia*. New York: Oxford Univ. Press, 1982.

Bartleman, Frank. *How Pentecost Came to Los Angeles*: *At the Beginning*. Los Angeles: Bartleman, 1925.

Barzun, Jacques. *The Culture We Deserve*. Middletown, CT: Wesleyan Univ. Press, 1989.

_____. *The House of the Intellect*. New York: Harper & Brothers, 1959.

_____. *From Dawn to Decadence*. New York: Harper Collins, 2000.

Bauer, Susan, and Jessie Wise. *The Well-Trained Mind*. New York: Norton, 1999.

Baxter, Richard. *Baxter's Practical Works*. Vol. 1. Ligonier, PA: Soli Deo Gloria, Reprint 1990.

_____. *The Reformed Pastor*. Carlisle, PA: Banner of Truth Trust, 1983.

Beck, David. *Opening of the American Mind*. Grand Rapids: Baker, 1991.

Bede. *The Venerable Bede's Ecclesiastical History of England*. Ed. John Giles. London: Bohn, 1845.

Beecher, Lyman. *Address to the Charitable Society for the Education of Indigent Pious Young Men*. New Haven, CT: Yale Univ. Press, 1814.

Benedict, Ruth. *Patterns of Culture*. Boston: Houghton Mifflin, 1934.

Bennett, William. *Index of Leading Cultural Indicators*. New York: Simon & Schuster, 1994.

Berry, Wendell. *The Hidden Wound*. San Francisco: North Point, 1989.

Bettenson, Henry, ed. *Documents of the Christian Church*. New York: Oxford Univ. Press, 1982.

Bigg, Charles. *The Christian Platonists of Alexandria*. New York: Macmillan, 1886.

Birrell, Augustine, ed. *The Oxford Dictionary of Quotations*. 3rd ed. Oxford: Oxford Univ. Press, 1979.

Black, Jim Nelson. *When Nations Die*. Wheaton: Tyndale, 1994.

Blamires, Harry. *The Christian Mind*. Ann Arbor: Servant Books, 1978.

Bloch-Hoell, Nils. *The Pentecostal Movement*. Oslo, Norway: Universitetsforlaget, 1964.

Bloom, Allan. *The Closing of the American Mind*. New York: Simon & Schuster, 1987.

Bloom, Harold. *The American Religion*. New York: Simon & Schuster, 1992.

Blumhofer, Edith. *The Assemblies of God: A Chapter in the Story of American Pentecostalism*. 2 vols. Springfield, MO: Gospel Publishing, 1989.

Boles, John. *The Great Revival of 1800*. Philadelphia: Williams, 1872.

Bonar, Andrew. *Memoir and Remains of R. M. M'Cheyne*. Southampton, UK: Camelot, 1966.

Bonaventure. *Major and Minor Life of St. Francis*. Ed. Benen Fahy. Chicago: Franciscan, 1973.

Bradford, Gamaliel. *D. L. Moody: A Worker in Souls*. New York: Blomaster & Son, 1927.

Brinton, Crane. *The Shaping of Modern Thought*. Englewood Cliffs, NJ: Prentice-Hall, 1963.

Broad, William, and Nicholas Wade. *Betrayers of Truth*: *Fraud and Deceit in the Halls of Science*. New York: Simon & Schuster, 1982.

Brook, Benjamin. *The Lives of the Puritans*. Pittsburgh, PA: Soli Deo Gloria, 1994.

Brown, Colin, ed. *The New International Dictionary of New Testament Theology*. Grand Rapids: Zondervan, 1976.

_____. *Philosophy and the Christian Faith*. Downers Grove, IL: InterVarsity, 1968.

Brown, Harold. *The Sensate Culture*. Dallas: Word, 1996.

Brumback, Carl. *What Meaneth This?* Springfield, MO: Gospel Publishing, 1947.

Bruce, A. B. *Apologetics: Christianity Defended*. Edinburgh: T. & T. Clark, 1892.

Bruce, F. F. *The Defense of the Gospel in the New Testament*. Leicester, UK: Inter-Varsity Press, 1977.

_____. *The New Testament Documents*. Grand Rapids: Eerdmans, 1992.

Bruner, Fredrick Dale. *A Theology of the Holy Spirit*. Grand Rapids: Eerdmans, 1970.

Brunner, Emil. *Revelation and Reason*. Philadelphia: Westminster, 1946.

_____. *Christianity and Civilization*. New York: Scribner's, 1949.

Buckingham, Jamie. "Wasted Time." *Charisma* (December 1988).

Buechner, Frederick. *Telling the Truth*. San Francisco: Harper & Row, 1977.

_____. *The Hungering Dark*. New York: Seabury, 1969.

Burder, Henry Foster. *Mental Discipline*. New York: Jonathan Leavitt, 1830.

Burgess, Stanley, and Gary B. Mcgee, eds. *Dictionary of Pentecostal and Charismatic Movements*. Grand Rapids: Zondervan, 1988.

Burgess, William. *The Bible in Shakspeare*. Chicago: Winona, 1903.

Burke, Edmund. *A Philosophical Inquiry into the Origin of Our Ideas*. Notre Dame, IN: Univ. of Notre Dame Press, 1968.

Burnham, James. *The Suicide of the West*. Washington, D.C.: Regnery Gateway, 1985.

Burtner, R. W., and R. E. Chiles. *A Compend of Wesley's Theology*. Nashville: Abingdon, 1954.

Bush, Russ. *A Handbook for Christian Philosophy*. Grand Rapids: Zondervan, 1991.

Butterfield, Herbert. *The Origins of Modern Science*. New York: Free Press, 1957.

Cahill, Thomas. *How the Irish Saved Civilization*. New York: Doubleday, 1995.

Cairns, Earle. *An Endless Line of Splendor*. Wheaton: Tyndale, 1986.

Calvin, John. *Commentaries on the Pastoral Epistles*. Grand Rapids: Baker, 1996.

_____. *Institutes of the Christian Religion*. Ed. John T. McNeil. Library of Christian Classics vols. 20–21. Philadelphia: Westminster, 1960.

Campbell, Joseph. *The Pentecostal Holiness Church*. Franklin Springs, GA: Publishing House of the Pentecostal Church, 1951.

Canfield, Joseph. *The Incredible Scofield and His Book*. Vallecito, CA: Ross House, 1988.

Cantelon, Williard. *The Baptism of the Holy Spirit and Speaking with God in the Unknown Tongue*. Plainfield, NJ: Logos International, 1970.

Carden, Allen. *Puritan Christianity in America*. Grand Rapids: Baker, 1990.

Carmody, Denise. *Organizing a Christian Mind*. Valley Forge, PA: Trinity Press International, 1996.

Carnell, Edward John. *An Introduction to Christian Apologetics*. Grand Rapids: Eerdmans, 1948.

Carroll, Leonard. *The Glossolalia Phenomenon*. Ed. Wade H. Horton. Cleveland, TN: Pathway, 1966.

Casserley, J.V. Langmead. *The Christian in Philosophy*. New York: Charles Scribner's Sons, 1962.

Chapman, J. Wilbur. *The Life and Work of Dwight Lyman Moody*. London: James Nisbet, 1900.

Chesterton, G. K. *William Blake*. London: Duckworth, 1936.

_____. *What's Wrong with the World*. Peru, IL.: Sherwood Sudgen, 1989.

Christenson, Larry. *A Message to the Charismatic Movement*. Minneapolis: Dimension, 1972.

Clark, Davis W. *Mental Discipline*. New York: Nelson & Phillips, 1847.

Clark, Elmer. *The Psychology of Religious Awakening*. New York: Macmillan, 1929.

Clark, Gordon. *Faith and Saving Faith*. Jefferson, MD: Trinity Foundation, 1983.

_____. *Logic*. Jefferson, MD: Trinity Foundation, 1988.

Clark, James. *Philosophers Who Believe*. Downers Grove, IL.: InterVarsity Press, 1993.

Clement, Arthur. *Pentecost or Pretense? An Examination of the Pentecostal and Charismatic Movements*. Milwaukee: Northwestern, 1981.

Clough, Shepard. *The Rise and Fall of Civilization*. New York: Columbia Univ. Press, 1951.

Collins, Gary R. *The Magnificent Mind*. Waco, TX: Word, 1985.

Colson, Charles. *Against the Night*. Ann Arbor, MI: Servant, 1989.

Commager, Henry. *The American Mind*. New Haven: Yale Univ. Press, 1959.

Conn, Charles. *Like a Mighty Army*. Cleveland, TN: Church of God Publishing, 1955.

Connally, William. *History of Kansas State and People*. Chicago: American Historical Society, 1928.

Coulter, E. Merton. *College Life in the Old South*. New York: Macmillan, 1928.

Cousins, Ewert, ed. *The Soul's Journey into God*. New York: Paulist, 1978.

Cowan, Louise, and Os Guiness, eds. *Invitation to the Classics*. Grand Rapids: Baker, 1998.

Cox, Harvey. *Fire from Heaven*. Reading, MA: Addison-Wesley, 1995.

Croce, Benedetto. *History as the Story of Liberty*. New York: Norton, 1941.

Culpepper, Richard. *Evaluating the Charismatic Movement*. Valley Forge, PA: Judson, 1977.

Cuming, G. J., and Derek Baker. *Popular Belief and Practice*. Cambridge: Cambridge Univ. Press, 1972.

Czitrom, Daniel. *Media and the American Mind*. Chapel Hill: Univ. of North Carolina Press, 1982.

Dayton, Donald. *Theological Roots of Pentecostalism*. Peabody, MA: Hendrickson, 1991.

DeArteaga, William. *Quenching the Spirit*. Orlando: Creation House, 1992.

Deferrari, Roy, ed. *Early Christian Biographies*. The Fathers of the Church, vol. 15, Washington, D.C.: Catholic Univ. of America Press, 1964.

DeMar, Gary. *Last Days Madness: Obsession of the Modern Church*. Atlanta: American Vision, 1994.

_____. *God and Government*. Vol. 1. Atlanta: American Vision, 1983.

De Molen, Richard. ed. *Leaders of the Reformation*. London: Susquehanna Univ. Press, 1984.

Dewey, John. *How We Think*. Boston: Heath, 1910.

Dimnet, Earnest. *The Art of Thinking*. Greenwich, CT: Premier, 1963.

Ditmanson, Harold. *Christian Faith and the Liberal Arts*. Minneapolis: Augsburg, 1960.

Dobson, James, and Gary Bauer. *Children at Risk*. Dallas: Word, 1990.

_____. *Emotions: Can You Trust Them?* Ventura, CA: Regal, 1980.

Dollar, George. *The New Testament and New Pentecostalism*. Sarasota, FL: Nystrom, 1978.

Dooyeweerd, Herman. *In the Twilight of Western Thought*. Nurley, NJ: Craig, 1965.

Douglas, J. D, ed. *The New International Dictionary of the Christian Church*. Grand Rapids: Zondervan, 1978.

Draper, John William. *The Conflict between Religion and Science*. London: Henry King, 1876.

Drummond, A. L. *Edward Irving and His Circle*. London: James Clarke, 1934.

Durant, Will. *The Age of Reason Begins*. New York: Simon & Schuster, 1960.

Duvall, S. M. *The Methodist Episcopal Church and Education up to 1860*. New York: AMS Press, 1928.

Eby, Frederick. *The Development of Modern Education*. New York: Prentice-Hall, 1941.

Edwards, Bela Bates. "Influence of Piety on the Intellectual Powers." In *Writings*. Boston: Tilton, 1853.

_____. *Biographies of Self-Taught Men*. Boston: Tilton, 1859.

Edwards, Jonathan. *A Treatise Concerning Religious Affections*. In *Works of Jonathan Edwards*, 2 vols. Ed. Tryon Edwards. New York: Garland, 1987.

_____. *The Life of David Brainerd*. Grand Rapids: Baker, 1978.

Einstadt, Samuel. *The Decline of Empires*. Englewood Cliffs, N.J.: Prentice Hall, 1967.

Ellul, Jacques. *The Humiliation of the Word*. Trans. Joyce Main Hanks. Grand Rapids: Eerdmans, 1985.

_____. *The Subversion of Christianity*. Grand Rapids: Eerdmans, 1986.

Erickson, Millard. *The Evangelical Mind and Heart*. Grand Rapids: Baker, 1993.

Fairlie, Henry. *The Seven Deadly Sins Today*. Washington, D.C.: New Republic, 1978.

Faupel, David W. *The American Pentecostal Movement: A Bibliographical Essay*. Wilmore, KY: Fisher Library and Society for Pentecostal Studies, 1972.

Faust, C. H. "Edwards as Scientist." In *American Literature*, vol. 1. New York: American, 1930.

Fee, Gordon. *Gospel and Spirit: Issues in New Testament Hermeneutics*. Peabody: Hendrickson, 1991.

_____. *Listening to the Spirit in the Text*. Grand Rapids: Eerdmans, 2000.

Fenelon, François. *The Best of Fenelon*. Ed. Harold Chadwick. Gainsville, FL: Bridge-Logos, 2002.

Findlay, James Jr. *Dwight L. Moody: American Evangelist*. Chicago: Univ. of Chicago Press, 1969.

Finney, Charles. *Lectures on Revivals of Religion*. New York: F. H. Revell, 1868.

_____. *Memoirs*. New York: New York Press, 1876.

Fish, Henry. *Primitive Piety Revived*. Boston: Congregational Board of Publication, 1855.

Fitzgerald, Allan D. *Augustine through the Ages*. Grand Rapids: Eerdmans, 1999.

Frodsham, Stanley. *With Signs Following*. Springfield, MO: Gospel Publishing, 1946.

Frye, Northrop. *The Educated Imagination*. Bloomington, IN: Indiana Univ. Press, 1964.

Gaebelein. Frank E. *The Christian, the Arts, and Truth*. Portland: Multnomah, 1985.

Gallagher, Susan, and Roger Lundin. *Literature through the Eyes of Faith*. San Francisco: Harper, 1989.

Garrett, Clarke. *Spirit Possession and Popular Religion*. Baltimore: Johns Hopkins Univ. Press, 1987.

Gee, Donald. *The Pentecostal Movement: Including the Story of the War Years (1940–1947)*. London: Elim, 1949.

_____. *Concerning Spiritual Gifts*. Springfield, MO: Gospel Publishing, reprint, 1994.

_____. *The Ministry-Gifts of Christ*. Springfield, MO: Gospel Publishing, 1930.

Geisler, Norman, and Ronald M. Brookes. *Come, Let Us Reason: An Introduction to Logical Thinking*. Grand Rapids: Baker, 1990.

Gibbon, Edward. *Christianity and the Decline of Rome*. New York: Collier, 1966.

Gill, David W. *The Opening of the Christian Mind*. Downers Grove, IL.: Inter Varsity Press, 1989.

Godolphin, F. R. B., ed. "Cupid and Psyche," in *The Golden Ass*, by Lucius Apuleius. New York: Random House, 1964.

Graham, Stephen R. *Cosmos in the Chaos: Philip Schaff's Interpretation of Nineteenth-Century Religion*. Grand Rapids: Eerdmans, 1995.

Grant, Robert. *Greek Apologists of the Second Century*. Philadelphia, PA: Westminster, 1988.

Graubard, Stephen. *Reading in the 1980's*. New York: Bowker, 1983.

Green, Michael. *I Believe in the Holy Spirit*. Grand Rapids: Eerdmans, 1975.

Greene, Jay. *100 Great Thinkers*. New York: Washington Square, 1967.

Grenz, Stanely, and Roger Olson, *Who Needs Theology?* Downer's Grove, IL: InterVarsity Press, 1996.

Gromacki, Robert. *The Modern Tongues Movement*. Philadelphia: Presbyterian & Reformed, 1976.

Guiness, Os. *Fit Bodies Fat Minds*. Grand Rapids: Baker, 1994.

_____. *The Gravedigger File*. Downers Grove, IL: InterVarsity Press, 1983.

Gurnall, William. *The Christian in Complete Armour*: 3 vols. Edinburgh: Banner of Truth Trust, 1986 reprint of 1655 edition.

Hamilton, Michael P., ed. *The Charismatic Movement*. Grand Rapids: Eerdmans, 1975.

Hanks, Geoffrey. *Seventy Great Christians*. Bristol, UK: Christian Focus, 1992.

Hardman, Keith. *Issues in American Christianity*. Grand Rapids: Baker, 1993.

Harper, Michael. "Are You a Gnostic?" *Renewal* (October-November, 1972).

Harvard Classics: *Five-Foot Shelf of Books*. New York: Collier & Son, 1938.

Hatch, Edwin. *The Influence of Greek Ideas and Usages upon the Christian Church*. Peabody, MA: Hendrickson, 1995 reprint.

Hatch, Nathan O. *The Democratization of American Christianity*. New Haven, CT: Yale Univ. Press, 1989.

Hayford, Jack. *Worship His Majesty*. Waco, TX: Word, 1987.

_____. *Twelve Voices for Truth*. Nashville: Nelson, 1995.

_____. "A Remedy for Imbalance." *Charisma* (September, 1990).

Healy, Jane. *Endangered Minds*. New York: Simon & Schuster, 1990.

Henry, Carl F. *The Christian Mindset in a Secular Society*. Portland, OR: Multnomah, 1978.

_____. *Evangelicals at the Brink of Crisis*. Waco, TX: Word, 1967.

_____. *Twilight of a Great Civilization*. Westchester, IL: Crossway, 1988.

_____. *Christian Countermoves in a Decadent Culture*. Portland, OR: Multnomah, 1986.

Henry, G. W. *History of the Jumpers*: *Shouting Genuine and Spurious*. Waukesha, WI: Metropolitan Church Association, 1909.

Hergenhahn, B. R. *An Introduction to Theories of Personality*. Englewood Cliffs, NJ: Simon & Schuster, 1980.

Highet, Gilbert. *Paideia*. New York: Oxford Univ. Press, 1945.

Hoftstader, Richard. *Anti-intellectualism in American Life*. New York: Alfred A. Knopf, 1963.

Hollenweger, Walter. *The Pentecostals*. Peabody, MA: Hendrickson, 1979.

Holmes, Arthur. *The Making of a Christian Mind*. Downers Grove, IL: InterVarsity Press, 1985.

_____. *Philosophy*: *A Christian Perspective*. Downers Grove, IL: InterVarsity Press, 1975.

_____. *The Idea of a Christian College*. Grand Rapids.: Eerdmans, 1987.

_____. *Contours of a World View*. Grand Rapids: Eerdmans, 1983.

Hooykaas, R. J. *Religion and the Rise of Modern Science*. Edinburgh: Scottish Academic Press, 1972.

_____. *The Principle of Uniformity in Geology, Biology, and Theology*. Leiden: Free Univ. Press, 1959.

_____. *Science and Theology in the Middle Ages*. Leiden: Free Univ. Press, 1954.

Horton, Michael. *Made in America: The Shaping of Modern Evangelicalism*. Grand Rapids: Baker, 1991.

Horton, Stanley M. *The Holy Spirit*, Springfield, MO: Gospel Publishing, 1947.

_____. *Into All Truth*. Springfield, MO: Gospel Publishing, 1955.

Houston, James. *The Mind on Fire*. Portland, OR: Multnomah, 1989.

Howley, Craig, A. Howley, and E. Pendarvis. *Out of Our Minds*. New York: Teachers College Press, 1995.

Hudson, Winthrop. "The Methodist Age in America." *Methodist History* 12 (April 1974).

Hughes, George. *Days of Power in the Forest Temple*. Salem, OH: Allegheny Wesleyan Methodist, 1975.

Huse, Scott. *The Collapse of Evolution*. Grand Rapids: Baker, 1983.

Huxley, Julian. *Religion without Revelation*. New York: Mentor, 1957.

Jackson, Thomas. *The Life of the Rev. Charles Wesley, M. A.: Some Time Student of Christ-Church Oxford*. New York: Lane Sandford, 1842.

Jaki, Stanley. *Science and Creation*. Edinburgh: Scottish Academic Press, 1974.

_____. *Roads of Science and the Ways to God*. Chicago: Univ. of Chicago Press, 1978.

Jastrow, Robert. *God and the Astronomers*. New York: Norton, 1978.

Jeffrey, David. *People of the Book*. Grand Rapids: Eerdmans, 1996.

Jensen, Jerry. *Baptists and the Baptism of the Holy Spirit*. Los Angeles: Full Gospel Businessmen's Fellowship International, 1963.

Johnson, Arthur. *Faith Misguided: Exposing the Dangers of Mysticism*. Chicago: Moody Press, 1988.

Johnson, Paul. *Intellectuals*. New York: Harper & Row, 1988.

Johnson, Phillip E. *Reason in the Balance*. Downers Grove, IL.: InterVarsity Press, 1993.

Jones, Michael E. *Degenerate Moderns*. San Francisco: Ignatius, 1993.

Kaiser, Christopher. *Creation and the History of Science*. Grand Rapids: Eerdmans, 1991.

Kendrick, Klaude. *The Promise Fulfilled*. Springfield, MO: Gospel Publishing, 1961.

_____. "The Pentecostal Movement: Hopes and Hazards." *Christian Century* (May 8, 1963).

Kennedy, D. James, and Jerry Newcombe. *What If the Bible Had Never Been Written?* Nashville: Nelson, 1998.

_____. *What If Jesus Had Never Been Born?* Nashville: Nelson, 2005.

Kerr, Hugh. *A Compend of Luther's Theology*. Philadelphia: Westminster, 1966.

Kilpatrick, William Kirk. *Psychological Seduction*. Nashville: Nelson, 1983.

Klaaren, Eugene. *Religious Origins of Modern Science*. Grand Rapids: Eerdmans, 1977.

Knox, R. A. *Enthusiasm*. Oxford: Clarendon, 1950.

Koestler, Arthur. *The Act of Creation*. London: Penguin Books, 1964.

_____. *The Sleepwalkers: History of Man's Changing Ideas*. Harmondsworth, U.K.: Penguin, 1964.

Kozol, Jonathan. *Illiterate America*. Garden City, NY: Anchor/Doubleday, 1985.

Kreeft, Peter. *A Summa of the Summa: The Essential Philosophical Passages of St. Thomas Aquinas*. San Francisco: Ignatius, 1990.

_____. *Christianity for Modern Pagans: Pascal's Pensees*. Fort Collins, CO: Ignatius, 1993.

_____. *C. S. Lewis for The Third Millennium*. San Francisco: Ignatius, 1994.

Kuyper, Abraham. *The Work of the Holy Spirit*. Grand Rapids: Eerdmans, 1946.

Kyle, Richard. *The Religious Fringe: A History of Alternative Religions in America*. Downers Grove, IL: InterVarsity Press, 1993.

La Haye, Tim. *Faith of Our Founding Fathers*. Brentwood, TN: Wolgemuth and Hyatt, 1987.

Lamont, Ann. *21 Great Scientists Who Believed the Bible*. Brisbane, Australia: CS Foundation, 1995.

Land, Steven J. *Pentecostal Spirituality: A Passion for the Kingdom*. Sheffield: Sheffield Academic Press, 1993.

Langford, Jerome. *Galileo, Science, and the Church*. Ann Arbor, MI: Ann Arbor Paperbacks, 1971.

Lapsley, James, and J. Simpson. "Speaking in Tongues." *The Princeton Seminary Bulletin* 58 (February 1965).

Lasch, Christopher. *The Culture of Narcissism*. New York: Norton, 1978.

Laski, Marghanita. *Ecstasy*. New York: Greenwood, 1968.

Latourette, Kenneth Scott. *Christianity in a Revolutionary Age*. 5 vols. New York: Harper, 1958–1962.

_____. *A History of the Expansion of Christianity: First Five Centuries*. Vol. 1. New York: Harper, 1970.

LeClercq, Jean. *The Love of Learning and the Desire for God*. New York: Fordham Univ. Press, 1982.

Lewis, C. S. *God in the Dock*. Grand Rapids: Eerdmans, 1970.

_____. *Letters to Arthur Greeves*. Ed. Walter Hooper. New York: Collier/Macmillan, 1986.

_____. *The Discarded Image: Medieval and Renaissance Literature*. Cambridge: Cambridge Univ. Press, 1964.

_____. *The Pilgrim's Regress*. Grand Rapids: Eerdmans, 1981.

_____. *The Great Divorce*. New York: Simon & Schuster, 1974.

_____. *Mere Christianity*. New York: Macmillan, 1972.

Lewis, I. M. *Ecstatic Religion*. Baltimore: Penguin, 1972.

Lloyd-Jones, David Martyn. *Revival*. Wheaton, IL, Good News, 1987.

_____. *Life in the Spirit*. Grand Rapids: Baker, 1975.

_____. *Joy Unspeakable: Power and Renewal in the Holy Spirit*. Eastbourne: Kingsway, 1984.

_____. *The Sovereign Spirit*. Wheaton, IL: Harold Shaw, 1985.

Lubenow, Marvin. *Bones of Contention*. Grand Rapids: Baker, 1992.

Ludwig, Charles. *Francis Asbury: God's Circuit Rider*. Milford, MI: Mott Media, 1984.

Lunn, Arnold. *The Revolt against Reason*. New York: Sheed & Ward, 1951.

Luther, Martin. *Works of Martin Luther*. Philadelphia: Holman, 1915.

_____. *Letters of Spiritual Counsel*. Ed. Theodore Tappert. Philadelphia: Westminster, 1955.

Lutzer, Erwin. *Exploding the Myths That Will Destroy America*. Chicago: Moody Press, 1986.

Ma, Wonsuk, and Robert P. Menzies, eds. *Pentecostalism in Context: Essays on Honor of William W. Menzies*. Sheffield, England: Sheffield Academic Press, 1997.

Malik, Charles. *The Two Tasks*. Westchester, IL: Cornerstone, 1980.

_____. *A Christian Critique of the University*. Downers Grove, IL: InterVarsity Press, 1982.

Manguel, Alberto. *A History of Reading*. New York: Penguin, 1996.

Manna, A. and S. Misheff. "What Teachers Say about Their Own Reading." *Journal of Reading* (November, 1987).

Marsden, George. *Fundamentalism and American Culture*. New York: Oxford, 1980.

_____. *Religion and American Culture*. San Diego: Harcourt Brace, 1990.

_____. *The Outrageous Idea of Christian Scholarship*. New York: Oxford Univ. Press, 1997.

Marshall, Peter, and David Manuel. *Sounding Forth the Trumpet: God's Plan for America in Peril: 1837–1860*. Grand Rapids: Revell, 1997.

_____. *From Sea to Shining Sea*. Tarrytown, NY: Revell, 1986.

Martin, David. *Tongues of Fire: The Explosion of Protestantism in Latin America*. Oxford: Basil Blackwell, 1990.

Martin, Walter. *Kingdom of the Cults*, Rev. ed.. Minneapolis: Bethany, 1985.

Mayer, F. E. *The Religious Bodies of America*. 4th ed. Revised Arthur Carl Piepkorn. St. Louis: Concordia, 1961.

McCutcheon, George Barr. *Books Once Were Men*. New York: Dodd, Mead, & Company, 1931.

McDowell, Josh. *The Best of Josh McDowell*. Nashville: Nelson, 1993.

McGaw, Francis. *Praying Hyde*. Minneapolis: Bethany, 1970.

McGiffert, A. C. *Protestant Thought before Kant*. London: Duckworth, 1911.

McGrath, Alister. *A Cloud of Witnesses: Ten Great Christian Thinkers*. Grand Rapids: Zondervan, 1990.

McLoughlin, William G. *Billy Sunday Was His Real Name*. Chicago: Univ. of Chicago Press, 1955.

_____. *Modern Revivalism*. New York: Ronald, 1959.

Mead, Sydney. *The Lively Experiment: The Shaping of Christianity in America*. New York: Harper, 1963.

Menzies, William. *Anointed to Serve*. Springfield, MO: Gospel Publishing, 1971.

Merrigan, Terrence. *Clear Heads and Holy Hearts*. Louvain, Belgium: Peeters, 1991.

Merton, Robert K. *Science, Technology, and Society in Seventeenth Century England*. New York: Fertig, 1970.

Merton, Thomas. *Thoughts in Solitude*. London: Burns & Oates, 1958.

Meyer, Joyce. *Battlefield of the Mind*. Tulsa, OK: Harrison House, 1995.

Mill, John Stuart. *Dissertations and Discourses*, vol. 4. New York: Henry Holt, 1875.

Millard, Catherine. *The Rewriting of America's History*. Camp Hill, PA: Horizon House, 1991.

Miller, Graham. *Calvin's Wisdom*. Edinburgh: Banner of Truth, 1992.

Miller, Perry. *America: A Sketch of Its Political, Social and Religious Character*. Cambridge, MA: Harvard Univ. Press, 1961.

_____. *The Life of the Mind in America: From the Revolution to the Civil War*. New York: Harcourt, Brace & World, 1965.

_____. *Jonathan Edwards*. New York: Sloane Associates, 1949.

_____. *The New England Mind: From Colony to Province*. Cambridge, MA: Belknap, 1953; reprint 1998.

_____. *The New England Mind: The Seventeenth Century*. Cambridge, MA: Belknap, 1939; reprint 1982.

Mills, Watson. *Speaking in Tongues*. Waco, TX: Word, 1967.

Milton, John. *Areopagitica and of Education*. New York: Appleton, 1951.

Mitchell, Christopher. *The C. S. Lewis Reader's Encyclopedia*. Grand Rapids: Zondervan, 1998.

M'Nemar, Richard. *The Kentucky Revival*; or, *A Short History of the Late Extraordinary Outpouring of the Spirit of God*. New York, 1846.

Molnar, Thomas. *The Decline of the Intellectuals*. New York: World, 1961.

Monsma, John Clover. *The Evidence of God in an Expanding Universe*. New York: Putnam, 1958.

Montgomery, John Warwick. *Evidence for Faith*. Dallas: Probe, 1991.

Moreland, J. P. *Love Your God with All Your Mind*. Colorado Springs: NavPress, 1997.

_____. *Christianity and the Nature of Science: A Philosophical Investigation*. Grand Rapids: Baker, 1989.

_____, and David Ciocchi. *Christian Perspectives on Being Human*. Grand Rapids: Baker, 1993.

Morison, Frank. *Who Moved the Stone?* London: Faber and Faber, 1972.

Morison, Samuel Eliot. *The Founding of Harvard College*. Cambridge, MA: Harvard Univ. Press, 1935.

Morris, Henry. *The Genesis Record*. Grand Rapids: Baker, 1976.

_____. *The Long War against God: The History and Impact of the Creation/Evolution Conflict*. Grand Rapids: Baker, 1989.

_____. *Men of Science — Men of God*. San Diego: Master, 1988.

Morris, Thomas. *Making Sense of It All: Pascal and the Meaning of Life*. Grand Rapids: Eerdmans, 1992.

_____. *God and the Philosophers*. New York: Oxford Univ. Press, 1994.

Moyer, Elgin, and E. Cairns, eds. *Wycliffe Biographical Dictionary of the Church*. Chicago: Moody Press, 1982.

Muggeridge, Malcolm. *Chronicles of Wasted Time*. New York: Collins, 1972.

Murray, Iain. *Jonathan Edwards: A New Biography*. Carlisle, PA: Banner of Truth Trust, 1987.

_____. *Revival and Revivalism*. Carlisle, PA: Banner of Truth Trust, 1994.

_____. *The Invitation System*. Carlisle, PA: Banner of Truth Trust, 1967.

Myer, Kenneth. *All God's Children and Blue Suede Shoes*. Westchester, IL: Crossway, 1989.

Nash, Ronald. *The New Evangelicalism*. Grand Rapids: Zondervan, 1963.

_____. *The Word of God and the Mind of Man*. Grand Rapids: Zondervan, 1982.

Nathan, Rich, and Ken Wilson. *Empowered Evangelicals*. Ann Arbor, MI: Servant, 1995.

Nee, Watchman. *The Spiritual Man*. New York: Christian Fellowship, 1968.

Needham, Joseph. The *Grand Titration: Science/Society in East and West*. Toronto: Univ. of Toronto Press, 1969.

Neuhaus, Richard. *America against Itself*. Notre Dame, IN: Univ. of Notre Dame Press, 1992.

_____. *The Naked Public Square*. Grand Rapids: Eerdmans, 1984.

Newman, John Henry. *The Idea of a University*. New Haven, CT: Yale Univ. Press, 1996.

_____. *Apologia Pro Vita Sua*. Ed. David DeLaura. New York: Norton, 1968.

Nichol, John. *The Pentecostals*. Plainfield, NJ: Logos International, 1966.

Niebuhr, H. Richard. *Christ and Culture*. London: Faber & Faber, 1952.

Niebuhr, Reinhold. *Nature and Destiny of Man*. 2 vols. New York: Scribner's, 1966.

Noll, Mark. *The Scandal of the Evangelical Mind*. Grand Rapids: Eerdmans, 1994.

_____. *Turning Points*. Grand Rapids: Baker, 1997.

_____, Nathan Hatch, and George Marsden. *The Search for Christian America*. Westchester, IL: Crossway, 1983.

O'Connor, Edward. *The Pentecostal Movement in the Catholic Church*. Notre Dame, IN: Ave Maria, 1971.

O'Connor, Flannery. *Mystery and Manners*. Ed. Robert Fitzgerald. New York: Farrar & Giroux, 1957.

Olson, Richard. *Science Deified and Science Defied*. Berkeley: Univ. of California Press, 1982.

Oral Roberts University Library. *Pentecostal Periodicals*. Tulsa, OK., 1971.

Orr, Edwin. *The Event of the Century*: *The 1857–1858 Awakening*, Ed. Richard Owens Roberts. Wheaton: International Awakening, 1989.

Orwell, George. *1984*. New York: New American Library, 1984 reprint.

Painter, F. *Luther on Education*. St. Louis, MO: Concordia, 1889.

Palmer, Michael. *Elements of a Christian Worldview*. Springfield, MO: Logion, 1998.

Parham, Charles. *A Voice Crying in the Wilderness*. Baxter Springs, KS: Joplin Printing, 1944.

_____. *The Everlasting Gospel*. Baxter Springs, KS: Parham, 1942.

Parham, Sarah. *The Life of Charles F. Parham: Founder of the Apostolic Faith Movement*. Joplin, MO: Tri-State Printing, 1930.

Pascal, Blaise. *Pensées*. Trans. A. J. Krailsheimer. Harmondsworth, UK: Penguin, 1966.

Pearcey, Nancy, and Charles Thaxton. *The Soul of Science*: *Christian Faith and Natural Philosophy*. Wheaton, IL: Crossway, 1994.

Peck, Janice. *The Gods of Televangelism*. Cresskill, NJ: Hampton, 1993.

Pelikan, Jaroslav. *The Idea of a University*: *A Reexamination*. New Haven, CT.: Yale Univ. Press, 1992.

Percy, Walker. *Lost in the Cosmos*. New York: Washington Square, 1983.

Phillips, Timothy, and Dennis Okholm, eds. *Christian Apologetics in the Postmodern World*. Downers Grove, IL: InterVarsity Press, 1995.

Pieper, Josef. *In Defense of Philosophy*. Trans. Lothar Drauth. San Francisco: Ignatius, 1992.

Pike, Kenneth L. *With Heart and Mind*. Grand Rapids: Eerdmans, 1962.

Pinnock, Clark. *Set Forth Your Case*. Chicago: Moody Press, 1967.

Plantinga, Alvin, and Nicholas Wolterstorff, eds. *Faith and Rationality*. Notre Dame, IN: Univ. of Notre Dame Press, 1983.

Plato. *Phaedrus*: *Collected Dialogues*. Princeton, NJ: Princeton Univ. Press, 1961.

Polanyi, Michael. *Personal Knowledge: Toward a Post-critical Philosophy*. New York: Harper, 1964.

Poloma, Margaret. *The Assemblies of God at the Crossroads*. Knoxville: Univ. of Tennessee Press, 1989.

Postman, Neil. *Amusing Ourselves to Death*. New York: Penguin, 1985.

_____. *Conscientious Objections: Stirring Up Trouble about Language, Technology, and Education*. New York: Knopf, 1988.

Quebedeaux, Richard. *The New Charismatics*. San Francisco: Harper & Row, 1976.

Quiller-Couch, Sir Arthur. *On the Art of Reading*. New York: Putnam's Sons, 1920.

Ramm, Bernard. *The Christian View of Science and Scripture*. Grand Rapids: Eerdmans, 1955.

Ravitch, Diane, and C. E. Finn. *What Do Our Seventeen Year Olds Know?* New York: Harper & Row, 1987.

Reid, W. Stanford, ed. *John Calvin*: *His Influence in the Western World*. Grand Rapids: Zondervan, 1982.

Rhys, Hedley Howell. *Seventeenth Century Science and Arts*. Princeton, NJ: Princeton Univ. Press, 1961.

Richmond, Hugh. *The Christian Revolutionary*: *John Milton*. Berkeley: Univ. of California Press, 1974.

Rookmaaker, H. R. *Modern Art and the Death of a Culture.* Downers Grove, IL: InterVarsity Press, 1970.

Ruckman, Peter S. *The Anti-Intellectual Manifesto.* Pensacola, FL: Ruckman, 1991.

Rupp, E. G. *Patterns of Reformation.* London: Epworth, 1969.

Rutland, Mark. *Behind the Glittering Mask.* Ann Arbor, MI: Servant, 1996.

Ryken, Leland. *Culture in Christian Perspective.* Portland, OR: Multnomah, 1986.

_____. *Worldly Saints: The Puritans As They Really Were.* Grand Rapids: Zondervan, 1986.

Sacks, Oliver. *The Man Who Mistook His Wife for a Hat.* New York: Harper Perennial, 1985.

Sale, Kirkpatrick. *Rebels against the Future.* Reading, MA: Addison-Wesley, 1995.

Sanders, Oswald. *Spiritual Leadership.* Chicago: Moody Press, 1967.

Sargant, William. *The Battle for the Mind.* New York: Harper & Row, 1957.

Sayers, Dorothy L. *Christian Letters to a Post-Christian World.* Grand Rapids: Eerdmans, 1969.

_____. *The Mind of the Maker.* San Francisco: HarperSanFrancisco, 1987.

_____. *Unpopular Opinions.* London: Victor Gollanz, 1946.

Schaeffer, Francis. *The Collected Works of Francis Schaeffer.* 5 vols. Wheaton, IL: Crossway, 1982.

_____. *The Great Evangelical Disaster.* Wheaton, IL: Crossway, 1984.

_____. *Art and the Bible.* Downers Grove, IL: InterVarsity Press, 1973.

Schaff, David. *The Life of Philip Schaff: In Part Autobiographical.* New York: Scribner's, 1987.

Schaff, Philip. *The Principle of Protestantism.* Trans. John W. Nevin. Chambersburg, PA: German Reformed Church, 1845.

_____. *Church and State in the United States.* New York: Scribner's, 1888.

_____. *America: A Sketch of the Political, Social, and Religious Character of the United States.* Cambridge, MA: Harvard Univ. Press, 1961.

_____. *History of the Apostolic Church with a General Introduction to Church History.* Trans. Edward D. Yeomans. New York: Scribner's, 1854.

Schlultze, Quentin. *Televangelism and American Culture.* Grand Rapids: Baker, 1991.

Scougal, Henry. *The Life of God in the Soul of Man.* Chouteau, MT: Gospel Mission, 1986 reprint.

Sertillanges, A. G. *The Intellectual Life.* Washington, D.C.: Catholic Univ. of America Press, 1987.

Shaull, Richard, and Waldo Cesar. *Pentecostalism and the Future of the Christian Churches.* Grand Rapids: Eerdmans, 2000.

Sherrill, John. *They Speak with Other Tongues.* Westwood, NJ: Revell, 1964.

Simmons, E. L. *History of the Church of God.* Cleveland, TN: Church of God, 1938.

Sire, James W. *Discipleship of the Mind.* Downers Grove, IL: InterVarsity Press, 1980.

_____. *The Universe Next Door.* Downers Grove, IL: InverVarsity Press, 1976.

Smail, Tom. *The Love of Power, The Power of Love.* Minneapolis: Bethany, 1994.

Smith, Harold, ed. *Pentecostals from the Inside Out,* Wheaton: Victor Books, 1990.

Smith, Timothy L. *Revivalism and Social Reform in Mid-Nineteenth-Century America.* New York: Abingdon, 1957.

Solzhenitsyn, Aleksandr. *A World Split Apart: Commencement Address Delivered at Harvard University, June 8, 1978.* New York: Harper & Row, 1978.

Spence, O. Talmage. *Charismatism: Awakening or Apostasy?* Greenville, SC: Bob Jones Univ. Press, 1978.

Spittler, Russell P., ed. *Perspectives on the New Pentecostalism.* Grand Rapids: Baker, 1976.

Sproul, R. C. Cassette series, *The Consequences of Ideas*, AP 12.9/10.

_____. Three-tape video series entitled *The Battle for Our Minds*. Ligonier Ministries.

_____. *Reason to Believe*. Grand Rapids: Zondervan, 1978.

_____. "Burning Hearts, Empty Minds." *Christianity Today* 26 (Sept. 3, 1982).

Stead, Christopher. *Philosophy in Christian Antiquity*. Gateshead, UK: Athenaeum, 1995.

Stebbing, L. Susan. *Thinking to Some Purpose*. Harmondsworth, UK: Penguin, 1939.

Stein, Gordon, and Marie MacNee. *Scams, Shams, and Flimflams*. Farmington Hills, MI: UXL, 1994.

Stolee, J. *Speaking in Tongues*. Minneapolis: Augsburg, 1963.

Stott, John R. W. *Your Mind Matters*. Downers Grove, IL: InterVarsity Press, 1972.

Strachan, Gordon. *The Pentecostal Theology of Edward Irving*. Peabody, MA: Hendrickson, 1988.

Strickland, W. B. *Autobiography of Peter Cartwright*. Cinncinnati: Cranston & Curtis, 1856.

Stronstad, Roger. *The Charismatic Theology of St. Luke*. Peabody, MA: Hendrickson, 1984.

Strobel, Lee. *The Case for Christ*. Grand Rapids: Zondervan, 1998.

Sumner, Allene. "The Holy Rollers on Shin Bone Ridge." *The Nation* 121 (July 29, 1925).

Sweet, William. *The American Churches: An Interpretation*. New York: Ronald, 1959.

Sykes, Norman. *Church and State in England in the Eighteenth Century*. Cambridge: Cambridge Univ. Press, 1934.

Synan, Vinson. *The Holiness-Pentecostal Movement in the United States*. Grand Rapids: Eerdmans, 1971.

_____. *Aspects of Pentecostal-Charismatic Origins*. Plainfield, NJ: Logos International, 1975.

Taylor, Ian. *In the Minds of Men: Darwin and New World Order*. Toronto: TFE, 1984.

Teresa of Avila. *The Complete Works of Saint Teresa of Jesus*. Trans. and ed. by Allison Peers. London: Shield & Word, 1950.

Teresa of Lisieux. *The Autobiography of St. Therese of Lisieux*. Garden City, NY: Doubleday, 1957.

Thomas, Cal. *Book Burning: Censorship and Thought Control*. Westchester, IL: Crossway, 1983.

Thompson, H. *Bede: His Life, Times, and Writings*. Oxford, UK: Clarendon, 1969.

Tillich, Paul. *Culture and Faith*. Chicago: Univ. of Chicago Press, 1951.

Tiner, J. H. *Johannes Kepler: Giant of Faith and Science*. Milford, MI: Mott Media, 1977.

Tipple, Ezra S. *Francis Asbury: Prophet of the Long Road*. New York: Methodist Book Concern, 1916.

Tocqueville, Alexis de. *Democracy in America*. 2 vols. Toronto: Vintage, 1945.

Torrey, R. A. *The Baptism with the Holy Spirit*. New York: Revell, 1895.

Toynbee, Arnold. *A Study of History*. New York: American Heritage Press, 1972.

Tozer, A. W. "The Use and Abuse of Books." *The Alliance Weekly* (February 22, 1956).

_____. *The Size of the Soul*. Camphill, PA: Christian Publications, 1992.

Trask, Thomas E., and Wayde I. Goodall. *The Blessing: Experiencing the Power of the Holy Spirit Today*. Grand Rapids: Zondervan, 1998.

_____. *The Choice: Embracing God's Vision in the New Millennium*. Grand Rapids: Zondervan, 1999.

Trotter, F. Thomas. *Loving God with One's Mind*. Nashville: United Methodist Church, 1987.

Varghese, Roy Abraham. *The Intellectuals Speak about God*. Chicago: Regnery Gateway, 1984.

Veith, Gene Edward Jr. *Reading between the Lines: A Christian Guide to Literature*. Wheaton, IL: Crossway, 1990.

_____. *Postmodern Times*. Wheaton, IL: Crossway, 1994.

_____. *Loving God with All Your Mind*. Wheaton, IL: Crossway, 1987.

Villafañe, Eldin. *The Liberating Spirit*. Grand Rapids: Eerdmans, 1993.

Wacker, Grant. *Heaven Below: Early Pentecostals and American Culture*. Cambridge, MA: Harvard Univ. Press, 2001.

Wainwright, William. *Reason and the Heart*. Ithaca, NY: Cornell Univ. Press, 1995.

Warfield, Benjamin Breckinridge. *Works of B. B. Warfield*. 10 vols. Grand Rapids: Baker, 1981.

Watts, Isaac. *The Art of Reading English*. Menston, UK: Scolar Press, 1972 (1721 reprint).

_____. *The Improvement of the Mind*. Morgan, PA: Soli Deo Gloria, 1988 (1833 reprint).

Weaver, Richard. *Ideas Have Consequences*. Chicago: Univ. of Chicago Press, 1948.

Webb, Stephen. *Blessed Excess: Religion and the Hyperbolic Imagination*. Ithaca, NY: Univ. of New York Press, 1994.

Webster, Douglas. *Selling Jesus*. Downers Grove, IL: InterVarsity Press, 1992.

Weil, Simone. *Waiting for God*. Trans. Emma Craufurd. New York: Harper & Row, 1951.

Wells, David F. *No Place for Truth: Whatever Happened to Evangelical Theology?* Grand Rapids: Eerdmans, 1993.

_____. *God in the Wasteland: The Reality of Truth in a World of Fading Dreams*. Grand Rapids: Eerdmans, 1994,

Wells, Ronald. *History through the Eyes of Faith: Western Civilization and the Kingdom of God*. New York: HarperCollins, 1989.

Wesley, John. *The Works of John Wesley*. 10 vols. Grand Rapids: Baker, 1996.

_____. *The Letters of the Rev. John Wesley*. London: Epworth, 1931.

West, Robert. *Alexander Campbell and Natural Religion*. New Haven, CT: Yale Univ. Press, 1948.

Westfall, Richard. *Science and Religion in Seventeenth-Century England*. New Haven: Yale Univ. Press, 1958.

White, Andrew Dickson. *A History of the Warfare of Science and Theology*. New York: Braziller, 1955.

Whitehead, A. N. *Science and the Modern World*. New York: Free Press, 1969.

Whitefield, George. *George Whitefield's Journals*. Edinburgh: Banner of Truth Trust, 1960.

Williams, Charles. *Reason and Beauty in the Poetic Mind*. Oxford: Oxford Univ. Press, 1933.

Williams, Don. *Signs, Wonders, and the Kingdom of God*. Ann Arbor, MI: Servant, 1989.

Williams, J. Rodman. *Renewal Theology*. Grand Rapids: Zondervan, 1996.

Wilson, Bryon. *Social Aspect of Religious Sects*. Vol. 2. London: Univ. of London Press, 1955.

Wilson, Douglas. *Recovering the Lost Tools of Learning*. Wheaton, IL: Crossway, 1991.

Wimber, John. *A Brief Sketch of Signs and Wonders through the Church Age*. Placentia, CA: Vineyard, 1984.

Wise, John. *The Nature of the Liberal Arts*. Milwaukee: Bruce, 1947.

Wolterstorff, Nicholas. *Reason within the Bounds of Religion*. Grand Rapids: Eerdmans, 1976.

_____. *Educating for Responsible Action*. Grand Rapids: Eerdmans, 1980.

Wolfson, H. A. *The Philosophy of the Church Fathers*. Cambridge, MA: Harvard Univ. Press, 1970.

Womack, David. *Pentecostal Experience: The Writings of Donald Gee*. Springfield, MO: Gospel Publishing, 1993.

_____. *Wellsprings of the Pentecostal Movement*. Springfield, MO: Gospel Publishing, 1968.

Woodbridge, John D. *More than Conquerors*. Chicago: Moody Press, 1992.

_____, Mark Noll, and Nathan Hatch. *The Gospel in America: Themes in the Story of America's Evangelicals*. Grand Rapids: Zondervan, 1979.

Woodhouse, F. W. *A Narrative of Events Affecting the Position and Prospects of the Whole Christian Church*. London: Bedford, 1938.

Woodworth-Etter, Mary. *Signs and Wonders God Wrought in the Ministry for Forty Years*. Chicago: Woodworth-Etter, 1910.

Wordsworth, Charles. *On Shakspeare's Knowledge and Use of the Bible*. London: Smith and Co., 1864.

Yancey, Philip, ed. *The Classics We've Read, The Difference They've Made*. New York: McCracken, 1993.

_____. *Soul Survivor: How Thirteen Unlikely Mentors Helped My Faith Survive the Church*. New York: Doubleday, 2001.

Zacharias, Ravi. *Can Man Live without God?* Waco, TX: Word, 1994.

Zimmerman, Thomas. "Plea for the Pentecostals." *Christianity Today* 7 (January 4, 1963).

PERIODICALS

Apostolic Faith. Topeka, KS; Houston, TX; Zion City, IL, 1901 – 1909.

Apostolic Faith. Los Angeles, 1906 – 1908.

Apostolic Faith. Baxter Springs, AR., 1925 – 1927.

Bridal Call. Los Angeles, 1920 – 1923.

Christian and Missionary Alliance. Nyack, NY, 1906 – 1908.

Church of God Evangel. Cleveland, TN, 1908 – 1925.

Glad Tidings Herald. New York, 1918 – 1935.

Grace and Truth. Memphis, 1914 – 1915.

Latter Rain Evangel. Chicago, 1909 – 1915.

Pentecostal Evangel. Springfield, MO, 1922 – 1955.

Pentecostal Herald. Chicago, 1920.

Pentecostal Holiness Advocate. Franklin Springs, GA, 1916 – 1924.

Weekly Evangel. St. Louis, 1915 – 1918.

Word and Witness. Malvern, AR., 1914 – 1915.

Scripture Index

Subject Index

Name Index